Handbook of Distributed Sensor Networks

Volume I

Handbook of Distributed Sensor Networks
Volume I

Edited by **Marvin Heather**

CLANRYE INTERNATIONAL

New Jersey

Published by Clanrye International,
55 Van Reypen Street,
Jersey City, NJ 07306, USA
www.clanryeinternational.com

Handbook of Distributed Sensor Networks: Volume I
Edited by Marvin Heather

International Standard Book Number: 978-1-63240-266-0 (Hardback)

Contents

Preface

Distributed Sensor Networks is a concept which provides a smart communication, located in a network, with the potential to handle applications that iterate according to the user's requirement. Due to the recently developed technical advancements in the field, distributed sensor networks are gradually becoming an important part of human life. They are a big challenge for researchers these days, in terms of designing of algorithms and protocols. If the central node fails when a centralized architecture is applied in a sensor network, the entire network collapses. This problem can only be avoided by using distributed control architecture. There are numerous advantages of using distributed sensor networks, a crucial one being that it provides nodes with backup in case the central node fails, especially when better collection of data is priority.

Popular advanced techniques applied in sensor networks are localization algorithms in large-scale underwater acoustic sensor networks, mobility aware energy efficient congestion control in mobile wireless sensor network, continuous probabilistic skyline queries for uncertain moving objects in road network, fractal cross-layer service with integration and interaction in internet of things, etc.

Some of the chapters discussed in this book are provided with a close discussion of different applications such as load balanced routing for wireless multi-hop network applications and node placement analysis for overlay networks in iot applications. Several other technical aspects of the distributed sensor networks are elucidated.

I hope that this book will help engineers and researchers in the field of networking as well as computer technologies. Lastly, I wish to thank all the contributors and my family for all the support they provided for the completion of this project.

Editor

Traffic-Aware Data Delivery Scheme for Urban Vehicular Sensor Networks

Chunmei Ma and Nianbo Liu

School of Computer Science and Engineering, University of Electronic Science and Technology of China, Chengdu, Sichuan 611731, China

Correspondence should be addressed to Nianbo Liu; liunb@uestc.edu.cn

Academic Editor: Ming Liu

Vehicular sensor network (VSN) is a promising technology which could be widely applied to monitor the physical world in urban areas. In such a scenario, the efficient data delivery plays a central role. Existing schemes, however, cannot choose an optimal route, since they either ignore the impact of vehicular distribution on connectivity, or make some unreasonable assumptions on vehicular distribution. In this paper, we propose a traffic-aware data delivery scheme (TADS). The basic idea of TADS is to choose intersections to forward packets dynamically as the route from a source to destination based on link quality and remaining Euclidean distance to destination. Specifically, we first present an optimal utility function as the criteria of intersection selection. Besides the packet forwarding through intersections, we also propose an improved geographically greedy routing algorithm for packet forwarding in straightway mode. Moreover, in order to decrease the routing overhead brought by the traffic information gathering, we build a traffic condition prediction model to estimate the link quality. The simulation results show that our TADS outperforms existing works on packet delivery ratio, end-to-end delay, and routing overhead.

1. Introduction

With the advance of technology, most of the vehicles are equipped with on-board sensors; thus, a new network is the emerging-vehicular sensor network (VSN). Different from traditional sensor networks, VSN is not limited in energy consumption, owns much powerful processing units and wireless communication, and can determine the position of the nodes through GPS. Because of these properties, VSN has been envisioned to be useful in monitoring the physical world, especially in urban areas in which more vehicles equipped with sensors are available. For example, a vehicular network can be used to monitor traffic [1, 2] (e.g., jams, traffic accident, etc.), for improving driving convenience and efficiency. It can also be used in environmental surveillance [3], since urban areas are full of vehicles especially the taxis. To realize this vision, efficiently data transmission mainly relies on intervehicle communication in VSN. However, the special property of vehicle in mobility brings many challenges to VSN in throughput and latency of data transmission.

For the past decade or so, quite a few number of researchers and institutions were dedicated to improving transportation efficiency in urban VSN. Usually, these protocols mainly focus on selecting an intersection candidate to forward data according to the density of vehicles on the road [4, 5], such as VADD based on historical traffic condition to select a road with high density to forward packets. However, not only the density but also the distribution of vehicles on the road can affect the node connectivity. As shown in Figure 1, although the density is high (Figure 1(b)), unbalance traffic, caused by signal light and car-following driving, will lead to disconnection. Consequently, both the density and distribution of vehicles are needed to be taken into consideration for data transmission. In order to consider the vehicular distribution in routing protocol, some of protocols give unreasonable assumptions. For example, in [6, 7], they assume that the speed of the vehicles in the traffic flow is uniform, so the distribution of the space headway is exponential, which does not hold in reality scenario.

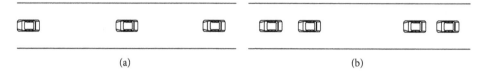

(a)   (b)

FIGURE 1: Connectivity in VSN.

In this paper, we solve the problem of efficient data delivery in vehicular sensor network when a vehicle sends a delay-tolerant data to some fixed site and how to efficiently route the packet to the destination. We propose a traffic-aware data delivery scheme (TADS), which emphasizes the intersection selection, that is, how to choose a robust route to forward packet. Different from existing routing protocols, TADS takes vehicular real-time spatial distribution together with vehicular density and the remaining Euclidean distance to the destination into consideration to choose an intersection for efficiently forwarding packet in VSN. For data delivery between intersections, we employ improved geographically greedy routing algorithm. We also build a vehicular density and vehicular spatial distribution prediction model based on the traffic pattern and road layout to estimate the link quality with time. Extensive simulations are conducted to evaluate the proposed protocol; the results show that TADS outperforms previous protocols in terms of packer delivery ratio, data packet delay, and routing overhead. TADS paves the way for delay-tolerant VSN applications like traffic surveillance and event reporting.

The major contributions of this paper are as follows.

(1) Uneven distribution of vehicles has great impact on routing performance; we present a method to denote the vehicular spatial distribution. Once the vehicular distribution can be obtained, the connectivity can be computed more accurately.

(2) Due to the traffic pattern and road layout, we establish a vehicular density and vehicular spatial distribution prediction model, through which TADS is efficient and resource efficient.

(3) We take vehicular density, distribution, and the remaining distance to the destination into account to design a routing protocol for VSN. The simulation results show that TADS outperforms most of the existing protocols.

The rest of the paper is organized as follows. In Section 2, we present a brief overview of related work on data delivery. In Section 3, we introduce the model of TADS. The detailed traffic-aware data delivery scheme will be introduced in Section 4. Section 5 evaluates the performance of TADS, and Section 6 summarizes the paper.

2. Related Work

In the last few years, a number of researchers have made many contributions to the routing protocol of ad hoc network.

These routing algorithms are divided into two categories: topology-based and position-based routings. Topology-based protocols [8–10] should establish the route from source to the destination and maintain it in a table before the packet is sent, which are suitable for dense networks. Position-based protocols [11–13] leverage geographic positioning information to select the next forwarding hop; there is no need to create and maintain the global route between source and destination. As more and more vehicles are equipped with GPS and digital maps, position-based routing strategy is more convenient for urban vehicular sensor network. Owing to that the connectivity in urban vehicle networks heavily relies on the traffic condition, we classify position-based routing algorithms into two categories. One category exploits the historical traffic information to assist packet forwarding, and the other exploits the real-time traffic information to forward packet.

For the first category algorithms, there is no need to collect traffic information or make prediction. With the help of the navigation system, the traffic conditions are priori known before the packet to be sent. Vehicle-assisted data delivery (VADD) [4] is a kind of geographic routing protocol. It assumes that vehicles can obtain traffic statistics such as traffic density and vehicular speed on the road at different times of the day through preloaded digital map. The shortest expected delivery delay to the destination of the data depends on each road vehicular density. A drawback is that the historical information will not confirm to the realist traffic conditions that may cause routes to be incorrectly computed.

For the second category, the traffic conditions are gathered through an on-the-fly collection process. Greedy traffic-aware routing protocol (GyTAR) [6] is an intersection-based geographical routing protocol. For the intersection selection process, an estimation score is given to each junction by combining the road density and the curve metric distance to the destination. The junction with the highest value will be chosen for data delivery. The work in [14] selects an optimal route with the best network transmission quality model that takes into account vehicle real-time density and traffic light periods to estimate the probability of network connectivity and data delivery ratio for transmitting packets. Both of these two protocols divide the road into segments, and the vehicle headers in each of the segments, which are highly dynamic, are needed to exchange information. Intersection-based routing protocol (IBR) [15] finds a minimum delay routing path in various vehicular densities. Moreover, vehicles reroute each packet according to real-time road conditions in each intersection, and the packets sent to a node at the intersections depend on the moving direction of the next vehicle. All of these protocols are needed to periodically collect road information, which significantly increases the routing overhead.

Most of these routing protocols do not take into account the vehicular distribution on the road where there may exist traffic hole [16], which means that it may be possible to lose some good candidate intersections when they try to forward a packet. Moreover, some of these protocols divide roads into segments, which are too complicated to be realized in the networking protocol design. To provide a solution to the aforementioned problems, in this paper, we take the vehicular density and distribution into account to design a new intersection-based routing protocol. The proposed protocol is easy to operate. In the following section, we will give a detailed description of our approach and present its added value compared with other existing vehicular routing protocols.

3. The TADS Model

3.1. Assumptions. We assume that each vehicle in the network is equipped with GPS, which enables them to acquire their own position and speed, and vehicles maintain a neighbor table that is built through beacon messages. The neighbor table records each neighboring vehicle's position, velocity, and moving direction. Furthermore, vehicles are equipped with preloaded with digital map, with the help of which we can determine the current geographical position of the destination. Finally, we assume that the traffic condition will not change significantly for a period of time.

3.2. Problem Statement. In city scenarios, data delivery has two modes: intersection mode and straightway mode. The most important issue is to select a robust route that can reduce delivery latency and improve delivery ratio. Although some of the routing protocols, such as ACAR [14] which always selects route with high density, are sometimes very inefficient for data delivery, as they ignore the distribution of vehicle on the road. As shown in Figure 2, the source node S wants to send a message to the destination D at the corner of intersection I_d. To forward the message through $I_a \rightarrow I_c \rightarrow I_d$ would be better than through $I_a \rightarrow I_b \rightarrow I_d$, even though the route $I_a \rightarrow I_b$ owns higher density. The reason is that the uneven distribution caused by traffic accidents or signal lights may lead to disconnection of the message that has to be carried by the vehicle. Since wireless communication is far faster than vehicle moving, the routing protocols should do their effort to leverage wireless communication.

Therefore, a proper routing protocol is important to forward the packet in VSN, and it is determined by several factors such as vehicular density, vehicular distribution, and road length. In this paper, we first model the link quality and then propose an approach to select the optimal route that can achieve the lowest forwarding delay.

3.3. TADS Model. TADS is an intersection-based multihop routing protocol that is capable of finding optimal route

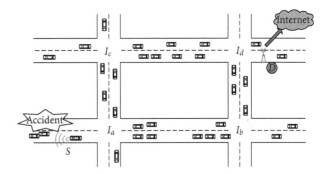

FIGURE 2: The problem of routing in VSN.

according to the real-time traffic condition. Owing to that the traffic flow will not change rapidly within a short time in urban scenario, we can build the link quality prediction model to increase the beacon cycle. To reach these objectives, TADS is organized into two schemes: (1) a scheme for the selection of the optimal route through which packets at each junction make decision to forward the packet to the destination; (2) a mechanism for the estimation of vehicular density and vehicular distribution to estimate link quality with time, which can significantly reduce the overhead of the routing protocol. Using TADS, packets will ultimately reach to the destination.

3.3.1. Intersection Selection. Similar to GPSR, TADS is a partial routing protocol and dynamically chooses the next intersection. When the packet carrier is approaching an intersection, it will calculate the utility function which depends on the link quality and the Euclidean distance from the candidate to the destination. Usually, the optimal route is the geographically closer candidate intersection to the destination and the route having higher link quality.

To better understand how the next intersection is chosen, it is illustrated by Figure 3 as an example. Since the source node S is approaching the intersection, it computes link quality of each neighboring road based on the traffic density and distribution. In order to guarantee the package forward to destination, the shorter distances from the candidate intersection to the destination will make a contribution to selecting the intersection. The source node knows the Euclidean distance from each candidate intersection to the destination through map. Thus, Swill not select the intersection far away from destination. Intersection I_a has the optimal utility function and is chosen as the next one.

To formally calculate the utility function, we define the following notations.

    (i) r_{ij} : The road from intersection I to intersection J;

    (ii) L_{ij} : The Euclidean distance on r_{ij};

    (iii) p_{ji_k} : The position of vehicle k on r_{ij};

    (iv) N_{ij} : The number of vehicles on r_{ij};

    (v) σ : The vehicular distributions on r_{ij};

    (vi) D_J : The Euclidean distance from the candidate intersection J to the destination.

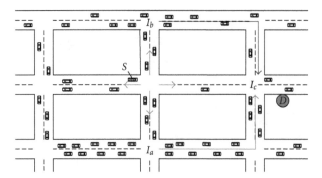

FIGURE 3: An example of selecting an intersection.

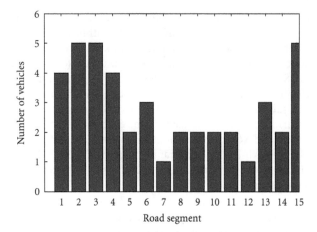

FIGURE 4: Vehicle spatial distribution on road.

Vehicular density depicts the status of the road segment that owns the ability to forward packets, it can be formulated on the road r_{ij} as

$$\rho_{ij} = \frac{N_{ij}}{L_{ij}}. \tag{1}$$

Before giving the vehicular distribution on road r_{ij}, we propose a definition called relative distance degree, which indicates the relative distance between the intersection and the current position of the vehicle.

Definition 1. For any node k and its position is p_{ij_k} on the road r_{ij}, the relative distance degree is

$$l_{ij_k} = \frac{p_{ij_k}}{L_{ij}}. \tag{2}$$

We can apply (2) to all vehicles on road r_{ij} and then acquire the vehicular spatial distribution. For each road, we employ a histogram to obtain the statistics results. Since the radio range is 200 m–250 m, we set the interval of histogram to 100 m; x-axis represents the road segments, the y-axis indicates the number of vehicles per segment, and the fluctuation of the graph indicates the vehicular unbalance distribution. Figure 4 is an example of a single road of length 1500 m. In the graph, the first 100 m has five vehicles, and

there is only one vehicle between 600 m–700 m, which will significantly affect the routing performance.

Histograms of all the road segments are calculated based on the collected beacons from vehicles on the road. Suppose that n_m denotes the number of vehicles in the ith interval zone, the deviation (it indicates the balance or unbalance vehicular distribution) of the road r_{ij} can be expressed as

$$\begin{aligned} \sigma_{ij} &= \frac{\sum_{m=1}^{N} \left(n_m - \sum_{m=1}^{N}\left(n_m/N\right)\right)^2}{N} \\ &= \frac{\sum_{m=1}^{N} n_m^2 - 2\sum_{m=1}^{N} n_m + \left(N_{ij}^2/N\right)}{N} \\ &= \frac{N\sum_{m=1}^{N} n_m^2 - N_{ij}^2}{N^2}. \end{aligned} \tag{3}$$

Hence, the utility function can be formulated as

$$\Theta_{\rho\sigma D_J} = \left(1 - \alpha \frac{D_J}{D_K + D_H}\right)\frac{\rho_{ij}}{1 + \sigma_{ij}}. \tag{4}$$

α is used as a weighting factor for the distance. $D_K = \max(D_1, D_2, \ldots, D_m)$ and $D_H = \min(D_1, D_2, \ldots, D_m)$.

As we can see, the utility function depends on three parameters (ρ, σ, D_J). For a given street, (1) provides the traffic density ρ and through the statistics results of the relative position of vehicles, the deviation σ (indicates if the road is balanced or not) is calculated using (3), whereas $D_J/(D_K + D_H)$ represents distance degree of different route, which guarantees that the packet is forwarded to the destination. $\rho_{ij}/(1 + \sigma_{ij})$ determines how high the whole street link quality is. Thus, by multiplying $\rho_{ij}/(1 + \sigma_{ij})$ with $\alpha(D_J/(D_K + D_H))$, we provide the streets with a correct value since this corresponds to scenarios where the candidate intersections are far away destination.

3.3.2. The Traffic Condition Prediction Model. In order to achieve the intersection selecting, we need to periodically collect the road information (e.g., the vehicle moving direction, speed, and position) to calculate the link quality, which consumes large resources, especially the bandwidth, and has bad impact on routing performance, for example, increasing routing overhead. However, owning to that the traffic flow may keep steady within a short time period, the traffic condition can be predicted based on the intersection historical traffic flow and moving vehicles on the road.

Link quality depends on the vehicular density and vehicular spatial distribution on the road; thus, in this section, we propose a vehicular density and vehicular spatial distribution prediction model to estimate the link quality. For prediction, each packet carrier maintains a road table where three tuples, $s_i(p, v, a)$, are recorded; here the three elements represent the position, velocity, and moving direction of vehicles on the road, and the table is divided into two sets $T1$ and $T2$ according to the vehicle moving direction. Each road periodically broadcasts its state to update the road table.

The problem of prediction of the link stability at time t is to compute the future density $\rho(t)$ and the deviation

$\sigma(t)$. The deviation is determined by the statistics results of relative distance degree; therefore, we just need to predict the vehicular number and their positions on the road. The vehicular number is affected by two parts: (1) the new coming vehicles and (2) the vehicles that have left. Suppose the vehicle arrivals at each intersection follow Poisson distribution. Thus, the probability of i of vehicles coming at time t is

$$P(A(t) = i) = e^{(-\lambda t)} \frac{(\lambda t)^i}{i!}. \tag{5}$$

When $P(A(t) = w) < h_c$, we ignore the possibility of coming vehicles; thus, the average number of arriving vehicles $A(t)$ is

$$A(t) = \sum_{i=1}^{w-1} e^{(-\lambda t)} \frac{i(\lambda t)^i}{i!} = \sum_{i=1}^{w-1} e^{(-\lambda t)} \frac{(\lambda t)^i}{(i-1)!}. \tag{6}$$

At time τ, the packet carrier receives the information from each road, then, it can compute the vehicle arrival rate of each intersection and applies (6) to estimate the number of the new coming vehicles. For the vehicles that have left, it is much simpler. The vehicles moving in the packet expectation direction belong to $T1$, and the others belong to $T2$. In this paper, we use D to denote the number of vehicles that have left. In $T1$, when $P_k + V_k t > L$, we can determine the vehicle has left the road, that is, $D = D + 1$ and in the same way, in $T2$, when $P_K - V_k t < 0$, $D = D + 1$. Thus, the number of vehicles on the road at time t is

$$N'(t) = N(t) + A(t) - D. \tag{7}$$

And then, we can apply (1) to compute the vehicular density on the road. For the vehicular distribution, it is essential to determine the relative distance of the new coming vehicles. We first consider the situation for moving in the packet expectation direction.

For Poisson distribution, N vehicles arrive at the intersection at time t, w_i denotes the ith arrival waiting time, and the conditional probability of waiting time is

$$f(t) = \begin{cases} \dfrac{n!}{t^n}, & \text{if } 0 < w_1 < w_2 < \cdots < w_n < t, \\ 0, & \text{otherwise.} \end{cases} \tag{8}$$

Suppose the new coming vehicles move at the average speed of road, and y_n denotes the nth vehicular position; thus, its relative position is

$$y_n = (t - w_n) V. \tag{9}$$

Hence, the conditional probability density function of the new arrival vehicles relative position is

$$f(y) = \begin{cases} -\dfrac{n!}{(t - y/V)^n}, & \text{if } 0 < y_1 < y_2 < \cdots < y_n < L, \\ 0, & \text{otherwise.} \end{cases} \tag{10}$$

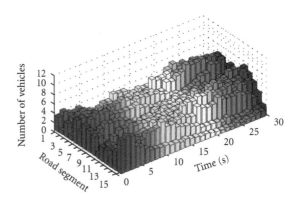

FIGURE 5: Prediction model.

The estimation position of nth vehicle is

$$E(y_n) = \int_0^L -\frac{yn!}{(t - y/v)^n} dy. \tag{11}$$

If the first arrival vehicle belongs to the first zone, the following ones do not need to be calculated, since they will not pass it; else, the second one is also computed until the one falling into the first zone emerges. For the vehicles on the opposite of the expectation direction, the relative position is

$$Y_n = L - y_n. \tag{12}$$

For the vehicles on the road, the relative distance is $P_K + v_k t$, v is a vector. When obtaining all the relative distances, we apply (2) to compute the relative degree and then apply (3) to compute vehicular spatial distribution.

Figure 5 shows an example of the change of vehicular spatial distribution over time. In this scenario, the vehicle arrivals rates of two intersections on the road are 0.6 and 0.3, respectively.

4. Traffic-Aware-Based Data Delivery Protocol

TADS is designed for city scenarios VSN routing, which only has two modes: intersection and straightway. In this section, we orderly present the protocol for the two modes.

4.1. TADS Used in the Intersection Mode. When approaching the intersection, the packet carrier can determine the best forward path deriving from (4) and then check if there is an available relay node to forward packets toward that intersection. As Figure 6(a) shows, vehicle A at intersection has a packet to forward to certain destination. Assume that north is the optimal direction for this packet. Both B and C are available relay nodes, for difference, B moving north and C moving south. TADS will select B as the next hop instead of vehicle C, since it can guarantee that the packet is forwarded to the optimal road. If there is only vehicle C available which is geographically closer to north, A will select C as the relay node, since C has the possibility to forward the packet to D immediately. Due to that the moving direction of C is on the opposite of the expectation direction, A always

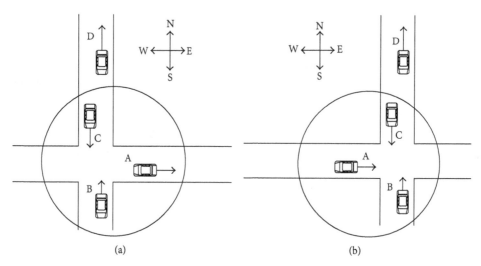

FIGURE 6: Packet forwarding in the intersection mode.

restores the packet until it receives the ACK message from C. If A failed to meet any relay node at current intersection, it will keep holding the packet and move ahead, it still has the opportunity to forward the packet to the expectation direction, as Figure 6(b) shown. When A passes through current intersection, nodes B and C are likely to emerge into the communication scope of A, and it can make a routing planning.

4.2. TADS Used in the Straightway Mode.

In the straightway mode TADS applies improved geographically greedy routing algorithm to forward the packets to the destination intersection (the intersection ahead). To implement the scheme, all packets are marked by the location of the next intersection, and the packet carrier needs to record the velocity vector information of each neighbor vehicle. When a packet is received, the forwarding vehicle uses the corresponding recorded information to select the next neighbor that is closest to the destination among the nodes moving in the packet expectation direction. For instance, as shown in Figure 7(a), A has a packet to forward to the next intersection, both B and C are its neighbors, A will select C which is geographically closer to destination to forward the packet. In Figure 7(b), even though B is further from the destination, A will select B to forward the packet, since this seems like better than selecting C. This is because if there is no relay node for C, it will pass the packet to B shortly, which increases the delay, and B can ensure the packet to be sent to destination.

5. Performance Evaluation

In this section, we analyze the weighting factor α and evaluate the performance of the prediction model and TADS. We use VanetMobiSim-1.1 [17], a flexible framework for vehicles mobility modeling, to generate the real traces that can be used by NS2. Since the simulation should be offered a network environment as close as possible to the real world one, we make an effort to define a realistic scenario where VSN may be deployed.

5.1. The Weighting Factor Analysis.

In this section, we analyze the weighting factor of the utility function to determine the good balance between distance and link quality. We simulated the packet delivery ratio of TADS for different values of α. The simulation scenario is shown in Figure 10, and we set the number of vehicles to be 250. As Figure 8 shows, in most of the cases, $\alpha = 0.4$ achieves the highest packet delivery ratio. This is mainly because the vehicle moving speed is much slower than the wireless communication, and it is better to favor a higher link quality to forward the packet.

5.2. Evaluation of the Prediction Model.

We simulated a 1500 m long straight road with two bidirectional lanes and set the period of vehicle light to 60 s. The traffic light can cause unbalanced vehicle distribution in various degrees, which has great impact on the performance of prediction model. In order to analyze the performance in various situations, we must set the simulation time to be greater than 60 s (in this section we set the simulation time to be 70 s). Since the different vehicles arrival rate of each intersection has impact on the performance of prediction accuracy, we extract different arrival rate to display our algorithm. In order to give the analysis result of the prediction model, firstly we define the error rate.

Definition 2. $\sigma(t)$ and $\sigma * (t)$ are the estimated and real deviation of road L at time t, respectively, and the error rate is given as

$$\text{err} = \frac{|\sigma(t) - \sigma * (t)|}{\sigma * (t)}. \tag{13}$$

Figure 9 plots the error rate of the prediction of vehicular spatial distribution over time. The figure shows that the error rate is lower than 10% for the low arrival rate and lower than 13% for the higher arrival rate when the estimation time is under 30 s, which means that the estimated deviation

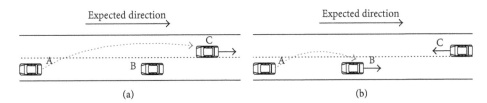

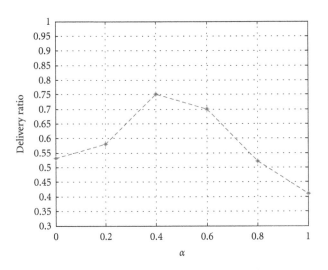

FIGURE 7: Packet forwarding in straightway mode.

FIGURE 8: The delivery ratio versus weighting factor.

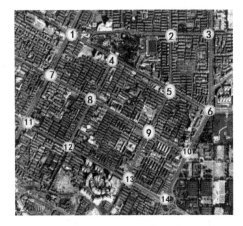

FIGURE 10: Road topology of simulation area.

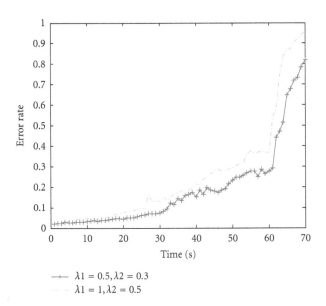

$\lambda 1 = 0.5, \lambda 2 = 0.3$
$\lambda 1 = 1, \lambda 2 = 0.5$

FIGURE 9: The error rate of road over time.

is close to the actual deviation, and it is observed that longer estimation time causes more errors rate. This is mostly explained by the fact that the vehicles are highly dynamic; by contrast, in our model we set a constant arrival rate during the estimation process which causes larger error rate with time increases. Furthermore, it is observed that when the time exceeds 60 s, the error rate sharply increases. This is because,

in reality scenario, the traffic red light is working beyond 60 s, and at the current intersection the vehicles stop moving into the road, which is consistent with the reality scenarios.

5.3. Evaluation of TADS. To evaluate the performance of the TADS, we conduct a more complex simulation and compare our algorithm with two existing protocols: GSR [18] and ACAR [14]. Since GSR always selects the forwarding node that is closest in geographical distance to the destination and drops packets when the network is disconnected, to have a fair comparison, we extend GSR by adding carry-and-forward schemes in it.

5.3.1. Simulation Setup. The simulation was based on a real street map with the range of 1600 m × 1400 m, which is extracted from an urban area of Chengdu, a city of China. As shown in Figure 10, it consists of 14 intersections and 21 bidirectional roads. At the beginning of the simulation, a number of vehicles are located on the position to the map following the predefined value, and each of them chooses one of the intersections as its destination. Then, they start moving along the road on both directions with an average speed range from 40 to 80 km/h that depends on the speed limit of a specific road. To produce traffic change, the total numbers of nodes are deployed in the region ranging from 100 to 300, and the traffic light period is set to 60 s to produce unbalanced vehicular distribution. Among all vehicles, 10 of them are source nodes to send CBR data packets at 0.1 to 1 per second with a packet size of 512 B. All the key simulation parameters are listed in Table 1.

TABLE 1: Simulation parameters.

Parameter	Value
Simulation time (s)	400
Simulation area (m)	1600×1400
Number of intersections	14
Period of traffic lights (s)	60
Number of vehicles	100150200250300
Communication range (m)	250
Vehicle velocity (km/h)	40–80
CBR (packet per second)	0.1–1
Packet size (B)	512
Vehicle beacon interval (s)	1.0, 30

5.4. Simulation Results. We mainly evaluate our algorithm on packet delivery ratio, end-to-end delay, and routing overhead as a function of the data transmission rate and the vehicular density in simulation. As a static metric, packet delivery ratio is the number of successfully received packets at the destination divided by the total number of packets in the networks, which is significantly affected by the simulation of time. End-to-end delay reflects transmission duration between two nodes, which indicates how long it takes for a packet to be forwarded across the network from the source to the destination. Routing overhead denotes the ratio between the total number of the control packets and the number of data packets sent into the networks and the control packets.

The routing protocols are compared under various data transmission rates that set the number of vehicles as 150 and various vehicular densities that set the packet sending rate as 0.3 pkt/s.

Packet Delivery Ratio. Figure 11(a) shows that GSR has the lowest packet delivery ratio, even if it is implemented in a carry-and-forward way, as it always chooses the geographically shortest path to destination without considering the vehicular traffic. Consequently, some data packets cannot reach their destination due to that the wireless transmission quality is low on some sections of the road. On the other hand, for almost all packet sending rates, TADS gives the highest packet delivery ratio, since it forwards packets along the route on the road following the road traffic density, vehicular spatial distribution, and the Euclidean distance to the destination. Hence, a packet will successively arrive at the destination along the streets with the highest transmission quality. ACAR has a lower delivery ratio than TADS, and this is because it just considers vehicular density to estimate the probability of network for transmitting packets. Consequently, some data packets cannot reach their destination due to the problem of traffic hole.

In Figure 11(b), it is observed that as the vehicular density increases, GSR achieves very good delivery ratio, and since the connectivity is much better than the previous scenario, there are more nodes that can help carry and forward the packets to the destination. For ACAR, its packet delivery ratio will increase when the network density is low, as it will forward packets along the path with higher connectivity. However, when network density is larger than 150 nodes, its packet delivery ratio slightly increases. When the network density becomes larger, ACAR may choose the highest density road to forward the packet, which causes MAC layer collisions, so the delivery ratio cannot drastically increase and sometimes may decrease. Due to full consideration of connectivity in TADS, the optimal utility function may be different; thus, there are few collisions, and the packet delivery ratio of TADS increases when network density increases.

End-to-End Delay. As Figure 12(a) shows, the end-to-end delay is a function of packet sending rates. When the packet sending rates increase, more opportunities are obtained to forward the packet to the destination; thus, the forwarding delay will decrease. GSR has the largest end-to-end delay compared to ACAR and TADS, which is mainly due to the long time vehicles carry packets as there is no next hop available. ACAR has relatively lower end-to-end delay at most of the packet sending rates. An interesting observation is that when the packet sending rate is closer to 0.9 prt/s or when the vehicular density increases (in Figure 12(b)) to 200 nodes, GSR shows lower delay. This is because of the forwarding rules in ACAR; when more packets are injected into the same route, there are more packet collision and longer queuing time. In this case, the end-to-end delay in ACAR will increase.

In Figure 12(b), TADS achieves the lowest end-to-end delay; this is because in TADS, it has an efficient scheme of selecting intersection that guarantees that the packet is sent to the destination with the least delay, and in straightway, the chosen sending node is the one closest to the candidate intersection which reduces the number of hops involved in delivering packets, which to some degree reduces the delivery delay.

Routing Overhead. In this section, we evaluate the routing overhead of these protocols. For certain packet sending rates, the total number of packets sent into the networks is similar for all protocols; thus, the routing overhead is determined by the control message. As Figure 11 shows, although the packet delivery ratio of ACAR is higher than GSR, when the packet sending rate increases, GSR outperforms ACAR in routing overhead (Figure 13(a)), and the major reason is the on-the-fly density collection scheme in ACAR. Due to the prediction scheme, the periodic beacon interval of TADS is much longer (30 s in the simulation) than the other two protocols; thus, TADS has the lowest routing overhead.

As shown in Figure 13(b), the routing overhead will increase along with the increase in vehicular density, since the size of control messages is proportional to the number of vehicles in the networks. Although GSR needs to send hello message to maintain its neighbor table, it achieves lower routing overhead than ACAR for different vehicular density. This is because the cost is lower compared with the real-time density collection for a whole street. In TADS, even if the size of control message increases similarly, the long periodic beacon interval decreases the ratio between the control packets and the total packets sent into the networks.

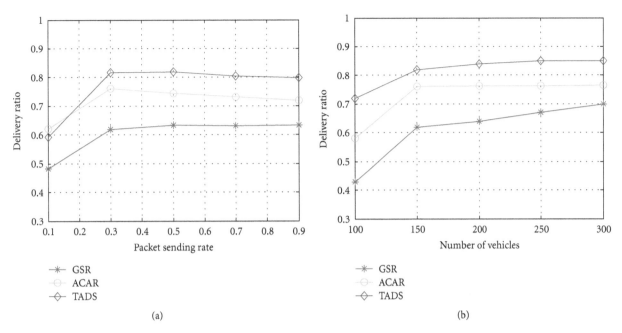

FIGURE 11: Data delivery ratio versus (a) packet sending rate and (b) number of vehicles.

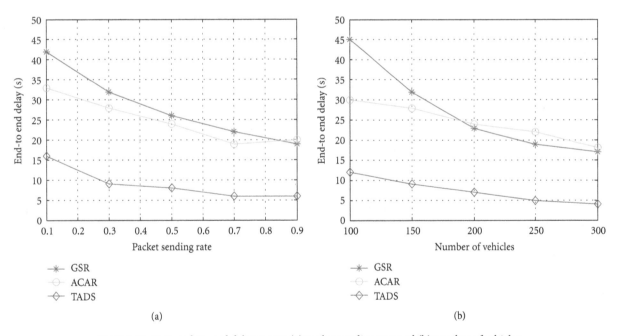

FIGURE 12: Data end-to-end delay versus (a) packet sending rate and (b) number of vehicles.

6. Conclusions

Motivated by the great impact of uneven distribution on the performance of routing protocol, we propose an efficient and a lightweight traffic aware-based data delivery scheme (TADS) to achieve data delivery, which will benefit many applications for urban VSN. The selection of intermediate intersection is based on the optimal utility function to each road. The utility function is determined by the dynamic traffic density, the Euclidean distance to the destination, and the vehicular distribution. Different from most of the existing protocols, we make use of real realistic vehicular distribution. In this paper, we first give a definition of relative distance degree, which can reflect the real distribution of vehicles. Then, we make use of the mathematical statistics method to calculate the deviation of road per 100 m. The result reflects the different distribution among road segments. Due to the character of vehicle mobility, which is constrained by

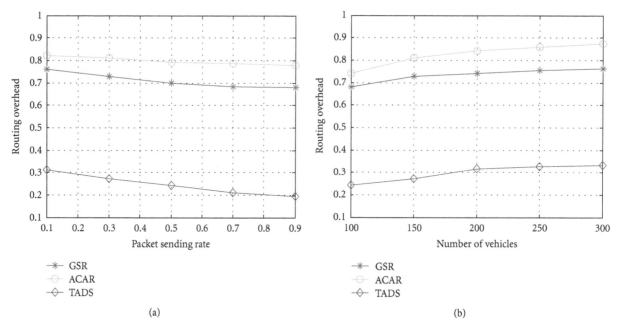

FIGURE 13: Data routing overhead versus (a) packet sending rate and (b) number of vehicles.

the road topology and traffic pattern, we build a prediction model. Our simulation results show that TADS achieves a higher successful throughput and lower delay with low cost compared to GSR and ACAR.

Acknowledgments

The authors sincerely thank their shepherd and the anonymous reviewers for their invaluable feedback which helped improve this paper. This work was supported in part by the National Natural Science Foundation of China under Grants (nos. 61003226, 61170256, 61173171, 61173172, 61103226, 61103227, and 61272526), the Fundamental Research Funds for the Central Universities under Grants (nos. ZYGX2011J060, ZYGX2011J073, and ZYGX2011J074).

References

[1] T. ElBatt, S. K. Goel, G. Holland, H. Krishnan, and J. Parikh, "Cooperative collision warning using dedicated short range wireless communications," in *Proceedings of the 3rd ACM International Workshop on Vehicular Ad Hoc Networks (VANET '06)*, pp. 1–9, September 2006.

[2] C. L. Robinson, L. Caminiti, D. Caveney, and K. Laberteaux, "Efficient coordination and transmission of data for cooperative vehicular safety applications," in *Proceedings of the 3rd ACM International Workshop on Vehicular Ad Hoc Networks (VANET '06)*, pp. 10–19, September 2006.

[3] L. E. Cordova-Lopez, A. Mason, J. D. Cullen, A. Shaw, and A. I. Al-Shamma'A, "Online vehicle and atmospheric pollution monitoring using GIS and wireless sensor networks," *Journal of Physics: Conference Series*, vol. 76, no. 1, Article ID 012019, 2007.

[4] J. Zhao, "VADD: vehicle-assisted data delivery in vehicular adhoc networks," in *Proceedings of the 25th IEEE International Conference on Computer Communications*, pp. 1–12, 2006.

[5] Q. Yang, "Connectivity aware routing in vehicular networks," in *Proceedings of the IEEE Wireless Communications and Networking Conference (WCNC '08)*, pp. 2218–2223, Piscataway, NJ, USA, 2008.

[6] M. Jerbi, S. M. Senouci, T. Rasheed, and Y. Ghamri-Doudane, "Towards efficient geographic routing in urban vehicular networks," *IEEE Transactions on Vehicular Technology*, vol. 58, no. 9, pp. 5048–5059, 2009.

[7] N. Wisitpongphan, F. Bai, P. Mudalige, V. Sadekar, and O. Tonguz, "Routing in sparse vehicular ad hoc wireless networks," *IEEE Journal on Selected Areas in Communications*, vol. 25, no. 8, pp. 1538–1556, 2007.

[8] G. Pei, M. Gerla, and T.-W. Chen, "Fisheye state routing: a routing scheme for ad hoc wireless networks, Communications," in *Proceedings of the IEEE International Conference on Communications (ICC '00)*, vol. 1, pp. 70–74, New Orleans, La, USA, 2000.

[9] C. Perkins, E. Belding-Royer, and S. Das, "Ad Hoc on-demand distance vector (AODV) routing," in *RFC 3561, Network Working Group*, 2003.

[10] Z. J. Haas, "The zone routing protocol (ZRP) for ad hoc networks," in *Internet Draft*, 1997.

[11] B. Karp and H. T. Kung, "GPSR: greedy perimeter stateless routing for wireless networks," in *Proceedings of the 6th Annual International Conference on Mobile Computing and Networking (MOBICOM '00)*, pp. 243–254, August 2000.

[12] C. Lochert, M. Mauve, H. Fler, and H. Hartenstein, "A routing strategy for vehicular ad hoc networks in city environments," in *Proceedings of the IEEE Intelligent Vehicles Symposium*, pp. 156–161, June 2003.

[13] B. C. Seet, G. Liu, B.-S. Lee, C.-H. Foh, K.-J. Wong, and K. K. Lee, "A-STAR: a mobile Ad Hoc routing strategy for

metropolis vehicular communications," in *Mobile and Wireless Communications*, vol. 3042, pp. 989–999, 2004.

[14] L. D. Chou, J. Y. Yang, Y. C. Hsieh, D. C. Chang, and C. F. Tung, "ACAR: adaptive connectivity aware routing for vehicular Ad Hoc networks in city scenarios," *Mobile Networks and Applications*, vol. 15, no. 1, pp. 36–60, 2010.

[15] L.-D. Chou, J.-Y. Yang, Y.-C. Hsieh, D.-C. Chang, and C.-F. Tung, "Intersection-based routing protocol for VANETs," in *Proceedings of the 2nd International Conference on Ubiquitous and Future Networks (ICUFN '10)*, pp. 105–124, June 2010.

[16] C. Song, M. Liu, Y. Wen, G. Chen, and J. Cao, "Towards the trafic hole problem in VANETs," in *Proceedings of the 9th ACM International Workshop on Vehicular Inter-Networking, Systems, and Applications*, pp. 139–140, 2012.

[17] J. Harri, F. Filali, C. Bonnet, and M. Fiore, "VanetMobiSim: generating realistic mobility patterns for VANETs," in *Proceedings of the 3rd International Workshop on Vehicular ad hoc Networks (VANET '06)*, pp. 96–97, 2006.

[18] C. Lochert, M. Mauve, H. Fubler, and H. Hartenstein, "Geographic routing in city scenarios," *ACM SIGMOBILE Mobile Computing and Communications Review*, vol. 9, no. 1, pp. 69–72, 2005.

2

On the Security of Certificateless Signature Schemes

Gaurav Sharma, Suman Bala, and Anil K. Verma

Computer Science and Engineering Department, Thapar University, Patiala 147004, India

Correspondence should be addressed to Gaurav Sharma; gaurav.sharma@thapar.edu

Academic Editor: J. Barbancho

Wireless Sensor Network (WSN) has proved its presence in various real time applications and hence the security of such embedded devices is a vital issue. Certificateless cryptography is one of the recent paradigms to provide security. Certificateless public key cryptography (CL-PKC) deals effectively with the twin issues of certificate management in traditional public key cryptography and key escrow problem in identity-based cryptography. CL-PKC has attracted special attention in the field of information security as it has opened new avenues for improvement in the present security architecture. Recently, Tsai et al. proposed an improved certificateless signature scheme without pairing and claimed that their new construction is secure against different kinds of attacks. In this paper, we present a security analysis of their scheme and our results show that scheme does not have resistance against malicious-KGC attack. In addition, we have found some security flaws in the certificateless signature scheme of Fan et al. and proved the scheme vulnerable to Strong Type I attack.

1. Introduction

The validation of public keys by a trusted third party, also known as Certificate Authority (CA), makes traditional Public Key Infrastructure (PKI) uneconomical. The user selects a public key and then CA provides a digital certificate to associate the public key with the user's identity. The management of these certificates is a complex issue and increases the computation and storage cost manifold. To resolve the issues of PKC a revolutionary ID-based infrastructure was introduced by Shamir [1] in 1984. This seminal concept of Identity Based Cryptography (IBC) allows the user to choose a public key of its own choice such as email ID, phone number, and name. In IBC, users do not generate their own private keys as in traditional PKC. Private keys are generated by Key Generation Centre (KGC), maintains the private keys of all the users, but there is always a possibility of the misuse of these private keys as they can be used to decrypt any ciphertext and forge the signature of user on any message for signature generation. Eventually, this new paradigm solved the problem of certificate management but gave birth to inherent problem of key escrow.

In 2003, Al-riyami and Paterson [2] proposed a novel approach to eliminate the inherent key escrow problem of IBC as well as the use of certificates in traditional PKC.

This approach is known as CL-PKC, where KGC generates a partial-private key for the user while user's secret key and partial-private key are used to generate the public key of the user. In other words, CL-PKC differs from IBC in terms of arbitrary public key, and when a signature is transmitted, user's public key is attached with it but not certified by any of the trusted authority. Moreover, KGC is not aware of the secret key of the user.

However, Al-riyami and Paterson's [2] scheme has been proved insecure against Type I adversary by Huang et al. [3] and proposed an improved scheme. A generic construction has been proposed by Yum and Lee [4] in 2004 which is based on identity based signature. Later, Hu et al. [5] found it insecure against key replacement attack and proposed an improved version. Meanwhile Libert and Quisquater [6] proposed another generic construction without precomputations, which is based on Al-riyami and Paterson's work. In 2005, Gorantla and Saxena [7] proposed an efficient CLS scheme but it was found to be insecure against the key replacement attack by Cao et al. [8]. Li et al. [9] and Zhang et al. [10] proposed CLS schemes based on elliptic curve but verification algorithms in their schemes require four pairing computations. To improve the performance, Yap et al. [11] proposed an efficient CLS scheme which required only two bilinear pairings. However, Park and Kang [12] found that the scheme [11] is insecure against a key replacement attack. Recently, Au et al. [13] suggested a new kind of malicious-but-passive-KGC attack where adversary may get access to the secret/public key of KGC and then modified Hu et al.'s model [5] for capturing the attack. In 2007, Huang et al. [14] proposed two new short CLS schemes and claimed their first scheme is provably secure against a Normal Type I adversary as well as Super Type II adversary and the second scheme is secure against Super Type I and Type II adversaries. Unfortunately, Shim [15] claimed that the first scheme in [14] is universally forgeable by the Type I adversary. Later, Tso et al. [16–18] presented efficient short CLS schemes. Recently two CLS schemes were proposed by Xu et al. in [19, 20] for mobile wireless cyber-physical systems, and emergency mobile wireless cyber-physical systems respectively. They were claimed to provide high efficiency and provable security. However, Zhang et al. [21] has shown that these two schemes are universally forgeable against public key replacement attack. Wang et al. [22] proposed a scheme which need not compute the pairing $e(P, P) = g$ at the sign stage, rather it precomputes and publishes the system parameters.

Recently, Du and Wen [23] presented a short CLS scheme and claimed that it is secure against Strong adversaries. However, Fan et al. [24] and Choi et al. [25] independently showed it to be insecure against Strong Type I adversary. Further, Fan et al. [24] proposed a CLS scheme from bilinear pairing with additional property of nonrepudiation but later it was found in [26] that the scheme does not acheive Girault's level 3 security. Later, Tian et al. [27] claimed that the scheme [25] didnot withstand against Strong Type II adversary.

In certificateless infrastructure, the majority of the schemes lacks in some common security issue. To attack a CLS scheme broadly two types of adversaries have been defined: Type I and Type II. A Type I adversary can replace a user's public key but is not able to obtain KGC's master secret key and a Type II adversary is a malicious KGC who knows the master secret key but cannot replace user's public key. Although Huang et al. [28] divide the potential adversaries according to their attack power and enrich the CL-PKC with three more categories. A clear definition of all the three categories of adversaries, Normal, Strong, and Super, has been provided together with the security models. On association with the existing categorization of Type I and Type II adversaries, six types of adversaries can be obtained. These are Normal Type I, Strong Type I, Super Type I, Normal Type II, Strong Type II, and Super Type II. In fact, if a scheme is secure against a Super Type I (II) adversary, it will guarantee the security against Normal and Strong Type I (II) adversaries but the reverse may not be true.

In any certificateless scheme, it is always a good idea to avoid pairing operation as it leads to the increase in computation cost manifold as compared to any other operation. An interesting attempt has been made by He et al. [29] in 2011. He et al. developed an efficient short CLS scheme without pairing. The advantage of the scheme is that it does not use any pairing operation and the length of signature is short. However, in 2012, Tian and Huang [30] proved that the scheme cannot resist against Strong Type II adversary having an access to the master secret key of the KGC. Later

Tsai et al. [31] discovered that the short CLS scheme [29] cannot withstand against Type II adversary and proposed an improved scheme to overcome the weaknesses of He et al.'s [29] scheme. In this paper, we provide a cryptanalysis on the Tsai et al. [31] scheme by using two Type II attacks.

As all the schemes based on ID-based cryptography have been implemented on sensor network, so these schemes are similarly applicable to Wireless Sensor Network [32]. Mica2, Micaz, Tmote sky, and TelosB are the commonly available motes and can be used for implementation. Evaluation of these schemes can be on the basis of various factors like energy consumption, computation time, and security provided. The schemes discussed here in this papers are very much of interest because they are free from pairing, so easily applicable to WSN. But with less resource consumption scheme should not compromise with security. These schemes are found to be vulnerable and few flaws have been reported. In this paper few attacks have been given which will help to improve the scheme.

The rest of the paper is organized as follows. Section 2 presents some preliminaries and complexity assumptions. Section 3 reviews the Tsai et al.'s scheme [31]. In Section 4, we discuss the security analysis of Tsai et al.'s scheme and prove that the scheme is insecure against Strong Type II attack. Section 5 reviews the Fan et al.'s scheme [24]. In Section 6, we discuss the security analysis of Fan et al.'s scheme and proved in insecure against Strong Type I attack followed by the concluding remarks on the presented work.

2. Preliminaries

This section revisits the fundamentals used in the CLS scheme.

2.1. Overview of Elliptic Curve Cryptography. An elliptic curve [33, 34] is a set of points over a finite field $GF(p)$, a Galois Field of order p, which satisfies the Weierstra $\mathscr{B}$ equation [35]

$$y^2 + a_1xy + a_3y = x^3 + a_2x^2 + a_4x + a_6 \qquad (1)$$

but for simplification of computations, cryptographic applications prefer the simple form of Weierstra $\mathscr{B}$ equation as

$$y^2 = x^3 + ax + b, \qquad (2)$$

where $a, b \in GF(p)$.

2.2. Complexity Assumptions. The security of elliptic curve based cryptosystem is based on the assumption that the Elliptic Curve Discrete Logarithm Problem (ECDLP) is hard, which can be defined as follows.

Let E be an elliptic curve over a finite field F_p. Suppose, there are points P, Q on the curve $E(F_p)$ for given generator P. Determine k such that $Q = [k]P$.

3. Review of Tsai et al.'s Short CLS Scheme

In this section, we briefly review the short certificateless signature scheme based on ECDLP [31]. The scheme works as follows.

Setup. Let G be a cyclic additive group, let E/F_p be an elliptic curve E over a prime finite field F_p defined by an equation $y^2 = x^3 + ax + b$, and let p be k-bit prime number, where $p \in G$. Initially, the KGC computes its master public key $P_{pub} = xP$ and chooses two secure one-way hash functions: $H_1 : \{0,1\}^* \times G \times G \to Z_n^*$ and $H_2 : \{0,1\}^* \times G \times G \times G \to Z_n^*$, where $x \in Z_n^*$ is the master key chosen by KGC. The KGC then publishes public parameters $\{F_p, E/F_p, G, P, P_{pub}, H_1, H_2\}$ and keeps master key x secret.

Set-Secret Value. A signer chooses his/her identity ID and his/her secret value x_{ID}. The signer then computes $P_{ID} = x_{ID}P$ and keeps master key x secret x_{ID}.

Partial-Private-Key Extract. The KGC computes $R_{ID} = r_{ID}P$ and $h_{ID} = H_1(ID, R_{ID}, P_{ID})$ for each signer with his/her identity ID $\in \{0,1\}^*$, where $r_{ID} \in Z_n^*$ is a random number. The KGC then computes $s_{ID} = r_{ID} + h_{ID}x \bmod n$ and sends (s_{ID}, R_{ID}) to the user via a secure channel. Notably, the tuple (s_{ID}, R_{ID}) is the partial-private key of the user and the user can confirm its validity by checking the following equation: $s_{ID}P = R_{ID} + h_{ID} \cdot P_{pub}$. If the equation holds, the partial-private key (s_{ID}, R_{ID}) is valid; otherwise, the signer rejects the partial-private key (s_{ID}, R_{ID}).

Set-Private Key. The signer uses $sk_{ID} = (x_{ID}, s_{ID})$ as his/her private key.

Set-Public Key. The signer adopts $pk_{ID} = (P_{ID}, R_{ID})$ as his/her public key.

Sign. Assume a signer wants to sign a message m, he/she performs the following steps to generate signature (R, s) on chosen message m.

(i) The signer computes $R = l \cdot P$, $h_1 = H_2(m, R, P_{ID}, R_{ID})$, $h_2 = H_2(m, R, P_{ID}, R_{ID}, P_{pub})$, where r_{ID} is a random number.

(ii) The signer checks whether $gcd(l + h_1, n)$ equals 1. If it does not hold, the signer returns to step (i).

(iii) The signer computes $s = (l+h_1)^{-1}(h_2 \cdot x_{ID} + s_{ID}) \bmod n$ and then sends (R, s) to the verifier.

Verify. Upon receiving the signature (R, s) on message m from the signer, the verifier can confirm the validity of signature (R, s) using the following equation:

$$s \cdot (R + h_1 \cdot P) = h_2 \cdot P_{ID} + R_{ID} + h_{ID} \cdot P_{pub}, \tag{3}$$

where $h_1 = H_2(m, R, P_{ID}, R_{ID})$, $h_2 = H_2(m, R, P_{ID}, R_{ID}, P_{pub})$, and $h_{ID} = H_1(ID, R_{ID}, P_{ID})$.

If the above equation holds, signature (R, s) is valid; otherwise, the verifier rejects the signature.

4. Cryptanalysis of Tsai et al.'s Short CLS Scheme

In this section, we prove that the He et al. [29] CLS scheme is forgeable by the Strong Type II adversary; that is, the adversary can forge users certificateless signatures by using malicious-KGC attack. Tsai et al. proposed an improvement in the He et al.'s [29] scheme and claimed that the scheme is secure under discrete logarithm assumption in random oracle model. Unfortunately, the scheme was found to be insecure against the malicious-KGC attack.

4.1. Attack 1. The adversary $\mathscr{A}_{II}$ will perform the following steps.

(i) The adversary $\mathscr{A}_{II}$ choose random numbers $t, l' \in Z_n^*$ and a message m' and computes

$$R' = l'P. \tag{4}$$

The adversary $\mathscr{A}_{II}$ replaces the KGC's master public key P_{pub} with

$$P'_{pub} = \frac{t - R_{ID}}{h'_{ID}}, \tag{5}$$

where, $h'_{ID} = H_1(ID, P_{ID}, R_{ID})$.

And, the adversary generates the signature as

$$s' = \frac{t + h'_2 P_{ID}}{(l' + h'_1) P} \bmod n, \tag{6}$$

where $h'_1 = H_2(m', R', P_{ID}, R_{ID})$, $h'_2 = H_2(m', R', P_{ID}, R_{ID}, P'_{pub})$. Clearly, (R', s') is the forged signature on the message m'.

(ii) To check the validity of the signature, the verifier can perform the following verification by using the following equation:

$$\begin{aligned} s' \cdot (R' + h'_1 \cdot P) &= \frac{t + h'_2 P_{ID}}{(l' + h'_1) P} \cdot (l'P + h'_1 P) \\ &= t + h'_2 P_{ID} \\ &= h'_2 \cdot P_{ID} + \left[\frac{t - R_{ID}}{h'_{ID}} \cdot h'_{ID} + R_{ID} \right] \\ &= h'_2 \cdot P_{ID} + R_{ID} + h'_{ID} \cdot P'_{pub}. \end{aligned} \tag{7}$$

4.2. Attack 2. The adversary $\mathscr{A}_{II}$ will perform the following steps to forge a signature.

(i) The adversary $\mathscr{A}_{II}$ selects a random number $t' \in Z_n^*$ and computes $R' = t' \cdot P$.

(ii) $\mathscr{A}_{II}$ chooses a random number $r'_{ID} \in Z_n^*$ and computes $R'_{ID} = r'_{ID} \cdot P$.

(iii) The adversary obtains the hash values $h_1' = H_2(m', R', P_{\mathrm{ID}}, R_{\mathrm{ID}}')$, $h_2' = H_2(m', R', P_{\mathrm{ID}}, R_{\mathrm{ID}}', P_{\mathrm{pub}})$, and $h_{\mathrm{ID}}' = H_1(\mathrm{ID}, P_{\mathrm{ID}}, R_{\mathrm{ID}}')$.

(iv) $\mathscr{A}_{\mathrm{II}}$ assesses whether $gcd(l + h_1, n)$ equals 1. If it does not hold, the signer returns to step (i).

(v) As the the adversary is of Type II, the value of x is known. Then, $\mathscr{A}_{\mathrm{II}}$ computes

$$s' = \left(t' + h_1'\right)^{-1}\left(r_{\mathrm{ID}}' + h_{\mathrm{ID}}' \cdot x + \frac{h_2' \cdot P_{\mathrm{ID}}}{P}\right) \bmod n. \quad (8)$$

The signature is (R', s') on message m'.

(vi) To check the validity of the signature, the verifier can perform the following verification as follows:

$$s' \cdot \left(R' + h_1' \cdot P\right) = h_2' \cdot P_{\mathrm{ID}} + R_{\mathrm{ID}} + h_{\mathrm{ID}}' \cdot P_{\mathrm{pub}}, \quad (9)$$

where $h_1' = H_2(m', R', P_{\mathrm{ID}}, R_{\mathrm{ID}}')$, $h_2' = H_2(m', R', P_{\mathrm{ID}}, R_{\mathrm{ID}}', P_{\mathrm{pub}})$, and $h_{\mathrm{ID}}' = H_1(\mathrm{ID}, P_{\mathrm{ID}}, R_{\mathrm{ID}}')$

$$s' \cdot \left(R' + h_1' \cdot P\right)$$

$$= \left(t' + h_1'\right)^{-1}\left(r_{\mathrm{ID}}' + h_{\mathrm{ID}}' \cdot x + \frac{h_2' \cdot P_{\mathrm{ID}}}{P}\right)$$

$$\times \left(t' \cdot P + h_1' \cdot P\right)$$

$$= \left(t' + h_1'\right)^{-1}\left(r_{\mathrm{ID}}' + h_{\mathrm{ID}}' \cdot x + \frac{h_2' \cdot P_{\mathrm{ID}}}{P}\right)\left(t' + h_1'\right) \cdot P$$

$$= \left(r_{\mathrm{ID}}' + h_{\mathrm{ID}}' \cdot x + \frac{h_2' \cdot P_{\mathrm{ID}}}{P}\right) \cdot P$$

$$= \left(r_{\mathrm{ID}}' \cdot P + h_{\mathrm{ID}}' \cdot x \cdot P + h_2' \cdot P_{\mathrm{ID}}\right)$$

$$= R_{\mathrm{ID}}' + h_2' P_{\mathrm{ID}} + h_{\mathrm{ID}}' \cdot P_{\mathrm{pub}}. \quad (10)$$

5. Review of Fan et al.'s Short CLS Scheme

In this section, we briefly review the short certificateless signature scheme based on ECDLP [24]. The scheme works as follows.

Setup. Let G_1, G_2, and G_T be three cyclic additive groups of prime order $q \leq 2^k$ where k is a security parameter, and let e be an efficiently computable bilinear pairing $e : G_1 \times G_2 \to G_T$, which satisfies the properties of bilinearity and nondegeneracy. Suppose that a message m which will be signed is an element in Z_q^*. KGC chooses two random generators $P_1 \in G_1$ and $P_2 \in G_2$ and a random integer $s \in Z_q^*$. It then computes $P_{\mathrm{pub}} = sP_2 \in G_2$ and $g = e(P_1, P_2) \in G_T$. It then selects two distinct cryptographic hash functions $H_1 : \{0, 1\}^* \to Z_q^*$ and $H_2 : \{0, 1\}^* \times G_2 \to Z_q^*$. KGC publishes the system

parameters, params = $\{k, G_1, G_2, e, q, P, g, P_{\mathrm{pub}}, H_1, H_2\}$, and keeps its master key s secret.

User-Key Gen. A user with identity ID randomly chooses $r \in Z_q^*$ and then computes $pk_{\mathrm{ID}} = rP_2$ and $pk_{\mathrm{ID}}' = r(P_{\mathrm{pub}} + Q_{\mathrm{ID}}P_2)$ where $Q_{\mathrm{ID}} = H_1(\mathrm{ID})$. The user keeps r secretly and sets $(pk_{\mathrm{ID}}, pk_{\mathrm{ID}}')$ as its public key.

Partial-Private-Key Gen. KGC takes params, the user's partial public information $(Q_{\mathrm{ID}}, pk_{\mathrm{ID}})$ as inputs, and then generates the user's partial-private key $d_{\mathrm{ID}} = 1/(s + Q_{\mathrm{ID}} + H_1(\mathrm{ID} \parallel pk_{\mathrm{ID}}))P_1$. Then KGC returns d_{ID} to the user via a secure manner. After receiving d_{ID}, the user checks the correctness of d_{ID} by examining if $e(d_{\mathrm{ID}}, P_{\mathrm{pub}} + Q_{\mathrm{ID}}P_2 + H_1(\mathrm{ID} \parallel pk_{\mathrm{ID}})P_2) = g$. The private key of the user is (d_{ID}, r).

CL Sign. To produce the signature on message $m \in \{0, 1\}^*$, the user with identity ID performs the following steps:

(i) set $h = H_2(m, pk_{\mathrm{ID}})$,

(ii) compute $S = (1/(r + h))d_{\mathrm{ID}}$, where S is the signature on message m of the user.

CL Verify. Given params, message m, pk_{ID}, pk_{ID}', and the signature S on message m of the user with identity ID, the signature can be verified as follows:

(i) let $h = H_2(m, pk_{\mathrm{ID}})$;

(ii) if the following formula holds, the signature S is valid:

$$e\left(S, pk_{\mathrm{ID}}' + H_1(\mathrm{ID} \parallel pk_{\mathrm{ID}})\, pk_{\mathrm{ID}}\right.$$
$$\left. + h\left(P_{\mathrm{pub}} + Q_{\mathrm{ID}}P_2 + H_1(\mathrm{ID} \parallel pk_{\mathrm{ID}})P_2\right)\right) = g. \quad (11)$$

6. Cryptanalysis of Fan et al.'s Short CLS Scheme

In this section, we demonstrate that the Fan et al. [24] CLS scheme is forgeable by the Strong Type I adversary; that is, adversary can replace a user's public key but is not able to obtain KGCs master secret key. $\mathscr{A}_{\mathrm{I}}$ is able to retrieve the partial-private key of the user.

6.1. Attack. The $\mathscr{A}_{\mathrm{I}}$ will perform the following steps.

(i) The adversary $\mathscr{A}_{\mathrm{I}}$ chooses a random number $r' \in Z_n^*$ and replaces a user's public key PK_{ID} with $PK_{\mathrm{ID}}^* = r'P_2$ and PK_{ID}' with $PK_{\mathrm{ID}}'^* = r'(P_{\mathrm{pub}} + Q_{\mathrm{ID}}P_2)$.

(ii) $\mathscr{A}_{\mathrm{I}}$ makes a strong sign query with ID, m, and r' as input and then the challenger returns a valid signature $S' = (1/(r' + h'))d_{\mathrm{ID}}$ where $h' = H_2(m, PK_{\mathrm{ID}}^*)$.

(iii) $\mathscr{A}_{\mathrm{I}}$ obtains the hash value h' on m, PK_{ID}^* by making a hash query.

(iv) $\mathscr{A}_{\mathrm{I}}$ can then compute the user's partial-private key $d_{\mathrm{ID}} = (r' + h')S'$ as he knows the value of r' and h'.

7. Conclusion

The schemes discussed here are of much interest because they are free from pairing and hence can easily be applicable to WSN. But less resource consumption is not enough reason to compromise security. In this paper, security attacks have been applied on two different schemes. Tsai et al. proposed the CLS scheme without pairing which is claimed to be more efficient than the existing schemes (since pairing is always an expensive operation). An exhaustive cryptanalysis has been shown in Section 4 and the results indicate that the improved scheme by Tsai et al. does not resist against the Strong Type II attacks and hence is forgeable. Moreover, we have found that Fan et al's. CLS scheme is forgeable by the Strong Type I adversary. Therefore, to construct a secure certificateless signature scheme without bilinear pairing needs more attention.

References

[1] A. Shamir, "Identity-based cryptosystems and signature schemes," in *Advances in Cryptology*, vol. 196 of *Lecture Notes in Computer Science*, pp. 47–53, Springer, Berlin, Germany, 1984.

[2] S. S. Al-riyami and K. G. Paterson, "Certificateless public key cryptography," in *Advances in Cryptology-ASIACRYPT 2003*, vol. 2894 of *Lecture Notes in Computer Science*, pp. 452–473, Springer, Berlin, Germany, 2003.

[3] X. Huang, W. Susilo, Y. Mu, and F. Zhang, "On the security of certificateless signature schemes from asiacrypt 2003," in *Cryptology and Network Security*, vol. 3810 of *Lecture Notes in Computer Science*, pp. 13–25, Springer, Berlin, Germany, 2005.

[4] D. H. Yum and P. J. Lee, "Generic constructin of certificateless signature," in *Information Security and Privacy*, vol. 3108 of *Lecture Notes in Computer Science*, pp. 200–211, Springer, Berlin, Germany, 2004.

[5] B. C. Hu, D. S. Wong, Z. Zhang, and X. Deng, "Key replacement attack against a generic construction of certificateless signature," in *Information Security and Privacy*, vol. 4058 of *Lecture Notes in Computer Science*, pp. 235–246, Springer, Berlin, Germany, 2006.

[6] B. Libert and J. J. Quisquater, "On constructing certificateless cryptosystems from identity based encryption," in *Proceedings of the 9th International Conference on Theory and Practice of Public-Key Cryptography (PKC '06)*, vol. 3958 of *Lecture Notes in Computer Science*, pp. 474–490, Springer, Berlin, Germany, 2006.

[7] M. Gorantla and A. Saxena, "An efficient certificateless signature scheme," in *Computational Intelligence and Security*, vol. 3802 of *Lecture Notes in Computer Science*, pp. 110–116, Springer, Berlin, Germany, 2005.

[8] X. Cao, K. G. Paterson, and W. Kou, "An attack on a certificateless signature scheme," Cryptology EPrint Archive 2006/367, 2006, http://eprint.iacr.org/.

[9] X. Li, K. Chen, and L. Sun, "Certificateless signature and proxy signature schemes from bilinear pairings," *Lithuanian Mathematical Journal*, vol. 45, no. 1, pp. 76–83, 2005.

[10] Z. Zhang, D. S. Wong, J. Xu, and D. Feng, "Certificateless public-key signature: security model and efficient construction," in *Applied Cryptography and Network Security*, vol. 3989 of *Lecture Notes in Computer Science*, pp. 293–308, Springer, Berlin, Germany, 2006.

[11] W. S. Yap, S. H. Heng, and B. M. Goi, "An efficient certificateless signature scheme," in *Emerging Directions in Embedded and Ubiquitous Computing*, vol. 4097 of *Lecture Notes in Computer Science*, pp. 322–331, Springer, Berlin, Germany, 2006.

[12] J. Park and B. Kang, "Security analysis of the certificateless signature scheme proposed at Sec Ubiq 2006," in *Emerging Directions in Embedded and Ubiquitous Computing*, vol. 4809 of *Lecture Notes in Computer Science*, pp. 686–691, Springer, Berlin, Germany, 2007.

[13] M. H. Au, J. Chen, J. K. Liu, Y. Mu, D. S. Wong, and G. Yang, "Malicious KGC attacks in certificateless cryptography," in *Proceedings of the 12th Australasian Conference on Information Security and Privacy (ACISP '07)*, vol. 4586 of *Lecture Notes in Computer Science*, pp. 308–322, Springer, 2007.

[14] X. Huang, Y. Mu, W. Susilo, D. S. Wong, and W. Wu, "Certificateless signature revisited," in *Information Security and Privacy*, vol. 4586 of *Lecture Notes in Computer Science*, pp. 308–322, Springer, Berlin, Germany, 2007.

[15] K. Shim, "Breaking the short certificateless signature scheme," *Information Sciences*, vol. 179, no. 3, pp. 303–306, 2009.

[16] R. Tso, X. Yi, and X. Huang, "Efficient and short certificateless signature," in *Cryptology and Network Security*, vol. 5339 of *Lecture Notes in Computer Science*, pp. 64–79, Springer, Berlin, Germany, 2008.

[17] R. Tso, X. Yi, and X. Huang, "Efficient and short certificateless signatures secure against realistic adversaries," *Journal of Supercomputing*, vol. 55, no. 2, pp. 173–191, 2011.

[18] R. Tso, X. Huang, and W. Susilo, "Strongly secure certificateless short signatures," *Journal of Systems and Software*, vol. 85, no. 6, pp. 1409–1417, 2012.

[19] Z. Xu, X. Liu, G. Zhang, W. He, G. Dai, and W. Shu, "A certificateless signature scheme for mobile wireless cyber-physical systems," in *28th International Conference on Distributed Computing Systems Workshops, ICDCS Workshops 2008*, pp. 489–494, chn, June 2008.

[20] Z. Xu, X. Liu, G. Zhang, and W. He, "MeCLS: certificateless signature scheme for emergency mobile wireless cyber-physical systems," *International Journal of Computers, Communications and Control*, vol. 3, no. 4, pp. 395–411, 2008.

[21] F. Zhang, S. Miao, S. Li, Y. Mu, W. Susilo, and X. Huang, "Cryptanalysis on two certificateless signature schemes," *International Journal of Computers, Communications and Control*, vol. 5, no. 4, pp. 586–591, 2010.

[22] C. Wang, D. Long, and Y. Tang, "An efficient certificateless signature from pairings," *Journal of Information Science and Engineering*, vol. 8, no. 1, pp. 96–100, 2009.

[23] H. Du and Q. Wen, "Efficient and provably-secure certificateless short signature scheme from bilinear pairings," *Computer Standards and Interfaces*, vol. 31, no. 2, pp. 390–394, 2009.

[24] C. Fan, R. Hsu, and P. Ho, "Truly non-repudiation certificateless short signature scheme from bilinear pairings," *Journal of Information Science and Engineering*, vol. 27, no. 3, pp. 969–982, 2011.

[25] K. Y. Choi, J. H. Park, and D. H. Lee, "A new provably secure certificateless short signature scheme," *Computers and Mathematics with Applications*, vol. 61, no. 7, pp. 1760–1768, 2011.

[26] Y. C. Chen and G. Horng, "On the security models for certificateless signature schemes achieving level 3 security," IACR Cryptology EPrint Archive 554, 2011.

[27] M. Tian, L. Huang, and W. Yang, "On the security of a certificateless short signature scheme," Cryptology EPrint Archive, 2011, http://eprint.iacr.org/2011/419.

[28] X. Huang, Y. Mu, W. Susilo, D. S. Wong, and W. Wu, "Certificate-less signatures: new schemes and security models," *Computer Journal*, vol. 55, no. 4, pp. 457–474, 2012.

[29] D. He, J. Chen, and R. Zhang, "An efficient and provably-secure certificateless signature scheme without bilinear pairings," *International Journal of Communication Systems*, vol. 25, no. 11, pp. 1432–1442, 2011.

[30] M. Tian and L. Huang, "Cryptanalysis of a certificateless signature scheme without pairings," *International Journal of Communication Systems*, 2012.

[31] J. Tsai, N. Lo, and T. Wu, "Weaknesses and improvements of an efficient certificateless signature scheme without using bilinear pairings," *International Journal of Communications Systems*, vol. 25, no. 11, pp. 1432–1442, 2012, Wiley-Blackwell.

[32] I. F. Akyildiz, W. Su, Y. Sankarasubramaniam, and E. Cayirci, "Wireless sensor networks: a survey," *Computer Networks*, vol. 38, no. 4, pp. 393–422, 2002.

[33] "2000. *Standards for efficient cryptography SEC 1: Elliptic curve cryptography*," Certicom Research, http://www.secg.org/collateral/sec1_final.pdf.

[34] "2000. *Standards for efficient cryptography SEC 2: Recommended Elliptic Curve Domain Parameters. Standards for Efficient Cryptography*," Version 1.0. Certicom Research, http://www.secg.org/collateral/sec2_final.pdf.

[35] D. Hankerson, A. J. Menezes, and S. Vanstone, *Guide to Elliptic Curve Cryptography*, Springer, New York, NY, USA, 2004.

An Energy-Efficient CKN Algorithm for Duty-Cycled Wireless Sensor Networks

Lei Wang,[1] **Zhuxiu Yuan,**[1] **Lei Shu,**[2] **Liang Shi,**[3] **and Zhenquan Qin**[1]

[1] *School of Software, Dalian University of Technology, Dalian 116621, China*
[2] *Department Multimedia Engineering, Osaka University, Osaka 565-0871, Japan*
[3] *School of Electronics Engineering and Computer Science, Peking University, Beijing 100871, China*

Correspondence should be addressed to Lei Shu, lei.shu@ieee.org

Academic Editor: Yunhao Liu

To prolong the lifetime of a wireless sensor network, one common approach is to dynamically schedule sensors' active/sleep cycles (i.e., duty cycles) using sleep scheduling algorithms. The connected K-neighborhood (CKN) algorithm is an efficient decentralized sleep scheduling algorithm for reducing the number of awake nodes while maintaining both network connectivity and an on-demand routing latency. In this paper, we investigate the unexplored energy consumption of the CKN algorithm by building a probabilistic node sleep model, which computes the probability that a random node goes to sleep. Based on this probabilistic model, we obtain a lower epoch bound that keeps the network more energy efficient with longer lifetime when it runs the CKN algorithm than it does not. Furthermore, we propose a new sleep scheduling algorithm, namely, Energy-consumption-based CKN (ECCKN), to prolong the network lifetime. The algorithm EC-CKN, which takes the nodes' residual energy information as the parameter to decide whether a node to be active or sleep, not only can achieve the k-connected neighborhoods problem, but also can assure the k-awake neighbor nodes have more residual energy than other neighbor nodes in current epoch.

1. Introduction

Wireless sensor networks (WSNs) are normally powered by batteries with limited energy, which are difficult or impossible to be recharged or replaced. A common approach for saving the sensor nodes' energy is to select a subset of nodes to remain active/awake and let others go to sleep in a given epoch. Most of current literatures on sleep scheduling in WSNs are to achieve *point coverage* and/or *node coverage* problems [1]. *Point coverage* problem (also called *spatial coverage*) focuses on selecting a set of active nodes in an epoch so that every point of the deployment space is covered, while considering some optimization goals, for example, minimizing energy consumption [2], minimizing average event detection latency [3]. *Node coverage* problem (also called *network coverage*) focuses on choosing a set of active nodes, in which (1) they construct a connected backbone and (2) sleeping nodes are direct neighbors of at least one active node [4]. This node coverage problem is to ensure that any

two nodes in the network can communicate with each other through the connected backbone.

The Connected K-Neighborhood (CKN) algorithm is a distributed sleep scheduling algorithm [1], which can reduce the number of active nodes efficiently. It keeps the network k-connected and optimizes the geographic routing performance. Supporting the geographic routing performance is not studied in any previous *point coverage* and *node coverage* researches. Although, the CKN algorithm performs well with the geographic routing protocols, the following questions are not addressed in paper [1]. (1) *How frequently should the CKN algorithm be executed in the network so that it can really help to save energy, for each time executing the CKN algorithm also consumes energy?* Intuitively, executing the CKN algorithm will consume a mass of energy with substantial data transmission to exchange local information between nodes and their neighbors, which influences the energy consumption distribution of network. (2) *Do all active sensor nodes in the CKN algorithm* [1] *consume the*

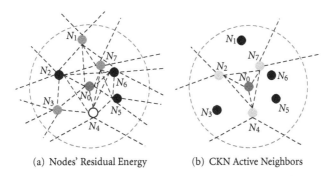

(a) Nodes' Residual Energy   (b) CKN Active Neighbors

FIGURE 1: Nonuniform energy consumption problem. In (a), the black nodes represent the nodes which have more residual energy than those of node N_0, the grey and white nodes have less energy than N_0's, and the white node has the least energy. In (b), the green nodes represent the active nodes according to the CKN algorithm in a WSN, and the sensor nodes with less residual energy are selected.

energy uniformly in each epoch? We identify the *nonuniform energy consumption* problem, as shown in Figure 1. It is recognized that when executing the CKN algorithm in WSNs, sensor nodes with less residual energy are possible to be selected, which may result in that the energy of these sensor nodes can be fast consumed. The problem is caused by: *the CKN algorithm chooses the active nodes absolutely based on the* ranks *that are randomly given at the beginning of executing the CKN algorithm in each epoch.* In other words, the CKN algorithm cannot ensure the network energy is balancedly consumed.

Motivated by above two major issues, we conduct theoretical studies on two important questions based on the CKN algorithm. The first question is as follows. *Is the CKN algorithm energy saving for any given value of k and the epoch? If not, how frequently should the CKN algorithm be executed so that the network is energy saving?* In order to find out the relationship between the epoch and the energy consumption, we build a probabilistic model for the CKN algorithm to compute the probability that each random node goes to sleep and the expected total number of epochs during each node's lifetime. We formulate the lower bound of an epoch to keep the CKN algorithm energy efficient.

We address the second question based on the analysis for the first problem: *How do we design a new sleep scheduling algorithm based on the CKN algorithm that can balance the energy consumption to prolong network lifetime further?* Satisfying all those requirements that the CKN algorithm holds, a new decentralized sleep scheduling algorithm is challenging. In the light of the discussions for the question 1, we propose a new sleep scheduling algorithm, named energy-consumption-based CKN (EC-CKN), to prolong the network lifetime. The advantage of the EC-CKN algorithm over the original CKN algorithm is that it takes the nodes' residual energy information as parameter to decide whether a node to be active or sleep. The EC-CKN algorithm inherits all the major properties of the CKN algorithm, that is, solving the k-connected neighborhoods problem. Meanwhile, it also makes a significant new contribution to the energy efficiency by assuring the k-active neighbor nodes have more residual energy than other neighbor nodes in the current epoch. A

theoretical analysis on the energy consumption of the EC-CKN algorithm is given to show the correctness of the new contribution.

The rest of the paper is as follows. Section 2 shows the network model. Section 3 presents the original CKN algorithm regulation and its properties. Section 4 builds a probabilistic model to compute the probability that a random node goes to sleep. Section 5 presents the EC-CKN algorithm. Section 6 demonstrates the properties of the EC-CKN algorithm. Section 7 shows the simulation results about the original CKN algorithm and the EC-CKN algorithm, comparing theoretical values and simulation results. Finally, Section 9 concludes the paper.

2. Network Model

2.1. Communication Network Model. A multihop sensor network is modeled by a graph $G = (S, E)$, where $S = \{s_1, s_2, \ldots, s_n\}$ is the set of sensor nodes and E is the set of directed links. Each node has a uniform transmission radius of r_t, and the necessary condition of $(s_i, s_j) \in E$ is $|s_i - s_j| \le r_t$ and a node s_j is the next hop of s_i to the sink by the routing protocol. If $(s_i, s_j) \in E$, we use $l_{i,j}$ to denote (s_i, s_j). Each node also has a uniform interference radius of r_f. An node s_j is interfered by the signal from s_i, if $|s_i - s_j| \le r_f$ and s_j is not the intended receiver. Let I_i be the interference region that centers at s_i with the interference radius r_f. Each node is only equipped with a single radio interface and has the uniform initial energy $\mathcal{E}_0$. The entire network lifetime is divided into epochs, and each epoch is T. At the beginning of each epoch, a node transmits packets in T_1, and then it runs the sleep scheduling algorithm to decide the state of the next epoch in T_2 (where $T = T_1 + T_2$) as shown in Figure 2.

2.2. Event Generation Model. Assume each node has a uniform sensing radius r_s. Let C_u denote the sensing region of the node s_u, which centers at s_u with the sensing radius r_s. An event occurs when the sensing unit of a node s_u picks up a signal with the power above a predetermined threshold within the sensing region C_u [5]. Suppose the

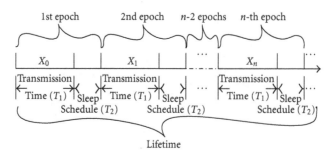

FIGURE 2: The lifetime of a node s_u consists of many epochs. Each epoch includes packet transmission time and sleep scheduling algorithm's execution time.

temporal event behavior over the entire sensing region, $\mathcal{A}$, is a Poisson process with an average event rate λ. Let $p_{XY}(x, y)$ denote an independent probability distribution of the spatial distribution of events. Let p_e denote the probability that an event is detected by a node s_u, given the fact that it occurred in $\mathcal{A}$:

$$p_e = \frac{\int_{C_u} p_{XY}(x, y)\, dx\, dy}{\int_{\mathcal{A}} p_{XY}(x, y)\, dx\, dy}, \qquad (1)$$

where $p_{XY}(x, y)$ is the spatial distribution of events that is characterized by an independent probability distribution. Let $p_m(T, n)$ denote the probability that n events occur in an epoch T at a node s_u. Therefore, the probability of no events occurring in C_u over an epoch T is given by

$$p_m(T, 0) = \sum_{i=0}^{\infty} \frac{e^{-\lambda T}(\lambda T)^i}{i!} (1 - p_e)^i$$
$$= e^{-p_e \lambda T}. \qquad (2)$$

Let $p_m(T)$ denote the probability that at least one event occurs in an epoch T at a node s_u:

$$p_m(T) = 1 - p_m(T, 0) = 1 - e^{-p_e \lambda T}. \qquad (3)$$

That is the probability of at least one event occurring at the node s_u is an exponential distribution characterized by a spatially weighted event arrival rate $\lambda_{u,u} = \lambda \times p_e$.

2.3. Buffer Analysis.
Now, we consider two sources of traffic as an input to the buffer of each node [6].

Generated Packets. The sensing unit of a node senses events and generates packets as discussed in Section 2.2. These packets are *generated packets*. For a node s_u, the rate of the generated packets is denoted by $\lambda_{u,u}$.

Relay Packets. A node also receives packets from its upstream nodes and then forwards them to the sink node. (Along the data stream from a source node to the sink node by the routing protocol, downstream nodes are closer to the sink node, and receive packets sent by the node. Upstream nodes are far away from the sink node, and transmit packets to the

node). These packets are referred as *relay packets*. The rate at which a node s_u receives relay packets from a node s_v is denoted as $\lambda_{v,u}$.

Therefore, the input packet rate of s_u's buffer, λ_u, can be written as

$$\lambda_u = \lambda_{u,u} + \lambda_{u,r} = \lambda_{u,u} + \sum_{v \in \mathcal{N}_u^{\text{in}}} \lambda_{v,u}, \qquad (4)$$

where $\lambda_{u,r}$ is the total relay packet rate at the node s_u, $\mathcal{N}_u^{\text{in}}$ is the set of nodes that have the node s_u as the next hop, and $\lambda_{v,u}$ is the packet rate from the node s_v to the node s_u. Let γ_u be the output rate of a node, which is given by

$$\gamma_u = (1 + e_u)\lambda_u, \qquad (5)$$

where e_i is the packet error rate.

2.4. Channel and Energy Consumption Model.
The energy consumption model characterizes energy consumption of a node in the network. Suppose there is no energy consumption when a node is sleep. If a node is active, we classify the energy consumption into three general categories.

(1) The Constant Energy Consumption. is the minimum energy needed to sustain a node when it is active without the packet transmission. It includes, for example, the battery leakage, energy consumed during the state transformation.

(2) The Additional Energy Consumption. is the energy consumed by the data transmission during the sleep scheduling algorithm running time.

(3) The Conventional Energy Consumption. includes the receiving energy consumption and the transmitting energy consumption except the local information exchange in the sleep scheduling algorithm, which is based on the first-order radio model [7].

The energy loss is due to the channel transmission, ϵ_{amp} is the transmit amplifier. And the transmitting energy consumption for a bit packet is

$$E_{tx} = \mathcal{E} + \epsilon_{\text{amp}} \cdot r_t^2, \qquad (6)$$

and the receiving energy consumption is

$$E_{rx} = \mathcal{E}, \qquad (7)$$

where $\mathcal{E}$ is energy consumed by the transmitter or receiver circuitry.

2.5. Lifetime Definition.

There is no universally agreed definition of network lifetime as it depends on the specific application. The lifetime can be measured by the time when the first node exhausts its energy, or when a certain fraction of nodes is dead, or even when all nodes are dead. Alternately, it may be reasonable to measure the network lifetime by application-specific parameters, such as the time when the network can no longer relay sensory data packets. In this paper, we define the network lifetime is the time when the first sensor node run out its energy from the beginning. The general network lifetime is the exact individual lifetime of each active node [8].

Theorem 1. *For a sensor network, each node has nonrecharge-able initial energy $\mathcal{E}_0$, the average general network lifetime $\mathbb{E}[\mathcal{L}]$, is given by*

$$\mathbb{E}[\mathcal{L}] = \frac{\mathcal{E}_0}{E_c + \lambda_r \mathbb{E}[E_{rx}] + \gamma \mathbb{E}[E_{tx}]}, \qquad (8)$$

where E_c is the constant energy consumption on the first died node, $\mathbb{E}[E_{rx}]$ is the expected receiving energy consumption, and $\mathbb{E}[E_{tx}]$ is the expected transmitting energy consumption.

Proof. Suppose there are M independently and identically distributed trials on the same sensor network to record the network lifetime $\mathcal{L}$, the receiving energy consumption of each bit E_{rx}, and the transmitting energy consumption of each bit E_{tx}. For the mth trial ($1 \le m \le M$), the total energy consumed by the first died node during the whole lifetime is

$$\mathcal{E}_0 = E_c \mathcal{L}^m + \sum_{i=1}^{N_{rx}^m} E_{rx}^m(i) + \sum_{i=1}^{N_{tx}^m} E_{tx}^m(i), \qquad (9)$$

where N_{rx}^m is the number of bits to be received, and N_{tx}^m is the number of bits to be transmitted of the first died node during the network lifetime of the mth trial. Summing (9) up over the M trials and dividing both sides by M, we obtain

$$
\begin{aligned}
\mathcal{E}_0 = \frac{1}{M} \sum_{m=1}^{M} \mathcal{L}^m \Bigg[& E_c \\
& + \left(\frac{\sum_{m=1}^{M} N_{rx}^m}{\sum_{m=1}^{M} \mathcal{L}^m} \right) \times \left(\frac{\sum_{m=1}^{M} \sum_{i=1}^{rx} E_{rx}^m(i)}{\sum_{m=1}^{M} N_{rx}^m} \right) \\
& + \left(\frac{\sum_{m=1}^{M} N_{tx}^m}{\sum_{m=1}^{M} \mathcal{L}^m} \right) \times \left(\frac{\sum_{m=1}^{M} \sum_{i=1}^{N_{tx}^m} E_{tx}^m(i)}{\sum_{m=1}^{M} N_{tx}^m} \right) \Bigg].
\end{aligned}
\qquad (10)
$$

Note that $\lim_{M \to \infty} (\sum_{m=1}^{M} N_{rx}^m)/(\sum_{m=1}^{M} \mathcal{L}^m) = \lambda_r$ is the average receiving rate and $\lim_{M \to \infty} (\sum_{m=1}^{M} N_{tx}^m)/(\sum_{m=1}^{M} \mathcal{L}^m) = \gamma$ is the average transmitting rate.

The average receiving energy consumed in the ith received bit can be written as

$$\mathbb{E}[E_{rx}] = \lim_{M \to \infty} \frac{\sum_{m=1}^{M} E_{rx}^m(i) \mathcal{X}_m(i)}{D_{rx}(i)}, \qquad 1 \le i \le N_{rx}, \qquad (11)$$

where $\mathcal{X}_m(i) = 1$ for $1 \le i \le N_{rx}^m$ and 0 otherwise. $D_{rx}(i) = \sum_{m=1}^{M} \mathcal{X}_m(i)$ is the total number of the occurrence of the ith received bit among the M trials, and $N_{rx} = \max_m \{N_{rx}^m\}$ is the maximum number of received bits during the network lifetime. The probability that the received bit chosen randomly happens to the ith received bit is given by

$$p_{rx}(i) = \lim_{M \to \infty} \frac{D_{rx}(i)}{\sum_{m=1}^{M} N_{rx}^m}, \qquad 1 \le i \le N_{rx}. \qquad (12)$$

Averaging (11) over the received bit chosen randomly indexing i, the expected receiving energy consumption is defined as

$$
\begin{aligned}
\mathbb{E}[E_{rx}] & \triangleq \mathbb{E}_{rx}^i \{\mathbb{E}[E_{rx}(i)]\} \\
& = \lim_{M \to \infty} \frac{\sum_{m=1}^{M} \sum_{i=1}^{N^m} E_{rx}^m(i)}{\sum_{m=1}^{M} N_{rx}^m},
\end{aligned}
\qquad (13)
$$

where $\mathbb{E}[E_{rx}(i)]$ is the average energy consumed in ith bit packet, $\mathbb{E}_{rx}^i\{\cdot\}$ denotes the expectation over the randomly chosen received packet indexing i.

Similarly, the expected transmitting energy consumption is

$$
\begin{aligned}
\mathbb{E}[E_{tx}] & \triangleq \mathbb{E}_{tx}^i \{\mathbb{E}[E_{tx}(i)]\} \\
& = \lim_{M \to \infty} \frac{\sum_{m=1}^{M} \sum_{i=1}^{N_{tx}^m} E_{tx}^m(i)}{\sum_{m=1}^{M} N_{tx}^m},
\end{aligned}
\qquad (14)
$$

where $\mathbb{E}[E_{tx}(i)]$ is the average energy consumed in ith transmitted packet, $\mathbb{E}_{tx}^{(i)}\{\cdot\}$ denotes the expectation over the randomly chosen transmitted packet indexing i.

3. A Brief Description of CKN

In [1], the studied WSN is represented as an undirected communication graph $G = (S, E)$. N_u is the set of s_u's neighbors. The connected K-neighborhood problem is defined as (i) each node has at least $\min\{k, |N_u|\}$ active neighbors, which can be called awake neighbors; (ii) all active nodes are connected. To solve the problem, the authors developed a sleep scheduling algorithm: connected K-neighborhood (CKN).

In CKN, each node s_u picks a random rank rank_u, broadcasts the rank_u, and collects its neighbors' ranks in R_u. And then, s_u broadcasts R_u and collects R_v from its neighbors, where $s_v \in N_u$. If s_u or its neighbors has less than k neighbors, s_u will remain awake. Otherwise, s_u computes a subset C_u of N_u that is a set of nodes having rank $< \text{rank}_u$. "Before the node s_u goes to sleep it needs to make sure that all nodes in C_u are connected by nodes with rank $< \text{rank}_u$ and each of its neighbors has at least k neighbors from C_u" [1].

The CKN algorithm has the following properties: first, each node s_u (awake or not) with $|N_u|$ neighbors must have at least $\min\{k, |N_u|\}$ awake neighbors in each epoch; second, there is the minimal average number of awake nodes per epoch; finally, awake nodes change from epoch to epoch. For any $k \ge 1$, there are more than $4(k + \ln N)$ neighbors for each node, where N is the number of nodes in the network. Then,

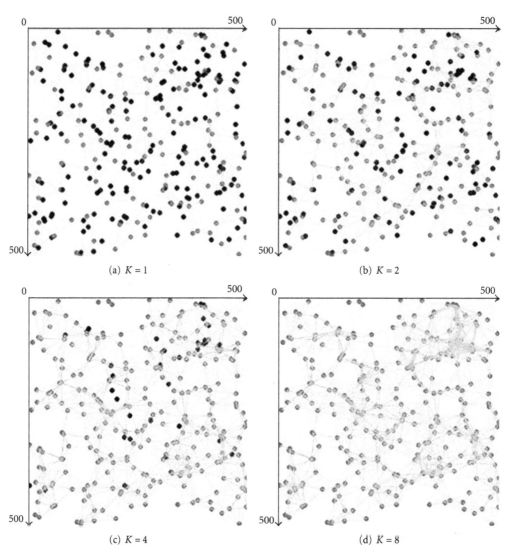

(a) $K = 1$ (b) $K = 2$

(c) $K = 4$ (d) $K = 8$

FIGURE 3: Four examples of executing the CKN algorithm with different values for k. When $k = 1$, a large number of sensor nodes can turn to sleep mode, but, when $k = 8$, almost all sensor nodes have to be always-on. Here, black and unconnected sensor nodes are sleeping nodes.

with high probability, $|CKN_k| = O(\ln N) \cdot |OPT_k|$, where $|CKN_k|$ is the number of awake nodes by the CKN algorithm and $|OPT_k|$ is the number of awake nodes by an optimal algorithm that finds a minimum connected k-neighborhood as Figure 3.

4. Analysis of the CKN Algorithm

In this section, we build up a probabilistic model for the CKN algorithm to compute the probability that one node s_u goes to sleep in each epoch. Based on the probability, we formulate the lower bound of an epoch to keep the CKN algorithm energy efficient.

Notations used in this section. N_u is the set of s_u's neighbors, and N'_u is the set of s_u's 2-hop neighbors. C_u and C'_u are the subsets of N_u and N'_u having rank $\leq$ rank$_u$. $|N_u|$, $|N'_u|$, $|C_u|$, and $|C'_u|$ are the number of the elements in N_u, N'_u, C_u, and

C'_u, respectively. Graphs G_{C_u} and $G_{C'_u}$ are composed of nodes and potential links in C_u and C'_u.

For a homogeneous Poisson point process in two dimensions, the probability that a random node has n neighbors is [9]

$$P(|N_u| = n) = \frac{(\rho \pi r_t^2)^n}{n!} \cdot e^{-\rho \pi r_t^2}, \tag{15}$$

where $\rho = N/\mathcal{A}$ is the nodes density. And a node is isolated with a probability of $P(|N_u| = 0) = e^{-\rho \pi r_t^2}$. The expectation of the number of s_u's neighbors is

$$\mathbb{E}[|N_u|] = \rho \pi r_t^2. \tag{16}$$

If there are at least k different paths connecting any two different vertices in the graph G, the graph is *k-connected*

$(k = 1, 2, \ldots)$. The probability that the graph G is k-connected is

$$P\left(G^k\right) = \left(1 - \sum_{n}^{k-1} \frac{(\rho \pi r_t^2)^n}{n!} \cdot e^{-\rho \pi r_t^2}\right)^N. \quad (17)$$

4.1. Sleep Probability in the CKN Algorithm. For the CKN algorithm, when a node s_u has at least k neighbors, whether it goes to sleep is decided by two factors: (1) "any two nodes in C_u are connected either directly or indirectly through s_u's 2-hop neighbors that have rank less than rank_u" and (2) "any node in N_u has at least k neighbors for C_u" [1].

Lemma 2. $|C_u| \sim B(|N_u|, p)$ and $|C_u'| \sim B(|N_u'|, p)$ are binomial distributions, where p is the probability that a node has rank $< \text{rank}_u$.

Proof. Let $\{\text{rank}_1, \text{rank}_2, \ldots, \text{rank}_{|N_u|}\}$ be the random ranks for nodes in N_u. Suppose $\text{rank}_i \in (0, 1)$ and $i \in [1, |N_u|]$. Let

$$x_i = \begin{cases} 1, & \text{if } \text{rank}_u - \text{rank}_i > 0, \\ 0, & \text{otherwise,} \end{cases}$$

$$p = p_i(x_i = 1) = E(P_{\text{rank}_u - \text{rank}_i > 0}) = \frac{1}{2}, \quad (18)$$

$$q = p_i(x_i = 0) = 1 - p.$$

Let $Z = \sum_{i \in N_u} x_i$, and the probability $z_j = j$ is

$$\begin{aligned} p_j &= \binom{|N_u|}{j} \cdot p^j \cdot q^{|N_u| - j} \\ &= \binom{|N_u|}{j} \cdot p^{|N_u|}, \end{aligned} \quad (19)$$

where $j \in [0, |N_u|]$ and $|C_u| \sim B(|N_u|, p)$. Similarly, $|C_u'| \sim B(|N_u'|, p)$.

Theorem 3. *Under the CKN algorithm, the sleep probability of a node s_u is*

$$p_s(|C_u|) = \text{Prob}_1 \cdot \text{Prob}_2, \quad (20)$$

and the awake probability is

$$p_a(|C_u|) = 1 - p_s(|C_u|), \quad (21)$$

where Prob_1, the probability a node s_u satisfies the first condition, is defined as

$$\text{Prob}_1 \triangleq \left(1 - e^{-\rho_1 \pi r_t^2}\right)^{|C_u'|}, \quad (22)$$

and Prob_2, the probability s_u satisfies the second condition, is defined as

$$\text{Prob}_2 \triangleq P(|C_u| \geq k + 1) \cdot P\left(G_{C_u}^k\right) \cdot P\left(C_{u N_u - C_u}^k\right). \quad (23)$$

Proof. If s_u and its neighbors have at least k neighbors, the two conditions deciding s_u whether to sleep or not can be interpret as the following corresponding conditions: (1) the graph $G_{C_u'}$ is connected, and (2) the graph G_{C_u} is k-connected

and each node in the set $N_u - C_u$ has at least k neighbors in C_u.

The probability that the graph $G_{C_u'}$ is k-connected is

$$\begin{aligned} \text{Prob}_1 &\leq \text{Prob}\left(G_{C_u'} \text{ is connected}\right) \\ &\leq P(|N_u|_{\min} \geq 1) \\ &= \left(1 - e^{-\rho_1 \pi r_t^2}\right)^{|C_u'|}, \end{aligned} \quad (24)$$

where $|N_u|_{\min}$ is the minimum degree in the graph $G_{C_u'}$, and $\rho_1 = |C_u'|/(4\pi t_r^2)$ is the node density in the graph $G_{C_u'}$.

The probability of the condition (2) is

$$\text{Prob}_2 = P(|C_u| \geq k + 1) \cdot P\left(G_{C_u}^k\right) \cdot P\left(C_{u N_u - C_u}^k\right), \quad (25)$$

where $P(G_{C_u}^k)$, the probability that the graph G_{C_u} is k-connected, can be expressed as

$$P\left(G_{C_u}^k\right) \leq \left(1 - \sum_{n=0}^{k-1} \frac{(\rho_2 \pi r_t^2)^n}{n!} \cdot e^{-\rho_2 \pi r_t^2}\right)^{|C_u|}, \quad (26)$$

and $P(C_{u N_u - C_u}^k)$ is the probability that a node $s_v \in (N_u - C_u)$ has at least k neighbors in C_u, which is

$$P\left(C_{u N_u - C_u}^k\right) = \left(1 - \sum_{n=0}^{k-1} \frac{(\rho_2 \pi r_t^2)^n}{n!} \cdot e^{-\rho_3 \pi r_t^2}\right)^{|N_u - C_u|}, \quad (27)$$

where $\rho_2 = |C_u|/(\pi t_r^2)$, $\rho_3 = (|C_u| + 1)/(\pi t_r^2)$, and $|N_u - C_u|$ is the number of the elements in the set $N_u - C_u$.

4.2. Energy Consumption of the CKN Algorithm. Based on the result of the probability a random node goes to sleep, we can now analyze the node energy consumption for two cases: (1) it runs the CKN algorithm; (2) it does not run the CKN algorithm.

Lemma 4. *When a node s_u executes the CKN algorithm, its energy consumption is*

$$\mathcal{E}_{\text{ckn}}(s_u) = \mathcal{E}_c^1 + 2(E_{tx} + |N_u| \cdot E_{rx}), \quad (28)$$

and the energy consumption of a node during each epoch is

$$\mathcal{E}_{\text{epoch}}(s_u) = \mathcal{E}_c^2 + T_1\left(\lambda_r E_{rx} + \gamma E_{tx}\right), \quad (29)$$

where $\mathcal{E}_c^1$ and $\mathcal{E}_c^2$ are the constant energy consumptions of a node during the time of the CKN algorithm executed and an epoch, respectively.

Theorem 5. *Under the CKN algorithm, the lower bound of an epoch keeping the network energy efficient is*

$$\underline{T} \geq \frac{\mathbb{E}[\mathcal{L}]\left(\mathbb{E}[\mathcal{E}_{\text{ckn}}] + p_a \cdot \mathbb{E}[\mathcal{E}_{\text{epoch}}]\right)}{\mathcal{E}_0}, \quad (30)$$

where $\mathbb{E}[\mathcal{E}_{\text{ckn}}]$ and $\mathbb{E}[\mathcal{E}_{\text{epoch}}]$ are the expectation energy consumption during the time of the CKN algorithm executed and the expectation of the energy consumption during an epoch.

Input: The least number of neighbors k

Output: Connected k-Neighborhood Network

(1) Get the current residual energy $Erank_u$;

(2) Broadcast $Erank_u$ and receive the residual energy of its neighbors N_u. Let R_u be the set of the residual energy of nodes in N_u.

(3) Broadcast R_u and receive R_v from each node s_v where $s_v \in N_u$.

(4) If $|N_u| < k$ or $|N_v| < k$ for any $s_v \in N_v$, remain awake.

  Return.

(5) Compute $E_u = \{s_v \mid s_v \in N_u$ and $Erank_v > Erank_u\}$;

(6) Go to sleep if both the following conditions hold. Remain awake otherwise.

  (i) Any two nodes in E_u are connected either directly or indirectly through nodes that are the s_u's 2-hop neighbors that have $Erank_v$ larger than $Erank_u$;

  (ii) Any node in N_u has at least k neighbors from E_u.

(7) Return.

ALGORITHM 1: Energy-consumption-based CKN (*run the following at each node s_u^*).

Proof. Suppose there are M *i.i.d.* trials on the same network that runs the CKN algorithm as the sleep schedule to record the network lifetime, $\mathcal{L}_{\text{ckn}}$, and the epoch is T in each trial. For the mth trial, the total energy consumed by the first died node during the lifetime is

$$\mathcal{E}_0 = \mathcal{N}_{\text{epoch}}^m \mathcal{E}_{\text{ckn}} + \sum_{i=1}^{\mathcal{N}_{\text{epoch}}^m} \mathcal{E}_{\text{epoch}}^m(i), \qquad (31)$$

where $\mathcal{N}_{\text{epoch}}^m$ is the number of epochs in the mth trial. Summing (31) up to the M trials and dividing both sides by M, we obtain

$$\mathcal{E}_0 = \frac{1}{M}\left[\mathcal{E}_{\text{ckn}} \sum_{m=1}^{M} \mathcal{N}_{\text{epoch}}^m + \sum_{m=1}^{M} \sum_{i=1}^{\mathcal{N}_{\text{epoch}}^m} \mathcal{E}_{\text{epoch}}^m(i) \right]. \qquad (32)$$

Note that $T \lim_{M \to \infty} (1/M) \sum_{m=1}^{M} \mathcal{N}_{\text{epoch}}^m = \mathbb{E}[\mathcal{L}_{\text{ckn}}]$.

The average energy consumed in the ith epoch can be written as

$$\mathbb{E}\left[\mathcal{E}_{\text{epoch}} \right] = \lim_{M \to \infty} \frac{\sum_{m=1}^{M} E_{\text{epoch}}^m(i) \mathcal{Y}_m(i)}{D_{\text{epoch}}(i)}, \qquad (33)$$
$$1 \le i \le \mathcal{N}_{\text{epoch}},$$

where $\mathcal{Y}_m(i) = 1$ if $1 \le i \le \mathcal{N}_{\text{epoch}}^m$ and the node is awake in the ith epoch, and 0 otherwise. $D_{\text{epoch}}(i) = \sum_{m=1}^{M} \mathcal{Y}_m(i)$ is the total number of the ith epoch that the node is awake among the M trials, and $\mathcal{N}_{\text{epoch}} = \max_m \{\mathcal{N}_{\text{epoch}}^m\}$ is the maximum number of epochs during the network lifetime. The probability that a randomly chosen awake epoch of a node happens to the ith epoch is given by

$$p_a(i) = \lim_{M \to \infty} \frac{D_{\text{epoch}}(i)}{\sum_{m=1}^{M} \mathcal{N}_{\text{epoch}}^m} = \lim_{M \to \infty} \frac{1}{M} \sum_{m=1}^{M} p_a(m), \qquad (34)$$

where $p_a(m)$ is the nodes awake probability in the mth trial. Averaging (33) over the randomly chosen epoch indexing i,

the expected ith epoch energy consumption except for the energy consumed by the CKN algorithm is defined as

$$\mathbb{E}\left[\mathcal{E}_{\text{epoch}} \right] \triangleq \lim_{M \to \infty} \sum_{m=1}^{M} \frac{E_{\text{epoch}}^m(i) \mathcal{Y}_m(i)}{\mathcal{N}_{\text{epoch}}^m}. \qquad (35)$$

5. The Energy-Consumption-Based CKN Algorithm

We develop a new sleep scheduling algorithm to extend the network lifetime, which can still have all properties of the CKN algorithm.

A scalable distributed solution to the connected k-neighborhoods problem based on the nodes' current residual energy information is challenging for several reasons. First, a node can go to sleep assuming that there are at least k neighbors being awake to keep it k-connected. Second, the outcome of the algorithm must change over epochs so that all nodes have opportunities to sleep. Third, even though nodes decide to sleep or wake up based on their local information, the whole network must be globally connected. The aforementioned three challenges have been achieved by the CKN algorithm [1], which keep the network duty-cycled and connected k-neighborhood. Fourth, awake neighbors of any node s_u have k-top residual. The last one makes sure the energy of the network consumed balancedly, which is the main strength that the EC-CKN algorithm has over the original CKN algorithm.

We address the challenges by proposing the EC-CKN algorithm. The pseudocode of Algorithm 1 depicts the EC-CKN algorithm, which is repeated in each epoch on each node. The algorithm takes an input parameter, k, the required minimum number of per node's awake neighbors. In EC-CKN algorithm, a node s_u broadcasts its current residual energy information $Erank_u$ (Step 1). It computes a subset E_u of neighbors having E rank $<$ $Erank_u$ (Step 5). Before s_u goes to sleep, it makes sure that any two nodes in E_u are connected either directly or indirectly through the node that is in the s_u's 2-hop neighbors having E rank $<$ $Erank_u$, and its neighbors have at least k neighbors from E_u (Step 6). These requirements ensure that when a node has less than k neighbors, none of its neighbors goes to sleep, and when it has more than k neighbors, at least k neighbors decide to remain awake. Note that these requirements are easy to keep by computing locally with 2-hop neighborhood information. The current residual energy is exchanged in Steps 2 and 3.

6. Properties of the EC-CKN Algorithm

This section analyzes the network lifetime, the awake probability, and the energy consumption of the network under the EC-CKN algorithm.

Theorem 6. *For any $k \geq 1$, the average network lifetime of the EC-CKN algorithm increases with the increases of the ratio of the network size N and k, N/k.*

Proof. Suppose N nodes are placed uniformly at random within a deployment area such that the average number of neighbors per node is $\xi \geq 4(k + \ln N)$. Let $\delta = (ck \ln N)/\xi$, for constant $c > 96$ determined by the analysis. Consider executing the algorithm EC-CKN on the network, and let $Erank^{(i)*}$ be the residual energy of the δth largest residual energy selected by a node in the ith epoch. We claim that, *w.h.p.*, all nodes with residual energy $<$ $Erank^{(i)*}$ go to sleep. Because there are at most δ nodes with residual energy at least $Erank^{(i)*}$, we have the average number of the awake nodes in each epoch is

$$|EC|_k \leq \delta = \frac{ck \ln N}{\xi}. \tag{36}$$

And the average network lifetime under the algorithm EC-CKN can be written as

$$\mathbb{E}[\mathscr{L}_{EC}] = \frac{NT\mathscr{E}_0}{|EC|_k \cdot \mathscr{E}_{epoch} + (N - |EC|_k) \cdot \mathscr{E}_{EC}}, \tag{37}$$

where $\mathscr{E}_{EC} = \mathscr{E}_{ckn}$ is the energy consumed by executing the EC-CKN algorithm, and T is the length of an epoch. In comparison with the energy consumed by the awake nodes in an epoch, the energy consumed by the sleep nodes in an epoch is considered negligible:

$$\mathbb{E}[\mathscr{L}_{EC}] \approx \frac{NT\xi\mathscr{E}_0}{ck \ln N \cdot \mathscr{E}_{epoch}}. \tag{38}$$

For the algorithm EC-CKN, a node could have four states: *Init, Awake, Sleep,* and *Dead.* Let $\mathscr{S} = \{Init = 0, Awake = 1, Sleep = 2, Dead = 3\}$ be the set of the node's states, and $N_s = |\mathscr{S}|$ is the capacity of the states. Nodes can turn into the states *Awake,* and *Sleep* from the states *Init, Awake* and *Sleep,* respectively. And the state *Dead* can be

only transformed from the states *Awake* and *Sleep*. Figure 4 shows the states transition graph in the algorithm EC-CKN, in which vertices are the states of nodes and the weights of edges are the transition probability between the two states in the ith epoch.

Theorem 7. *Under the algorithm EC-CKN, the difference of the energy consumption between nodes s_u and s_v in the ith epoch is*

$$d^n = \begin{cases} T_2(\Lambda E_{rx} + \Gamma E_{tx}), & \text{if } n = 0, \\ T_2 p_u^a(i-1)(\Lambda E_{rx} + \Gamma E_{tx}), & \text{otherwise,} \end{cases} \tag{39}$$

where Λ and Γ are both the Skellam distributions and $p_u^a(i-1)$ is the average probability that a node is awake in the $(i-1)$-th epoch.

Proof. Let $\mathscr{S}_u = \{\mathscr{S}_u^0, \mathscr{S}_u^1, \ldots, \mathscr{S}_u^i, \ldots\}$ denote the states of s_u in epochs, and let the chain

$$d : d^0, d^1, \ldots, d^i, \ldots \tag{40}$$

denote the difference between the energy consumed by nodes s_u and s_v in each epoch, where $s_v \in N_u$. $d^i = \alpha\mathscr{E}_{v,epoch}(i) - \beta\mathscr{E}_{u,epoch}(i)$, where $\mathscr{E}_{u,epoch}(i)$ and $\mathscr{E}_{v,epoch}(i)$ are the conventional energy consumption of nodes s_u and s_v if they are awake in the ith epoch. The factors α and β depend on the state of nodes s_u and s_v. If $\mathscr{S}_u^i = 0$ *or* 1, $\alpha = 1$, and if $\mathscr{S}_u^i = 3$, $\alpha = 0$, which is the same with β.

Suppose there are M independently and identically distributed trials. For the mth trial ($1 \leq m \leq M$), the difference between the energy consumption of the two nodes in the ith epoch is

$$d_m^i = \alpha\mathscr{E}_{v,epoch}^m(i) - \beta\mathscr{E}_{u,epoch}^m(i). \tag{41}$$

The average difference of energy consumption in the ith epoch can be defined as

$$d^{(i)} = \lim_{M \to \infty} \frac{T_2}{M} \left[\frac{\sum_{m=1}^M \left[\left(\alpha N_{v,rx}^{m,i} - \beta N_{u,rx}^{m,i}\right) E_{rx} \right]}{T_2} \right. $$
$$\left. + \frac{\sum_{m=1}^M \left[\left(\alpha N_{v,tx}^{m,i} - \beta N_{u,tx}^{m,i}\right) E_{tx} \right]}{T_2} \right], \tag{42}$$

where $N_{u,rx}^{m,i}$ and $N_{u,tx}^{m,i}$ are the number of received bits and transmitted bits of the node s_u in the ith epoch during the mth trial. T_2 is the time of the conventional data transmission time of each epoch. We discuss the difference between the energy consumption of two nodes in the following two cases.

Case 1 ($i = 0$). According to (33) and (14), we obtain

$$d_{(0)} = T_2[(\lambda_{v,r} - \lambda_{u,r})E_{rx} + (\gamma_v - \gamma_u)E_{tx}]. \tag{43}$$

Case 2 ($i > 0$). According to (33) and (34), we obtain

$$d_{(i)} = T_2 p_u^a(i-1)[(\lambda_{v,r} - \lambda_{u,r})E_{rx} + (\gamma_v - \gamma_u)E_{tx}], \tag{44}$$

where $p_u^a(i-1)$ is the expected probability that the node is awake in the $(i-1)$-th epoch.

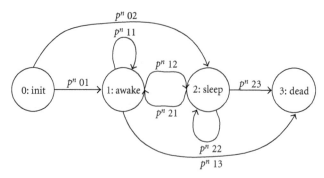

FIGURE 4: The Markov state transition probability graph of the EC-CKN algorithm.

Note for $\lambda_{v,r}$ and $\lambda_{u,r}$ are two independent Poisson distributions, $\Lambda = \lambda_{v,r} - \lambda_{u,r}$ is the Skellam distribution. Similarly, $\Gamma = \gamma_v - \gamma_v$ is also the Skellam distribution.

Theorem 8. *Consider a random node s_u, which has more than k neighbors, the probability that a node s_u is awake in the ith epoch under the EC-CKN algorithm is*

$$p_a^i = \begin{cases} p_a(|E_u^0|), & \text{if } i = 0, \\ p_a(|E_u^i|), & \text{otherwise.} \end{cases} \tag{45}$$

Proof. We introduce a new chain

$$D : 0, d^0, D^0, d^1, D^1, \ldots, d^i, D^i, \ldots, \tag{46}$$

to denote the difference between the residual energy of the two nodes s_u and s_v, where $s_v \in s_u$. Then, we obtain

$$D^i = \begin{cases} d^0, & \text{if } i = 0, \\ D^{(i-1)} + d^0, & \text{otherwise.} \end{cases} \tag{47}$$

Therefore, the number of elements in the set E_u^i is $|E_u^i| = |N_u|\varrho^i$, where

$$\varrho^{(i)} = \begin{cases} \dfrac{D^0}{\max\{d^0\} - \min\{d^0\}} & \text{if } i = 0, \\ \dfrac{D^i}{\max\{D^i\} - \min\{D^i\}} & \text{otherwise.} \end{cases} \tag{48}$$

Theorem 9. *Under the EC-CKN algorithm, the upper bound of the network lifetime is*

$$\overline{\mathcal{L}}_{\text{EC-CKN}} = \frac{\mathcal{E}_0}{\min \sum_i \sum_a \sigma_{i,a} \mathcal{E}_{\text{epoch}}^n}, \tag{49}$$

where $\sigma_{i,a}$ is the steady-state probability that the action a is chosen when the chain is in the state i under the policy $\mathcal{K}$.

Proof. Now, we construct a Markov State Decision chain for each node s_u:

$$\mathcal{S}_u^0, a^0, \mathcal{S}_u^1, a^1, \ldots, \mathcal{S}_u^n, a^n, \ldots, \tag{50}$$

where $\mathcal{S}_u^0 = 0$, and $\mathcal{S}_u^n \in \{1, 2, 3\}$ denotes the state in the nth epoch ($n \geq 1$), and a^n is the action under the state $\mathcal{S}_u^n$

$$a^n = \begin{cases} \mathcal{E}_{u,\text{epoch}}^n, & \text{if } n = 0 \text{ or } \mathcal{S}_u^n = 1, \\ 0, & \text{otherwise.} \end{cases} \tag{51}$$

Let the policy $\mathcal{K} = \{\kappa_{u,i}^n(a)\}$ denote the probability that the action a is chosen when $\mathcal{S}_u = i$, which satisfies the following two conditions:

$$0 \leq \kappa_{u,i}(a) \leq 1, \quad \forall i, a,$$
$$\sum_a \kappa_{u,i}(a) = 1, \quad \forall i. \tag{52}$$

Under the policy $\mathcal{K}$, the sequence of states $\mathcal{S}_u^n$ constitutes a Markov chain with the transition probability $p_u^n(\mathcal{K}, i, j)$, which can be written as

$$\begin{aligned} p_u^n(\mathcal{K}, i, j) &= p_u\{\mathcal{S}_u^{n+1} = j \mid \mathcal{S}_u^n = i\} \\ &= \sum_a p_u^n(i, j)\kappa_{u,i}(a). \end{aligned} \tag{53}$$

For the policy $\mathcal{K}$, let $\sigma_{i,a}$ denote the steady-state probability that the chain is in the state i and the action a is chosen:

$$\sigma_{i,a} = \lim_{n \to \infty} P_{\mathcal{K}}\{\mathcal{S}_u^n = i, a^n = a\} \tag{54}$$

The vector $\sigma = \{\sigma_{i,a}\}$ satisfies

$$\begin{aligned} &\text{(i)} \quad \sigma_{i,a} \geq 0, \quad \forall i, a, \\ &\text{(ii)} \quad \sum_i \sum_a \sigma_{i,a} = 1, \quad \forall i, a, \\ &\text{(iii)} \quad \sum_a \sigma_{j,a} = \sum_i \sum_a \sigma_{j,a} p_{i,j}, \quad \forall i, a, j, \end{aligned} \tag{55}$$

Equations (55)(i) and (55)(ii) are obvious, and (55)(iii) follows as the left-hand side equals the steady-state probability of being in the state j and the right-hand side is the same probability computed by conditioning on the state and action chosen one epoch earlier.

Suppose that a reward $\mathcal{R}(Y_i^n, a_i^n) = a^n$ is earned whenever the action a_i^n is chosen in the state i in the n'th epoch. Since $\mathcal{R}(Y_i^n, a_i^n)$ denotes the reward earned at the epoch n, the expected average reward per epoch under the $\mathcal{K}$ policy can be written as

$$
\begin{aligned}
\mathbb{E}[\mathcal{R}(\mathcal{K})] &= \lim_{n \to \infty} \frac{\sum_n \sum_{i \in \mathcal{S}} \mathcal{R}(Y_i^n, a_i^n)}{n} \\
&= \sum_i \sum_a \sigma_{i,a_i^n} \mathcal{R}(Y_i^n, a_i^n) \\
&= \sum_i \sum_a \sigma_{i,a_i} a^n.
\end{aligned}
\tag{56}
$$

Therefore, $\mathbb{E}[\mathcal{R}(\mathcal{K})]$ can be interpreted as the following linear program:

$$
\begin{aligned}
\min \sum_i \sum_a &\sigma_{i,a} \mathcal{R}(Y_i^n, a_i^n) \\
\text{subject to } &\sigma_{i,a} \geq 0, \quad \forall i, a, \\
&\sum_i \sum_a \sigma_{i,a} = 1, \quad \forall i, a, \\
&\sum_a \sigma_{ja} = \sum_i \sum_a \sigma_{i,a} p_{i,j}, \quad \forall i, a, j,
\end{aligned}
\tag{57}
$$

$\mathbb{E}[\mathcal{R}(\mathcal{K})]$ is a special case of the linear programm and is solved by a standard linear linear programming algorithm known as *the simplex algorithm*. The simplex algorithm solves the linear program by moving from an extreme point of the feasibility region to a better extreme point until the optimal is reached. So we can figure out the lower bound and upper bound of the lifetime by the linear programming (57).

Lemma 10. *Under the EC-CKN algorithm, the upper bound network lifetime is*

$$
\mathcal{L}_{\text{EC-CKN}} = \frac{\mathcal{E}_0}{\max \sum_i \sum_a \sigma_{i,a} \mathcal{E}_{\text{epoch}}^n},
\tag{58}
$$

where $\sigma_{i,a}$ is the steady-state probability that the action a is chosen when the chain is in the state i under the policy $\mathcal{K}$.

7. Simulation

Simulation Setup. In NetTopo [10], we conduct extensive simulation experiments. The studied WSN has the network size $800 \times 600 \, \text{m}^2$. The number of deployed sensor nodes are increased from 100 to 1000 (each time increased by 100). The value of k is changed from 1 to 10 (each time increased by 1). For every number of deployed sensor nodes, we use 100 different seeds to generate 100 different network deployment. A source node is deployed at the location of $(50, 50)$, and a sink node is deployed at the location of $(750, 550)$. The transmission radius for each node is 60 m.

Routing Algorithm. TPGF routing algorithm [11] is one of the earliest geographical multipath routing algorithms designed for facilitating the multimedia stream data transmission in static and always-on wireless sensor networks (WSNs). It focuses on exploring the maximum number of optimal node-disjoint routing paths in network layer in terms of minimizing the path length and the end-to-end transmission delay. TPGF routing algorithm includes two

phases. Phase 1 is responsible for exploring the possible routing path. Phase 2 is responsible for optimizing the found routing path with the least number of hops. The simulation results with changed k values in this figure reflect the comparison between the original average length of paths and the optimized average length of paths.

Sleep Probability of the CKN Algorithm. The node's sleep probability has been analyzed in Section 4.1. Figure 5 describes the node's theoretic sleep probability based on the probability model that has been set up and covers the comparison between the simulation results and the theoretic value. We enlarge the some factors of the probabilistic model so that the theoretic value is greater than the simulation when $N/k > 100$. While $N/k < 100$, the theoretical results and simulation results approximate every much. Moreover, the same variation trend proves that our model is ponderable for nodes' sleep probability in the CKN algorithm.

Network Lifetime Under the CKN Algorithm. Based on the node sleep probability from the probabilistic model and simulation, we can get the relative probability stretch variation curve with the epoch. *Relative probability stretch* is defined as a function of the expected number of epochs with k active neighbors compared to the expected number of epochs with a larger $|N_u|$ active neighbors. In our work, we assume that the radio dissipates $E_{\text{elec}} = 50 \, \text{nJ/bit}$ to the transmitter or receiver circuity and $\epsilon = 100 \, \text{pJ/bit/m}^2$, and the data rate is 20 kbps. In Figure 6, there is a key value of the length of the epoch time $(M \cdot t)$ when N and k are certain, which is the intersection of relative probability stretch and reference axis. The CKN algorithm is energy efficient if the epoch is less than the key value. Otherwise, the node will consume more energy by the CKN algorithm than it is always active.

Network Lifetime Comparison between the CKN Algorithm and the EC-CKN Algorithm. The network lifetime of the CKN algorithm and the EC-CKN algorithm in a WSN is represented by the number of epochs. We conduct simulation for the CKN algorithm and the EC-CKN algorithm in a WSN and compare the network lifetime under the same situation in Figures 7 and 8. Results in Figures 7(a) and 7(c) confirm that the energy consumption of the EC-CKN algorithm is better managed and balanced than the CKN algorithm. Results in Figures 7(b) and 7(d) reveal the influence of changing the value of k: decreasing the value of k in the EC-CKN algorithm can prolong the network lifetime, particularly when the network nodes are densely deployed. Figures 7(a) and 7(b) show the whole distribution and tendency varying from the different combinations between k and N (the total number of deployed nodes in the network). Correspondingly, Figures 7(c) and 7(d) have the same meaning for the EC-CKN algorithm. Figure 8 compares the network lifetime between the CKN algorithm and the EC-CKN algorithm, by conducting the two algorithms under the same scenario. And the results give a straight proof that the

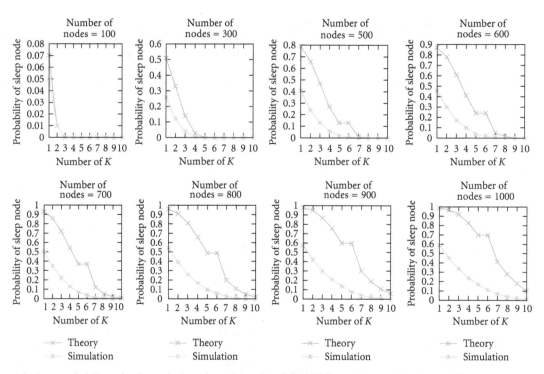

FIGURE 5: Node's sleep probability. The theoretical results and simulation results do not match well when the network size gets bigger, such as $N = 700\ 1000$. The reason is that we enlarge the probability that any two nodes in C_u are connected either directly themselves or indirectly through s_u's 2-hop neighbors.

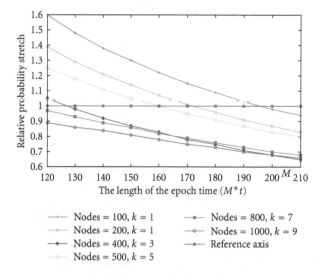

FIGURE 6: Relative probability stretch varies with epoch.

EC-CKN algorithm can provide longer network lifetime than the CKN algorithm.

8. Related Work

Network lifetime has been defined in various ways [12–17], and an energy-efficient mechanism may choose to maximize a certain type of network lifetime. One useful mechanism is the MAC layer power saving scheme, which reduces energy consumption by minimizing radio transceivers' idle time. SMAC [18] is an important MAC protocol designed for sensor networks, which forces sensor nodes to operate at low duty cycle by putting them into periodic sleep instead of idle listening. The timeout-MAC protocol (TMAC) improves SMAC by using an adaptive duty cycle [19]. Data-gathering MAC (DMAC) also uses an adaptive duty cycle, which provides low node-to-sink latency in convergecast communication by staggering the wake-up times of the nodes in the convergecast tree [20]. Pattern MAC (PMAC)

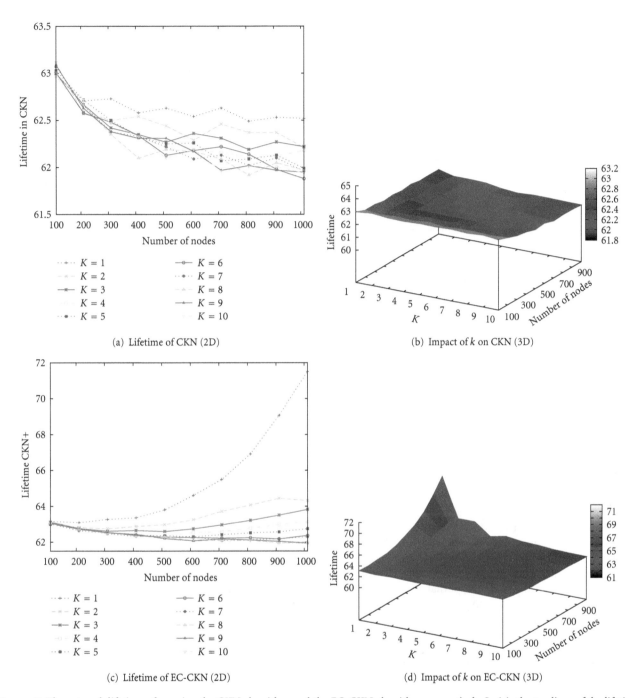

(a) Lifetime of CKN (2D)

(b) Impact of k on CKN (3D)

(c) Lifetime of EC-CKN (2D)

(d) Impact of k on EC-CKN (3D)

FIGURE 7: The network lifetime of running the CKN algorithm and the EC-CKN algorithm, respectively. In (a), the ten lines of the lifetime results according to the CKN algorithm have a lot intersections, which means the energy consumption by the CKN algorithm in a WSN is not managed towards the energy-balancing direction. However, in (c), the ten lines of the lifetime results by the EC-CKN algorithm present smooth changing when the number of nodes and the value of k are changed and the lifetime increases when the ratio N/k increases. This point clearly reflects that the energy consumption by the EC-CKN algorithm in a WSN is well managed towards the energy-balancing direction. Furthermore, simulation results in (b) and (d) also reveal that decreasing the value of k (let more nodes sleep) can definitely help to prolong the network lifetime of the EC-CKN algorithm in a WSN, but not the CKN algorithm.

[21] allows each sensor node determines the sleep-wake-up schedules based on its own traffic and the traffic patterns of its neighbors. BMAC [22] and XMAC [23] are two asynchronous duty-cycle-based protocols. In BMAC, each sensor node periodically wakes up to check whether there is any activity currently on the wireless channel or not. If so, the node remains active to receive a possible incoming packet. In this way, the node will receive one or more packets that are actually destined for other nodes. XMAC uses a strobed preamble to solve the overhearing

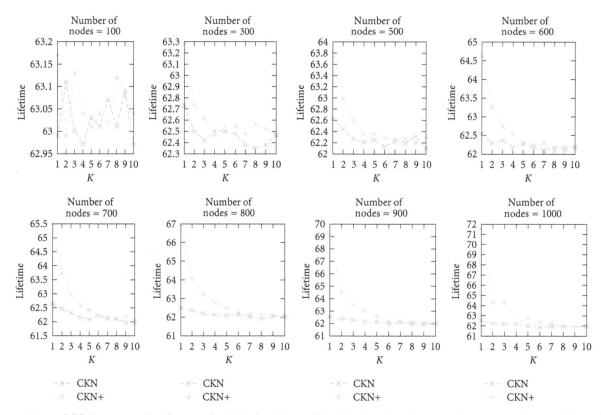

FIGURE 8: Network lifetime comparison between the CKN algorithm and the EC-CKN algorithm. Y-axle represents the recorded number of epochs when the first node runs out of its energy.

problem in BMAC. A strobed preamble includes a sequence of short preambles prior to DATA transmission. Obviously, the preamble transmission of BMAC and XMAC occupies the wireless medium for a long time under the light traffic load. To solve the problem, WiseMAC [24] is proposed. WiseMAC is similar to BMAC except that senders efficiently reduce the length of the wake-up preamble by exploiting the sampling of the schedules of its neighbors.

Another common technique to minimize the energy consumption and extend the network lifetime is to put some sensors in the sleep state and put others in the active state for the sensing and communication tasks. When a sensor is in the sleep state, its processor is turned off, but a timer or some other triggering mechanism may be running to wake up the sensor. On the other hand, all the components in the sensor are turned on when it is in the active state. Therefore, the energy consumed in the sleep state is only a tiny fraction of that consumed in the active state. One complexity here is that different types of sensors may support different sets of states. For example, the μAMPS sensor has three sleep states: *Monitor*, *Observe*, and *Deep Sleep* [25]. A sleep scheduling mechanism allows each sensor to determine when it should switch its state and what state it will switch to. Kumar et al. adopt the randomized independent scheduling (RIS) mechanism extending network lifetime while achieving asymptotic K-coverage [26]. RIS assumes that time is divided into epochs based on a time synchronization method. At

the beginning of a epoch, each sensor independently decides weather to become active with probability p or go to sleep with probability $1 - p$. Thus, the network lifetime is increased by a factor close to $1/p$. Berman et al. presented a centralized and a distributed algorithm to maximize network lifetime while achieving K-coverage [27]. In the distributed algorithm, each sensor is in one of three states: *active, idle,* or *vulnerable*. In the vulnerable state, if the sensor discovers that part of its sensing area cannot be covered by any of its active or vulnerable neighbors, it immediately enters the active state. Otherwise, it enters the idle state if its sensing area can be monitored by either active neighbors or vulnerable neighbors with a higher energy level. Another distributed scheduling mechanism named lightweight deployment aware scheduling (LDAS) is proposed in [16]. Unlike the aforementioned distributed algorithm, LDAS does not ask if the sensor nodes are equipped with GPS or other devices to obtain location information. It assumes that each active node knows the number of its active neighbors. If the number of the active nodes exceeds a threshold, the node randomly selects some of its neighbors and sends tickets to them. When a node receives enough tickets from its neighbors, it may enter the sleep state after a random backoff period. Probing environment and adaptive sensing (PEAS) mechanism was designed for high-density sensor networks in a harsh environment [17]. Each node broadcasts a message with a transmission range of t_r after sleeping for a random period. A node will go to the active state only if it receives no replies from its active neighbors. PEAS assumes that sensor nodes may fail frequently and unexpectedly, which makes synchronized sleeping algorithm infeasible. Coverage configuration protocol (CCP) is an integrated coverage and connectivity configuration protocol [4]. The protocol defines that nodes have three states: ACTIVE, LISTEN, and SLEEP. Each node is initially ACTIVE. When it receives a message, it goes to the LISTEN state and starts a random LISTEN timer. The node will go to SLEEP if it satisfies the following conditions: (i) its LISTEN timer expires; (ii) the network is still connected when it goes to SLEEP. In the SLEEP state, a node will set a random SLEEP timer. When the timer expires, it will enter the LISTEN state. PECAS (probing environment and collaborating adaptive sleeping) is an extension of PEAS. A active node in PECAS will go back to sleep after a specified period of time. It piggybacks the remaining ACTIVE time in its reply messages to its neighbors' probe message. Therefore, an active neighbor who will go to SLEEP can schedule itself to wake up before the node goes to SLEEP, which prevents the occurrence of blind spots. Adaptive self-configuring sensor networks topologies (ASCENT) is similar to PEAS, which is also designed for high-density sensor networks. However, unlike PEAS, ASCENT does not guarantee network connectivity. Low-energy adaptive clustering hierarchy (LEACH) [28] is a cluster-based protocol, which utilizes randomized rotation of cluster heads to distribute work load among the sensors. In LEACH, the lifetime of network is divided into epochs, and each epoch includes a *set-up* phase and a *steady* phase. During the set-up phase, cluster heads are selected and each sensor joins a cluster by choosing a cluster that needs the minimum communication energy. During the steady phase, each cluster head aggregates the data from the sensors in its cluster and then forwards them to the sink. To conserve energy, nonhead sensors go to sleep at all time except that they are transmitting data. E-LEACH [15] is an extension of LEACH, which adapts the cluster heads selection algorithm to the nonuniform starting energy level among the sensors and the required number of cluster heads.

9. Conclusion

When deploying real WSNs for practical applications, it is extremely important to have a good sleeping scheduling algorithm to balance sensor nodes' energy consumption and a reasonable length for an epoch towards energy saving is extremely important. In this paper, we make the following major contributions for supporting the real WSNs applications. (1) A theoretical study is given for the CKN algorithm, which formulates the lower bound of an epoch to keep the CKN algorithm feasible. (2) A new sleep scheduling algorithm, named as EC-CKN, is proposed to balance the energy consumption and prolong the network lifetime. (3) Extensive simulation work is conducted, which proved the energy consumption in the EC-CKN algorithm is well balanced.

Acknowledgments

This work is partially supported by Natural Science Foundation of China under Grant no. 61070181 and Natural Science Foundation of Liaoning Province under Grant no. 20102021. L. Shu's research in this paper was supported by Grant-in-Aid for Scientific Research (S)(21220002) of the Ministry of Education, Culture, Sports, Science and Technology, Japan.

References

[1] S. Nath and P. B. Gibbons, "Communicating via fireflies: geographic routing on duty-cycled sensors," in *Proceedings of the 6th International Symposium on Information Processing in Sensor Networks (IPSN '07)*, pp. 440–449, April 2007.

[2] C. F. Hsin and M. Liu, "Network coverage using low duty-cycled sensors: random & coordinated sleep algorithms," in *Proceedings of the 3rd International Symposium on Information Processing in Sensor Networks (IPSN '04)*, pp. 433–442, April 2004.

[3] Q. Cao, T. Abdelzaher, T. He, and J. Stankovic, "Towards optimal sleep scheduling in sensor networks for rare-event detection," in *Proceedings of the 4th International Symposium on Information Processing in Sensor Networks (IPSN '05)*, pp. 20–27, April 2005.

[4] X. Wang, G. Xing, Y. Zhang, C. Lu, R. Pless, and C. Gill, "Integrated coverage and connectivity configuration in wireless sensor networks," in *Proceedings of the 1st International Conference on Embedded Networked Sensor Systems (SenS '03)*, pp. 28–39, November 2003.

[5] A. Sinha and A. Chandrakasan, "Dynamic power management in wireless sensor networks," *IEEE Design and Test of Computers*, vol. 18, no. 2, pp. 62–74, 2001.

[6] I. F. Akyildiz, M. C. Vuran, and O. B. Akan, "A cross-layer protocol for wireless sensor networks," in *Proceedings of the 40th Annual Conference on Information Sciences and Systems (CISS '06)*, pp. 1102–1107, March 2006.

[7] W. R. Heinzelman, A. Chandrakasan, and H. Balakrishnan, "Energy-efficient communication protocol for wireless microsensor networks," in *Proceedings of the 33rd Annual Hawaii International Conference on System Siences (HICSS '00)*, p. 223, January 2000.

[8] Y. Chen and Q. Zhao, "On the lifetime of wireless sensor networks," *IEEE Communications Letters*, vol. 9, no. 11, pp. 976–978, 2005.

[9] C. Bettstetter, "On the minimum node degree and connectivity of a wireless multihop network," in *Proceedings of the 3rd ACM International Symposium on Mobile Ad Hoc Networking and Computing (MOBIHOC '02)*, pp. 80–91, June 2002.

[10] L. Shu, C. Wu, Y. Zhang, J. Chen, L. Wang, and M. Hauswirth, "NetTopo: beyond simulator and visualizer for wireless sensor networks," in *Proceedings of the 2nd International Conference on Future Generation Communication and Networking (FGCN '08)*, pp. 17–20, December 2008.

[11] L. Shu, Z. Zhou, M. Hauswirth, D. Le Phuoc, P. Yu, and L. Zhang, "Transmitting streaming data in wireless multimedia sensor networks with holes," in *Proceedings of the 6th International Conference on Mobile and Ubiquitous Multimedia (MUM '07)*, pp. 24–33, Oulu, Finland, December 2007.

[12] A. Cerpa and D. Estrin, "ASCENT: adaptive self-configuring sensor networks topologies," in *Proceedings of the IEEE Computer and Communications Societies (INFOCOM '02)*, pp. 1278–1287, June 2002.

[13] J. Deng, Y. S. Han, W. B. Heinzelman, and P. K. Varshney, "Scheduling sleeping nodes in high density cluster-based sensor networks," *Mobile Networks and Applications*, vol. 10, no. 6, pp. 825–835, 2005.

[14] T. He, S. Krishnamurthy, J. A. Stankovic et al., "Energy-efficient surveillance system using wireless sensor networks," in *Proceedings of the 2nd International Conference on Mobile Systems, Applications and Services (MobiSys '04)*, pp. 270–283, 2004.

[15] W. B. Heinzelman, A. P. Chandrakasan, and H. Balakrishnan, "An application-specific protocol architecture for wireless microsensor networks," *IEEE Transactions on Wireless Communications*, vol. 1, no. 4, pp. 660–670, 2002.

[16] K. Wu, Y. Gao, F. Li, and Y. Xiao, "Lightweight networks," *Mobile Networks and Applications*, vol. 10, no. 6, pp. 837–852, 2005.

[17] F. Ye, G. Zhong, J. Cheng, S. Lu, and L. Zhang, "PEAS: a robust energy conserving protocol for long-lived sensor networks," in *Proceedings of the 23th IEEE International Conference on Distributed Computing Systems (ICDCS '03)*, pp. 28–37, May 2003.

[18] W. Ye, J. Heidemann, and D. Estrin, "An energy-efficient MAC protocol for wireless sensor networks," in *Proceedings of the IEEE Computer and Communications Societies (INFOCOM '02)*, pp. 1567–1576, New York, NY, USA, June 2002.

[19] T. Van Dam and K. Langendoen, "An adaptive energy-efficient MAC protocol for wireless sensor networks," in *Proceedings of the 1st International Conference on Embedded Networked Sensor Systems (SenSys '03)*, pp. 171–180, Los Angeles, Calif, USA, November 2003.

[20] G. Lu, B. Krishnamachari, and C. S. Raghavendra, "An adaptive energy-efficient and low-latency MAC for data gathering in wireless sensor networks," in *Proceedings of 18th International Parallel and Distributed Processing Symposium (IPDPS '04)*, pp. 3091–3098, April 2004.

[21] T. Zheng, S. Radhakrishnan, and V. Sarangan, "PMAC: an adaptive energy-efficient MAC protocol for wireless sensor networks," in *Proceedings of the 19th IEEE International Parallel and Distributed Processing Symposium (IPDPS '05)*, p. 237, April 2005.

[22] J. Polastre, J. Hill, and D. Culler, "Versatile low power media access for wireless sensor networks," in *Proceedings of the 2nd International Conference on Embedded Networked Sensor Systems (SenSys '04)*, pp. 95–107, November 2004.

[23] M. Buettner, G. V. Yee, E. Anderson, and R. Han, "X-MAC: a short preamble MAC protocol for duty-cycled wireless sensor networks," in *Proceedings of the 4th International Conference on Embedded Networked Sensor Systems (SenSys' 06)*, pp. 307–320, November 2006.

[24] A. El-Hoiydi and J. D. Decotignie, "WiseMAC: an ultra low power MAC protocol for multi-hop wireless sensor networks," in *Proceedings of the 1st International Workshop on Algorithm Aspects of Wireless Sensor Networks*, vol. 3121 of *Lecture Notes in Computer Science*, pp. 18–31, 2004.

[25] E. Shih, S. H. Cho, N. Ickes et al., "Physical layer driven protocol and algorithm design for energy-efficient wireless sensor networks," in *Proceedings of the 7th Annual International Conference on Mobile Computing and Networking (MOBICOM '01)*, pp. 272–286, July 2001.

[26] S. Kumar, T. H. Lai, and J. Balogh, "On k-coverage in a mostly sleeping sensor network," in *Proceedings of the 10th Annual International Conference on Mobile Computing and Networking (MOBICOM '04)*, pp. 144–158, October 2004.

[27] P. Berman, G. Calinescu, C. Shah, and A. Zelikovsky, "Power efficient monitoring management in sensor networks," in *Proceedings of the IEEE Wireless Communications and Networking Conference (WCNC '04)*, pp. 2329–2334, 2004.

[28] W. R. Heinzelman, A. Chandrakasan, and H. Balakrishnan, "Energy-efficient communication protocol for wireless microsensor networks," in *Proceedings of the 33rd Annual Hawaii International Conference on System Siences (HICSS '00)*, p. 223, January 2000.

[29] A. Sinha and A. Chandrakasan, "Dynamic power management in wireless sensor networks," *IEEE Design and Test of Computers*, vol. 18, no. 2, pp. 62–74, 2001.

4

BRS-Based Robust Secure Localization Algorithm for Wireless Sensor Networks

Ning Yu, Lirui Zhang, and Yongji Ren

School of Instrumentation Science and Optoelectronics Engineering, Beijing University of Aeronautics and Astronautics (Beihang University), Beijing 100191, China

Correspondence should be addressed to Ning Yu; nyu@buaa.edu.cn

Academic Editor: Sunho Lim

Localization is the key supporting technology for wireless sensor networks (WSNs). Security and accuracy are the premise of the localization application. Real-world applications of wireless sensor networks are often subject to a variety of adverse circumstances interference, and the localization performance is seriously affected. In this paper, we propose a BRS-based robust secure localization (BRSL) algorithm in order to reduce the impact of the malicious attackers in WSNs. The BRSL method includes two phases. In the first stage, the trust evaluation framework is established on the basis of beta reputation system. In the second phase, we employ the weighted Taylor-series least squares method to estimate the coordinates of sensor nodes. Simulation results demonstrate that the proposed algorithm is robust and effective.

1. Introduction

Wireless sensor networks (WSNs) are based on the technology of sensor, wireless communication, tiny embedded devices, and distributed computing. They exchange information with the environment through sensors and implement the function of collecting and dealing with data. Wireless sensor networks have been widely used in the fields of environmental monitoring, target tracking, military applications, disaster management, and so forth [1–3].

Self-localization technology of nodes is the prerequisite and basis for the application of wireless sensor networks, especially the position information that is needed for the perceived data. Node localization of WSNs is to determine the positions of normal nodes based on the positions of beacon nodes and the constraint relations between normal and beacon nodes. Positions or coordinates of normal nodes are unknown. Beacon nodes usually get their positions or coordinates through global positioning system (GPS) modules or by manual deployments. Being an essential support technology of wireless sensor networks, node localization has got more and more attention in the recent years [4–10].

Most localization methods depend on measuring the distances or hops between normal and beacon nodes to obtain the coordinates of normal nodes. In many typical localization algorithms [11–13], the coordinates of beacon nodes are generally assumed to be completely correct without any disturbs of adverse factors, and the normal nodes can use beacon information in security. However, in the actual hostile situations, some malicious nodes may intrude into sensor networks. They pretend to be true beacon nodes or attack other anchor nodes and make them declare false coordinates [14, 15]. The false coordinates or distance estimation will cause a major localization error for normal sensor nodes [16]. In this case, some methods should be explored to eliminate or reduce the adverse influence caused by malicious beacon nodes and ensure safe localization in wireless sensor networks.

In this paper, we develop a BRS-based robust secure localization (BRSL) algorithm for solving the node self-localization problem in the case of malicious nodes existence. In BRSL, normal sensor node first observes the anchor nodes in its communication range and evaluates the trust values of these anchor nodes. Specially, the concepts of the beta reputation system are employed to deal with the uncertain factors in trust evaluation. Then, each anchor node obtains a final trust value, and sensor nodes compare the final trust values of anchor nodes in their multihop communication range with the stored threshold. Finally, the normal sensor nodes utilize the trustful anchor nodes to estimate their coordinates. All the above operations can be carried out by each node. The method is a completely distributed localization approach. Through simulations, we demonstrate that the BRSL method can efficiently reduce the influence of malicious attackers in WSNs.

The remainder of the paper is organized as follows: Section 2 introduces related works on secure localization algorithms. Section 3 presents the network model, attack model, and related definitions. Section 4 provides the details of the BRS-based robust secure localization (BRSL) algorithm. Section 5 presents the simulation results. Section 6 concludes the paper.

2. Related Works

Alfaro et al. [17] consider the localization security of sensor nodes under limited trust anchor nodes. It introduces three algorithms to enable the sensor nodes to determine their positions, but it would fail when the malicious anchor nodes are in colluding conditions.

Liu et al. [18] propose two secure localization algorithms. One is attack-resistant minimum mean square estimation, which excludes malicious anchor nodes by the consistency check. The other is voting-based location estimation. The algorithms are difficult to work for the malicious anchor nodes in colluding conditions.

Zhu et al. [19] propose an attack detection module which can detect compromised beacons and provide a localization service in terms of bounded estimation error by secure localization module, but it mainly concentrates on the one-hop localization.

Liu et al. [20] present a secure localization mechanism that detects malicious anchor nodes claiming fake positions. It uses redundant anchor nodes instead of normal nodes in the sensing field to verify malicious anchors. The method relies on a centralized base station for the detection.

Li et al. [21] introduce a secure scheme "Bilateration" which is derived from multilateration. It calculates the weight of anchor nodes and decides which anchor nodes are malicious. After ignoring the coordinates caused by compromised nodes, it uses the average value of the left candidate positions as the estimated location of the sensor node, but it mainly focuses on the one-hop localization.

3. Preliminaries

3.1. Network Model. We consider a network consisting of two types of nodes, namely, anchor nodes and sensor nodes. The anchor nodes are specially equipped and aware of their coordinates after deployment. The sensor nodes, whose positions are yet to be discovered, estimate their locations by measuring distances to neighboring anchor nodes. All nodes are randomly distributed in a 2D spatial region. Every node has a unique identity (ID). The transmission range or ranging radius of each node is R. Every node is capable of measuring the distance to any of its immediate neighbors.

The ranging error e follows a Gaussian distribution $N(u, \lambda^2)$, where the mean u is 0 and the standard deviation λ is within a threshold. Measurement error e is bounded by $|e_i| \leq e_{\max}$, and the maximum physical inaccuracy $e_{\max}$ can be obtained experimentally. In multihop localization, each anchor node broadcasts a message that carries its declared position to its one-hop neighbors. Then, the message is propagated in the network in a controlled flooding manner. When a sensor node obtains three or more anchor messages, the sensor node can estimate its location by the localization algorithm.

3.2. Attack Model. We assume that the WSN is in a hostile environment, that is, there are malicious attackers in the network. The attackers attack the anchor nodes in order to make them declare dishonest coordinates. When an anchor node is attacked and broadcasts erroneous locations, we call it malicious anchor node. The nodes claiming actual coordinates are called benign anchor nodes. We consider an adversarial environment where the malicious anchor nodes are in noncolluding scenario or colluding scenario. If the malicious anchor nodes are noncolluding, they cannot know whether other anchor nodes are malicious or not. They can only fake their own declared locations to affect the localization process. While the malicious anchor nodes are colluding, they can detect whether other anchor nodes are the same type, and each pair of colluding malicious anchor nodes can revise the measure distance between them by changing their declared locations.

As shown in Figure 1, when a sensor node M gets enough measurement distances d_{mi} ($i = 1, 2, \ldots, k$), where $k \geq 3$, to anchor nodes A_i, a system of the Euclidean equations can be set up:

$$
\begin{aligned}
&\|X_m - X_1\|_2 = d_{m1} \\
&\|X_m - X_2\|_2 = d_{m2} \\
&\qquad\qquad \vdots \\
&\|X_m - X_k\|_2 = d_{mk},
\end{aligned}
\tag{1}
$$

where $X_m = [x_m, y_m]^T$ is M's coordinates that need to be estimated and $X_i = [x_i, y_i]^T$ is anchor node A_i's declared position.

If the anchor node A_1 is attacked, it will become a malicious anchor node A_1' with fake coordinates. When M utilizes A_1' to compute its position, its estimated position M' will deviate far from its physical position, and its location accuracy will be very low.

3.3. Related Definitions. To be convenient, some necessary definitions are given in the following.

(i) Measurement distance: node i is in the communication radius of node j. The physical measurement distance from i to j (through RSSI, TDOA, etc.) is called measurement distance.

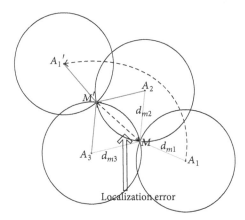

FIGURE 1: Node localization with malicious anchor node.

(ii) The Euclidean distance: the distance between the declared coordinates of two anchor nodes i and j, that is,

$$d_{ij} = \left\| X_i - X_j \right\|_2 = \sqrt{\left(x_i - x_j\right)^2 + \left(y_i - y_j\right)^2}, \quad (2)$$

where $X_i = [x_i, y_i]^T$ and $X_j = [x_j, y_j]^T$ denote, respectively, the declared coordinates of anchors i and j.

(iii) Multihop communication range: the range that a node's propagation packet can reach through multihop forwarding.

(iv) Multihop count: the hops count of the shortest path between a pair of nodes. For example, if the shortest path between nodes i and j passes T nodes (including i and j), the multihop count of nodes i and j is $\text{HOP}_{ij} = T - 1$.

4. BRS-Based Robust Secure Localization (BRSL) Algorithm

In BRSL method, every sensor node has the detecting function. The sensor node examines each of the anchor nodes that are available to it and evaluates the reliability of each anchor node according to the geometric relationship among anchor nodes. After the sensor node obtains the final trust values of each anchor node, a weighted Taylor-series least squares method is utilized to compute the sensor nodes' coordinates. In general, the BRSL method includes two main phases: trust evaluation of anchor nodes and the localization of sensor nodes.

4.1. Trust Evaluation of Anchor Nodes. In this subsection, we employ the concepts of the beta reputation system [22] to construct the trust evaluation framework of anchor nodes. In contrast to most other intuitive reputation systems, the beta reputation system has a firm basis on the theory of statistics, that is, the beta probability density function. The beta

distribution $B(a, \beta)$ can be expressed by using the gamma function as

$$f\left(x \mid \alpha, \beta\right) = \frac{\Gamma\left(\alpha + \beta\right)}{\Gamma\left(\alpha\right)\Gamma\left(\beta\right)} x^{\alpha-1}(1-x)^{\beta-1}, \quad (3)$$

where $0 < x < 1$, $\alpha > 0$, $\beta > 0$, and $\Gamma(a)$ is the gamma function.

The gamma function [23] (represented by the capital Greek letter Γ) is an extension of the factorial function, with its argument shifted down by 1, to real and complex numbers. If n is a positive integer, we get the formula $\Gamma(n) = (n-1)!$. If z is a complex number, we get the formula $\Gamma(z) = \int_0^\infty (t^{(z-1)}/e^t)dt$, where the real part of z must be larger than zero ($Re(z) > 0$). The gamma function is applicable in the fields of probability and statistics. It is also a component in various probability-distribution functions.

The beta reputation system consists of two elements (α, β) that can be used separately or in combination to provide a flexible framework for reputation services of WSNs applications. We use the beta reputation system to establish the trust evaluation framework of anchor nodes. In the network, anchor nodes have two types: benign anchor nodes and malicious anchor nodes. And the two elements (α, β) of beta reputation system are the most appropriate parameters here to judge the anchor nodes. The probability expectation value of the beta distribution is given by

$$E\left(x\right) = \frac{\alpha}{\alpha + \beta}, \quad (4)$$

and the variance is

$$\text{Var}\left(x\right) = \frac{\alpha\beta}{\left(\alpha + \beta\right)^2\left(\alpha + \beta + 1\right)}. \quad (5)$$

In the network, every anchor node has a unique ID, and the sensor node is assumed to have the detecting function. We utilize the beta reputation system to detect the malicious anchor nodes. The detecting process is considered with two possible outcomes (benign anchor node and malicious anchor node). Let $(a + 1)$ be the observed outcome number of benign anchor nodes, and let $(b + 1)$ be the observed outcome number of malicious anchor nodes. Then, we have a beta function expressed as $f(x \mid (a + 1), (b + 1))$, where x denotes the benign anchor node. The observed number of benign anchor nodes and malicious anchor nodes is used in the beta function to estimate the probability of anchor nodes to be benign ones, which equals to the expectation value of x. As we do not know whether the anchor nodes are benign or not at the beginning, we initially assume all anchor nodes to be benign ones.

Let Rep_T denotes the reputation of anchor nodes and $Rep\_T \sim B(a + 1, b + 1)$. Let Tru_T denotes the trust value of the anchor node. From the beta reputation system, we know that the expectation value of Rep_T is equal to Tru_T, that is, $E(Rep\_T) = Tru\_T$. Assume that there are $N_1 + N_2$ anchor nodes and N_3 sensor nodes randomly deployed in the network. Assume n ($n \leq N_1 + N_2$) anchor nodes $(A_1, A_2, \ldots, A_n)$ are available to an arbitrary sensor node M_j.

We deploy the network Q times in total. The detail of the detecting process is given as follows.

(1) Compute a_i and b_i through the geometric relationship among anchor nodes. The values of a_i and b_i are set to 0 initially. The value of d_{ij} is the Euclidean distance between A_i and A_j, and d'_{ij} denotes the measurement distance between A_i and A_j (if A_i and A_j are neighbors).

  (a) If inequality $|d_{ij} - d'_{ij}| \leq e_{\max}$ or $0 < d_{ij} < 2R$ is satisfied, let $a_i^j = 1$. Otherwise, let $a_i^j = 0$.

  (b) If inequality $|d_{ij} - d'_{ij}| > e_{\max}$ or $d_{ij} > 2R > 0$ is satisfied, let $b_i^j = 1$. Otherwise, let $b_i^j = 0$.

For example, Figure 2 shows the geometric relationship among anchor nodes, in which A_i $(i = 1, 2, \ldots, 6)$ represents the anchor nodes and M_j $(j = 1, 2, \ldots, 5)$ represents the sensor nodes. Anchor node A_2 is attacked, and A'_2 is the declared position of A_2. As anchor node A_3 is not the neighbor of A_2, we can only obtain the Euclidean distance d_{23} between them. A set of inequalities can be set up: $|d_{12} - d'_{12}| > e_{\max}$, $|d_{14} - d'_{14}| \leq e_{\max}$, $|d_{15} - d'_{15}| \leq e_{\max}$, $|d_{16} - d'_{16}| \leq e_{\max}$, and $0 < d_{23} < 2R$. Sensor nodes M_1 and M_3 are in anchor node A_1's communication range. Therefore, we can get $a_1^1 = 2, b_1^1 = 1$ and $a_1^3 = 2, b_1^3 = 0$.

(2) Compute the trust value of anchor node A_i in each network deployment.

  (a) Assume that m $(m \leq N_3)$ sensor nodes $(M_1, M_2, \ldots, M_m)$ are available to anchor node A_i. These m sensor nodes utilize step (1) to detect anchor node A_i. The observed number of anchor node A_i to be a benign one is

$$a'_i + 1 = \sum_{j=1}^{m} a_i^j + 1 \qquad (6)$$

  and the observed number of anchor node A_i to be a malicious one is

$$b'_i + 1 = \sum_{j=1}^{m} b_i^j + 1. \qquad (7)$$

  (b) The $Rep\_T_{A_ip} \sim B(a'_i + 1, b'_i + 1)$. The trust value of anchor node A_i is

$$Tru\_T_{A_ip} = E\left(Rep\_T_{A_ip}\right) = \frac{a'_i + 1}{a'_i + b'_i + 2}, \qquad (8)$$

  and the variance of anchor node A_i is

$$\sigma_{A_ip} = \frac{\left(a'_i + 1\right) \times \left(b'_i + 1\right)}{\left(a'_i + b'_i + 2\right)^2 \left(a'_i + b'_i + 3\right)}. \qquad (9)$$

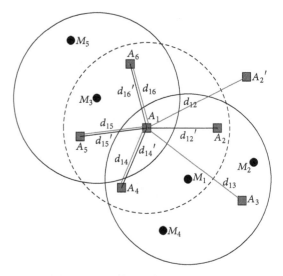

FIGURE 2: Geometric relationship among anchor nodes.

(3) Compute the trust value of anchor node A_i after the Q times network deployment. Let p denotes the current deployment time. Repeat step (1) and step (2) until $p > Q$. The final trust value of anchor node A_i is

$$Tru\_T_{A_i} = \frac{\left(\sum_{p=1}^{Q} Tru\_T_{A_ip}\right)}{Q}, \qquad (10)$$

and the final variance of anchor node A_i is

$$\sigma_{A_i} = \frac{\left(\sum_{p=1}^{Q} \sigma_{A_ip}\right)}{Q}. \qquad (11)$$

(4) Judge whether anchor node A_i is a benign anchor node.

  (a) After the anchor node A_i obtains the final trust value $Tru\_T_{A_i}$, it broadcasts $Tru\_T_{A_i}$ to the network in a multihop flooding manner. The sensor nodes store the final trust values they obtained, based on which they can decide whether A_i is a benign anchor node.

  (b) The sensor nodes compare the $Tru\_T_{A_i}$ that they received from step (3) with threshold ∇. If $Tru\_T_{A_i} \geq \nabla$, sensor nodes will consider anchor node A_i as a benign anchor node and utilize A_i in the localization phase. If $Tru\_T_{A_i} < \nabla$, sensor nodes will take anchor node A_i as a malicious anchor node, and A_i will be revoked before the localization stage.

The determination of threshold ∇ depends on the final trust value of each anchor node. The threshold ∇ is defined as follows

$$\nabla = \sum_{q=1}^{N_1+N_2} \left(\left(\frac{\sigma_q}{\sum_{q=1}^{N_1+N_2} \sigma_q} \right) \times Tru\_T_q \right), \qquad (12)$$

where $N_1 + N_2$ is the total number of anchor nodes, q is the ID of anchor node, and σ_q is the final variance of anchor node q.

From the above steps, we will get the trust evaluation of anchor nodes. The situation we investigated in this paper is that the percentage of malicious anchor nodes is less than half of the number of anchor nodes. When the malicious anchor nodes are noncolluding, they will not cooperate with each other. Therefore, it is hard for these malicious anchor nodes to obtain high value of a_i'. As the number of malicious anchor nodes is less than that of benign ones, the colluding malicious anchor nodes will be given more value on b_i'. When malicious anchor nodes are cooperated, some malicious anchor nodes may obtain more value on a_i' than b_i', but such nodes are very few. Generally, a_i' is smaller than b_i' for malicious anchor nodes, and a_i' is bigger than b_i' for benign anchor nodes. Therefore, most benign anchor nodes' trust values are larger than that of malicious anchor nodes in each network deployment.

Formula (8) shows that the bigger a_i' is, the larger Rep_T is. Similarly, the bigger b_i' is, the smaller Rep_T is. The variance of anchor node q denotes the deviating degree of anchor node q's trust value from the expectation value. If the final variance of anchor node q is big, it means the distribution of anchor node q's trust values $(Tru\_T_{q_1}, Tru\_T_{q_2}, \ldots, Tru\_T_{q_Q})$ is relatively discrete in Q times network deployment. While the final variance of anchor node q is small, it means that the distribution of anchor node q's trust values is relatively concentrated. The differences between most benign anchor nodes' trust values and their average trust value are larger than those of malicious anchor nodes, that is, $\sigma_{\text{benign}} > \sigma_{\text{malicious}}$. The weight $\sigma_q / \sum_{q=1}^{N_1+N_2} \sigma_q$ of trust values of anchor nodes in formula (12) demonstrates that the trust values of benign anchor nodes account for a higher proportion than malicious anchor nodes' trust values in the judging threshold, which is helpful in excluding malicious anchor nodes. Therefore, formula (12) indicates the most appropriate threshold here.

4.2. The Localization of Sensor Nodes. When utilizing malicious anchor nodes to localize the sensor nodes, the localization accuracy of sensor nodes is very low. To resolve this problem, we eliminate the malicious anchor nodes before the localization phase. The sensor node M utilizes all its multihop communication anchor nodes to estimate its coordinates. The traditional method like maximum likelihood estimation (MLE) has a high computational complexity and always loses much coordinates information.

We employ the weighted Taylor-series least squares algorithm to estimate the coordinates of sensor nodes and the final trust values Tru_T_1, Tru_T_2, ..., Tru_T_K $(q = 1, 2, \ldots, K, K \geq 3)$ of benign anchor nodes are used as the weight in the localization stage. The weighted Taylor-series least squares method can make better use of the anchor information, and the computing accuracy can be greatly improved. The localization processes are as follows.

Assume d_{mi} $(i = 1, 2, \ldots, K)$ are the measurement distances from the k anchor nodes to the sensor node M and $X_i = (x_i, y_i)$ is the declared coordinates of anchor node i. The position of sensor node M is denoted as $X = (x_0, y_0)$. Therefore, we have a set of the Euclidean equations:

$$Tru\_T_i \times \|X - X_i\|_2 = Tru\_T_i \times d_{mi}. \tag{13}$$

Firstly, calculate the centroid coordinates $X_C = (x_C, y_C)$ of K anchor nodes, that is, $X_C = (1/K) \sum_{i=1}^{K} X_i$.

Secondly, expand the function $f(X) = \|X - X_i\|_2$ in Taylor series at X_C, and ignore the high-order terms. Equation (13) is transformed into the following modus:

$$Tru\_T_1 \left(\frac{x_C - x_1}{d_{1C}} \Delta x + \frac{y_C - y_1}{d_{1C}} \Delta y \right) = Tru\_T_1 (d_1 - d_{1C})$$

$$Tru\_T_2 \left(\frac{x_C - x_2}{d_{2C}} \Delta x + \frac{y_C - y_2}{d_{2C}} \Delta y \right) = Tru\_T_2 (d_2 - d_{2C})$$

$$\vdots$$

$$Tru\_T_K \left(\frac{x_C - x_K}{d_{KC}} \Delta x + \frac{y_C - y_K}{d_{KC}} \Delta y \right) = Tru\_T_K (d_K - d_{KC}), \tag{14}$$

where d_{ij} denotes the Euclidean distance between X_i and X_j. Therefore, $\Delta X_C = (\Delta x_C, \Delta y_C)$ can be obtained by $\Delta X_C = (A^T W^T W A)^{-1} A^T W^T W B$, where

$$W = \begin{bmatrix} Tru\_T_1 & 0 & 0 \\ & Tru\_T_2 & \\ & & \ddots & 0 \\ 0 & 0 & Tru\_T_K \end{bmatrix},$$

$$B = \begin{bmatrix} d_1 - d_{1C} \\ d_2 - d_{2C} \\ \vdots \\ d_K - d_{KC} \end{bmatrix}, \tag{15}$$

$$A = \begin{bmatrix} \dfrac{x_C - x_1}{d_{1C}} & \dfrac{x_C - x_2}{d_{2C}} & \cdots & \dfrac{x_C - x_K}{d_{KC}} \\ \dfrac{y_C - y_1}{d_{1C}} & \dfrac{y_C - y_2}{d_{2C}} & \cdots & \dfrac{y_C - y_K}{d_{KC}} \end{bmatrix}^T.$$

Thirdly, let $d = \sqrt{\Delta x_C^2 + \Delta y_C^2}$, and judge whether the iteration termination condition $d \leq \eta$ is satisfied, where η is a prior-defined threshold. If $d \leq \eta$, we stop the iteration process. Otherwise, we set $X_C = X_C + \Delta X_C$ and go to the second step.

Finally, repeat the second step and the third step until the iteration termination condition is satisfied or the maximum iteration number is reached. The final output X_C is the estimated coordinates of sensor node M.

Table 1: Default network configuration parameters.

Parameters	Values
Network size (A)	200 m × 200 m
Deployment strategy	Random
Number of nodes ($N = N_1 + N_2 + N_3$)	200
Number of benign anchor nodes (N_1)	20
Number of malicious anchor nodes (N_2)	10
Number of normal sensor nodes (N_3)	170
Number of simulation rounds (Q)	1000
TTL	4
Trust threshold value ∇	Formula (12)
Communication radius (R)	30 m
$e_{\max}$	0.1R
The standard deviation λ	1
Network connectivity	8~12

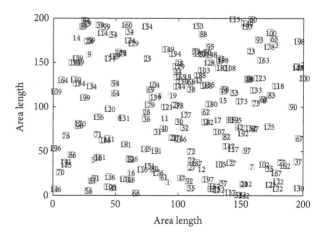

Figure 3: Network deployment.

5. Performance Evaluation

In this section, the performance of the BRSL algorithm is tested. All simulations are executed in MATLAB.

The WSN is in a hostile environment, and the malicious anchor nodes are in two conditions: noncolluding or colluding. The default network configuration parameters are shown in Table 1. Unless specified, the default parameters are used in the simulations.

Figure 3 shows the random network deployment, and each anchor node has a unique ID in all the simulations, where benign anchor nodes' IDs are from 1 to 20 and malicious anchor nodes' IDs are from 21 to 30.

5.1. Trust Evaluation of Anchor Nodes. Firstly, we analyze the trust evaluation of anchor nodes. Figures 4 and 5 show that the final variances of benign anchor nodes are bigger than those of the malicious anchor nodes, no matter whether the malicious anchor nodes are noncolluding or colluding. Therefore, the weight $\sigma_q / \sum_{q=1}^{N_1+N_2} \sigma_q$ is proper in this paper. When malicious anchor nodes are in noncolluding condition, from Figure 6, we can see that the final trust values of benign anchor nodes are much larger than those of malicious anchor nodes, and the threshold ∇ is about 0.267032. Therefore, we can remove all the malicious anchor nodes before the localization stage. When malicious anchor nodes are colluding, as Figure 7 shows, some of the malicious anchor nodes' final trust values are bigger than those of benign anchor nodes, and the threshold ∇ is about 0.297201. Although all the malicious anchor nodes can be excluded by the threshold, some benign anchor nodes are also removed. But in Section 5.2, it proves that the localization accuracy is still high although some benign anchor nodes are excluded.

5.2. Evaluation of BRSL Algorithm. In this subsection, we compare the average localization error (ALE) of the BRSL algorithm with other localization techniques: RMLA2 [15], RMLA1 [15], Bilateration [21], and the traditional multihop

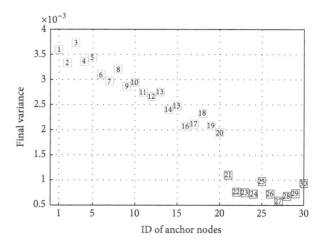

Figure 4: Final variances of anchor nodes when malicious anchors are in noncolluding condition.

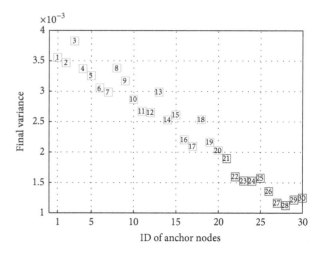

Figure 5: Final variances of anchor nodes when malicious anchors are in colluding condition.

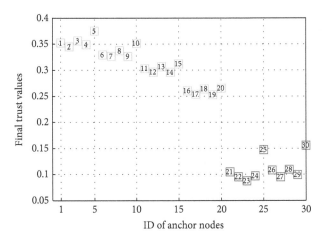

FIGURE 6: Final trust values of anchor nodes when malicious anchor nodes are in noncolluding scenario.

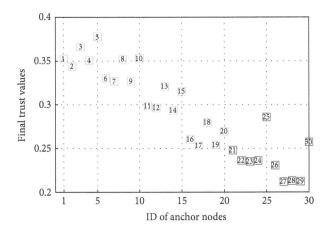

FIGURE 7: Final trust values of anchor nodes when malicious anchors are in colluding scenario.

localization method without trust evaluation in which Taylor-series least squares solver is used (t-TLS for short). Based on our simulations, we show that BRSL has superior performance in localization accuracy.

The ALE is normalized by the nodes' communication radius R:

$$\text{ALE} = \frac{1}{N_3 R} \sum_{i=N_1+N_2+1}^{N} \left\| X_i - X_i' \right\|_2, \qquad (16)$$

where X_i is the estimated coordinates of sensor node i and X_i' is the real coordinates of sensor node i.

Figures 8 and 9 show the impact of malicious anchor number on the localization accuracy of BRSL, RMLA2, RMLA1, Bilateration, and t-TLS. With the increase of number of malicious anchor nodes, the ALE of RMLA2, RMLA1, Bilateration, and t-TLS rises obviously, while that of BRSL remains stable (no more than 22% in noncolluding scenario and 30% in colluding scenario). Therefore, BRSL is robust for multihop localization and can greatly improve the average

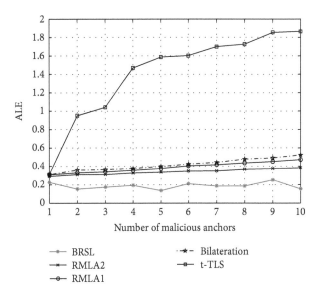

FIGURE 8: ALE versus malicious anchor number when malicious anchor nodes are noncolluding.

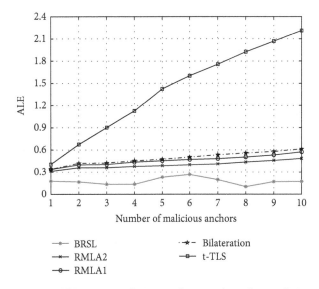

FIGURE 9: ALE versus malicious anchor number when malicious anchor nodes are colluding.

localization accuracy no matter the malicious anchor nodes are noncolluding or colluding.

Figures 10 and 11 show the comparison results of ALE under different standard deviation λ of ranging errors in noncolluding and colluding scenario, respectively. The ALE of each algorithm increases with standard deviation λ. Compared with RMLA2, RMLA1, Bilateration, and t-TLS, BRSL may approximately improve the localization accuracy by 10%, 15%, 55%, and 110%, respectively, in noncolluding scenario and 15%, 20%, 65%, and 150% in colluding scenario. The BRSL performs much better than other algorithms.

Figures 12 and 13 illustrate the relationship of ALE with the times of network deployment. The number of simulation rounds equals to the times of network deployment. The

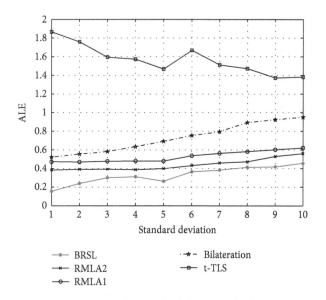

FIGURE 10: ALE versus the standard deviation λ when malicious anchor nodes are in noncolluding scenario.

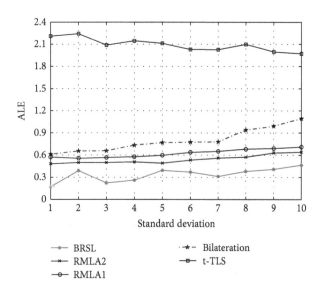

FIGURE 11: ALE versus the standard deviation λ when malicious anchor nodes are in colluding scenario.

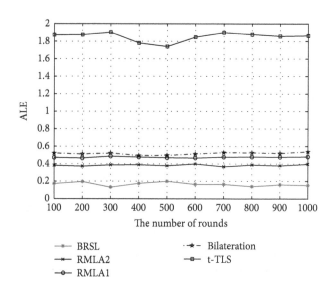

FIGURE 12: ALE versus rounds number when malicious anchor nodes are noncolluding.

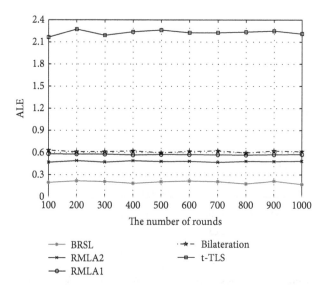

FIGURE 13: ALE versus rounds number when malicious anchor nodes are colluding.

ALE almost does not change with the number of simulation rounds whether the malicious anchor nodes are in noncolluding or colluding condition. The variety of network topology does not affect the detecting and localization process.

5.3. Cost Analysis. Finally, we analyze the costs of five algorithms. Assume a sensor node M_j can hear n anchor nodes in its one-hop range. In BRSL method, M_j needs to compute $\binom{n}{2}$ times to detect each anchor node. Thus, the cost of reputation computation in the network is $O(N_3 \cdot n^2)$. The computation complexity of the localization stage in our method is $O(n)$. Then the total cost of BRSL method is $O(N_3 \cdot n^2) + O(n)$. The costs of RMLA2 equals to that of RMLA1. The communication complexity of RMLA1 or RMLA2 is $O(N_3 \cdot$

$n^2)$. And the computation complexity of RMLA1 or RMLA2 is $O(n)$. Thus, the total cost of RMLA1 or RMLA2 is $O(N_3 \cdot n^2) + O(n)$, which is the same as BRSL algorithm. The costs of Bilateration and t-TLS mainly focus on the computation stage. The computation complexity of Bilateration is $O(n^2)$, while that of t-TLS is $O(n)$. Therefore, the cost of our method is moderate and acceptable.

6. Conclusions

In this paper, we propose a BRS-based robust secure localization algorithm for the case of presence of malicious anchor nodes. Based on the beta reputation system and the trust evaluation, the malicious anchor nodes are detected and excluded. By utilizing the weighted Taylor-series least squares method, the coordinates of sensor nodes are estimated. The simulation results demonstrate that the BRSL algorithm can effectively distinguish malicious anchor nodes and improve localization accuracy, as well as resist topology variety and ranging uncertainties. In the future, our work will focus on the secure localization when there are multiple and different attacks in complex environments.

Acknowledgments

The authors are grateful to the anonymous reviewers for their industrious work and insightful comments. This work is supported by National Natural Science Foundation of China under Grant nos. 61001138 and 61201317.

References

[1] J. Albowicz, A. Chen, and L. Zhang, "Recursive position estimation in sensor networks," in *Proceedings of the 9th International Conference on Network Protocols*, pp. 35–41, 2001.

[2] H. A. Oliveira, E. F. Nakamura, A. A. F. Loureiro, and A. Boukerche, "Directed position estimation: a recursive localization approach for wireless sensor networks," in *Proceedings of the 14th IEEE International Conference on Computer Communications and Networks*, pp. 557–562, San Diego, Calif, USA, 2005.

[3] T. He, C. Huang, B. M. Blum, J. A. Stankovic, and T. Abdelzaher, "Range-free localization schemes for large scale sensor networks," in *Proceedings of the 9th Annual International Conference Mobile Computing and Networking (MobiCom '03)*, pp. 81–95, ACM Press, San Diego, Calif, USA, 2003.

[4] M. L. Sichitiu and V. Ramadurai, "Localization of wireless sensor networks with a mobile beacon," in *Proceedings of the 1st IEEE International Conference on Mobile Ad-Hoc and Sensor Systems*, pp. 174–183, Fort Lauderdale, Fla, USA, October 2004.

[5] X. L. Guo, R. J. Feng, Y. F. Wu, and J. W. Wan, "Grid-Scan-Based multi-hop Localization algorithm for wireless sensor networks," in *Proceedings of IEEE Sensors Conference*, pp. 668–672, Waikoloa, Hawaii, USA, 2010.

[6] D. Niculescu and B. Nath, "DV based positioning in ad hoc networks," *Telecommunication Systems*, vol. 22, pp. 267–280, 2003.

[7] K. Yu, Y. J. Guo, and M. Hedley, "TOA-based distributed localisation with unknown internal delays and clock frequency offsets in wireless sensor networks," *IET Signal Processing*, vol. 3, no. 2, pp. 106–118, 2009.

[8] J. Wan, N. Yu, R. Feng, Y. Wu, and C. Su, "Localization refinement for wireless sensor networks," *Computer Communications*, vol. 32, pp. 1515–1524, 2009.

[9] H. Lim and J. C. Hou, "Localization for anisotropic sensor networks," in *Proceedings of 24th Annual Joint Conference of the IEEE Computer and Communications Societies*, vol. 1, pp. 138–149, 2005.

[10] J. W. Wan, X. L. Guo, N. Yu, Y. F. Wu, and R. J. Feng, "Multi-hop localization algorithm based on grid-scanning for wireless sensor networks," *Sensors*, vol. 11, no. 4, pp. 3908–3938, 2011.

[11] Y. Shang, H. Shi, and A. A. Ahmed, "Performance study of localization methods for ad-hoc sensor networks," in *Proceedings of the IEEE International Conference on Mobile Ad-Hoc and Sensor Systems*, pp. 184–193, October 2004.

[12] S. Y. Wong, J. G. Lim, S. V. Rao, and W. K. G. Seah, "Multihop localization with density and path length awareness in non-uniform wireless sensor networks," in *Proceedings of the IEEE 61st Vehicular Technology Conference*, vol. 4, pp. 2551–2555, Stockholm, Sweden, June 2005.

[13] Q. J. Xiao, B. Xiao, J. N. Cao, and J. P. Wang, "Multihop range free localization in anisotropic wireless sensor networks: a pattern-driven scheme," *IEEE Transactions On Mobile Computing*, vol. 9, no. 11, pp. 1592–1607, 2010.

[14] J. Hwang, T. He, and Y. Kim, "Detecting phantom nodes in wireless sensor networks," in *Proceedings of the 26th IEEE International Conference on Computer Communications (INFOCOM '07)*, pp. 2391–2395, May 2007.

[15] R. J. Feng, X. L. Guo, N. Yu, and J. W. Wan, "Robust multihop localization for wireless sensor networks with unreliable beacons," *International Journal of Distributed Sensor Networks*, vol. 2012, Article ID 972101, 13 pages, 2012.

[16] H. L. Chen, W. Lou, and Z. Wang, "A novel secure localization approach in wireless sensor networks," *Eurasip Journal on Wireless Communications and Networking*, vol. 2010, article 12, 2010.

[17] J. G. Alfaro, M. Barbea, and E. Kranakis, "Secure localization of nodes in wireless sensor networks with limited number of truth tellers," in *Proceedings of the 7th Annual Communication Networks and Services Research Conference (CNSR '09)*, pp. 86–93, May 2009.

[18] D. Liu, P. Ning, A. Liu, C. Wang, and W. K. Du, "Attack-resistant location estimation in sensor networks," in *Proceedings of the 4th International Symposium on Information Processing in Sensor Networks (IPSN '05)*, vol. 11, no. 4, pp. 99–106, 2005.

[19] W. T. Zhu, Y. Xiang, J. Y. Zhou, R. H. Deng, and F. Bao, "Secure localization with attack detection in wireless sensor networks," *International Journal of Information Security*, vol. 10, no. 3, pp. 155–171, 2011.

[20] D. Liu, P. Ning, and W. L. Du, "Detecting malicious beacons for secure localization discovery in wireless sensor networks," in *Proceedings of the 25th IEEE International Conference on Distributed Computing Systems (ICDCS '05)*, pp. 609–619, 2005.

[21] X. Li, B. Hua, Y. Shang, Y. Guo, and L. H. Yue, "Bilateration: an attack-resistant localization algorithm of wireless sensor network," in *Embedded and Ubiquitous Computing*, Lecture Notes in Computer Science, pp. 321–332, 2007.

[22] A. Jsang and R. Ismail, "The beta reputation system," in *Proceedings of the 15th Bled Electronic Commerce Conference*, pp. 41–55, 2002.

[23] G. E. Andrews, R. Askey, and R. J. Roy, *Special Functions*, Cambridge University Press, Cambridge, UK, 2001.

5

A Street Parking System Using Wireless Sensor Networks

Zusheng Zhang,[1] **Xiaoyun Li,**[2] **Huaqiang Yuan,**[1] **and Fengqi Yu**[2]

[1] *Dongguan University of Technology, No. 1 University Road, Songshan Lake Sci.&Tech. Industry Park, Dongguan, Guangdong 523808, China*
[2] *Shenzhen Institute of Advanced Technology, Chinese Academy of Sciences/The Chinese University of Hong Kong, 1068 Xueyuan Avenue, Shenzhen University Town, Nanshan District, Shenzhen 518055, China*

Correspondence should be addressed to Zusheng Zhang; zushengzhang@gmail.com

Academic Editor: Sabah Mohammed

Recently, with the explosive increase of automobiles in cities, parking problems are serious and even worsen in many cities. This paper proposes a street parking system (SPS) based on wireless sensor networks. The system can monitor the state of every parking space by deploying a magnetic sensor node on the space. For accurately detecting a parking car, a vehicle detection algorithm is proposed. And an adaptive sampling mechanism is used to reduce the energy consumption. Eighty-two sensor nodes are deployed on the street parking spaces to evaluate the performance of SPS. By running the system for more than one year, we observed that the vehicle detection accuracy of the SPS is better than 98%, and the lifetime of the sensor node is more than 5 years with a pair of 2500 mAh Li batteries.

1. Introduction

Due to the explosive growth of automobiles, parking near the center of the city gradually becomes one of the most annoying things to carowners. In most cases, they find the indoor parking spaces nearby are always full, and they have to drive around to search available parking space on the street. Then a traffic jam may occur. With the continuous growth of automobiles, the situation becomes worse and worse [1]. So the demand for street parking guidance service is expected to grow rapidly in the near future. Wireless sensor networks [2] have lots of potential toward providing an ideal solution for street parking service, such as their low power, small size, and low cost.

Almost all road vehicles have significant amounts of ferrous metals in their chassis and engine (iron, steel, nickel, cobalt, etc.), so AMR sensor is a good candidate for detecting vehicles [3–5]. It determines whether a space is occupied or not by detecting the presence of a vehicle based on a change in the environment's magnetic field. Some algorithms [6–8] have been proposed for parking vehicle detection by AMR sensor. However, these algorithms have the following problems.

(a) A whole parking period of a vehicle can be divided into three phases: entering, parking stop and leaving. Most existing algorithms [6–8] only consider the signal's characteristic of the parking stop, phase. These algorithms perform well when the interferences are relatively low. However, if the low SNR (signal-to-noise ratio) is low, they will lead to increased false detection rate.

(b) Existing algorithms typically sample the magnetic field at a fixed interval. This interval poses a basic tradeoff. A small interval can obtain more details of magnetic signals, but with higher energy consumption. A larger interval uses less energy but reduces the fidelity of the magnetic signal and may result in a false detection.

This paper proposes a street parking system based on WSN. Our main contributions are given as follows (a) A vehicle detection algorithm is proposed based on the integrated magnetic signal characteristics of a vehicle's entering, parking stop, and leaving phases. (b) To balance the energy consumption and accuracy of the algorithm, we design an adaptive sampling mechanism. (c) We deployed a street parking system which includes eighty-two sensor nodes. The system has been running reliably for more than one year. Experiment results show that the system detection accuracy is better than 98%, and it is energy efficient.

The remainder of this paper is organized as follows. Section 2 introduces the related works. Section 3 describes the overview of SPS. Section 4 proposes the vehicle algorithm. Section 5 describes the adaptive sampling and analyzes the energy consumption. Section 6 conducts experiments to prove the performance of SPS. Finally, Section 7 makes a brief conclusion.

2. Related Works

At present, the sensors used in vehicle information acquisition mainly include the following types: inductive loop detector [9], image (camera) sensor [10, 11], acoustic sensor [12, 13], infrared sensor [14], and ultrasonic sensor [15], The image sensor acquires an abundance of information, but it is vulnerable to bad weather and nighttime operation. The acoustic sensor and infrared sensor are vulnerable to noise in deployed environments. Magnetic sensors based on magnetoresistors have recently been proposed for vehicle detection [16, 17] because they are quite sensitive, small, and more immune to environmental factors such as rain, wind, snow, or fog than sensing systems based on video cameras, ultrasound, or infrared radiation.

Many algorithms have been proposed for moving vehicle monitoring. The PATH program of the University of California, Cheung and Varaiya [4], had first extensively explored magnetic sensor network based vehicle detection system. Cheung and Varaiya [4] had explored the applications for vehicle detection, speed estimation, and classification. Experiment results show that the vehicle detection accuracy rate is more than 99%, and the accuracy rate to estimate length and speed of vehicle is more than 90%.

Zhang et al. [16] proposed a Similarity Based Vehicle Detection (SBVD) algorithm to detect vehicles in low SNR conditions by calculating the similarity between on-road signals and a referential signal. Besides, data fusion algorithm based on fuzzy logic theory has also been proposed to monitor parking space in the parking lot using magnetic sensor [17]. Both kinds of algorithms have high computational complexity.

The research for parking vehicle detection mainly based on ultrasonic technology. Kim et al. [18] introduced wireless sensor networks based parking management system. They used an ultrasonic sensor as vehicle detection module and adopted a clustered network topology. The system provides monitoring information through individual sensor nodes installed at each parking space.

The works of [15, 19] also used ultrasonic sensors to implement a parking system. Additionally, the work of [15] implemented the shortest path algorithm to calculate the shortest distance from the parking berth to the nearest preferred entrance. In [19], Lee et al. implement and deploy a solar powered wireless sensor network in an outdoor car park to provide parking guidance. Although the ultrasonic sensor has a high accurate rate of vehicle detection, its performance

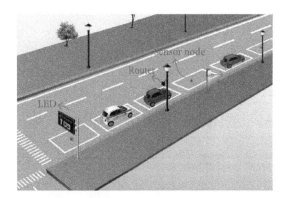

FIGURE 1: Diagram of street parking system.

is affected by environment, such as air turbulence and temperature change, especially the shielding of leaves or soil.

The work of [6] discussed the effect of detecting vehicles by comparing the acoustic, visual light, infrared, temperature, ultrasonic, and magnetic sensors. Their experiments verified that ultrasonic and magnetic sensors have better accuracy and reliability in parking space. Commercial sensors, such as SENSIT system [20], can detect parking occupancy. Each node was equipped with two sensors: infrared and magnetic, and its vehicle detection accuracy rate is nearly 100%.

3. Overview of the Street Parking System

3.1. System Introduction. The proposed SPS consists of a base station, routers, sensor nodes, and a remote server. The diagram of SPS is shown in Figure 1. Sensor nodes are deployed alongside the roadside and each node is mounted on the center floor of a parking space. Each sensor node detects the earth's magnetic field periodically. When a node detected a car entering or leaving, it transmits a message to the router. The router forwards the packet to a base station that is one or more hops away. In the base station, information from different nodes will be merged, and parking guidance information will be transmitted to LED board and remote server.

3.2. Hardware Design. We adopt ZigBee [21] as the wireless communication stack. Sensor node consists of HMC5883L [22] magnetic sensor. When deploying the sensor nodes in the complicated realistic environment, we faced several problems. One is the crush-resistant issue. Using high-strength PVC-steel material as node shell is a good choice for resisting the crush of the parking vehicles. Figure 2(a) shows the nodes with high-strength PVC-steel material. Another problem is to protect against the permeating rainwater through our node shell in bad weathers, we incised a circled lines around the chip location and fill with waterproof adhesive. As shown in Figure 2(b), considering the power issue, routers are equipped with solar panel for frequent data forwarding.

3.3. Test Field Setup. In the experiments, we place the sensor node in the middle of the parking space. HMC5883L is a 3-axis magnetic sensor. Figure 3 describes the deployment of sensor nodes: the Z-axis is vertical, the Y-axis is parallel with the direction of vehicle entering, and the X-axis is pointing

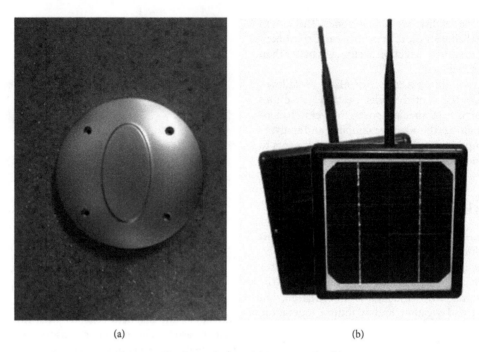

(a)   (b)

FIGURE 2: Hardware devices. (a) Sensor node. (b) Router.

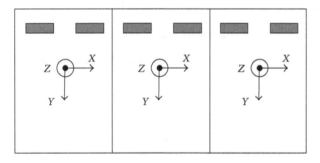

FIGURE 3: The coordinate position of the sensor.

to adjacent space. HMC5883L has temperature drift, and the method of temperature compensation refers to its datasheet [22].

4. Vehicle Detection Algorithm

Sensor nodes have limited computing power and memory. Therefore the data processing algorithm must be simple. By referring to the prior work [4], an algorithm based on the threshold and state machine was designed for parking vehicle detection. The threshold detection mechanism is used to reduce the computational requirement of the algorithm so that it can be implemented on the sensor node's processor and generate detection results in real time.

4.1. Characterization of Magnetic Signal. As shown in Figure 4, it is the three-axis magnetic signature of a vehicle parking process. A whole parking period includes three phases: entering, parking stop, and leaving. Initially, the parking space is vacant, and the values of x, y, z are the environment's

magnetic fields. Then a car enters the parking space and creates a fluctuation of the magnetic field. After the car parking stop, the car creates a stable disturbance on the environment's magnetic field. The parking space is occupied. Then the car is leaving the parking space and also has a fluctuation signature. Finally, the parking space is vacant, and the values of x, y, z recover to the environment's magnetic field.

4.2. Signal Preprocessing. For vehicle presence applications, the amplitude and direction of the magnetic field are not important, but the detection of a significant shift in the magnetic field is the key factor. The vector magnitude shift from the environment's magnetic field would be the most reliable method. Using digitized measurements of three-axis sensor outputs after amplification, the vector magnitude would be:

$$G(i) = \sqrt{X_i^2 + Y_i^2 + Z_i^2}. \tag{1}$$

A smoothing filter, which takes a running average of the signal, is used to smooth the signal. The running average is given by

$$A(i) = \begin{cases} \dfrac{G(i) + G(i-1) + \cdots + G(1)}{i} & \text{for } i < L, \\[2ex] \dfrac{G(i) + G(i-1) + \cdots + G(i-L+1)}{L} & \text{for } i \geq L. \end{cases} \tag{2}$$

$G(i)$ is the vector magnitude and L is the predefined running average buffer size. For implementation, we use G_{buf} to store the values of $[G(i), G(i-1), \ldots, G(i-L+1)]$.

4.3. Fluctuation Detection. Since the fluctuation of the magnetic signal is a key characteristic of the vehicle entering and

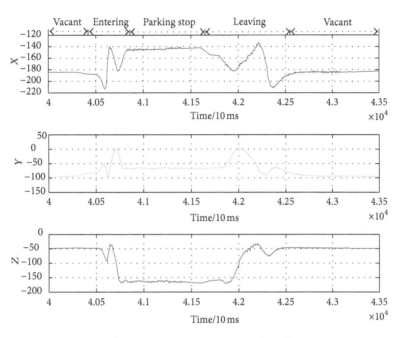

FIGURE 4: Three-axis magnetic signature of a parking space.

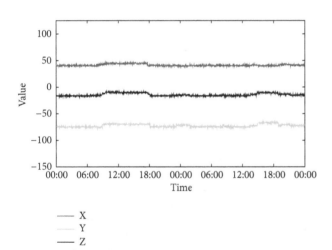

FIGURE 5: Drift in the magnetic signal of a parking space.

leaving. Exact detection of the fluctuation signature is important for the vehicle detection algorithm. $C(i)$ is the stable states of the magnetic signal. If there has one up-or-down fluctuation sample of the magnetic signal in the G_{buf}, the signal is unstable and $C(i) = 1$, otherwise, the signal is stable and $C(i) = 0$. $C(i)$ can be described as (3). $F(i)$ is used to track the singular point. T_1 and T_2 are thresholds, $T_2 > T_1$. The vehicle entering and leaving fluctuation can be detected by the pseudocode program, as shown in Pseudocode 1. One has

$$C(i) = \begin{cases} 1 & \text{if } \forall k \in (i, i-1, \ldots, i-L+1): \\ & \quad |G(k) - A(i)| \geq T_1, \\ 0 & \text{otherwise,} \end{cases} \quad (3)$$

$$F(i) = \begin{cases} 1 & \text{if } |G(i) - A(i)| \geq T_2, \\ 0 & \text{otherwise.} \end{cases} \quad (4)$$

4.4. Stable Disturbance Detection. There is an uncontrollable drift in the magnetic signal, which is mainly caused by the interference of adjacent parking spaces' vehicles. As shown in Figure 5, it is the magnetic signal of a parking space which is vacant in consecutive two days. All the three axes have different drift in two days. The drift has a negative effect on the detection of a vehicle in parking duration. In order to account for the drift in the long term, an adaptive baseline is used to track the background magnetic reading. The adaptive baseline is given by the following equations:

$$B(i) = \begin{cases} B(i-1) \times (1-\alpha) + A(i) \times \alpha & \text{if the state} \\ & \text{machine is in} \\ & \text{vacant state,} \\ B(i-1) & \text{otherwise.} \end{cases} \quad (5)$$

$B(i)$ is the adaptive baseline, α is the forgetting factor, and $A(i)$ is the smoothed magnetic data. The adaptive baseline is only updated by the magnetic reading when there is no signal fluctuation and no vehicle is detected. With this adaptive baseline, two over threshold Boolean flags $R(i)$ and $L(i)$ are generated according to following equations. T_{up} and T_{down} are the corresponding threshold levels, and $T_{\text{up}} > T_{\text{down}}$. The main reason of using two thresholds is to detect the stable

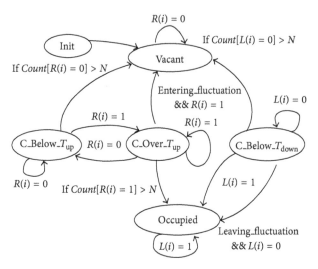

FIGURE 6: Detection state machine.

disturbance which is incurred by a vehicle parking stop on the space. One has

$$R(i) = \begin{cases} 1 & \text{if } |A(i) - B(i-1)| \geq T_{\text{up}}, \\ 0 & \text{otherwise}, \end{cases}$$

$$L(i) = \begin{cases} 1 & \text{if } |A(i) - B(i-1)| \geq T_{\text{down}}, \\ 0 & \text{otherwise}. \end{cases}$$

$$(6)$$

4.5. State Machine. Figure 6 shows the block diagram of a state machine which is designed for detecting parking vehicles in SPS. The state machine consists of

State: {Init, Vacant, C_Over_T_{up}, C_Below_T_{up}, Occupied, C_Below_T_{down}}

Input [$R(i)$, $L(i)$, fluctuation]: {0, 1, Entering_ fluctuation, Leaving_fluctuation}

Output[$D(i)$]: {0, 1}.

The Boolean flags $R(i)$ and $L(i)$ are passed to the state machine. Their main objective is to filter out spurious signals that are not caused by a parking stop and to output binary detection flag. $D(i)$ is the output of the detection state machine. Only when the state machine is in "Occupied" or "C_Below_T_{down}", $D(i) = 1$, otherwise, $D(i) = 0$. The following section is a walkthrough of the state machine's logical flow.

S1: "Init"

Assuming there is no vehicle in the parking space when the sensor node is being deployed. It will go into state S1 and start initializing the baseline with the environmental magnetic field.

S2: "Vacant"

After a predefined initializing time, it will jump to state S2 where the baseline is updated adaptively. It will jump to state S3 that has an Enter_fluctuation and a stable disturbance is over threshold T_{up}.

S3: "C_Over_T_{up}"

It was found that a vehicle signature produces a successive sequence of "1" in $R(i)$ and this state is used to track such a sequence. If there is any "0" reading from $R(i)$, it will immediately jump to state S4. Otherwise, if the number of successive $R(i) = 1$ has reached a critical value N, it will jump to state S5.

S4: "C_Below_T_{up}"

Within this state, it will jump back to state S2 after the number of successive $R(i) = 0$ has reached a critical value N. In order not to lose a potential vehicle detection, it will jump back to state S3 again in case there is any $R(i) = 1$ reading.

S5: "Occupied"

Staying in this state implies the magnetic change is strong as the vehicle is on the sensor node, and the parking space is occupied. It will jump to S6 when the sensor detected a Leaving_fluctuation and the stable disturbance is below threshold T_{down}.

S6: "C_Below_T_{down}"

Within this state, it will jump back to state S2 after the number of successive $L(i) = 0$ has reached a critical value N. In order to filter out spurious signals that are not caused by a car leave, it will jump back to state S5 again in case there is any $L(i) = 1$ reading.

5. Adaptive Sampling and Energy Consumption

5.1. Adaptive Sampling. Usually, the time cost of the phase of a vehicle entering or leaving is between 0 s and 60 s. So the sensor requires a much higher sampling frequency to obtain the fluctuation signature. For example, a vehicle traveling at 10 mph will travel 10 feet before it comes to a parking stop. This entering phase will take less than one second. If the sampling frequency is 50 HZ, the sensor can sample about 50 numbers of magnetic data about the entering phase. On the other hand, if there is no a moving vehicle interference, the magnetic signal is stable and the drift in the magnetic field is smaller than 5. To balance the energy consumption and accuracy of the vehicle detection algorithm, we design an adaptive sampling mechanism. When there is one up-or-down fluctuation sample of the magnetic signal, *if $C(i) = 1$,* it samples the magnetic field faster until the biggest value (50 HZ). Otherwise, *if $C(i) = 0$,* it decreases the sampling rate exponentially until less than the smallest value (5 HZ). Thus, the sensor can quickly respond to the magnetic signal dynamics while incurring low overhead in the long term.

5.2. Analysis of Energy Consumption. For battery powered wireless sensor networks, the network lifetime is a critical factor because replacing batteries for sensor nodes is a laborious task. The sensor node has no specific responsibility for maintaining the network infrastructure because it is an enddevice [21]. So the sensor node does not exchange packet for network maintaining when it has been joined the network. Sensor node samples the magnetic signal periodically. When

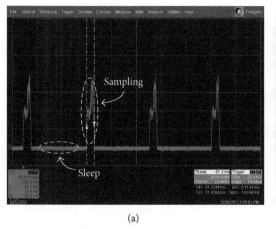
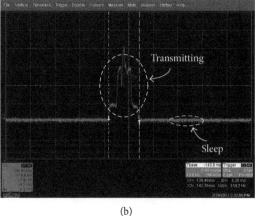

(a)   (b)

FIGURE 7: Energy consumption (a) sampling and (b) transmitting.

it detected a car arrival or leave, it transmits one binary detection flag to base station. And it goes to sleep when no task. Ignoring the energy consumption in joining or rejoining the network, the energy consumption of a sensor node consists of energy consumed by detection flag transmission (E_{tran}), magnetic field sampling (E_{sample}), and sleep (E_{sleep}).

In energy consumption experiments, a sensor node and a 10 Ω resistor are in series connection. So the sensor node's current can be obtained by measuring the voltage of the resistor ($I = V/10$). We found the greatest contribution of power consumption is sampling unit. As shown in Figure 7(a), the energy consumption of a sensor node whose sampling interval is 50 ms. We can see that the measurement period of magnetic sensor is $S_{period} = 6$ ms, the average current of sample is about $I_{sample} = 10$ mA, and the current of sleep is $I_{sleep} = 2$ uA. According to the adaptive sampling mechanism, the energy consumption of sampling can be described as

$$E_{sample} = I_{sample} * T_{sample\_per\_second} * V,$$

$$T_{fast\_sample} = N_{inter} * T_{inter} * F_{biggest} * S_{period},$$

$$T_{slow\_sample} = \left(T_{one\_day} - N_{inter} * T_{inter}\right) * F_{smallest} * S_{period},$$

$$T_{sample\_per\_second} = \frac{\left(T_{fast\_sample} + T_{slow\_sample}\right)}{T_{one\_day}}. \tag{7}$$

T_{fast_sample} and T_{slow_sample} are the total time in one day of sampling using the biggest and smallest frequency, respectively. N_{inter} is the interference times in one day. T_{inter} is the average duration of once interference. $F_{biggest}$ and $F_{smallest}$ are the biggest and smallest frequency, respectively. T_{one_day} is the total seconds of one day.

As shown in Figure 7(b), the period of one packet's transmission is about $T_{tran} = 6$ ms, and the average current

of transmission is about $I_{tran} = 30$ mA. So the energy consumption of transmission can be described as E_{tran}:

$$E_{tran} = I_{tran} * T_{tran\_per\_second} * V,$$

$$T_{tran\_per\_second} = \frac{N_{tran} * T_{tran}}{T_{one\_day}}. \tag{8}$$

N_{tran} is the average number of transmissions in one day. And $T_{tran\_per\_second}$ is the proportion of transmission per second. The energy consumption for sleep can be described as E_{sleep}:

$$E_{sleep} = I_{sleep} * T_{sleep\_per\_second} * V, \tag{9}$$

$$T_{sleep\_per\_second} = 1 - T_{sample\_per\_second} - T_{tran\_per\_second}, \tag{10}$$

$$L = \frac{E}{\left(E_{sample} + E_{tran} + E_{sleep}\right)}. \tag{11}$$

Using a pair of 2500 mAh AA Li batteries parallel connected, with the voltage of each battery being 3 V, the lifetime of the sensor node is calculated by (11). Given the parameters in Table 1, we can draw a conclusion that the sensor node can continuously work for 5 years without changing battery.

6. Experiments

To test the proposed system, we deploy eighty-two sensor nodes in the street parking of SIAT (Shenzhen Institute of Advanced Technology). As shown in Figures 8(a) and 9(b). Devices with magnetic sensors are nailed in the center of the parking spaces. The routers which are equipped with a solar panel for forwarding parking message are fixed on the street light, as shown in Figure 8(c).

We developed a server system using Java language and MySQL database. As shown in Figure 9, using the graphical client interface, users can know which parking space is vacant or occupied and the occupied duration of each parking space. As shown in Figure 9(a), the nodes which ID signed as

(a)   (b)   (c)

FIGURE 8: Devices are deployed in roadside parking spaces. (a)-(b) Senor nodes in parking spaces. (c) A solar powered router is mounted on the roadside light.

TABLE 1: Related parameters.

Notation	Description	Value
I_{tran}	Transmission current	30 mA
I_{sample}	Sampling current	10 mA
I_{sleep}	Sleep current	2 uA
N_{inter}	Interference times	100
N_{tran}	Number of transmission	100
F_{biggest}	Biggest frequency	50 HZ
F_{smallest}	Smallest frequency	5 HZ
T_{inter}	Duration of once interference	30 s
S_{period}	Sampling time	6 ms
T_{tran}	Transmission time	6 ms
$T_{\text{one\_day}}$	Total seconds of one day	86400 s
V	Voltage	3 V
E	Battery capacity	5000 mAh

TABLE 2: Experiment parameters.

Parameter	Description	Value
L	Smooth buffer length	30
α	Forgetting factor	0.1
T_1	A threshold for $C(i)$	10
T_2	A threshold for $F(i)$	50
T_{up}	A threshold for $R(i)$	20
T_{down}	A threshold for $L(i)$	10
N	The successive count number	10
Count	The threshold for fluctuation detection	5

TABLE 3: Car parking detection result.

The number of times of vehicle parking	The detected number of vehicle parking of SPS	Accuracy of SPS
32896	32402	0.985

integer, such as 6, 3, and 5, are router nodes. The nodes are sensor nodes whose ID started with "B," such as B27 and B26. The sensor node to be colored as a green dot indicates the according parking space is vacant; on the other hand, a red dot means the parking space is occupied. In Figure 9(b), these blue lines with arrow describe the wireless network topology.

In our experiments, parameters related to the vehicle detection algorithm are given in Table 2. Figure 10 shows the detection results of a parking space B19 for successive 8 days. X, Y, Z are the raw magnetic field, and their value refer to the right coordinate axis. $D(i)$ is the detection result whose value refer to the left coordinate axis, where value 0 indicates the parking is "vacant," and 1 stands for "occupied." As shown in

Figure 11, it describes the daily occupancy time of the parking space B19 for successive 8 days.

Our SPS has been deployed in SIAT and worked for more than one year. Table 3 shows the average accuracy of our vehicle detecting algorithm is about 98.5%. The prior work [4] proposed an Adaptive Threshold Detection Algorithm (ATDA for short). Using the magnetic signal collected from sensor nodes, we run our algorithm and ATDA on PC, respectively. Table 4 shows the test results of our algorithm and ATDA. The experiment results show that in the first case two algorithms have best performance. In the case 1–3, interference signal caused by vehicles on neighbor parking spaces has a negative impact on the detection performance.

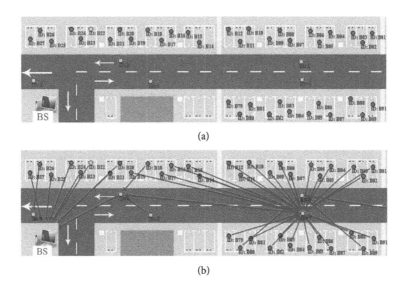

(a)

(b)

FIGURE 9: Pictures of the management system. (a) Sensor nodes deployed on the parking spaces. (b) Topology of the network.

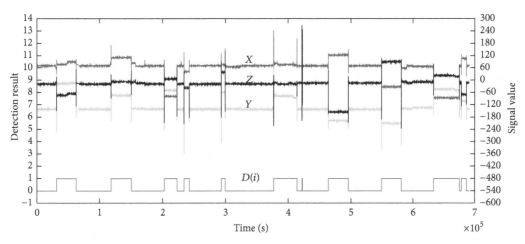

FIGURE 10: The detection results of a parking space for successive 8 days.

TABLE 4: Car parking detection result: group 2.

Case	Situation	The number of vehicle parking	Accuracy of SPS	Accuracy of ATDA
1	No car on left or right	720	0.997	0.96
2	A car on the left	720	0.985	0.95
3	A car on the right	720	0.986	0.95
4	Two cars on both left and right	720	0.980	0.94

And our algorithm is more accurate for vehicle detection than ATDA. ATDA smooths out the entering and leaving fluctuation of the magnetic signal, and it is only considers the signal's characteristic of the parking stop phase. As shown in Figure 12, there is no exit a threshold to distinguish the characteristic between parking stop and interference. In the low SNR (signal-to-noise ratio) situation, the frequent up-and-down fluctuation of the magnetic signal is a key characteristic for the vehicle detection algorithm. With the feature being designed, our algorithm has a better performance than ATDA.

7. Conclusions

In this paper, a street parking system based on wireless sensor networks is presented. It focuses on the accuracy of the parking system. A parking algorithm and an adaptive sampling mechanism are proposed. Our SPS has been in operation in SIAT for more than one year. The experiment results show that the system detection accuracy is better than 98%, and it is energy efficient. However, there is a tradeoff between sensitivity and specificity of magnetic signal that may result in the detection of vehicles in adjacent parking

```
//F_count counts the number of F(i) = 1
//Entering_fluctuation is a flag of detection of the entering fluctuation
//Leaving_fluctuation is a flag of detection of the leaving fluctuation
//COUNT is a threshold

if(C(i) = 1)
{ if(F(i) = 1) F_count++; }
else if(C(i) = 0)
{ F_count = 0; }

if( The space status is vacant && F_count > COUNT )
{ Entering_fluctuation = 1; }
Else if( The space status is occupied && F_count > COUNT )
{ Leaving_fluctuation = 1; }
```

PSEUDOCODE 1: Pseudocode for vehicle entering or leaving detection.

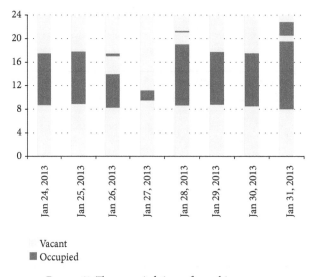

FIGURE 11: The occupied time of a parking space.

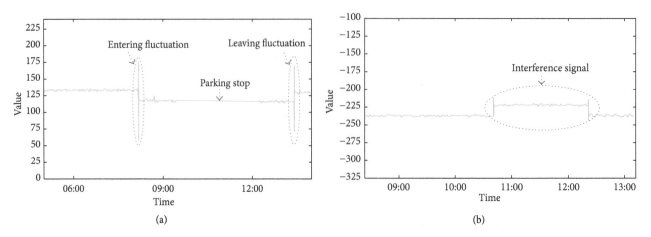

FIGURE 12: The signal comparison of parking and interference. (a) The signal of a car parking. (b) The signal of interference.

places. In the future, we will concentrate on the characteristic of the interference signal caused by adjacent vehicles and develop more accurate algorithm to improve the system performance.

Acknowledgments

This work was supported by the National Natural Science Foundation of China (Grant no. 61271005), the Key Laboratory Project (Grant no. CXB201104220033A), the Technology Research and Development Project of Shenzhen (CXZZ20120831173053551), and the research Projects KQC201109050096A and JC201005270368A of Shenzhen.

References

[1] D. Schrank, T. Lomax, and B. Eisele, *Urban Mobility Report 2011*, Texas Transportation Institute, The Texas A&M University System, College Station, Tex, USA, 2011.

[2] P. Baronti, P. Pillai, V. W. C. Chook, S. Chessa, A. Gotta, and Y. F. Hu, "Wireless sensor networks: a survey on the state of the art and the 802.15.4 and ZigBee standards," *Computer Communications*, vol. 30, no. 7, pp. 1655–1695, 2007.

[3] A. Haoui, R. Kavaler, and P. Varaiya, "Wireless magnetic sensors for traffic surveillance," *Transportation Research C*, vol. 16, no. 3, pp. 294–306, 2008.

[4] S. Y. Cheung and P. Varaiya, "Traffic surveillance by wireless sensor networks: final report," Tech. Rep., California PATH, University of California, Berkeley, Calif, USA, 2007.

[5] R. Wang, L. Zhang, R. Sun, J. Gong, and L. Cui, "EasiTia: a pervasive traffic information acquisition system based on wireless sensor networks," *IEEE Transactions on Intelligent Transportation Systems*, vol. 12, no. 2, pp. 615–621, 2011.

[6] S. Lee, D. Yoon, and A. Ghosh, "Intelligent parking lot application using wireless sensor networks," in *Proceedings of the International Symposium on Collaborative Technologies and Systems (CTS '08)*, pp. 48–57, May 2008.

[7] S.-E. Yoo, P. K. Chong, T. Kim et al., "PGS: parking guidance system based on wireless sensor network," in *Proceedings of the 3rd International Symposium on Wireless Pervasive Computing (ISWPC '08)*, pp. 218–222, May 2008.

[8] J. Chinrungrueng, S. Dumnin, and R. Pongthornseri, "IParking: a parking management framework," in *Proceedings of the 11th International Conference on ITS Telecommunications (ITST '11)*, pp. 63–68, August 2011.

[9] Q.-J. Kong, Z. Li, Y. Chen, and Y. Liu, "An approach to Urban traffic state estimation by fusing multisource information," *IEEE Transactions on Intelligent Transportation Systems*, vol. 10, no. 3, pp. 499–511, 2009.

[10] G. Alessandretti, A. Broggi, and P. Cerri, "Vehicle and guard rail detection using radar and vision data fusion," *IEEE Transactions on Intelligent Transportation Systems*, vol. 8, no. 1, pp. 95–105, 2007.

[11] P. N. Pathirana, A. E. K. Lim, A. V. Savkin, and P. D. Hodgson, "Robust video/ultrasonic fusion-based estimation for automotive applications," *IEEE Transactions on Vehicular Technology*, vol. 56, no. 4, pp. 1631–1639, 2007.

[12] J. Ding, *Vehicle detection by sensor network nodes [Ph.D. thesis]*, University of California, Berkeley, Calif, USA, 2003.

[13] V. Cevher, R. Chellappa, and J. H. McClellan, "Vehicle speed estimation using acoustic wave patterns," *IEEE Transactions on Signal Processing*, vol. 57, no. 1, pp. 30–47, 2009.

[14] T. M. Hussain, A. M. Baig, T. N. Saadawi, and S. A. Ahmed, "Infrared pyroelectric sensor for detection of vehicular traffic using digital signal processing techniques," *IEEE Transactions on Vehicular Technology*, vol. 44, no. 3, pp. 683–689, 1995.

[15] M. Y. I. Idris, E. M. Tamil, N. M. Noor, Z. Razak, and K. W. Fong, "Parking guidance system utilizing wireless sensor network and ultrasonic sensor," *Information Technology Journal*, vol. 8, no. 2, pp. 138–146, 2009.

[16] L. Zhang, R. Wang, and L. Cui, "Real-time traffic monitoring with magnetic sensor networks," *Journal of Information Science and Engineering*, vol. 27, no. 4, pp. 1473–1486, 2011.

[17] J. Zhu, H. Cao, J. Shen, and H. Liu, "Data fusion for magnetic sensor based on fuzzy logic theory," in *Proceedings of the 4th International Conference on Intelligent Computation Technology and Automation (ICICTA '11)*, pp. 87–92, March 2011.

[18] J. Kim, H. Kim, H. Jeong, Y. Seo, and P. Mah, "Field deployment of a large-scale WSN for parking management system," in *Proceedings of the 7th Annual IEEE Communications Society Conference on Sensor, Mesh and Ad Hoc Communications and Networks (SECON '10)*, pp. 1–3, June 2010.

[19] P. Lee, H.-P. Tan, and M. Han, "Demo: a solar-powered wireless parking guidance system for outdoor car parks," in *Proceedings of the 9th ACM Conference on Embedded Networked Sensor Systems (SenSys '11)*, pp. 423–424, November 2011.

[20] SENSIT, December 2012, http://www.nedapavi.com/products/sensit/.

[21] ZigBee Alliance, "ZigBee PRO specification," November 2012, http://www.zigbee.org/Specifications.aspx.

[22] Three-axis magnetic sensor HMC5883L, December 2012, http://www.magneticsensors.com/three-axis-digital-compass.php.

6

A Traffic Parameters Extraction Method Using Time-Spatial Image Based on Multicameras

Jun Wang and Deliang Yang

School of Electronic Information and Control Engineering, Beijing University of Technology, Beijing 100124, China

Correspondence should be addressed to Jun Wang; wangjun88100720@emails.bjut.edu.cn

Academic Editor: Liguo Zhang

Based on the traffic monitoring system consisting of image processing units (IPUs), network communication, and data fusion server, this paper proposes an approach for the extraction of traffic parameters in the highway based on time-spatial image and data fusion. This system used a simple method to install cameras, which can capture the video images from the left to the right perspectives synchronously, for the sake of reducing the influence from vehicles height or width by fusing the image plane information of multicameras. Firstly, based on the synchronous and adaptive camera calibration method, images from different cameras are projected onto a same world coordinate, which is a top view picture of the same detecting region. Secondly, in order to improve the environment adaptability, an advanced method of time-spatial image is proposed to extract traffic information. At the same time, through network communication, traffic information picked up by each camera is transformed to the SDF timely. Finally, combined with probability fusion map, SDF fuses information grabbed by all cameras to improve the accuracy of traffic parameters extraction. The experimental results show that the proposed method can be implemented quickly and accurately either in crowed state or in fluent state.

1. Introduction

With the development of image processing technology, traffic monitoring system based on multicameras has received more and more attention. Many research achievements have been transformed into commercial products, such as the vehicle infrastructure integration (VII) project in the USA, SARETEA project in Europe, and advanced cruise assist highway system (AHS) project in Japan. Among them, papers [1, 2] describe a traffic monitoring system which is composed of three parts by ATUs, Network Communications, and SDF, based on the architecture of TRAVIS. Based on background updating technology, each ATU, composed of a series of video sensors, extracts the traffic information such as vehicle type and location from the video frames. Using the grid-based fusion or foreground probability map fusion technology, SDF fuses the traffic information from the ATUs connected with SDF via the internet. The experimental results show that this system is flexible, versatile, and practical. Based on the vehicle infrastructure integration (VII) system and the theory of shock wave, Koutsia et al. [3] designed a traffic monitoring

system by placing video sensors on different road sections. The model calculates the average vehicle velocity of every road section, tracks the moving target using Spatial-Temporal Markov Random Field model (S-T MRF model), predicts traffic state of the current road section and downstream sections, and reduces the incidence of traffic incidents such as traffic congestion.

Currently, on the area of microcosmic traffic parameters extraction, such as the length of the vehicle, most researches focused on the technology of 3D model reconstruction using multiple cameras, which can get a high accuracy and prolific information about the shape of the vehicle, but it is more time consuming and complex simultaneously. Generally, macroscopic traffic parameters are extracted by background updating and optical flow through tracking the moving vehicles, which is more precise at the cost of simplicity of algorithm attributed to updating background and retrieving optical flow points in time and prone to become invalid under the traffic jam. Fujimura et al. and Lamosa et al. [4, 5] proposed an image fusion method based on multilevel probability fusion maps, which analyzes each pixel's foreground probability to obtain a new foreground image firstly, then analyzes the plane projective map of diverse height between the object and its plane to detect the existence of vehicles and compute their height and width. This method can segment the vehicles accurately, but shape information is detected imprecisely. A method of traffic parameters extraction based on time-spatial image using a single camera was proposed by Zhu et al. [6]. It will extract macroscopic traffic parameters, for instance, traffic flow and average speed, and microcosmic parameters containing height and width of the vehicle, through the analysis of PVI (the panoramic view image and EPI (the epipolar plane image)). The way is resilient to circumstances and less demanding for background update, while it has more sophisticated mathematical operation. Reference [7] adopts multivirtual line (MVDL), of which the method sets up several vehicle-detecting lines along the direction of the lane to obtain a series of PVI images. The idea is excellent in traffic flow statistics, but the method is more reliable on the angle of cameras, which is difficult to avoid.

Based on the traffic monitoring system consisting of image processing units (IPUs), network communication, and data fusion server (SDF), this paper proposes an approach for traffic parameters extraction in the highway, such as vehicle number, vehicle velocity and vehicle type, based on time-spatial image [6] and image fusion. This system used a simple method to install cameras, which can capture the video images from the left to the right perspectives synchronously, for the sake of reducing the influence from vehicles height or width by fusing the image plane information of multicameras. Firstly, based on the synchronous and adaptive camera calibration method [8, 9], project images from different cameras onto a same world coordinate, which is a top view picture of the same detecting region. Secondly, in order to improve the environment adaptability, an advanced method of time-spatial image is proposed to process the video images and extract traffic parameters. At the same time, through network communication, traffic information picked up by each camera is transformed to the data fusion server (SDF) in time. Finally, combined with probability fusion maps (PFM) [1, 2, 4, 5], information grabbed by all of related cameras is fused to improve the accuracy of traffic parameter extraction by the SDF. The experimental results show that the proposed method can be implemented quickly and accurately either in crowed state or in fluent state. Therefore, in the future, combined with pattern recognition and data mining technology, this method can be used to realize the traffic state identification and prediction and provide basis for section optimization.

This paper is organized as follows. Section 2 will demonstrate the system architecture, including the functions and implementation methods of IPUs, network communication, and SDF. The procedure of image processing and parameters extracting concerning IPU will be elaborated in Sections 3. Sections 4 and 5 will briefly describe the realization process or basic theories concerning the functions of SDF and network communication, respectively. Section 6 gives the experimental results, and a brief conclusion is also presented in Section 6.

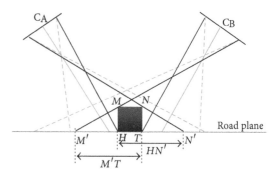

FIGURE 1: Perspective projection of cameras with different angle. Green lines denote the visual range of cameras.

2. Problem Description and System Framework

2.1. Problem Description. In order to guarantee the accuracy of the information extraction, in the existing methods based on computer vision, the video cameras, which are mounted in the position near the target section, access the road traffic information by using nearly perspective method. Thus the shape information of vehicles will be greatly affected in the 2D plane. Just as what is shown in Figure 1.

Assume that the THMN plane is the section along the vehicle width direction and HT is the vehicle width. Affected by the height of the vehicle, the vehicle width in the image flat is HN' in the perspective C_A, while it is $M'T$ in the perspective C_B. $M'T$.

If we fuse the image plane information of the two cameras into D ($D = A \cap B$), the influences on the vehicle width shown in the 2D plane from cameras of different perspective could be cancelled each other out, and thus the vehicle width range can be compressed to HT ($HN' \cap M'T = HT$). By this way the vehicle position can be detected accurately. As shown in Figure 2(e) and in Figure 2(d), the green, red, and yellow regions denote the vehicle contours in the camera 1, 2, in Figures 2(a), and 2(b) and the fusion image, respectively.

Therefore, in order to guarantee the accuracy of the information extraction, this paper will, on the one hand, access the clear and abundant traffic image information by using the nearly perspective method with multicameras video sensors. On the other hand, in order to reduce the influence from vehicles such as height and width, put forward a method to realize the traffic monitoring system consisting of IPU, network communication, and SDF, to extract the traffic parameters such as road vehicle number, vehicle velocity, and vehicle type.

2.2. System Introduction. Based on the traffic monitoring system consisting of IPUs, network communication, and SDF, this paper proposes an approach for traffic parameters extraction in the highway, such as vehicle number, vehicle velocity, and vehicle type, as shown in Figure 3.

(A) *Image Processing Unit (IPU).* There is a corresponding relationship between cameras and IPUs. And each IPU is

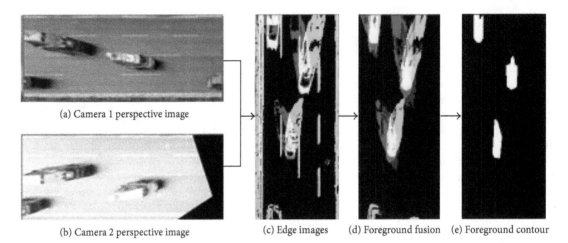

(a) Camera 1 perspective image

(b) Camera 2 perspective image

(c) Edge images   (d) Foreground fusion   (e) Foreground contour

FIGURE 2: Foreground fusion.

PVI, EPIs of each road,
traffic ,parameters and so on

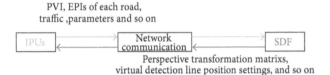

Perspective transformation matrixs,
virtual detection line position settings, and so on

FIGURE 3: Traffic monitoring system.

used to capture related video streaming, to process vision information, and to extract real traffic formation. In this paper, an advanced method based on the method mentioned in [6, 10] will be used to generate PVI and EPI, which are useful for traffic information extraction, such as traffic flow, vehicle velocity, type, and so on.

There is no requirement on the camera number, height, and shooting mechanism of each camera in this paper, but the following installation conditions should be satisfied.

(1) The target road section should be highway.

(2) The cameras should be installed on the left and the right perspectives simultaneously on the target road section, in order to capture the video images from the left and the right perspectives synchronously.

(3) The cameras should be installed on the same road section, upstream road section, or downstream road section, to ensure that the directions of all the moving vehicles in the target road section are the same.

(B) *Network Communication.* Each IPU, which is an independent unit, exchanges information with SDF by the internet. In this paper, based on method of [1, 2], the internet protocol (IP), including the transmission control protocol (TCP) and the user datagram protocol (UDP), will be used to transmit traffic information from IPUs to SDF, and the configuration information of IPUs can be controlled by the SDF using the IP protocol similarly. In this way, time-spatial image and traffic parameters can be transmitted to SDF synchronously from IPUs. Accordingly, the image perspective switching matrix of

each IPU and the position of virtual detecting lines can be set flexibly by SDF.

(C) *Sensor Date Fusion Server (SDF).* The following three functions can be achieved by SDF.

(1) IPUs camera calibration: this paper will use the method of [8, 9, 11] to calibrate the camera group synchronously and adaptively and calculate the perspective transformation matrix of each camera to ensure that the images from different cameras can be projected onto a top view picture with the same size and direction, as shown in the perspective images of the camera 1 and camera 2 in Figures 2(a) and 2(b).

(2) Virtual detection and tracking lines position settings: based on the perspective images and the methods of [7, 10, 12], the position of the detection line vertical to the direction of traffic movement to detect whether the vehicle is passing and the lines parallel to the direction of traffic movement to track the existing vehicles, which are shown in Figure 4 by red lines, can be set to generate the time-spatial image.

(3) IPUs information fusion: based on time-spatial image of each IPU and the method of PFM [1, 2, 4, 5], the fused image of the PVI and EPIs can be obtained, respectively, by image fusion on the pixel level. And then a series of traffic parameters can be extracted using the traffic parameter extraction strategy based on the time-spatial fusion image.

3. Image Processing Unit

In order to improve environment adaptability of the system, the method of time-spatial image [6, 7, 10, 13] will be used to process the video image. First of all, the images from all cameras should be projected onto the same horizontal area by the method of perspective transformation. Secondly, the PVI and the EVI of each lane will be obtained using the method of time-spatial image. Finally, the traffic parameters such as vehicle type, vehicle velocity, and traffic flow of the vehicles

FIGURE 4: The set of virtual detecting lines.

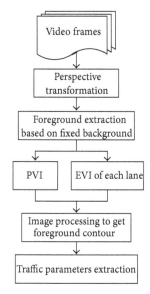

FIGURE 5: The traffic parameters extraction method of IPU.

through the virtual detection line can be obtained. The traffic parameters extraction method of IPU is shown in Figure 5.

3.1. Generation and Processing of Time-Spatial Image.

As shown in Figure 4, based on the perspective images and the methods of [7, 10, 12], the position of the detection line vertical to the direction of traffic movement to detect whether the vehicle is in the road and the line parallel to the direction of traffic movement to track the existing vehicles can be set, and the corresponding PVI and EPIs of each lane can also be generated. Then extract the binary image of vehicle outline from the PVI and EPIs based on the image processing technology such as morphology.

(A) *Generation of Time-Spatial Image.* The generation process of PVI and EPI is shown in Figure 6. FPI $t - i$ $(1 \le i < N)$ is defined as the perspective image of video frame $t - i$; the red line vertical to the direction of traffic movement, defined as $dvdl$, is the virtual detecting line for vehicle detecting, and the other red line parallel to the direction of traffic movement, defined as $tvdl$, is the virtual detecting line for vehicle tracking.

The relation between PVI and EPI is shown in Figure 7. Both numbers of pixels in f axis of PVI and EPI are N, which is the number of frames used to create time-spatial image one time. And l_{dvdl} and l_{tvdl} are the number of pixels of $dvdl$ and $tvdl$ in Figure 6, respectively.

The value of pixel (f, y_dvdl) in PVI is defined as formula (1). The value of pixel (f, y_tvdl) in EPI is defined as formula (2).

$$
\begin{aligned}
\text{PVI} &\left(f, y\_dvdl\right) \\
&= \text{FPI}_{t+i}\left(dvdl\_x, \min \_y\_dvdl + y\_dvdl\right),
\end{aligned}
\tag{1}
$$

$$
\begin{aligned}
\text{EPI} &\left(f, y\_tvdl\right) \\
&= \text{FPI}_{t+i}\left(dvdl_x - l_{tvdl} + x_{tvdl}, tvdl_y\right),
\end{aligned}
\tag{2}
$$

$$
f = (t + i) \% N + 1.
\tag{3}
$$

In formula (1) and (2), FPI_{t+i} denotes the FPI $t + i$, $dvdl\_x$ and $tvdl\_y$ are the x coordinate of $dvdl$ and the y coordinate of $tvdl$ in Figure 6, respectively, and $\min \_y\_dvdl$ is the minimum of y coordinate of $dvdl$ in Figure 6.

(B) *Image Processing of Time-Spatial Image.* Based on the image processing technology, such as morphology [7, 12], extracting the binary image of vehicle outline from the PVI and EPIs, one example of processing result is shown in Figure 8.

3.2. Traffic Parameters Extraction.

This paper proposed a simple and effective method to extract traffic parameters, based on the hypothesis that vehicles move with constant speed when passing the virtual detection line ($dvdl$ and $tvdl$). Based on time-spatial images of PVI and EPIs analyses, basic traffic information, including vehicle existence, approximate length, and velocity, is extracted.

Firstly, through the analysis of PVI and EPIs synchronously, vehicle existence detection of each lane is achieved. Then, the vehicle approximate length is extracted. Next, the vehicle velocity can be calculated readily. Finally, based on the three kinds of traffic information mentioned previously, variety of traffic parameters such as the number of passed vehicles, the vehicle velocity, the vehicle type, the distance between successive vehicles, and the road occupancy rate can be obtained easily:

$$
\text{counts} = \sum_{t=1}^{N-1} D(t) \wedge D(t+1),
\tag{4}
$$

$$
D(t) =
\begin{cases}
\text{true}, & \text{if } P(t) \cap E(t) = \text{true}, \\
\text{false}, & \text{others},
\end{cases}
\tag{5}
$$

$$
P(t) =
\begin{cases}
\text{true}, & \text{if } \text{PVI}(t, y\_dvdl) = 255, \\
& \quad 0 \le y\_dvdl \le l_{dvdl}, \text{ exists}, \\
\text{false}, & \text{others},
\end{cases}
\tag{6}
$$

$$
E(t) =
\begin{cases}
\text{true}, & \text{if } \text{EPI}(t, y\_dtdl) = 255, \\
& \quad 0 \le y_{dtdl} \le l_{tvdl}, \text{ exists}, \\
\text{false}, & \text{others}.
\end{cases}
\tag{7}
$$

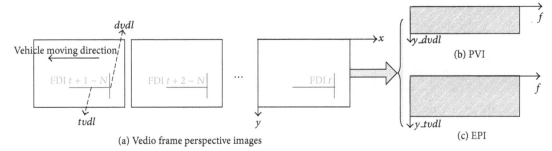

(a) Vedio frame perspective images

(b) PVI

(c) EPI

FIGURE 6: Generation process of PVI and EPI.

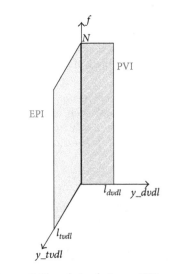

FIGURE 7: The relation between PVI and EPI.

In Figure 9 and formula (4), counts is defined as the existing number of vehicles in the time interval of PVI and EPI related. The area between two adjacent dotted red lines denotes that a vehicle is detected, while the area between two adjacent dotted green lines denotes that no vehicle is detected. Therefore, only foreground is detected simultaneously in PVI and EVI, vehicle can be inspected in this period, as shown in formula (4)–(7), among which t is defined as the horizontal ordinate of time-spatial images, and it represents the time label of video frame as discussed in Section 3.1, and $D(t)$, $P(t)$, and $E(t)$ denotes the ultimate detecting result of vehicle existence, the detecting result of PVI and EPI at the moment of video frame t, respectively.

4. Sensor Data Fusion Server

The SDF server mainly realizes multicameras synchronous calibration, virtual detection and tracking lines position settings, time-spatial image collecting and fusion using a constant polling cycle, and traffic parameter extraction based on the fusion image using the method descried in Section 3.2. Among them, the method of virtual detection and tracking lines position settings has been discussed in Section 3.1. This section describes the basic theories of multicameras synchronous calibration and image fusion.

4.1. Multicameras Synchronous Calibration. A calibration technique, which is based on a 3×3 homographic transformation and uses both point and line correspondences, was proposed in paper [11] to map images into a reference world coordinate system corresponding to an approximate bird's eye view of the real scene, so that any point can be converted from image coordinates to ground coordinates and vice versa.

Assume that the surface of the road is flat; this paper refers to paper [11] and ignores the height information in the world coordinate system, to map multicameras into the same reference world coordinate system corresponding to an approximate bird's eye view of the same real scene. Define $C^w = (x^w, y^w)$ and $C^I = (x^I, y^I)$ as the point of the world coordinate system and the image coordinate, respectively. So there exists a fixed perspective transformation matrix M and variable λ meeting formula (8), and between them λ is a variable related to corresponding coordinate point:

$$\lambda \begin{bmatrix} x^w \\ y^w \\ 1 \end{bmatrix} = M \cdot \begin{bmatrix} x^I \\ y^I \\ 1 \end{bmatrix},$$

$$M = \begin{bmatrix} m_{11} & m_{12} & m_{13} \\ m_{21} & m_{22} & m_{23} \\ m_{31} & m_{32} & 1 \end{bmatrix}. \tag{8}$$

According to Figure 10, define the direction and the vertical direction of lane lines as the x^w axis and y^w axis in the world coordinate system, respectively. Denoting that (x_j^w, y_j^w) and (x_j^I, y_j^I) are one of point correspondence in the world and the image coordinate systems, respectively, and one of corresponding calibration line is defined as $y^w + c_i^w = 0$ and $a_i^I \cdot x^I + b_i^I \cdot y^I + c_i^I = 0$ in the world and the image coordinate systems, respectively. Referencing paper [11], variables are defined as follows:

$$P_j = \begin{bmatrix} x_j^I & y_j^I & 1 & 0 & 0 & 0 & -x_j^w \cdot x_j^I & -x_j^w \cdot y_j^I \\ 0 & 0 & 0 & x_j^I & y_j^I & 1 & -y_j^w \cdot x_j^I & -y_j^w \cdot y_j^I \end{bmatrix},$$

$$T_j^P = \begin{bmatrix} x_j^w, y_j^w \end{bmatrix},$$

$$L_i = \begin{bmatrix} 0 & 0 & 0 & 1 & -\dfrac{a_i^I}{b_i^I} & 0 & c_i^w & -\dfrac{c_i^w \cdot a_i^I}{b_i^I} \\ 0 & 0 & 0 & 0 & -\dfrac{c_i^I}{b_i^I} & 1 & 0 & -\dfrac{c_i^w \cdot c_i^I}{b_i^I} \end{bmatrix}, \tag{9}$$

$$T_i^L = [0, c_i^w].$$

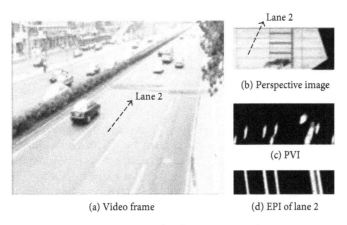

FIGURE 8: Example of processing result.

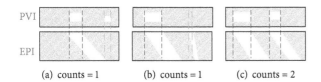

FIGURE 9: Vehicle existence detection: PVI and EPI analyses to detect passed vehicles.

FIGURE 10: Coordinate systems and calibration points and lines. The red circles and purple lines respectively represent point and line correspondences.

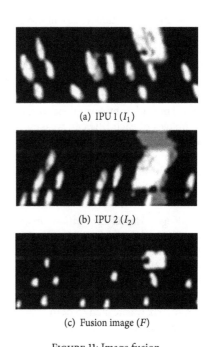

FIGURE 11: Image fusion.

Consequently, related equations defined below can be deduced, and with at least two line correspondences, parameters such as m_{22}, m_{31}, and m_{32} can be calculated, and then using at least three point correspondences, rest parameters of $\overline{M}$ can be figured out:

$$A \cdot \overline{M} = B,$$
$$A = \left[P_1^T, P_2^T, P_3^T, L_1^T, L_2^T, \ldots \right]^T,$$
$$B = \left[T_1^P, T_2^P, T_3^P, T_1^L, T_2^L, \ldots \right]^T, \qquad (10)$$
$$\overline{M} = \left[m_{11}, m_{12}, m_{13}, m_{21}, m_{22}, m_{23}, m_{31}, m_{32} \right]^T.$$

$\overline{M}$ can be solved by the method of the least square, as shown in formula (11):

$$\overline{M} = \left(A^T \cdot A \right)^{-1} A^T \cdot B. \qquad (11)$$

In the SDF platform, utilizing perspective matrix, all of images related to specific cameras are projected to a same bird's eye view in the same world coordinate system. And then check the contact ratio with respect to all bird's eye views. If the contact ratio is too low, the SDF could adjust the point coordinate or linear equation correspondences. The procedure is repeated until the contact ratio of all bird's eye views is high enough in order to realize multicameras synchronous calibration.

4.2. Probability Fusion Map (PFM). As discussed in Section 2.1, because of the fact that height information is ignored in camera calibration and internal and external

FIGURE 12: Network communication procedure.

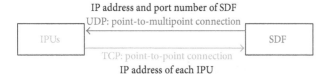

FIGURE 13: Network connection process.

camera factors including the camera orientation, the aperture angle, and the off-plane distance of the world point, there exists certain distortion to show moving targets in the bird's eye view through the perspective transformation, where the closest points to the surface will be the least distorted.

For any pixel in the 2D plane, it is only falsely projected as the foreground of vehicle by several video cameras. So that weighting the images of each IPU can weaken the influence, as can be seen in Figure 2. In this paper, the method of probability fusion map (PFM), which is firstly mentioned in paper [5], is adopted and optimized in terms of camera weight estimation and image fusion formula.

4.2.1. Camera Weight-Matrix Estimation. According to the characteristics of error transmissibility, paper [11] deduced that visual error generated by the conversion process from 2D image plane to 3D physical plane is related not only to camera pixels error but also to both inside and outside camera parameters. Paper [5] has demonstrated that the perspective transformation matrix was related to both inside and outside camera parameters, namely that based on the perspective transformation matrix and the camera pixels error, the deviation in the corresponding bird's eye view, which is called visual error before, can be estimated.

From formula (8), it is known that the world coordinate point (x^w, y^w) and the camera image coordinate point (x^I, y^I) have relations described in formulas (12) and (13). Therefore, the relationship between the visual error of bird's eye view about the world coordinate system and the system error of camera can be defined in formulas (14) and (15).

$$x^w = \frac{m_{11} \cdot x^I + m_{12} \cdot y^I + m_{13}}{\lambda}, \quad (12)$$

$$y^w = \frac{m_{21} \cdot x^I + m_{22} \cdot y^I + m_{23}}{\lambda}, \quad (13)$$

$$\sigma_{x^w,i} = \frac{m_{11}^2 \cdot \sigma_{x^I} + m_{12}^2 \cdot \sigma_{y^I}}{\lambda_i^2}, \quad (14)$$

$$\sigma_{y^w,i} = \frac{m_{21}^2 \cdot \sigma_{x^I} + m_{22}^2 \cdot \sigma_{y^I}}{\lambda_i^2}. \quad (15)$$

Assume that the deviation of all cameras is the same, that is, $\sigma_{x^I} = \sigma_{y^I}$, to define a bigger camera weight when the visual deviation is smaller while to define a smaller camera weight when the visual deviation is bigger, the relationship between visual error and the weight of the related camera is evaluated as follows:

$$
\begin{aligned}
w_{(x^w, y^w),i} &= \frac{1/\left(\sigma_{x^w,i} \cdot \sigma_{y^w,i}\right)}{\sum_{i=1}^{n} 1/\left(\sigma_{x^w,i} \cdot \sigma_{y^w,i}\right)} \\
&= \frac{\lambda_i^{4}/\left[\left(m_{11}^2 + m_{12}^2\right) \cdot \left(m_{21}^2 + m_{22}^2\right)\right]}{\sum_{i=1}^{n} \lambda_i^{4}/\left[\left(m_{11}^2 + m_{12}^2\right) \cdot \left(m_{21}^2 + m_{22}^2\right)\right]}.
\end{aligned}
\quad (16)
$$

In formula (16), $w_{(x^w, y^w),i}$ is defined as the weight about point (x^w, y^w) of camera i related to IPU i.

4.2.2. Image Fusion. Traffic parameter extraction methods based on data fusion are mainly divided into 2 kinds, data fusion on feature layer and on pixel layer [2, 3]. Through grid-based fusion on feature layer [3], traffic parameters from each IPU are fused to estimate traffic parameters precisely with less network bandwidth demand. Compared with those kinds of method, methods of data fusion on pixel layer have increased computational and network bandwidth requirements, but they can very robustly resolve occlusions among multiple views, just as what is discussed in Section 2.1.

Denoting the value of pixel to be $I_i(x^w, y^w)$ about point (x^w, y^w) in IPU i. Assume that there are n IPUs in the system. F represents the result image of image fusion, and $F(x^w, y^w)$ denotes the value of pixel about point (x^w, y^w) in F. The result image of image fusion is generated as follows:

$$
F(x^w, y^w) = \begin{cases} 255, & \text{if } \sum_{i=1}^{n} w_{(x^w, y^w),i} \cdot I_i(x^w, y^w) \geq T, \\ 0, & \text{others.} \end{cases}
\quad (17)
$$

In formula (17), $w_{(x^w, y^w),i}$ has the same meaning described in Section 4.2.1. T denotes a threshold used for vehicle existence detection. Figure 11 gives the result of image fusion using the method of PFM when $T = 500$.

5. Network Communication

The traffic monitoring system proposed in this paper is based on client-server network model where each IPU acts as a client, while the SDF plays the role of listening server. With the help of wired or wireless local area network (LAN) facilitates, each IPU sends video information, such as time-spatial images, to the server via point-to-point connection using TCP protocol, and each IPU is remotely controlled by

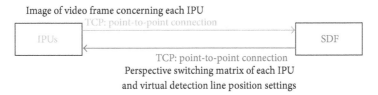

Image of video frame concerning each IPU

FIGURE 14: Transmission process concerning video image configuration information.

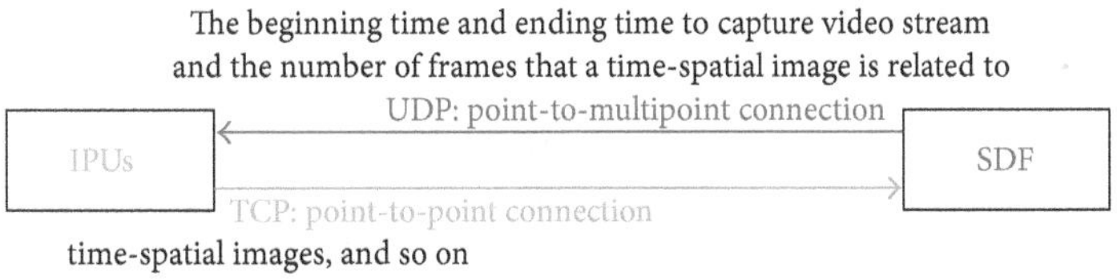

FIGURE 15: Process of synchronous image transmission.

FIGURE 16: Set of cameras.

(a) Camera left

(b) Camera right

FIGURE 17: Coordinate systems and calibration points and lines. The red circles and purple lines respectively represent point and line correspondences. The thick black line indicates the image coordinate system C_I, and the thick orange line indicates the world coordinate system C_w.

the SDF server through an independent signaling channel via point-to-point or point-to-multipoint connection, which enables the SDF server user to start or stop capturing frames, transmit perspective switching matrix and the settings of virtual detection line, and so on.

This paper is based on software platforms to realize real-time information fusion of multicameras; therefore, the system shall satisfy 3 key points. Firstly, it would be better that all cameras connected to a unique IPU separately have the same pattern. Hence, in this paper all cameras in the system have the same mode, resolution, and frame rate. Secondly, IPUs and SDF should be in the state of clock synchronization. Thirdly, within a certain time cycle, SDF must receive synchronous time-spatial images from each IPU. To fulfill the second and third points, on one hand, the network time protocol (NTP) is used in order to synchronise the system clocks of each related computer in the traffic monitoring system with reference to SDF server's system clock. On the other hand, considering network transmission delay caused by factors such as the capacity of internet channel and software processing speed, this paper references [2, 3, 14] to adjust parameters of the beginning time and ending time to capture video stream and the number of frames that a Time-Spatial image related to, according to the accuracy and time efficiency of receiving information, in order to ensure that each IPU cannot only synchronously capture video streaming but also generate and send time-spatial image within a certain time window to SDF. And then SDF issues the parameters to each IPU to ensure synchronization.

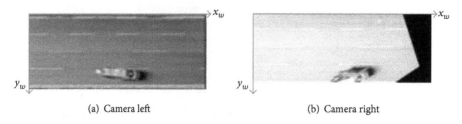

(a) Camera left

(b) Camera right

FIGURE 18: Calibration result: approximate bird's eye views of the testing region.

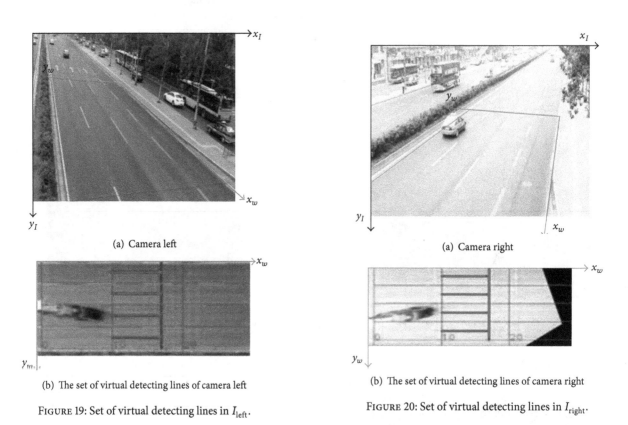

(a) Camera left

(a) Camera right

(b) The set of virtual detecting lines of camera left

(b) The set of virtual detecting lines of camera right

FIGURE 19: Set of virtual detecting lines in I_{left}.

FIGURE 20: Set of virtual detecting lines in I_{right}.

In general, network communication is realized through socket, and network communication procedure is divided into three steps, as shown in Figure 12.

(A) *Network Connection Process*. After installation, all IPUs in the traffic monitoring system are set in standby mode. At this phase, each IPU is listening in a UDP port for information in an independent signaling channel from the SDF. The UDP port has been set up before connection, and the signaling channel is specifically defined in order to separate data transmission of the IPUs from signals sent by SDF.

When SDF server sends the information packet which consists of SDF's IP address and its listening port number using UDP to the IPUs, network connection process starts. The next step is for each IPU to send respective IP address and request TCP connection to the listening SDF server. After all handshake procedures have been established and the meeting time has been reached, the network connection

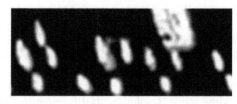

FIGURE 21: PVI of camera left (I_{left}) generated by video frames from frame 24,000 to frame 24,300.

process succeeds, and the system enters the next stage. The process of network connection is briefly shown in Figure 13.

(B) *Transmission Process concerning Video Image Configuration Information*. At this stage, each IPU captures several video frames and then transmits them to the SDF based on TCP. Next, on the basis of video images about each IPU, SDF accomplishes synchronous camera calibration, to map each IPU frames into a same reference world coordinate system corresponding to an approximate bird's eye view of the same

(a) Lane 1   (b) Lane 2   (c) Lane 3   (d) Lane 4

FIGURE 22: EPIs of camera left (I_{left}) generated by video frames from frame 24,000 to frame 24,300.

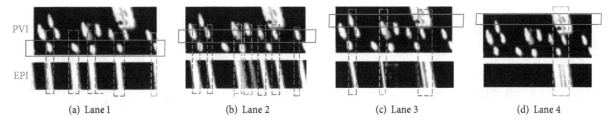

(a) Lane 1   (b) Lane 2   (c) Lane 3   (d) Lane 4

FIGURE 23: Vehicle existence detection of camera left generated by video frames from frame 24,000 to frame 24,300. In the figure, the orange rectangular box represents the position of homologous lane. And the red rectangular box and green rectangular box, respectively, represent the correct-detected and false-segmented vehicles.

FIGURE 24: PVI of camera right (I_{right}) generated by video frames from frame 24,000 to frame 24,300.

scene. Finally, the results of camera calibration, including the perspective switching matrix of each IPU and the settings of virtual detection lines, are sent to the homologous IPU, respectively.

After this stage, the system enters normal operation, in the phase of which, SDF and IPU software maintain timers to control frame capture, generate and transform synchronous time-spatial image with a const cycle. The transmission process is briefly shown in Figure 14.

(C) *Process of Synchronous Image Transmission*. The process of synchronous image transmission is the normal operation of the system. At this stage, firstly, through the first two phases, the network delay is estimated, based on which SDF sets a reasonable number of frames that a time-spatial image related to, which is defined as N in Section 3.1 and is related to the cycle of image transmission T. Secondly, IPU software maintains timers to control frame capture, generates synchronous time-spatial image with the period of N frames, and then transforms them timely to SDF with the cycle of T using TCP to achieve data fusion of multicameras in SDF server.

T is calculated by the formula below:

$$T = N \cdot f. \tag{18}$$

In formula (18), f is defined as camera's frame rate per second. In addition, as a secondary backup system, the IPUs support real-time media streaming directly to SDF server, in order to assist operators when an accident or other abnormal situation is reported. To confirm effective transmission, a new independent port is defined to receive synchronous video frame information. So there will be 2 independent ports to intercept disparate information, which are defined as time-spatial image listening port and video frame listening port. The process of synchronous image transmission is briefly shown in Figure 15.

6. Experimental Results

6.1. Experimental Environment

6.1.1. Camera Installation and the Set of IPUs. The proposed method is evaluated using two IPUs, which are all running in an independent PC with an Intel i3-2310M 2.10 GHz and 2 GB RAM with the aid of visual studio 2008. Both of them are related to a PAL video camera grabbing videos at the highway of Beijing Jinsong Bridge. Both of the two cameras have a 720×576 resolution at a frame rate of 25 frames per second. The cameras are fixed on the overpasses: one is set on the left and the other is set on the right of the interesting region, as shown in Figure 16, which are defined as I_{left} and I_{right}, respectively.

Each of the testing video streaming has 90,000 frames in all, representing the peak hour from 12:00 to 13:00. The testing region, which has 4 lanes, is in crowded state during the former one-fourth frames, while the rest is in fluent state. Therefore, from 12:00 to 12:15 the testing region is in crowded state, and from 12:15 to 13:00 the testing region is in fluent state.

6.1.2. Camera Calibration and the Settings of Virtual Detecting Lines in SDF. The SDF is also operating on an independent PC with an Intel i3-2310M 2.10 GHz and 2 GB RAM with the aid of visual studio 2008. On the basis of video images about each IPU received by SDF, point and line correspondences concerning the image and the reference world coordinate systems [10, 11], the images are mapped into a reference world coordinate system corresponding to an approximate bird's eye view of the real scene, as shown in Figures 17 and 18.

(a) Lane 1   (b) Lane 2   (c) Lane 3   (d) Lane 4

FIGURE 25: EPIs of camera right (I_{right}) generated by video frames from frame 24,000 to frame 24,300.

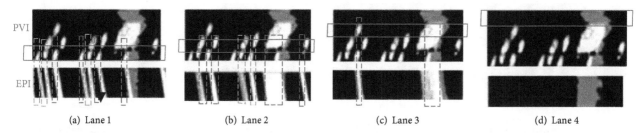

(a) Lane 1   (b) Lane 2   (c) Lane 3   (d) Lane 4

FIGURE 26: Vehicle existence detection of camera right generated by video frames from frame 24,000 to frame 24,300. In the figure, the meanings of color rectangular boxes are the same as those of Figure 23.

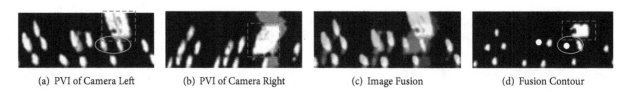

(a) PVI of Camera Left   (b) PVI of Camera Right   (c) Image Fusion   (d) Fusion Contour

FIGURE 27: PVI images generated by video frames from frame 24,000 to 24,300. In the image (c), fusion map is shown, where the green, red and yellow region denote the vehicle contours in the camera left, camera right and the fusion image, respectively.

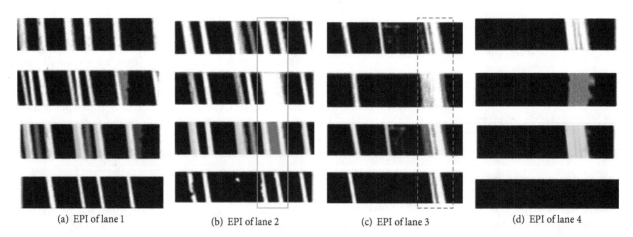

(a) EPI of lane 1   (b) EPI of lane 2   (c) EPI of lane 3   (d) EPI of lane 4

FIGURE 28: EPIs of each road generated by video frames from frame 24,000 to 24,300. The first and second row show the EPIs of each lane in camera left and camera right, respectively. In the third row, fusion map is shown, where the green, red and yellow region denote the vehicle contours in the camera left, camera right and the fusion image, respectively. The fusion contour is shown in the fourth row.

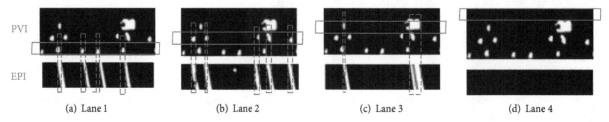

(a) Lane 1   (b) Lane 2   (c) Lane 3   (d) Lane 4

FIGURE 29: Vehicle existence detection with the method of PFM data fusion from frame 24,000 to frame 24,300. In the figure, the meanings of color rectangular boxes are the same as thos of Figure 23.

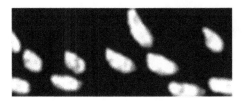

FIGURE 30: PVI of camera left (I_{left}) generated by video frames from frame 2,175 to frame 2,475.

Based on the results of calibration, virtual detecting and tracking lines are confirmed through SDF. Figures 19 and 20 show the results of camera calibration and virtual detecting lines settings. Between them, Figures 19(a) and 20(a) show the detecting region, which is surrounded by the pink color box. The thick red lines in Figures 19(b) and 20(b) are the settings of virtual detecting lines, of which the vertical and horizontal lines on each road denote the *dvdl* and *tvdls*, respectively. Horizontal pink lines in Figures 19(b) and 20(b) denote traffic lane lines.

6.2. The Experimental Results. To show the effectiveness of the method proposed in this paper, experimental results about traffic volume detection concerning the method of a single IPU and PFM data fusion with SDF, running under the experimental environment introduced in Section 6.1 which consists of 2 typical traffic states, are analysed and contrasted.

6.2.1. Experimental Results in Different Traffic State. The experimental environment introduced in Section 4.1 of this paper consists of 2 typical traffic states, fluent and crowed traffic states. In fluent state, both of traffic volume and velocity are relatively larger, while in crowed traffic state, traffic volume is large, but the velocity is relatively slower. In this paper, we randomly select two different time quantums, respectively, representing fluent and crowed traffic states, to proof the environmental suitability of our method.

To obtain real-time road traffic information, the time of delay-line is usually set as 10 s or so in time-spatial image [10, 13]. In our experiment environment, we set the time of delay-line as 12 s, namely, PVI and EPI images are constituted by 300 consecutive frames, so the width of time-spatial image is 300 pixels.

(i) *Fluent Traffic State.* From 12:15 to 13:00, the detecting region is in fluent state. So this paper randomly selects 12 s in this period, from 12:16:00 to 12:16:12, corresponding to video frames from frame 24,000 to frame 24,300, to analyze the experimental results concerning the method of a single IPU and PFM data fusion.

(A) *Experimental Results about a Single IPU.*

(1) *Camera Left (I_{left}).* Figure 21 shows the PVI image of the detecting road, and Figure 22 shows the EPIs of each lane, all of which are generated by the IPU related to camera left

TABLE 1: Experimental result about the IPU related to *camera left* in fluent traffic state.

Lane index	Lane 1	Lane 2	Lane 3	Lane 4	Total
Actual traffic volume (unit: number of vehicles)	4	5	2	0	11
Number of vehicles detected by IPU	5	7	3	1	16
Number of missed vehicles	0	0	0	0	0
Number of false-segmented vehicles	1	2	1	1	5
Detection error rate	25%	40%	50%	—	45.6%
Statistics error rate	25%	40%	50%	—	45.6%
The average computing time	About 32.5 ms per fame				

TABLE 2: Experimental result about the IPU related to *camera right* in fluent traffic state.

Lane index	Lane 1	Lane 2	Lane 3	Lane 4	Total
Actual traffic volume (unit: number of vehicles)	4	5	2	0	11
Number of vehicles detected by IPU	7	6	2	0	15
Number of missed vehicles	0	1	0	0	1
Number of false-segmented vehicles	3	2	0	0	5
Detection error rate	75%	60%	0	0	54.5%
Statistics error rate	75%	20%	0	0	36.4%
The average computing time (unit: s)	About 32.5 ms per fame				

(I_{left}). In Figure 23 the process and result of vehicle existence detection of camera left are described.

To measure the accuracy, we define the detection error rate γ_d and the statistics error rate γ_s, shown in lines 6 and 7 of Tables 1, 2, 3, 4, 5, and 6 as follows:

$$\gamma_d = \frac{n_m + n_f}{n_a} \times 100\%,$$

$$\gamma_s = \left| \frac{n_a - n_d}{n_a} \right| \times 100\%. \tag{19}$$

According to Figure 23, experimental result about the IPU related to camera left in fluent traffic state is summarized in Table 1.

(2) *Camera Right (I_{right}).* Figure 24 shows the PVI image of the detecting road, and Figure 25 shows the EPIs of each lane, all of which are generated by the IPU related to camera right (I_{left}). In Figure 26, the process and result of vehicle existence detection of camera right are described.

According to Figure 26, experimental result about the IPU related to camera right in fluent traffic state is summarized in Table 2.

(B) *PFM Data Fusion with SDF.* In SDF, on the basis of time spatial images from each IPU and PVI about detecting road

| (a) Lane 1 | (b) Lane 2 | (c) Lane 3 | (d) Lane 4 |

FIGURE 31: EPIs of camera left (I_{left}) generated by video frames from frame 2175 to frame 2475.

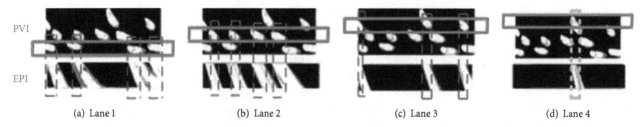

| (a) Lane 1 | (b) Lane 2 | (c) Lane 3 | (d) Lane 4 |

FIGURE 32: Vehicle existence detection of camera left generated by video frames from frame 2,175 to frame 2,475. In the figure, the meanings of color rectangular boxes are the same as those of Figure 23.

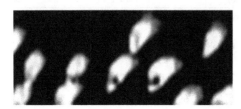

FIGURE 33: PVI of Camera Right (I_{right}) generated by video frames from frame 2,175 to frame 2,475.

TABLE 3: Experimental result with the method of PFM data fusion in fluent traffic state.

Lane index	Lane 1	Lane 2	Lane 3	Lane 4	Total
Actual traffic volume (unit: number of vehicles)	4	5	2	0	11
Number of vehicles detected by IPU	4	5	2	0	11
Number of missed vehicles	0	0	0	0	0
Number of false-segmented vehicles	0	0	0	0	0
Detection error rate	0	0	0	0	0
Statistics error rate	0	0	0	0	0
The average computing time	About 32.72 ms per fame				

TABLE 4: Experimental result about the IPU related to *camera left* in crowed traffic state.

Lane index	Lane 1	Lane 2	Lane 3	Lane 4	Total
Actual traffic volume (unit: number of vehicles)	4	4	3	0	11
Number of vehicles detected by IPU	4	4	3	1	12
Number of missed vehicles	0	0	0	0	0
Number of false-segmented vehicles	0	0	0	1	1
Detection error rate	0	0	0	—	9.1%
Statistics error rate	0	0	0	—	9.1%
The average computing time	About 32.5 ms per fame				

TABLE 5: Experimental result about the IPU related to *camera right* in crowed traffic state.

Lane index	Lane 1	Lane 2	Lane 3	Lane 4	Total
Actual traffic volume (unit: number of vehicles)	4	4	3	0	11
Number of vehicles detected by IPU	6	4	3	0	13
Number of missed vehicles	0	0	0	0	0
Number of false-segmented vehicles	2	0	0	0	2
Detection error rate	50%	0	0	0	18.2%
Statistics error rate	50%	0	0	0	18.2%
The average computing time (unit: s)	About 32.5 ms per fame				

and EPIs of each lane are revised with the method of PFM data fusion. Figure 27 described the process and the result of PFM data fusion about PVI of the detecting road, and Figure 28 described the process and the result of PFM data fusion about the EPIs of each lane.

In Figures 27 and 28, the dotted red boxes denote a bus in lane 3, but are mistakenly detected by camera left in lane 4 and by camera right in lane 2. And 2 cars in lane 2, which are surrounded by the green boxes or circles, are not detected by Camera Right. Through image fusion, all of the errors are revised.

According to Figure 29, experimental result with the method of PFM data fusion in fluent traffic state is summarized in Table 3.

(ii) *Crowed Traffic State*. From 12:00 to 12:15, the detecting region is in crowed state. So this paper randomly selects 12 s in

(a) Lane 1   (b) Lane 2   (c) Lane 3   (d) Lane 4

FIGURE 34: EPIs of camera right (I_{right}) generated by video frames from frame 2,175 to frame 2,475.

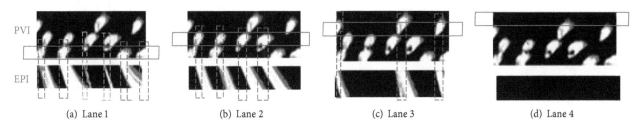

(a) Lane 1   (b) Lane 2   (c) Lane 3   (d) Lane 4

FIGURE 35: Vehicle existence detection of camera right generated by video frames from frame 2,175 to frame 2,475. In the figure, the meanings of color rectangular boxes are the same as those of Figure 23.

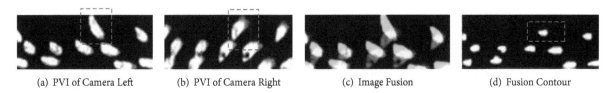

(a) PVI of Camera Left   (b) PVI of Camera Right   (c) Image Fusion   (d) Fusion Contour

FIGURE 36: PVI generated by video frames from frame 2,175 to frame 2,475. In the figure, the meanings of color shapes are the same as those of Figure 27.

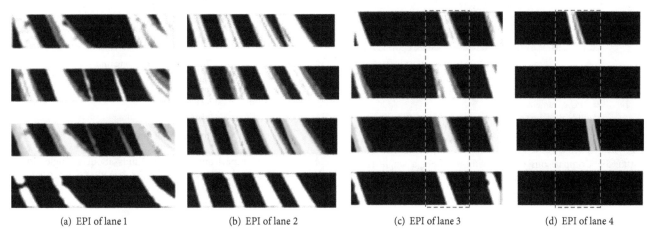

(a) EPI of lane 1   (b) EPI of lane 2   (c) EPI of lane 3   (d) EPI of lane 4

FIGURE 37: EPI of each road generated by video frames from frame 2,175 to frame 2,475. In the figure, the meanings of color shapes are the same as those of Figure 28.

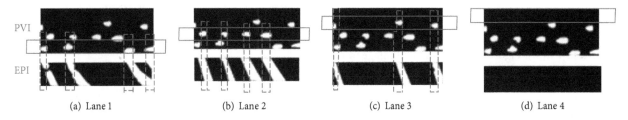

(a) Lane 1   (b) Lane 2   (c) Lane 3   (d) Lane 4

FIGURE 38: Vehicle existence detection with the method of PFM data fusion from frame 2,175 to frame 2,475. In the figure, the meanings of color rectangular boxes are the same as those of Figure 23.

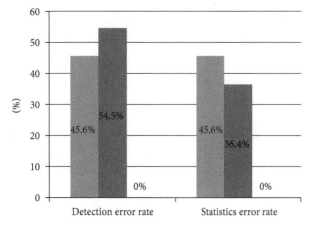

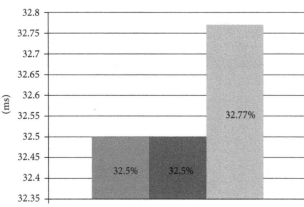

(a) Comparison of detection error rate and statistics error rate

(b) Comparison of time efficiency

FIGURE 39: Comparisons of the methods about a single IPU of camera left, a single IPU of camera right, and PFM data fusion with SDF in fluent traffic state.

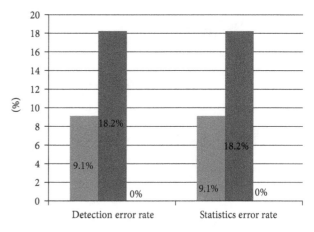

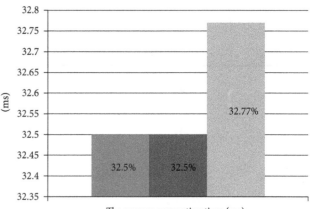

(a) Comparison of detection error rate and statistics error rate

(b) Comparison of time efficiency

FIGURE 40: Comparisons of the methods about a single IPU of camera left, a single IPU of camera right, and PFM data fusion with SDF in crowed traffic state.

this period, from 12:01:27 to 12:01:39, corresponding to video frames from frame 2,175 to 2,475, to analysis the experimental results concerning the method of a single IPU and PFM data fusion.

(A) *Experimental Results about a Single IPU.*

(1) *Camera Left* (I_{left}). Figure 30 shows the PVI image of the detecting road, and Figure 31 shows the EPIs of each lane, all of which are generated by the IPU related to camera left (I_{left}). In Figure 32, the process and the result of vehicle existence detection of camera left are described.

According to Figure 32, experimental result about the IPU related to camera left in crowed traffic state is summarized in Table 4.

(2) *Camera Right* (I_{right}). Figure 33 shows the PVI image of the detecting road, and Figure 34 shows the EPIs of each lane, all of which are generated by the IPU related to camera right (I_{left}). In Figure 35, the process and result of vehicle existence detection of camera right are described.

According to Figure 35, experimental result about the IPU related to camera right in crowed traffic state is summarized in Table 2.

(B) *PFM Data Fusion with SDF.* Figures 36 and 37, respectively, described the process and the result of PFM data fusion about PVI of the detecting road, and the EPIs of each lane.

In Figures 36 and 37, the dotted red boxes denote a car in lane 3 but are mistakenly detected by camera left in lane 4. Through image fusion, the error is revised.

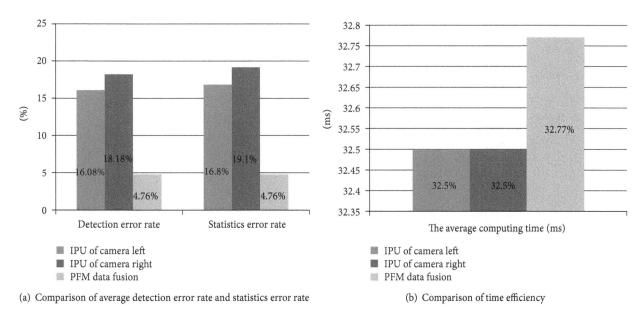

(a) Comparison of average detection error rate and statistics error rate

(b) Comparison of time efficiency

FIGURE 41: Comparisons of the methods about a single IPU of camera left, a single IPU of camera right, and PFM data fusion with SDF in crowed or in fluent traffic state.

TABLE 6: Experimental result with the method of PFM data fusion in crowed traffic state.

Lane index	Lane 1	Lane 2	Lane 3	Lane 4	Total
Actual traffic volume (unit: number of vehicles)	4	4	3	0	11
Number of vehicles detected by IPU	4	4	3	0	11
Number of missed vehicles	0	0	0	0	0
Number of false-segmented vehicles	0	0	0	0	0
Detection error rate	0	0	0	0	0
Statistics error rate	0	0	0	0	0
The average computing time	About 32.72 ms per fame				

According to Figure 38, experimental result with the method of PFM data fusion in crowed traffic state is summarized in Table 6.

(iii) *Analysis of Experimental Results in Different Traffic State.* Based on the Tables 1, 2, and 3, Figure 39 reflects the comparisons of detection error rate, statistics error rate, and time efficiency concerning the method of a single IPU and PFM data fusion with SDF in fluent traffic state. Similarly, based on the Tables 4, 5, and 6, Figure 40 reflects the comparisons in fluent traffic state.

To a large extent, the error happens because of the deviation of calibration, which depends on the vehicle height, as discussed in Section 2.1. And the proposed method weakens the effect of vehicle height and shadow greatly. So the error rate is approximately zero with a relatively high time efficiency using the proposed method in this paper, as shown in Figures 39 and 40.

6.2.2. Analysis of Experimental Results. With three Intel i3-2310M 2.10 GHz and 2 GB RAM PC, the average computing time is about 32.5 ms per fame in the IPU and 0.22 ms more in the data fusion process. In regard to vehicle existence detection in a different traffic state, through plenty of tests under the experimental environment introduced in Section 6.1 of this paper, the average detection error rate is 16.08%, 18.18%, and 4.76% in camera left, camera right, and the fusion images, respectively, and the average statistics error rate is 16.80%, 19.10%, and 4.76%, respectively, as shown in Figure 41. Therefore, the proposed method can be implemented quickly and accurately either in crowed state or in fluent state.

7. Conclusions

Based on the traffic monitoring system consisting of IPUs, network communication, and SDF, this paper proposes an approach for traffic parameters extraction in the highway, such as vehicle number, vehicle velocity, and vehicle type, based on time-spatial image and image fusion. The experimental results show that the proposed method can be implemented quickly and accurately either in crowed state or in fluent state. Further research to test the performance of the proposed method in more diversified circumstances, such as nighttime, and to optimize the algorithms of image processing and data fusion should be done. In addition, combined with pattern recognition and data mining technology, this method can be used to realize the traffic state identification and prediction, and to provide basis for section optimization.

Acknowledgments

This work was supported in part by Projects of International Cooperation and Exchanges of Natural Science Foundation of China (NSFC) under Grants 61111130119 and NSFC

60904069, the Doctoral Fund of Ministry of Education of China under Grant 20091103120008.

References

[1] L. Li, W. Huang, I. Y. H. Gu, and Q. Tian, "Foreground object detection from videos containing complex background," in *Proceedings of the 11th ACM International Conference on Multimedia (MM '03)*, pp. 2–10, November 2003.

[2] T. Semertzidis, K. Dimitropoulos, A. Koutsia, and N. Grammalidis, "Video sensor network for real-time traffic monitoring and surveillance," *IET Intelligent Transport Systems*, vol. 4, no. 2, pp. 103–112, 2010.

[3] A. Koutsia, T. Semertzidis, K. Dimitropoulos, N. Grammalidis, and K. Georgouleas, "Intelligent traffic monitoring and surveillance with multiple cameras," in *Proceedings of International Workshop on Content-Based Multimedia Indexing (CBMI '08)*, pp. 125–132, June 2008.

[4] K. Fujimura, K. Toshihiro, and K. Shunsuke, "Vehicle infrastructure integration system using vision sensors to prevent accidents in traffic flow," *IET Intelligent Transport Systems*, vol. 5, no. 1, pp. 11–20, 2011.

[5] F. Lamosa, Z. Flu, and K. Uchimura, "Vehicle detection using multi-level probability fusion maps generated by a multi-camera system," in *Proceedings of IEEE Intelligent Vehicles Symposium*, pp. 452–457, June 2008.

[6] Z. Zhu, G. Xu, B. Yang, D. Shi, and X. Lin, "VISATRAM: a real-time vision system for automatic traffic monitoring," *Image and Vision Computing*, vol. 18, no. 10, pp. 781–794, 2000.

[7] N. C. Mithun, N. C. Rashid, and S. M. M. Rahman, "Detection and classification of vehicles from video using multiple time-spatial images," *IEEE Transactions on Intelligent Transportation Systems*, vol. 13, no. 3, pp. 1215–1225, 2012.

[8] N. K. Kanhere and S. T. Birchfield, "A taxonomy and analysis of camera calibration methods for traffic monitoring applications," *IEEE Transactions on Intelligent Transportation Systems*, vol. 11, no. 2, pp. 441–452, 2010.

[9] Y. Shang, Q. Yu, and X. Zhang, "Analytical method for camera calibration from a single image with four coplanar control lines," *Applied Optics*, vol. 43, no. 28, pp. 5364–5369, 2004.

[10] D. Lee and Y. Park, "Measurement of traffic parameters in image sequence using spatio-temporal information," *Measurement Science and Technology*, vol. 19, no. 11, Article ID 115503, 2008.

[11] K. Dimitropoulos, N. Grammalidis, D. Simitopoulos, N. Pavlidou, and M. Strintzis, "Aircraft detection and tracking using intelligent cameras," in *Proceedings of IEEE International Conference on Image Processing (ICIP '05)*, pp. 594–597, September 2005.

[12] D. Yang, L. Xin, Y. Chen, Z. Li, and C. Wang, "A robust vehicle queuing and dissipation detection method based on two cameras," in *Proceedings of the 14th International IEEE Conference on Intelligent Transportation Systems (ITSC '11)*, pp. 301–307, 2012.

[13] L. Li, L. Chen, X. Huang, and J. Huang, "A traffic congestion estimation approach from video using time-spatial imagery," in *Proceedings of the 1st International Conference on Intelligent Networks and Intelligent Systems (ICINIS '08)*, pp. 465–469, November 2008.

[14] G. Litos, X. Zabulis, and G. Triantafyllidis, "Synchronous image acquisition based on network synchronization," in *Proceedings of IEEE Workshop on Three-Dimensional Cinematography*, June 2006.

7

Efficient and Secure Routing Protocol Based on Encryption and Authentication for Wireless Sensor Networks

Jiliang Zhou

Shanghai University of International Business and Economics, Shanghai 201620, China

Correspondence should be addressed to Jiliang Zhou; hnzhoujl@126.com

Academic Editor: Anfeng Liu

One concerned issue in the routing protocol for wireless sensor networks (WSNs) is how to provide with as much security to some special applications as possible. Another is how to make full use of the severely limited resource presented by WSNs. The existing routing protocols in the recent literatures focus either only on addressing security issues while expending much power or only on improving lifetime of network. None of them efficiently combine the above-mentioned two challenges to one integrated solutions. In this paper, we propose efficient and secure routing protocol based on encryption and authentication for WSNs: BEARP, which consists of three phases: neighbor discovery phase, routing discovery phase, and routing maintenance phase. BEARP encrypts all communication packets and authenticates the source nodes and the base station (BS), and it ensures the four security features including routing information confidentiality, authentication, integrity, and freshness. Furthermore, we still design routing path selection system, intrusion detection system, and the multiple-threaded process mechanism for BEARP. Thus, all the secure mechanisms are united together to effectively resist some typical attacks including selective forwarding attack, wormhole attacks, sinkhole attacks, and even a node captured. Our BEARP especially mitigates the loads of sensor nodes by transferring routing related tasks to BS, which not only maintains network wide energy equivalence and prolongs network lifetime but also improves our security mechanism performed uniquely by the secure BS. Simulation results show a favorable increase in performance for BEARP when compared with directed diffusion protocol and secure directed diffusion protocol in the presence of compromised nodes.

1. Introduction

A wireless sensor network (WSN) is a collection of nodes that can form a network without the need of a fixed infrastructure, which operates in an unattended, sometimes hostile, environment. Nodes can be connected arbitrarily, and all nodes take part in discovery and maintenance of routes to other nodes in the network [1]. Thus, one concerned issue when designing wireless sensor network is the routing protocol that requires the researchers to provide as much security to the application as possible [2]. Another important factor makes full use of the severely limited resource presented by WSNs, especially the energy limitation. Current presenters for routing protocols in sensor networks optimize for the limited capabilities of the nodes and the application specific nature of the networks, or they incorporate security into these proposed protocols; however, they have not been designed with security as a goal. When the defender has the liabilities of insecure wireless communication, limited node capabilities, and possible threats, and the adversaries can use powerful laptops with high energy and long-range communication to attack the network, therefore, designing a secure routing protocol for WSNs is crucial and nontrivial [3, 4].

1.1. Background. There are two secure problems to be considered when designing a secure routing protocol. On the one hand, different from the special router between conventional networks connected by wire cable, any node in sensor networks can be a router which can not only route to another node but also receive and send any routing information in a certain scope. On the other hand, one aspect of sensor networks that complicates the design of a secure routing protocol is in-network aggregation and inside attacks. In more conventional networks, a secure routing protocol is typically only required to guarantee message availability. Message confidentiality, authenticity, integrity, and freshness are handled at a higher layer by an end-to-end security mechanism. End-to-end security is possible in more conventional networks because it is absolutely unnecessary for intermediate routers to have access to the content of messages [5, 6]. However, in sensor networks, in-network processing makes end-to-end security mechanisms harder to deploy because intermediate nodes need direct access to the content of the messages. Link layer security mechanisms can help mediate some of the resulting vulnerabilities, but it is not enough for WSNs: we will now require much more from conventional routing protocols.

1.2. Related Works. In this section, we will discuss directed diffusion (DD) protocol and secure DD protocol (S-DD), possible attacks on routing protocol, securing routing protocols, and detecting compromised nodes. DD protocol and secure DD protocol, as our research and comparison representative, are very important, even a milestone, for the research of routing protocol for WSNs, and above all secure routing must exert to aim at some kinds of possible attacks. Moreover, it is necessary for the whole security mechanism to be improved by detecting the compromised nodes in case the routing protocol fails. The following is the current related work for them.

1.2.1. DD Protocol and S-DD Protocol. DD protocol [7] consists of several elements: interests, data messages, gradients, and reinforcements. An interest message is a query or an interrogation which specifies what a user wants. Each interest contains a description of a sensing task that is supported by a sensor network for acquiring data. In general speaking, in DD protocol, the setup and maintenance of extensive routing table are avoided. Instead, it relies on the broadcast propagation of queries, pruned by information content and geographical data. Sensor nodes maintain route caches which contain the source routes of the other nodes that are known. All in all, DD protocol is not resource aware or resource adaptive and especially suffers from many attacks for lack of encryption and authentication in course of packet receiving and transmitting.

Then, Wang et al. [8] present the design of a new secure directed diffusion protocol (S-DD), which provides a secure extension for the directed diffusion protocol. They mainly focus on secure routing and give a simple scheme to securely diffuse data, which uses an efficient one-way chain and do not use asymmetric cryptographic operations in this protocol. However, S-DD cannot work against any active attackers or compromised nodes in the network with the in-network aggregation. Especially, all sensor nodes do not have the ability to authenticate their neighbor nodes, so S-DD is also not robust without the in-network aggregation.

1.2.2. Possible Attacks on Routing Protocol. Two kinds of attacks can target routing protocols for WSNs [9]: passive attacks, where the attacker just eavesdrops on the routing information, and active attacks, where the attacker impersonates other nodes, drops packets, modifies packets, launches denial of service attacks, and so forth.

Most of the current routing protocols assume that all nodes in the network are trustworthy. The control information in the header of the packets carries the routing information, and intermediate nodes are assumed not to change this information. However, a compromised node can easily change the routing field of the packet and redirect the packet to anywhere it wants. The attacker can also redirect the route by changing the route sequence number in some protocols. In that case, the attacker can divert the traffic to itself by advertising a route to a node with the base station (BS) sequence number which is greater than the BS node's route. Redirecting the traffic can also be established by modifying the hop count. Route length is represented as hop count in routing protocol. A compromised node can direct all the traffic to itself by broadcasting the shortest hop count.

These attacks include impersonation, fabrication, and wormhole attacks. Compromised nodes can also create loops by changing the routes in the data packets. This will result in denial of service attacks. In impersonation, the attacker pretends to be another node after learning its address and changes it to its own address. Fabrication is another attack, where the compromised node generates false route messages, such as false error messages. In DD protocol, when links go down and routes break, the node which precedes this broken link broadcasts a "route error message." A compromised node can easily send false error messages for a working route. Another attack is the route cache poisoning attack. Any node can overhear the traffic, and if it finds route information, it adds it to its cache for future use. A compromised node can then broadcast spoofed packets with source route via itself. Then, neighboring nodes hear this and add the route to their cache. Also a compromised node can attack the routing table by overflowing it. It can attempt to initiate route discovery to nonexisting nodes. The worst attack is node captured, in which all information may be exposed and decrypted.

Finally, multihop routing in WSNs causes the packets to be delivered between one or more intermediate nodes. The security of routing information is harder to manage in this case.

1.2.3. Secure Routing Protocols for WSNs. Secure routing protocols for WSNs are difficult to be designed, especially when the nodes of a wireless sensor network have limited resources such as low battery power, CPU processing capacity, and memory. Since most routing protocols currently assume that nodes are trustworthy, security in WSNs mainly deals with authentication of the user nodes and security of the data packets that are being routed. Authentication is one goal, which verifies the identity of a node. A BS, a key, or the use of certificates can be implemented to perform authentications. Certificates can be thought of as a unique identification for every node. In Internet of Things, security mechanisms based on access control and secret communication channels regarding defending against outside attackers have been studied [10].

Zhou and Haas [11] proposed the idea of distributing a BS throughout the network in a threshold fashion. However, Zhou and Haas adopted public key and threshold cryptography, which are very expensive for sensor devices. Therefore, we do not consider this method practical for the time being. All the protocols below assume the preexistence and presharing of secret keys for all honest nodes in the beginning.

Adrian Perrig and Robert Szewczyk [3] present a suite of security protocols optimized for sensor networks: SPINS [5]. SPINS has two secure building blocks: SNEP and μTESLA. SNEP includes data confidentiality, two-party data authentication, and evidence of data freshness. μTESLA provides authenticated broadcast for severely resource-constrained environments. However, their system requires synchronized clocks for all the nodes in the network, and the SPINS is not robust for routing attacker because it is not based on the secure routing protocol.

Secure routing protocol (SRP) proposed by Papadimitratos and Haas guarantees correct route discovery [12]. They assume a security association between the end points in the beginning. The correctness of their protocol was only proven analytically.

Nasser and Chen proposed an efficient routing protocol, which we called SEEM [13], for WSNs. Compared to other proposed routing protocols, SEEM is designed based on utilizing multipath concept and considers energy efficiency and security simultaneously. However, SEEM is not really secure because its packets can be modified by attackers without any encryption and authentication.

Lee and Choi have presented SeRINS [14]: a secure alternate path routing in sensor networks. Their alternate path scheme makes the routing protocol resilient in the presence of compromised nodes that launch selective forwarding attacks. It also detects and isolates the compromised nodes, which try to inject inconsistent routing information, from the network by neighbor report system. In neighbor report system, a node's route advertisement is verified by its surrounding neighbor nodes so that the suspect node is reported to the BS and is excluded from the network. We think the SeRINS has not combined the authentication with encryption, and cooperation of several neighbor nodes can make the reported information good in order to cheat the BS, so the packet of the verified itself is not secure, and this leads the whole protocol not to be secure and trusted.

1.2.4. Detecting Compromised Nodes.
Compromised nodes in WSNs usually promise to forward packets but later drop the data packets and refuse to forward them. Current network protocols do not have a mechanism to detect such nodes. Link layer acknowledgment such as IEEE 802.11 MAC protocol can detect link layer failure. However, it cannot detect a forwarding failure. Some protocol acknowledgments can detect end-to-end communication failure, but it cannot detect which particular node caused the failure in between [15].

Some researchers propose the idea of having neighbor nodes detect each other's behaviors and then report to each other or to a network authority, which detects compromised nodes by observing the reports on several attacks in the network [14, 16, 17]. All nodes have a monitor and reputation records, trust records, and a path manager. All these adapt to changes in networks and find out the misbehaving nodes in the network. However, we think that compromised nodes acting in groups can make these records good for themselves without the authentication mechanism with encryption. Therefore, we believe that a special agent such as BS is necessary for intrusion detection system (IDS) to detect the compromised nodes.

1.3. Contributions.
In this paper, we propose a new routing protocol BEARP: efficient and secure routing protocol based on encryption and authentication for WSNs. In BEARP, we design to encrypt all communication packets, authenticate the source node and the BS, and ensure the four security features including routing information confidentiality, authentication, integrity, and freshness. Moreover, BEARP mitigates the load of sensor nodes by transferring routing-related tasks to the BS which operates routing paths selection and intrusion detection system. In routing paths selection system, the BS periodically selects a newly best path from many paths based on current energy level of nodes along each path. In the process of selecting route, especially, we design the algorithm *multi_shortest_path* to create another child thread, which executes the function *send_route* in time when finding a route to the source node. This thread helps decrease the delay for sending routing information. In intrusion detection system, detecting compromised nodes also performs uniquely by the secure BS. Therefore, the two approaches not only maintain network wide energy equivalence and prolong network lifetime but also improve our security mechanism. BEARP can effectively resist to some typical attacks including selective forwarding attack, wormhole attacks, sinkhole attacks, and even a node captured.

Compared to other proposed routing protocols, BEARP not only considers integration between energy efficiency and security simultaneously but regards security as our design goal for the first time. At the same time, the feature making BEARP distinct is that BEARP takes full advantage of the predominance of the BS. As a result, packet delivery ratios and network lifetime for operating BEARP in the WSN are more preferable and work better against some attacks, compared to operating DD protocol. The contributions of our work include the following: (1) we implement the four security features for WSNs including routing information confidentiality, authentication, integrity, and freshness, and BEARP works well under some typical attacks; (2) BEARP has much better packet delivery ratio than DD protocol in the presence of some compromised nodes; (3) the network lifetime is prolonged compared to insecure routing protocols, like DD protocol; (4) BEARP has almost no blocked nodes in WSNs and remarkably surpasses DD protocol.

1.4. Organization of the Paper.
Foregoing contents are our preliminary work before we propose BEARP. The following in this paper is organized as follows. Some used notations and assumptions are introduced in Section 2. In Section 3,

we present BEARP routing protocol and related algorithm and give some implementation details. Then, we discuss the security analysis for BEARP in Section 4, followed by performance evaluation in Section 5. Finally, we draw our conclusions in Section 6.

2. Notations and Assumptions

Sensor networks typically consist of one or multiple base stations and hundreds or thousands of inexpensive, small, and hardware-constrained nodes scattered over a wide area. Our sensor network model includes a powerful BS and numerous constrained sensor nodes. BS, which has greater capabilities, can directly transmit data to any node in the network. Resource-constrained sensor node, whose transmission range is limited, can send data along the multihop route to the BS. We consider that a BS is trustworthy, differently from sensor nodes. Moreover, we can extend naturally our scheme for a single BS to multiple BS as presented by Deng et al. [18].

Developing a proper threat model against our routing protocols, we consider two attack sources: outer or insider [19]. Outsider attackers do not have trusted keys. They typically rely on message replay or delay to influence routing protocols. Insider threats occur when a fully trusted node, with appropriate key material, is compromised. We assume the key management system is always secure, since there have been a lot of successful researches for them. The attacks launched from outsiders cannot join in the network because of the assumption, but we consider that the outsider attackers can interfuse in the network to be compromised nodes through any other special means.

Before presenting our BEARP protocol, we introduce some used notations and assumptions about sensor network in Tables 1 and 2, respectively, which are used in the following sections.

3. Routing Protocol Based on Encryption and Authentication (BEARP)

Now we present our BEARP protocol, which consists of three phases: neighbor discovery phase, routing discovery phase, and routing maintenance phase. In the following, each of them will be described in detail [13, 20, 21].

3.1. Neighbor Discovery Phase. Neighbor discovery takes place right after the deployment of all sensor nodes. However, neighbor discovery can be launched at any time by the BS during the lifetime of the sensor network. By doing this, the BS can request to reconstruct this network topology according to the great changes of the topology [13, 20].

To initiate the neighbor discovery, the BS selects broadcast key *BK* to encrypt the packet neighbor discovery (*ND*) and broadcasts the packet confidential *ND* (*CND*) to the whole network. After receiving this packet, each node does as follows (see Table 4):

(1) decrypt $ND = D_{BK}(CND)$ with the broadcast key *BK* of the node;

(2) record the address *prev_hop* from which the current node receives the packet and stores it in the list *neighbor_list* in ascending order of packet received time;

(3) change the address *prev_hop* to the address of itself;

(4) check if the broadcast packet has been received by searching *pkt_seq_num* in the table *rc_pkt_table*. If the packet has already been received once, the node drops this *CND* and does not rebroadcast it. Otherwise, it stores *pkt_seq_num* in table *rc_pkt_table*, encrypts $CND = E_{BK}(ND)$ with the broadcast key *BK*, and rebroadcasts the *CND* to its neighbor.

The fourth step insures that no *CND* packet is broadcasted more than one time for each node, which also applies to other control messages. Thus, the communication overheads for transmitting control packets are reduced to a low level.

Through the process of receiving, decrypting, segmenting, encrypting, and rebroadcasting *CND*, each node knows its real neighbor and stores them for using in the following phases.

The BS waits for a short time to ensure that the *CND* broadcast can be flooded through the network. Then, the BS broadcasts another packet confidential neighbor collection (*CNC*) in order to collect the neighbor information of each node. At the same time, the BS sets the current time T_B and the random number R_B to the packet *NC* in order to authenticate each node in the WSN. After receiving this packet, each node does as follows (see Table 5(a)):

(1) decrypt $NC = D_{BK}(CNC)$ with the broadcast key *BK* of the node and gets the two fields T_B and R_B for creating the reply packet *CNCR*;

(2) check if the address *prev_hop* from which the current node receives the packet has been saved in the list *neighbor_list*. If not then it stores it;

(3) change the address *prev_hop* to the address of itself;

(4) check if the broadcast packet has been received by searching *pkt_seq_num* in the table *rc_pkt_table*. If the packet has already been received once, the node drops this *CNC* and does not rebroadcast it. Otherwise, it stores *pkt_seq_num* in table *rc_pkt_table*, keeps the other fields in the packet, encrypts $CNC = E_{BK}(NC)$ with the broadcast key *BK*, and rebroadcasts the *CNC* to its neighbor.

When sensor node receives the *CNC* packet, it replies a confidential neighbor collection reply (*CNCR*) packet to the BS by flooding. In *NCR*, we add the session key field *SK*, time field T_B, and random number field R_B, and the source address is set to itself, and the destination address is set to the BS. The *CNCR* packet contains the following information:

(1) the address of the node,

(2) the list that has all addresses of its neighbors,

(3) the session key between the node and the BS,

(4) the authentication information.

TABLE 1: Basic notations.

BK	The initial key used to create the session key between BS and nodes and encrypt the routing message at beginning.
SK	Session key used for data encryption and authentication between BS and source.
T_B, T_S	Denote the current time of the BS and the current time of the source node, respectively.
R_B, R_S	Denote the random number of the BS selected and the random number of the source node selected, respectively.
$E_k(x)$	Encryption of message x with key k.
$D_k(x)$	Decryption of cipher message x with the key k.
$x\|y$	Concatenation of message x and y.
prev_hop	Denote the previous node address from which the current node receives the packet
next_hop	Denote the next node address to which the current node sends the packet.
neighbors_list	Neighbors address list.
pkt_seq_num	The sequent number of a packet.
rc_pkt_table	Received packet table that stores the sequent number of packets.
route_list	The routing list field in a packet.
route_table	The routing table in a node.
pkt_type	Packet type including CND, CNC, $CNCR$, CDE, and $CDER$.
source_add	The source node address.
data_length	The length of data packet.
itself_add	The current node address.
$A \xrightarrow{M} B$	Node A sends message M to node B.

TABLE 2: Assumptions.

A-1:	The links between these sensor nodes are always bidirectional. The communication patterns in WSNs fall into three categories: node to BS, BS to node, and BS to all nodes.
A-2:	The BS has sufficient battery power to surpass the lifetime of all sensor nodes and sufficient memory to store cryptographic keys, and it is very secure and cannot be compromised under any conditions.
A-3:	Each node in WSNs has unique identifier stored in BS, and it can forward a message towards the BS, recognize packets addressed to it, and handle message broadcasts.
A-4:	WSNs may be deployed in unauthentic locations, and basic wireless communication is not secure. Individual sensors are untrustworthy; any adversary can eavesdrop on traffic, inject wrong routing messages, and replay old routing messages.
A-5:	Each node can get a master secret key which it shares with the BS before its deployment. The secret key is used as authentication key by the BS.
A-6:	The BS can update all secret keys between any nodes after a certain period of time, and the key management system is always secure.

TABLE 3: Neighborhood matrix.

	BS	1	2	3	4	5	6
BS	0	∞	∞	0	0	0	0
1	1000	0	1000	1000	1000	0	0
2	1000	1000	0	1000	1000	0	0
3	0	1000	1000	0	1000	1000	1000
4	0	1000	1000	1000	0	1000	1000
5	0	0	0	1000	1000	0	1000
6	0	0	0	1000	1000	1000	0

Each node receiving this packet does as follows (see Table 5(b)):

(1) decrypt $NCR = D_{BK}(CNCR)$ with the broadcast key BK of the node;

(2) check if the address prev_hop from which the current node receives the packet has been saved in the list neighbor_list. If not then it stores it;

(3) change the address prev_hop to the address of itself;

(4) check if the broadcast packet has been received by searching pkt_seq_num in the table rc_pkt_table. If the packet has already been received once, the node drops this $CNCR$ and does not rebroadcast it. Otherwise, it stores pkt_seq_num in table rc_pkt_table, keeps the other fields in the packet, encrypts $CNCR = E_{BK}(NCR)$ with the broadcast key BK, and rebroadcasts the $CNCR$ to its neighbor.

When the BS receives the packet $CNCR$, at first, it must authenticate communication time cost by comparing the time field T_B with the current time and authenticate the freshness of the packet by comparing random number field R_B with the foregone random number R_B. If the authentication fails, the BS will drop the packet. Finally, after receiving neighbor information of all nodes, the BS has a vision of the topology of the whole networks.

To select a path that has the maximum available energy on each node, we introduce the concept weight. The weight of an edge in the corresponding graph of the network is

TABLE 4: Confidential neighbor discovery packet broadcasts.

BS (sender)		Neighbor of BS (receiver)
$ND = [pkt\_type\|BS\|prev\_hop\|pkt\_seq\_num]$; $CND = E_{BK}(ND)$.	$\xrightarrow{\text{CND}}$	$ND = D_{BK}(CND); prev\_hop \rightarrow neighbor\_list$; $itself\_address \rightarrow prev\_hop$; $pkt\_seq\_num \rightarrow rc\_pkt\_table$; $ND = [pkt\_type\|BS\|prev\_hop\|pkt\_seq\_num]$; $CND = E_{BK}(ND)$.
N_i (sender)		N_{i+1} (receiver, neighbor of node N_i)
$ND = D_{BK}(CND); prev\_hop \rightarrow neighbor\_list$; $itself\_address \rightarrow prev\_hop$; $pkt\_seq\_num \rightarrow rc\_pkt\_table$; $ND = [pkt\_type\|BS\|prev\_hop\|pkt\_seq\_num]$; $CND = E_{BK}(ND)$.	$\xrightarrow{\text{CND}}$	$ND = D_{BK}(CND); prev\_hop \rightarrow neighbor\_list$; $itself\_address \rightarrow prev\_hop$; $pkt\_seq\_num \rightarrow rc\_pkt\_table$; $ND = [pkt\_type\|BS\|prev\_hop\|pkt\_seq\_num]$; $CND = E_{BK}(ND)$.

TABLE 5: Confidential neighbor collection and confidential neighbor collection reply packet broadcasts.

(a) Confidential neighbor collection packet broadcasts

BS (sender)		N_i (receiver)
$NC = [pkt\_type\| BS\|prev\_hop$ $\|pkt\_seq\_num \| T_B\| R_B]$; $CNC = E_{BK}(NC)$.	$\xrightarrow{\text{CNC}}$	$NC = D_{BK}(CNC); get\ T_B, R_B$; $prev\_hop \rightarrow neighbor\_list$; $itself\_address \rightarrow prev\_hop$; $pkt\_seq\_num \rightarrow rc\_pkt\_table$; $NC = [pkt\_type\|BS\|prev\_hop\|pkt\_seq\_num \| T_B\| R_B]$; $CNC = E_{BK}(NC)$.

(b) Confidential neighbor collection reply packet broadcasts

Source node (sender)		N_i (receiver, neighbor of BS)
$NC = D_{BK}(CNC)$; $NCR = [pkt\_type\| source\_add\|neighbor\_list$ $\|prev\_hop\|pkt\_seq\_num\|SK \| T_B\| R_B - 1]$; $CNCR = E_{BK}(NCR)$.	$\xrightarrow{\text{CNCR}}$	$NCR = D_{BK}(CNCR)$; $prev\_hop \rightarrow neighbor\_list$; $itself\_address \rightarrow prev\_hop$; $pkt\_seq\_num \rightarrow rc\_pkt\_table$; $NCR = [source\_add\|neighbor\_list\|prev\_hop$ $\|pkt\_seq\_num\|SK\| T_B\| R_B - 1]$; $CNCR = E_{BK}(NCR)$.
N_i (sender)		BS (receiver)
$NCR = D_{BK}(CNCR) (prev\_hop) \rightarrow neighbor\_list$; $itself\_address \rightarrow prev\_hop$; $pkt\_seq\_num \rightarrow rc\_pkt\_table$ $NCR = [source\_add\|neighbor\_list\|prev\_hop\|$ $pkt\_seq\_num\|SK\| T_B\| R_B - 1]$; $CNCR = E_{BK}(NCR)$.	$\xrightarrow{\text{CNCR}}$	$NCR = D_{BK}(CNCR)$; $pkt\_seq\_num \rightarrow rc\_pkt\_table$; $get\ source\_add, neighbor\_list, SK, R_B - 1$; $authenticate\ T_B, R_B - 1$.

the available energy on the head node. The BS then constructs a directed graph marked weight with neighbor information. The weight decreases as the head node sends and receives packets. Figure 1 shows the subgraph derived from the network topology. In Figure 1, the weights of edges starting from BS are infinite, which means that the BS has much more energy than other sensor nodes.

The calculation of the weight is based on the formula

$$\text{Weight} = \frac{\text{total power of each node}}{\text{power for transmitting or receiving one packet}}. \tag{1}$$

We assume the total energy of each node initially is 10000 units and the total energy for sending one packet is about 10 units; then

$$\text{weight} = \frac{10000}{10} = 1000 \text{ units.} \tag{2}$$

We use neighborhood matrix to represent the neighborhood relations between nodes. Table 3 shows the weighted matrix corresponding to the graph in Figure 1. Each row except the first row contains the neighbor information of a specific node; for example, the second row shows neighbor information of the BS. Each column except the first column represents a node. If the value for some space is not zero, it means that the nodes corresponding to the row and the

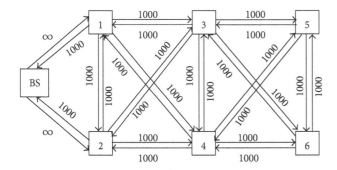

FIGURE 1: The subgraph derived from network topology.

column are neighbors. The value of each space is the weight of the edge from the node corresponding to the row to the node corresponding to the column. As we defined, weights of edges from the BS are infinite. For example, from Table 3 we know that *node 3* has five neighbors: *node 1, node 2, node 4, node 5,* and *node 6*.

3.2. Routing Discovery Phase.
The BS starts its task, routing discovery, beginning at phase two. The task is divided into three subtasks: data enquiry; routing path selection system (RPSS); sending routing information.

3.2.1. Data Enquiry.
By now, BEARP supports only data transmission requested by the BS; that is, the BS broadcasts enquiry for data with specific features. Sensor nodes have satisfied the enquiry response with enquiry reply. Data transmission follows these steps.

(1) The BS broadcasts an enquiry packet confidential data enquiry (*CDE*).

(2) Sensor nodes have satisfied the enquiry response with a reply packet confidential data enquiry reply (*CDER*).

(3) Sensor nodes that do not satisfy the enquiry rebroadcast *CDE*.

(4) The BS calculates a shortest path to the desired node in the weighted graph. The shortest path is a path from the source to the BS of which the total energy consumed on each node for sending one packet is the least, that is, usually the path with minimum hops.

Each node receiving *CDE* packet does as follows:

(1) check if it satisfies the enquiry itself;

(2) if not, the node rebroadcasts the *CDE* and saves the *pkt_seq_num* to avoid repeating broadcasting the *CDE* more than once;

(3) if it does, the node returns a *CDER* packet that contains the length of data sent soon to the BS by setting the *next_hop* to the first node in the *neighbor_list*. Because the *neighbor_list* is in the ascending order of the receiving time of *CND* and *CNC*, the first node in the *neighbor_list*, sometimes even the second and the

third and so on, must be one-hop close to the BS than the node itself. If the node is the neighbor of the BS, the BS must be the first node in its *neighbor_list*.

In packet *CDER*, we add the length of data field *data_length*, time field T_S, and random number field R_S, and the source address is set to itself, and the destination address is set to the BS. The packet *CDER* contains following information:

(1) the address of the source node, the previous hop, and the next hop,

(2) the length of data,

(3) the authentication information: time field T_S, random number field R_S.

Source node selects a broadcast key *BK* to encrypt the packet *DER*, selects the session key *SK* to encrypt $T_S \parallel R_S$, and broadcasts a confidential *DER* (*CDER*) packet to the whole network. After receiving this packet, each intermediate node does as follows (see Table 6):

(1) decrypt $DER = D_{BK}(CDER)$ with the broadcast key *BK* of the node;

(2) change the address *prev_hop* to the address of itself;

(3) get the address *prev_hop* in the first record of *neighbor_list* to set the *next_hop*;

(4) check if the broadcast packet has been received by searching *pkt_seq_num* in the table *rc_pkt_table*. If the packet has already been received once, the node drops this *CDER* and does not rebroadcast it. Otherwise, it stores *pkt_seq_num* in table *rc_pkt_table*, encrypts $CDER = E_{BK}(DER)$ with the broadcast key *BK*, encrypts $T_S \parallel R_S$ with the session key *SK*, and rebroadcasts the packet *CDER* to its neighbor.

When the BS receives the *CDER* packet, it decrypts $DER = D_{BK}(E_{BK}(CDER))$ with the broadcast key *BK* and $T_S \parallel R_S = D_{SK}(E_{SK}(T_S \parallel R_S))$ with the session key *SK*. It gets the *data_length* for the following calculations of the shortest path, through which we can get the energy for sending the data from the source node and random number field R_B and time T_B for authentication.

3.2.2. Routing Path Selection System (RPSS).
After the BS receives the packet *CDER*, in order to tell the source node a best routing path to BS, it starts to calculate the shortest path to the node. However, it is important for BS how to calculate the shortest path in WSNs. We design routing path selection system (RPSS) to solve the problem.

As mentioned above, the shortest path has the minimal sum of energy consumed for transmitting one packet, that is, usually the path with minimum hops. Thus it saves the energy from the view of the whole network. When there are more than two shortest paths, we use the maximal available power as the second criteria; that is, we select the path that has the maximal available energy on each sensor node.

To get the desired shortest path, we modify the breadth first search (BFS) algorithm [5] to get the relatively shortest

TABLE 6: Confidential data enquiry reply packet forwards.

Source node (sender)		Intermediate nodes (receiver)
$DER = [pkt\_type\|source\_add\|data\_length$ $\|prev\_hop\|next\_hop\|pkt\_seq\_num];$ $CDER = E_{BK}(DER)\|E_{SK}(T_S\|R_S)$	$\xrightarrow{\text{CDER}}$	$DER = D_{BK}(E_{BK}(CDER));$ $itself\_address \rightarrow prev\_hop;$ $First\ record\ of\ neighbor\_list \rightarrow next\_hop;$ $pkt\_seq\_num \rightarrow rc\_pkt\_table;$ $DER = [pkt\_type\|source\_add\|data\_length$ $\|prev\_hop\|next\_hop\|pkt\_seq\_num];$ $CDER = E_{BK}(DER)\|E_{SK}(T_S\|R_S)$
		The base station
	$\xrightarrow{\text{CDER}}$	$DER = D_{BK}(E_{BK}(CDER))$ $T_S\|R_S = D_{SK}(E_{SK}(T_S\|R_S));$ $Get\ data\_length.$

path from the BS to source node, as is shown in Algorithm 1. The BFS always finds the shortest path from the source to the destination, if there is one. Our modified version of BFS algorithm does not necessarily select the absolute shortest path because we also need to consider the left energy, that is, the weight corresponding to each edge, of each node into consideration. That is, if one node on the shortest path has energy left less than required level, we discard this shortest one and continue searching the second shortest path until success.

We assume that the BS wants to get data from source node N. We first define three levels of energy limitation. Each level is the half of the upper level. The main modification to the breadth-first search algorithm is that whenever it finds a shortest path to source node N, it checks if the weight of each edge on the path is greater than the predefined level. If so it returns this path as the shortest path. Otherwise, it continues the calculations until it finds the second shortest path. If the shortest path under current energy limitation cannot be found, it means that each path found has at least one node whose energy level is less than current energy limitation. Consequently, we degrade the energy limitation to the lower level and search again. If not any path is found from the first level to the third level, it means that source node N is unreachable [20, 21].

In a word, BS maintains an energy limitation array for all nodes, and the updating of energy limitation for each node is independent. This feature ensures the best use of each node in the sensor network. In the RPSS, BS can determine whether it has the routing path to the source node or not and how many routes it may be selected. If there are routes to the source, the BS will select the shortest route and send to it in time.

3.2.3. *Sending Routing Information.* In the algorithm *multi_shortest_path*, we introduce into multiple-threaded process mechanism. As is to know that a thread is a lightweight process which exists within a program and executed to perform a special task in operating system. A process that has only one thread is referred to as a single-threaded process, while a process with multiple threads is referred to as a multiple-threaded process [22]. In our design, a thread is placeholder information associated with a single use of a program that can handle multiple concurrent users,

and several threads of execution may be associated with a single process. In runtime environment designed by us, some threads exist in a common memory space and can share both data and code of a program, and they can increase the speed of any application.

We then present the process of executing the related function of RPSS. When any standalone application is running, it first executes the method *main* running in a one thread, called the main thread. The main thread creates another child thread which executes the function *send_route_to_source_node*, and the function schedules another function *multi_shortest_path*, which urgently creates another child thread which executes the function *send* when finding a route to the source node. Algorithm 2 shows code segments for sending route to source node algorithm. The method *main* execution can be finished, but the program will keep running until all threads have completed its execution. As is shown in Algorithms 1 and 2.

The multiple-threaded process mechanism mentioned above evidently decreases the delay with the multiple-threaded process because it can satisfy with multiple users and concurrent requests. If multiple users are using the function *multi_shortest_path*, the threads are created and maintained for each of them. Our design not only increases the speed of selecting a path to the source but also always saves memory space.

Once the BS has got the routing path to the source, the route is set to the field *route_list* of the packet RR. The BS then selects a broadcast key BK to encrypt the packet route reply (RB) including the route to the source, selects the session key SK to encrypt T_S and $R_S - 1$, and sends the confidential RR (CRR) packet to the second address of the route. Each intermediate node forwards this packet according to the corresponding of the route.

When the source node receives the *CRR*, at first, it must authenticate communication time cost by comparing the time field T_B with the current time and also authenticate the freshness of the packet by comparing random number field R_B with the foregone random number R_B. If the authentication fails, the source node can conclude that the sender of the packet is not real or the route is not credible and drops the packet. Otherwise, the source node stores *route_list* in table *route_table* and *pkt_seq_num* in table *rc_pkt_table*.

Multiple shortest path algorithm

```
vector<nsaddr_t> BEARP::multi_shortest_path(nsaddr_t
source_node, int packet_energy){
    bool visited[NODES_AMOUNT];
    nsaddr_t father[NODES_AMOUNT];
    nsaddr_t tmp, neighbor_node;
    vector<nsaddr_t> queue, route [PATHS_AMOUNT];
    bool found;
    int pointer, path_amount;

    found = false;
    path_amount = 1;
    nsaddr_t father_node;
    queue . reserve(NODES_AMOUNT);
    route . reserve(NODES_AMOUNT);

    while (!found){
        pointer = 0;
        for (int i = 0; i <NODES_AMOUNT; i++){
            visited[i] = false;
            father[i] = -1;
        }
        for (int i = 0; i <queue.size(); i++)
            queue · pop_out();

        visited[BASE_STATION] = true;
        queue . reserve(NODES_AMOUNT);
        queue . push_in((nsaddr_t)BASE_STATION);

        for (int i = 0; i <NODES_AMOUNT; i++){
            if (left_energy[i]- packet_energy >=
                current_energy_limit[source_node]){
                for (int j = 0; j<NODES_AMOUNT; j++){
                    if (weight_matrix[i][j] > 0 && weight
                        _matrix[i][j] < MAX_INT){
                    if (left_energy[j]- packet_energy >=
                        current_energy_limit[source_node])
                        all_neighbor_list[i] . push_in(j);
                    }
                }
            }
        }

        tmp = queue[pointer];
        visited[tmp] = true;
        while(queue · size() > pointer){
            for(int i = 0; i<all_neighbor_list[tmp] . size(); i++){
                neighbor_node = all_neighbor_list[tmp][i ];

                if (visited[neighbor_node])
                continue;
                father [neighbor_node] = tmp;

                if (neighbor_node == source_node){
                    father_node = neighbor_node;
                    while(father_node!= BASE_STATION){
                        route . push_in(father_node);
                        father_node = father[fa];
                    }
                    found = true;

                    if(path_amount = 1){
                        path_amount++;
                        threadbegin /*create a thread to send route*/
                        send(route[0], source_node);
```

ALGORITHM 1: Continued.

```
                              threadend
                          }
                      }
                      visited[neighbor_node] = true;
                      queue . push_in(neighbor_node);
                  }
              pointer++;
              tmp = queue[pointer];
          }
          if (found && path_amount = =PATH_MAX)
              break;
          update_energy_limit(source_node,
                  current_energy_limit[source_node]);
      }
      return route;
  }
```

ALGORITHM 1: Code segments for multiple shortest path algorithm.

```
Send_route_to_source_node(nsaddr_t source_node, int packet_energy){
    /*start multi_shortest_path algorithm*/
    vector<nsaddr_t> BEARP::multi_shortest_path(nsaddr_t source_node, int packet_energy);
    bool exchange;
    int high, low, path_amount;
    multi_shortest_path (nsaddr_t source_node, int packet_energy);
    count(int timer); exchange = true;
    high = path_amount; low = 1;
    while(timer >= TIME_MAX && listening(ACK) = false){
        if(high >= low){
            if(exchange){
                exchange = false;
                path_amount --;
                send(route[high --], source_node),
            }
}
            else{
                exchange = true;
                path_amount --;
                send(route[low + + ], source_node);
            }
        }
        else {
            multi_shortest_path(nsaddr_t source_node,
              int packet_energy);
            high = path_amount; low = 1; exchange = true;
        }
    }
    Return(1);
}
```

ALGORITHM 2: Code segments for sending route to source node.

Table 7 shows the process of forwarding the confidential route reply packet in the WSN.

At the same time, the *ACK* mechanism can also help the source node find a correct route to the BS. On receiving the *CRR* packet, the source node knows which path it can use to communicate with the BS. As a result, using the path transferred with the *CRR* packet, it returns an *ACK* packet to the BS to confirm the receipt of the *CRR*. The *ACK* packet also contains the number of data packets going to be sent, which to some extent guarantees that the receiver can detect the loss

TABLE 7: Confidential route reply packet forwards.

BS (sender)		Intermediate nodes (receiver)
$DER = D_{BK}(E_{BK}(CDER))$;		$RR = D_{BK}(E_{BK}(RR))$;
$T_S\|R_S = D_{SK}(E_{SK}(T_S\|R_S))$;	$\xrightarrow{\text{CRR}}$	*The corresponding of route_list* $\rightarrow$ *next_hop*;
$RR = [pkt\_type\|source\_add\|route\_list\|pkt\_seq\_num]$;		$pkt\_seq\_num \rightarrow rc\_pkt\_table$;
$CRR = E_{BK}(RR)\|E_{SK}(T_S\|R_S - 1)$.		$CRR = E_{BK}(RR)\|E_{SK}(T_S\|R_S - 1)$.
		Source node
	$\xrightarrow{\text{CRR}}$	$RR = D_{BK}(E_{BK}(CRR))$;
		route_list $\rightarrow$ *route_table*;
		$pkt\_seq\_num \rightarrow rc\_pkt\_table$;
		authenticate $T_S\|R_S - 1$: $T_S\|R_S - 1 = D_{SK}(E_{SK}(T_S\|R_S - 1))$.

of data due to communication problems, nodes failure, or misbehavior of compromised nodes. After sending the *ACK* packet, source node is ready to start transmitting the real data. If the BS does not receive the *ACK* packet within a predefined time, it deems the selected route as invalid and runs the function *multi_shortest_path* once more to find another path. If it receives the *ACK* packet, then it knows that this route is available and waits for data from the source node.

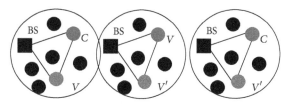

FIGURE 2: Network of including malicious nodes.

3.3. Routing Maintenance and IDS. In route maintenance, it is still the BS that works as the server to operate intrusion detection system (IDS) and to release control information. The purpose of the phase route maintenance is to overcome this potential risk by IDS and to prolong the network lifetime as much as possible [16–18, 23].

The BS must verify all nodes entering the network at the beginning. This is one of our assumptions. In our proposed solution, the BS detects any compromised node which possibly exists in the network by impersonating regular users. The BS detects the compromised node by sending each node arbitrary route requests one by one. Figure 2 shows a network of including compromised nodes. When a BS wants to test whether a node (let us say node *C*) is forwarding other nodes' data packets inside the network or not, the BS will first pick a validated destination node *V* that is close to node *C*. Then, the BS will send a *REQ* to node *C* for node *V*. Once node *C* agrees to participate in the route and a route is established between the BS, node *C*, and node *V*, the BS will send data packets to node *V* using this route. Then, by sending information and asking for the received packets to node *V* encrypted with its private shared key between the BS and node *V*, the BS will check whether node *V* has received the packets or not. Node *V* will send back an acknowledgment to BS whether it has received any data packets from node *C* or not. If it has not, the BS will test whether the node *C* and *V* are forwarding other nodes' data packets inside the network or not, so the BS will continue to pick another validated destination node *V'* and node *V*. Thus, the BS will check whether node *V'* has received the packets or not by sending information and asking for the received packets to the validated destination node *V'* encrypted with its private shared key between the BS and node *V'*. If it has not, the BS will mark node *C* or *V* as compromised nodes and will update the network key immediately. Algorithm 3 shows

code segments for detecting compromised node algorithm in intrusion detection system.

All nodes in the network except for the compromised nodes will receive the new network shared key. From that the compromised nodes will not be able to encrypt or decrypt any packet information [24]. The BS will know that the nodes are compromised and take them out of the network. At the same time, the BS will process the routing tree including the compromised nodes.

4. Security Analysis of BEARP

In this section, we will analyze the security properties of BEARP required by sensor networks and present how BEARP defends some typical attacks in the WSN.

4.1. Routing Message Confidentiality. A sensor network should not leak sensor readings, especially control packet, to neighboring networks. We have assumed that the key management system is secure, which is the underlying security for our BEARP, so the secret keys are confidential. The standard approach for keeping sensitive routing message secret is to encrypt them with a secret key that only intended receivers possess, hence our BEARP can distinctly achieve routing message confidentiality. Given the observed communication patterns, we set up secure channels between nodes and base stations and later bootstrap other secure channels as necessary.

4.2. Identity Authentication and Routing Message Authentication. Since an adversary may exert to personate or imitate a compromised node, identity authentication and routing message authentication are important for many applications in sensor networks [25]. The receiver needs to ensure that

```
Detect_compromised_node(compromised node C, validate node V )
/*Use the validate node V to confirm whether the node C is compromised node or not.*/
        { if (Base Station received the acknowledge packet of the validate node)
                 return (true);
            else {
        select another validate node V';
            if (detect_compromised_node(compromised
              node V, validate node V'))
             validate node C is compromised node;
             else
            {
            detect_compromised_node(compromised
              node C, validate node V');
            validate node V is compromised node;
            }
          }
        }
```

ALGORITHM 3: Code segments for detecting compromised node algorithm.

the routing message used in any decision-making process originates from a trusted source. Informally, routing message authentication allows a receiver to verify that the routing message was really sent by the claimed sender. In the two-party communication case of the BEARP, routing message authentication can be achieved through a purely symmetric mechanism: the sender and the receiver share a session secret key to compute the four particular parameters (T_B, R_B, T_S, and R_S) of all communicated routing message because they are correlative with the routing message. When a routing message with four correct particular parameters arrives, the receiver knows that it must have been sent by the sender. If the four particular parameters have some mistakes, the receiver concludes the sender or intermediate node may be adversary.

4.3. Routing Message Integrity.

In communication, routing message integrity ensures the receiver that the received routing message is not altered in transmission by an adversary [5]. In BEARP, we achieve routing message integrity through routing message authentication for the four particular parameters (T_B, R_B, T_S, and R_S), which is not a stronger property. It is very difficult that an adversary only alters routing information but does not alter the four particular parameters because the routing message is confidential as a whole. At the same time, the packet sequence number pkt_seq_num can also help authenticate routing message integrity.

4.4. Routing Message Freshness.

Routing message freshness means that the routing message is recent, and it ensures that no adversary replayed old messages. Sensor networks send measurements over time, so it is not enough to guarantee confidentiality and authentication [5]. In BEARP, to ensure each routing message is fresh, we design a real-time T_B or T_S field of the routing packet, which provides to conclude the freshness of the packet through computing and comparing the two particular parameters (T_B, T_S), the receiving time, allowing delay time.

4.5. Defending Some Typical Attacks.

The most direct attack against a routing protocol is to target the routing information exchanged between nodes. By spoofing, altering, or replaying routing information, adversaries may be able to create routing loops, attract or repel network traffic, extend or shorten source routes, generate false error messages, partition the network, increase end-to-end latency, and so forth. [9]. Apparently, routing information in BEARP which holds the above four security properties can defend adversaries to spoof, alter, or replay them.

Wormholes are hard to detect because they use a private, out-of-band channel invisible to the underlying sensor network. Sinkholes are difficult to defend against in protocols that use advertised information such as remaining energy or an estimate of end-to-end reliability to construct a routing topology because this information is hard to verify [26].

However, resistant to the two attacks is the most important of all secure targets of our designing the routing protocols [25]. Adversary cannot encrypt and decrypt the routing information with the secret key, and it cannot pretend to be another node to impersonate and fabricate any other information. Furthermore, all routing paths are selected uniquely by the BS which is very secure and cannot be compromised under any condition in our assumption. Therefore, protocols that construct a topology initiated by a BS are most susceptible to wormhole and sinkhole attacks, but BEARP can easily defend them.

In a selective forwarding attack, compromised nodes may intend to include themselves on the actual path of the data flow and refuse to forward certain messages and simply drop them, ensure that they are not propagated any further. However, once again the mechanism that BEARP selects routing paths prevents sensor nodes from selecting or joining routing path. All routing paths are selected uniquely by the BS, which defends adversaries to join in the WSN. A more subtle form of this attack is when an adversary selectively forwards packets. An adversary interested in suppressing or modifying packets originating from a select few nodes can reliably forward the remaining traffic and limit suspicion of its wrongdoing. Routing message confidentiality can prevent adversary to open any routing packets.

When an adversary captures a sensor node in WSNs and knows all its secret keys, BEARP also has two methods for secure process: one is routing paths selected uniquely by the secure BS, which reject a sensor node captured to imitate BS; another is IDS of detecting compromised nodes, which can take the sensor node captured out of the WSN.

5. Performance Evaluations and Analyses

The goal of our experiments is to evaluate and analyze the performance of our BEARP. To simplify the simulation, we generated random nodes and defined some of them as compromised nodes. In BEARP, these compromised nodes are kicked out of the network as soon as they discovered; however, in DD protocol and S-DD protocol, these nodes are not detected. In our simulations, no compromised nodes will be allowed to reenter the network before being certified by the BS, and therefore they will not be able to route packets again. In the following sections, We measured the packet delivery ratios, network lifetime, and nodes blocked by compromised attacks during data forwarding, which are very important for efficient and secure routing protocol for WSNs [3], and we then show the simulation results for different scenarios.

5.1. Simulation Metrics. To evaluate the performance of our secure routing mechanism in the presence of some compromised nodes which impact network performance, we have simulated BEARP on a network simulator, ns-2 [27]. In our simulations, we consider to generate a variety of sensor fields of different sizes. Some sensor nodes, ranging from 100 to 1200, are randomly deployed in $200 \times 200 \, \text{m}^2$ target area, and the network size is changeable according to different measure for network performance. Regarding the left-bottom corner of the target area as $(0, 0)$, we positioned a BS at a fixed point $(100, 100)$, almost in the center of the WSN. Each sensor node has a constant transmission range of 20 m. All sensor nodes are stable, and no node is moving, and every round each node sends 20 packets to the BS. We changed the scenario files each time for testing the BEARP protocol, DD, and S-DD protocol for different numbers of nodes, compromised nodes.

5.2. Packet Delivery Ratios. In this scenario, we increased the compromised nodes into the WSN for every test case. The simulation time was 90 s in test. In Figure 3, we show the packet delivery ratio when there are some compromised nodes amounts from 10 to 100 present in the WSN. As we can see from the figure, the BEARP has better packet delivery ratio than the DD protocol and S-DD protocol all the time. This is due to the fact that since compromised nodes are left out of the network because of encryption and authentication in BEARP, all data packets may not be sent to them. Therefore, the packet delivery ratios of the BEARP hold rather higher than those of the DD protocol and S-DD protocol.

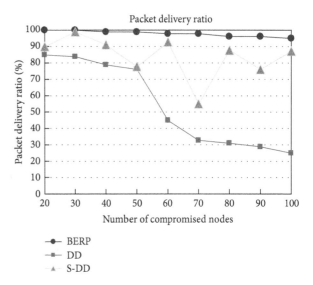

FIGURE 3: Packet delivery ratio (%) for 600 nodes.

At the same time, as the number of compromised nodes increases, the packet delivery ratio for both protocols goes down because the compromised nodes are dropping the packets. Especially, the packet delivery ratio for DD protocol descends sharply when the compromised nodes are more than 50. In S-DD protocol, without authentication mechanism between neighbors, the compromised node may transmit or not when the packets send to a compromised node. Thus, the packet delivery ratio for S-DD protocol is unstable. We think that since certain compromised nodes are chosen randomly, there is a chance that compromised nodes may occupy crucial positions for data transferring. In BEARP, there are not many nodes left in the WSN since the compromised nodes are being left out due to the mechanism of encryption and authentication. Therefore, it is taking a certain time to establish connections and for the packets to be delivered, and the packet delivery ratio for BEARP decreases slightly.

5.3. Network Lifetime. The most significant performance increase achieved in BEARP is the network lifetime. In Figure 4(a), we can see that BEARP increases the network lifetime over 15% and 8%, respectively, compared to DD protocol and S-DD protocol. Though the rule for reinforcing a particular path differs, it is always the fact that DD protocol and S-DD protocol use the same path for all communications between the same source and BS. The direct consequence is that nodes on this particular path may deplete energy very soon, while BEARP uses several shortest paths and maintains an energy limitation array for all nodes to avoid each node to exhaust energy quickly. Figure 4(b) is the simulation results for network lifetime when 10% of nodes misbehave. From this figure we can see that network lifetime of DD protocol suffers a significant decrease, and S-DD protocol's lifetime is increased but unstable while that of BEARP decreases slightly and be stable. When compromised nodes destroy the path for forwarding, both DD protocols and S-DD protocol

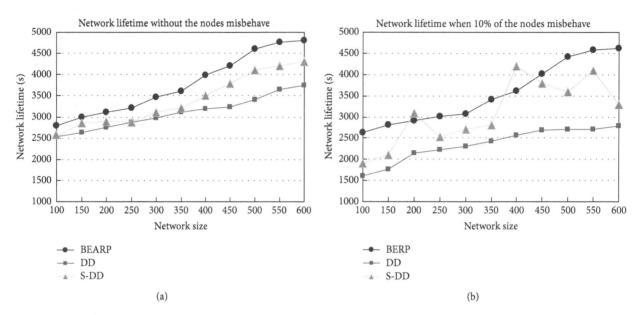

FIGURE 4: Compared average network lifetime between BEARP, DD, and S-DD protocol. (a) without the nodes misbehaving. (b) when 10% of the nodes misbehave.

have to select a new path, and the communication load spreads among a small number of available paths. Instability of lifetime for S-DD protocol is that it cannot detect and reject compromised nodes. Moreover, the lifetime of BEARP is 37% longer than DD protocol because BEARP can reject compromised node, resist their attacks, and distribute the load more evenly among several secure paths according to the algorithm *multi_shortest_path*.

5.1. Nodes Blocked by Compromised Attacks. We randomly distributed compromised nodes over the square area. In the simulations, we considered two types of compromised nodes: one drops all the relaying packets (type I), and the other drops all the relaying packets and also advertises inconsistent routing information (type II). In addition, we simulated two different density networks: one is 600 sensor nodes network, and the other is 1200 sensor nodes network.

We performed a set of experiments to measure the number of sensor nodes blocked by a set of compromised nodes in each round, increasing the number of compromised nodes in the network. In the presence of type I compromised nodes, we, respectively, measured the number of blocked nodes running on the BEARP, on the DD protocol, and on the S-DD protocol in both 600 and 1200 sensor nodes networks. We also measured the number of blocked nodes using the same scheme in the presence of type II compromised nodes.

Each simulation experiment was conducted using 10 different network topologies, and each result was averaged over 10 runs of different network topologies.

Simulation experiment results are shown in Figure 5. In the presence of type I compromised nodes which drop all the relaying packets, the effect of DD protocol, S-DD protocol, and our BEARP on a ratio of blocked nodes is shown in Figures 5(a) and 5(b). S-DD protocol is not stable to be blocked by type I compromised nodes. In 600

sensor nodes network, using DD protocol incurs blocked nodes from about 5% to 44%, while BEARP has almost no blocked nodes for compromised node to be entered to WSNs due to the secure authentication mechanism, as shown in Figure 5(a). In Figure 5(b), in 1200 sensor nodes network, using DD protocol has less blocked nodes than in 600 sensor nodes network. This is because, the number of sensor nodes scattered in the network is doubled, which makes the network denser. Also, each sensor node has more neighbor nodes so that it has more next-hop nodes. Thus, this increases the chances of bypassing the compromised nodes which drop relaying packets.

In the presence of type II compromised nodes which both drop all the relaying packets and advertise inconsistent routing information, the effect of secure authentic system on a ratio of blocked nodes is shown in Figures 5(c) and 5(d). Without secure authentic system, the influence of type II compromised nodes over the network is more devastating than that of type I nodes, since type II compromised nodes even attract the network traffic and drop them. Using secure authentic system, however, we see that more than 99% of sensor nodes are not blocked, as shown in Figures 5(c) and 5(d). Since, in the experiments, almost every type II nodes were excluded by secure encryption and authentication system from the network; legitimate nodes did not forward packets to the compromised nodes identified. Thus, with several type II nodes, almost all of them are excluded from the network so that more than 99% of sensor nodes are not blocked.

Out of control is the cause of network blocked. In WSN with compromised nodes, DD protocol cannot control the relaying for any packets, while S-DD protocol cannot control the relaying of neighbor's packets due to no secure authentic system. On the one hand, our secure authentic system in BEARP can protect the sensor nodes from compromising

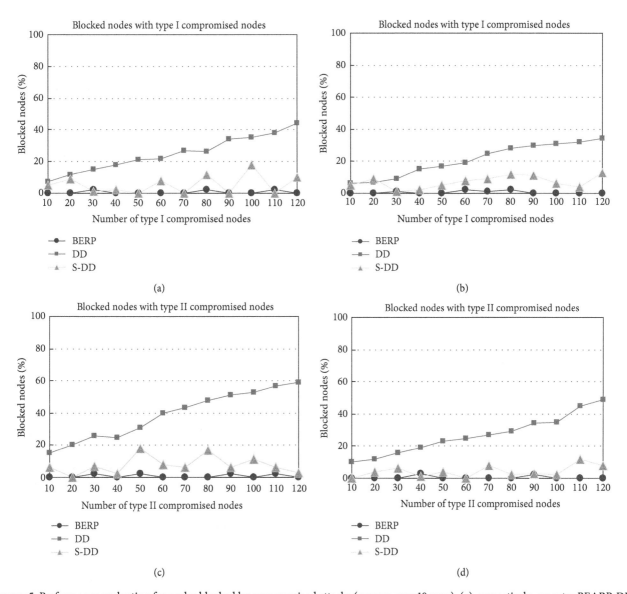

FIGURE 5: Performance evaluation for nodes blocked by compromised attacks (average over 10 runs). (a), respectively, executes BEARP, DD, and S-DD protocol in 600 sensor nodes network, in the presence of type I compromised nodes; (b), respectively, executes BEARP, DD, and S-DD protocol in 1200 sensor nodes network, in the presence of type I compromised nodes; (c), respectively, executes BEARP, DD, and S-DD protocol in 600 sensor nodes network, in the presence of type II compromised nodes; (d), respectively, executes BEARP, DD, and S-DD protocol in 1200 sensor nodes network, in the presence of type II compromised nodes.

in WSNs. On the other hand, even if the sensor nodes suffer insurmountable attacks of compromised nodes, the IDS including the algorithm *detect_compromised_node* has an ability to detect type I and type II compromised node, and makes them become no more a member of the network so that they cannot influence other legitimate nodes any more. However, seen in Figures 5(b) and 5(d), as the network gets denser and each node's degree becomes higher, our BEARP makes the network more resilient in the presence of type I or type II compromised nodes.

6. Conclusions

Nowadays, most of the wireless sensor network routing protocols are implemented with no security in mind. Incorporating security into these protocols can only solve some simple security problems, so we focus on security mechanisms for the WSN and design a security routing protocol as a goal, which is performed throughout the network. Simultaneity, using the power of network nodes for security is a necessary evil. Consequently, we propose the efficient and secure routing protocol called BEARP.

We presented the BEARP absolutely different from the well-known DD protocol and the other routing protocol incorporated security. BEARP can successfully not only achieve routing message confidentiality, authentication, integrity, and freshness but detect the compromised nodes in a network by IDS. We implemented an encryption and authentication mechanism to encrypt the data packets between any two nodes and authenticate BS and source node in the network. Moreover, BEARP has two methods for secure process: one is routing paths selected uniquely by the secure BS; another is our important IDS for detecting compromised node. All the secure mechanisms are united together to make our routing protocol BEARP effectively resilient in the presence of compromised nodes that launch selective forwarding attacks, wormhole attacks, sinkhole attacks, and even a node captured.

At the same time, we also make full use of the severely limited resource presented by WSNs, especially the energy limitation. Our BEARP mitigates the loads of sensor nodes by transferring routing-related tasks such as RPSS and IDS to the BS, which not only efficiently maintains network wide energy equivalence and prolongs network lifetime but also successfully improves our security mechanism. Especially, in algorithm *multi_shortest_path* of the RPSS, we design the multiple-threaded process mechanism, which not only increases the speed of selecting a path to the source but also always saves memory space and the contents of the register when RPSS is interrupted and restored. Furthermore, RPSS maintains an energy limitation array for all nodes, and the updating of energy limitation for each node is independent. This feature ensures the best use of each node's energy in the sensor network.

Simulation results show a favorable increase in the performance evaluation for BEARP when compared to DD protocol in the presence of compromised nodes. Our protocol surpasses the DD protocol and S-DD protocol in terms of the packet delivery ratios, network lifetime, and nodes blocked by compromised attacks during data forwarding.

However, we only considered the efficient and secure routing protocols of BS actively launch. In future work, we will focus the research on security mechanisms for other different WSNs, also for particular misbehaviors of some compromised nodes such as denial-of-service attacks and jamming attacks.

Acknowledgments

The authors would like to thank anonymous referees for their useful comments. This work is supported by the Special Research Funds of Educational Ministry of China under Grant no. 104086.

References

[1] I. F. Akyildiz, W. Su, Y. Sankarasubramaniam, and E. Cayirci, "A survey on sensor networks," *IEEE Communications Magazine*, vol. 40, no. 8, pp. 102–114, 2002.

[2] K. Akkaya and M. Younis, "A survey on routing protocols for wireless sensor networks," *Ad Hoc Networks*, vol. 3, no. 3, pp. 325–349, 2005.

[3] A. Perrig and R. Szewczyk, "SPINS: security protocols for sensor networks," *Wireless Networks*, vol. 9, pp. 534–548, 2002.

[4] A. Quintero, D. Y. Li, and H. Castro, "A location routing protocol based on smart antennas for ad hoc networks," *Journal of Network and Computer Applications*, vol. 30, no. 2, pp. 614–636, 2007.

[5] A. Perrig, R. Szewczyk, J. D. Tygar, V. Wen, and D. E. Culler, "SPINS: security protocols for sensor networks," *Wireless Networks*, vol. 8, no. 5, pp. 521–534, 2002.

[6] B. Awerbuch, D. Holmer, C. Nita-Rotaru, and H. Rubens, "An on-demand secure routing protocol resilient to byzantine failures," in *Proceedings of the ACM Workshop on Wireless Security*, pp. 21–30, September 2002.

[7] C. Intanagonwiwat, R. Govindan, and D. Estrin, "Directed diffusion: a scalable and robust communication paradigm for sensor networks," in *Proceedings of the 6th Annual International Conference on Mobile Computing and Networking (MOBICOM '00)*, pp. 56–67, Boston, Mass, USA, August 2000.

[8] X. Wang, L. Yang, and K. Chen, "SDD: secure directed diffusion protocol for sensor networks," in *Proceedings of the 1st European Workshop (ESAS '04)*, C. Castelluccia et al., Ed., Lecture Notes in Computer Science, pp. 205–214, August 2004.

[9] C. Karlof and D. Wagner, "Secure routing in wireless sensor networks: attacks and countermeasures," *Ad Hoc Networks*, vol. 1, no. 2-3, pp. 293–315, 2003.

[10] R. Roman, C. Alcaraz, J. Lopez, and N. Sklavos, "Key management systems for sensor networks in the context of the internet of things," *Computers & Electrical Engineering*, vol. 37, no. 2, pp. 147–159, 2011.

[11] L. Zhou and Z. J. Haas, "Securing wireless sensor networks," *IEEE Network Magazine*, vol. 6, pp. 30–37, 1999.

[12] P. Papadimitratos and Z. J. Haas, "Secure routing for mobile wireless sensor networks," in *Proceedings of the SCS Communication Networks and Distributed Systems (CNDS '02)*, pp. 27–31, 2002.

[13] N. Nasser and Y. Chen, "SEEM: secure and energy-efficient multipath routing protocol for wireless sensor networks," *Computer Communications*, vol. 30, no. 11-12, pp. 2401–2412, 2007.

[14] S. B. Lee and Y. H. Choi, "A secure alternate path routing in sensor networks," *Computer Communications*, vol. 30, no. 1, pp. 153–165, 2006.

[15] B. Wu, J. Wu, E. B. Fernandez, M. Ilyas, and S. Magliveras, "Secure and efficient key management in mobile ad hoc networks," *Journal of Network and Computer Applications*, vol. 30, no. 3, pp. 937–954, 2007.

[16] Y. C. Hu, A. Perrig, and D. B. Johnson, "Rushing attacks and defense in wireless Ad Hoc network routing protocols," in *Proceedings of the ACM Workshop on Wireless Security*, pp. 30–40, New York, NY, USA, September 2003.

[17] Y. C. Hu, D. B. Johnson, and A. Perrig, "SEAD: secure efficient distance vector routing for mobile wireless ad hoc networks," *Ad Hoc Networks*, vol. 1, no. 1, pp. 175–192, 2003.

[18] J. Deng, R. Han, and S. Mishra, "INSENS: intrusion-tolerant routing for wireless sensor networks," *Computer Communications*, vol. 29, no. 2, pp. 216–230, 2006.

[19] T. Ito, H. Ohta, N. Matsuda, and T. Yoneda, "A key predistribution scheme for secure sensor networks using probability density function of node deployment," in *Proceedings of*

the ACM Workshop on Security of Ad Hoc and Sensor Networks (SASN '05), pp. 69–75, November 2005.

[20] S. Marti, T. J. Giuli, K. Lai, and M. Baker, "Mitigating routing misbehavior in mobile ad hoc networks," in *Proceedings of the 6th Annual International Conference on Mobile Computing and Networking (MOBICOM '00)*, pp. 255–265, August 2000.

[21] A. Perrig, J. Stankovic, and D. Wagner, "Security in wireless sensornetworks," *Communications of the ACM*, vol. 47, no. 6, pp. 53–57, 2004.

[22] G. J. Narlikar, "Scheduling threads for low space requirement and good locality," *Theory of Computing Systems*, vol. 35, no. 2, pp. 151–187, 2002.

[23] S. Zhong, J. Chen, and Y. R. Yang, "Sprite: a simple, cheat-proof, credit-based system for mobile ad-hoc networks," in *Proceedings of the 22nd Annual Joint Conference on the IEEE Computer and Communications Societies*, pp. 1987–1997, April 2003.

[24] D. Liu and P. Ning, "Establishing pairwise keys in distributed sensor networks," in *Proceedings of the 10th ACM Conference on Computer and Communications Security (CCS '03)*, pp. 52–61, October 2003.

[25] H. Yang, F. Ye, Y. Yuan, S. Lu, and W. Arbough, "Toward resilient security in wireless sensor networks," in *Proceedings of the 6th ACM International Symposium on Mobile (MobiHoc '05)*, pp. 34–45, 2005.

[26] M. Abomhara, O. Zakaria, O. Khalifa, A. Zaidan, and B. Zaidan, "Enhancing selective encryption for H. 264/AVC using advanced encryption standard," *International Journal of Computer Theory and Engineering*, vol. 2, no. 2, pp. 223–229, 2010.

[27] G. Chen, J. W. Branch, M. Pflug, L. Zhu, and B. K. Szymanski, "SENSE: a wireless sensor network simulator," in *Advances in Pervasive Computing and Networking*, B. Szymanski and B. Yener, Eds., Springer, New York, NY, USA, 2005.

8

A Hybrid Energy- and Time-Driven Cluster Head Rotation Strategy for Distributed Wireless Sensor Networks

Guoxi Ma and Zhengsu Tao

Department of Electronic, Information and Electrical Engineering, Shanghai Jiaotong University, No. 800 Dongchuan Road, Shanghai 200240, China

Correspondence should be addressed to Zhengsu Tao; zstao@sjtu.edu.cn

Academic Editor: Wenzhong Li

Clustering provides an effective way to extend the lifetime and improve the energy efficiency of wireless sensor networks (WSNs). However, the cluster heads will deplete energy faster than cluster members due to the additional tasks of information collection and transmission. The cluster head rotation among sensors is adopted to solve this problem. Cluster head rotation strategies can be generally divided into two categories: time-driven strategy and energy-driven strategy. The time-driven strategy can balance energy consumption better, but it is not suitable for heterogonous WSNs. The energy-driven cluster head rotation strategy has high energy efficiency, especially in heterogonous networks. However, the rotation will become increasingly frequent with the reduction of the nodes residual energy for this strategy, which causes lots of energy waste. In this paper, we propose a hybrid cluster head rotation strategy which combines the advantages of both energy-driven and time-driven cluster head rotation strategies. In our hybrid rotation strategy, the time-driven strategy or energy-driven strategy will be selected according to the residual energy. Simulations show that the hybrid strategy can enhance the energy efficiency and prolong network lifetime in both homogeneous and heterogeneous networks, compared with either single time-driven or energy-driven cluster head rotation method.

1. Introduction

The advances in MEMS-based sensor technology and wireless communications recently have enabled the development of low-cost, low-power, multifunctional sensor nodes that are in small size and have short communication distance and low computational ability in wireless sensor networks (WSNs). These small sensor nodes are capable of sensing the environment, storing and processing the collected sensor data, and interacting and collaborating with each other within the network [1]. The major challenge in the design of WSNs is the energy management. Due to the strict energy constraint and nonrechargeable energy provision, the energy resource of sensors should be managed wisely to extend the lifetime of networks. Therefore, much attention has been paid to develop low-power hardware design, collaborative signal processing techniques, and energy-efficient algorithms at various WSNs [2, 3].

Neighboring sensor nodes usually have the data of similar events because they collect events within a specific area. If each node transmits the collected data to the sink individually, lots of energy will be wasted for transmitting similar data. In order to achieve high energy efficiency and extend the network lifetime, sensors are often hierarchically organized into clusters, each of which has its own cluster head (CH). Within each cluster, sensors transmit data to their CH over a relatively short distance, which in turn forwards the data (or it is further aggregated) to the sink via a single-hop or a multihop path through other CHs like the illustration in Figure 1. In hierarchical clustering protocol, network is operated based on rounds. Each round begins with the cluster set-up phase and follows with a steady-state phase. In cluster set-up phase, sensor nodes elect themselves to be CHs at any given time with a certain probability and local cluster network is formed by each CH. In steady-state phase, each noncluster head node, which we call a cluster member, collects events and transmits them to its cluster head. After that, each cluster head aggregates the collected data to prevent duplicated transmissions of similar events and transmits the aggregated data to the sink node.

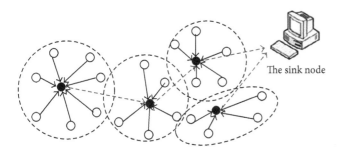

The sink node

● Cluster head
○ Cluster member

FIGURE 1: Clustering scheme of wireless sensor network.

From the description above, we can see that CHs undertake much heavier responsibilities than cluster members including long distance communication to sink node, intra-cluster data collection, and aggregation. Therefore, CHs consume much more energy than cluster members, and the fast energy depletion problem of them has become a serious issue in the cluster-based sensor networks. In traditional clustering schemes, powerful backbone nodes are proposed to serve as the cluster heads [4], which may increase the system deployment cost and is not suitable for many scenarios, for example, the intrusion detection and large-scale sensor networks which are often automatically deployed by the vehicles or planes. In such cases, the cluster heads are tiny and unattendant battery-powered sensors, which require innovative design techniques to ensure high energy efficiency. The only way to prolong the lifetime of CHs lies in organization method. Then, CHs rotation strategy has been exploited to balance the energy consumption among cluster members and heads in hierarchical clustering WSNs.

The CHs rotation strategy is a technology of cluster topology maintenance. It plays a very important role in the reconstruction of the hierarchical cluster structure for avoiding premature death of CH nodes and increasing network lifetime. Many cluster head rotation strategies have been proposed in the recent research literatures. Such strategies can be divided into two categories: time-driven strategy and energy-driven strategy. Heinzelman et al. [5] firstly proposed LEACH cluster protocol in which cluster head is rotated periodically among the sensor nodes to ensure the balanced energy consumption of networks. By such periodical rotation of cluster heads among the sensors, energy is evenly depleted among nodes and the premature exhaustion of battery in any sensor can be avoided. But the time-driven based CH rotation method doesnot consider the residual energy of cluster heads which will cause much unnecessary energy waste and low energy efficiency when the network energy is powerful, especially in heterogeneous WSNs. However, time-driven CH rotation method can maintain fixed energy efficiency at any time.

To better solve this problem, the CH rotation mechanism based on energy driven is proposed in EDAC [6] and EDCR [7, 8], where the cluster head candidacy election phase and rotation phases are triggered only when the residual energy of any cluster head falls below a dynamic threshold. This kind of energy-driven CH rotation strategy can mitigate the impact of the cluster head rotation on the network and achieve high energy efficiency in heterogeneous WSNs. But under this rotation mechanism, the cluster head rotation will become increasingly frequent along with the reduction of residual energy of the nodes. As a result, more and more energy will be used in rotation rather than data transmission, which will in turn reduce the energy efficiency of the network even to zero.

We notice that the residual energy of nodes will become almost equal in heterogeneous WSNs after a long period of network operation. The heterogeneous WSNs will become nearly the same as the homogeneous WSNs in terms of residual energy. Based on the respective features of time-driven and energy-driven CH rotation strategies above, we can develop new CHs rotation approach to achieve better energy balance and higher energy efficiency. We can use the energy-driven CH rotation strategy to achieve high energy efficiency when the energy of WSNs is abundant and unbalanced. After a long time of network operation, the energy of WSNs nodes is low and almost balanced, therefore; we adopt time-driven CH rotation strategy to ensure stable data transmission efficiency. This is the theoretical basis of our research. In this paper, we build the energy consumption model for contention-based CH selection and data transmission. By analyzing the energy consumption relationship between the cluster set-up phase and the steady-state data transfer phase, we propose a hybrid cluster head rotation strategy for WSNs in which the CH rotation strategy based on time or energy will be selected according to the network energy efficiency. We give the optimal mechanism that when we switch from energy-driven CH rotation to time-driven CH rotation to obtain the maximal energy efficiency for WSNs. Theoretical analysis and simulation results show that hybrid CH rotation strategy can successfully balance the energy consumption of the network and prolong the network lifetime. Moreover, it can obtain better energy efficiency and transfer more useful data to sink than either time-driven or energy-driven CH rotation method in both homogeneous and heterogeneous sensor networks. As a fundamental technology of cluster topology maintenance, our rotation strategy can be used in any cluster protocols.

The remainder of the paper is organized as below. Section 2 reviews research work in this area; Section 3 introduces the system assumptions used in this paper; Section 4 establishes and analyzes energy consumption for contention-based CHs selection and data transmission. Section 5 puts forward hybrid energy- and time-driven CH rotation strategy; Section 6 elaborates on our simulation efforts and the analysis results we obtained; Section 7 offers concluding remarks and points out future directions for research work.

2. Literature Review

As an important technology of cluster topology maintenance, cluster head rotation strategy has a great signification for the performance of cluster protocol in WSNs. By restoring the current topology and building a new one, it prolongs the network lifetime and prevents the premature death of sensors. However, it doesnot attract enough attention and extensive research work is only dedicated to the study of cluster organization and scheduling algorithms. In this section, we briefly describe the most popular research that is most relevant to our approach.

Clustering provides an effective way for extending the lifetime of WSNs. Experiments have proved that the networks based on cluster hierarchy structure protocol are 7~8 times more efficient than traditional dispersed flat nodes protocol in measuring the lifetime of nodes. So, more efficient hierarchical network algorithms based on cluster architecture are designed to extend the network lifetime. Heinzelman et al. [5] proposed the LEACH algorithm, in which the CH is dynamically rotated among all sensors in the cluster for a period of time. Although there are advantages in using this distributed cluster algorithm, it doesnot consider the residual energy of sensor nodes and creates lots of overhead frames. Heinzelman also proposed the improved LEACH named LEACH-C algorithm [5] that elects cluster head based on the residual energy of sensor nodes.

SEP [9] extends the LEACH by adding a small percentage of higher energy nodes than the normal nodes in the network. HEED [10] elects CHs according to their total residual energy and a secondary parameter such as node degree. It has a much higher overhead compared with other algorithms because of CHs selection and rotation. The energy-efficient clustering method proposed in ANTCLUST [11] assumes that nodes sense their locations either using GPS or some localization techniques. Such an assumption is suitable for location-based information gathering systems but less applicable to low-cost ad hoc sensor networks. ACE [12] is an emergent algorithm to produce uniform clusters. Meanwhile, many other cluster-based hierarchy algorithms are improved based on LEACH [13–20]. All of the above algorithms share a common feature that their CH rotation mechanisms are all time driven. That is, the CH will be changed after a predetermined number of data gathering rounds. EDAC [6] and EDCR [7, 8] algorithms use method based on dynamic energy threshold to initiate a new CH election phase. This energy driven CH rotation strategy can achieve better energy efficiency and produce less overhead, especially in heterogeneous sensor networks.

Both energy-driven and time-driven CH rotations are faced with an urgent issue that how to select the optimum number of data transmission rounds. If a CH election phase is triggered after a smaller number of data transmission rounds, it will result in excessive overhead during the CH election phase. On the other hand, after a large number of data transmission rounds, the CH nodes will not have enough energy to act as ordinary sensor nodes after relinquishing the CH role. In [21], the authors proved that the energy-driven CH rotation strategy is better than the time-driven CH rotation strategy in a single cluster analysis model, and they gave a suboptimal solution for rotation energy threshold in the single cluster model. In [22], authors provided a method to obtain the optimal energy threshold parameter for energy-driven CH rotation strategy. For our hybrid CH rotation strategy, the main challenge lies in the mechanism how to select the best CH rotation strategy, energy driven or time driven, to obtain the maximum energy efficiency and extend the network lifetime. In the latter part, we will study it theoretically and analyze the simulation result, which constitutes the major part of this paper.

3. Preliminaries

Before describing our proposed algorithm in detail, we will introduce the characteristics of the network model used in our implementations. We consider a WSN consisting of sensors and sink and make the following assumptions.

3.1. Assumptions on Node and Energy of the Network. As Figure 2 shows, we consider a sensor network of N nodes which is randomly dispersed in an $M \times M$ meters square area to continuously monitor the sense area, and all nodes including sink are stationary after disposition. Our assumptions about the sensor nodes and network are as below.

(1) Nodes are equipped with wireless transmission and reception equipment and they have the capability of data fusion and power adjusting.

(2) Time Division Multiple Access (TDMA) schedules the data transmission from normal nodes to its cluster head.

(3) Nodes can estimate the approximate distance to another node based on the received signal strength.

(4) Links between nodes are symmetric.

(5) The network runs a periodic data gathering application, in which the sensor generates traffic at an average rate of λ bits/second and sends it to its CH, which in turn delivers it to sink.

3.2. Energy Consumption Model. A typical sensor node includes three basic units: sensing unit, processing unit, and transceivers. For our energy model of communication and transmission scheme, we assume a free space propagation channel model [23]. We ignore the power consumption of node for sensing because it is constant at any time and cannot be reduced with whatever means. Therefore, the energy model of a sensor includes the power for data aggregating, data receiving, and data transmission, in accordance with the radio hardware energy dissipation, both the free space (d^2 Power loss) and the multipath fading (d^4 Power loss) channel models. If the distance is less than the fading threshold d_0, the free space model is used; otherwise, the multipath model is used. If E_{Tx} denotes the energy consumption of transmitting, E_{Rx} denotes the energy consumption of receiving, and E_{Dx} denotes the energy consumption of aggregating, the energy for transmitting, receiving, and aggregating l bits over distance d is computed as follows:

$$E_{Tx} = \begin{cases} \left(E_{elec} + \varepsilon_{fs} * d^2\right) l, & d < d_0, \\ \left(E_{elec} + \varepsilon_{amp} * d^4\right) l, & d \geq d_0, \end{cases} \tag{1}$$

$$E_{Rx} = E_{elec} l,$$
$$E_{Dx} = E_{DA} l, \tag{2}$$

The amplifier energy ε_{fs} and ε_{amp} are the energy required for power amplification in the two models, respectively.

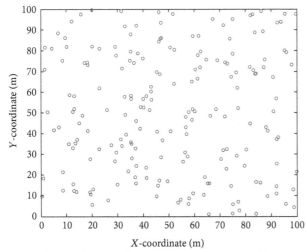

FIGURE 2: Data collection sensor network model.

The electronics energy E_{elec} depends on the factors such as the digital coding and modulation. E_{DA} is the energy used for aggregating unit sensor data. The typical values for the above parameters in current sensor technologies are as follows: E_{elec} = 50 nJ/bit, ε_{fs} = 10 pJ/bit/m^2, ε_{amp} = 0.0013 pJ/bit/m^4, and E_{DA} = 5 nJ/bit/signal.

3.3. Contention-Based Cluster Head Election Model. We assume that N nodes are divided into κ clusters. Then each cluster includes $n = N/\kappa$ nodes. We can guarantee the connectivity of clusters by adjusting the communication range and the number κ of cluster heads. One continuous cluster set-up phase and steady-state data transfer phase are regarded as a cluster round. Within a round, only one node can be elected as the cluster head in a cluster. For the sake of simplicity, we assume that the frame length of command frame and data frame is l bits. All sensor nodes initially consider themselves as potential candidates CH. We donot require that all sensor nodes are homogeneous in energy. The probability of being a cluster head depends on nodes' residual energy. Meanwhile, we assume that all nodes have data to transmit during each round. To ensure that all nodes die at approximately the same time, the nodes with more energy should be cluster heads rather than those with less energy. It means that a sensor node with more residual energy has more opportunity to be the cluster head than those with less residual energy in a neighboring circle within radius R. This can be achieved by setting the probability of becoming a cluster head as a function of a node's energy and the total energy of the network; thus

$$P_{ri} = \frac{E_{ri}}{E_{rtotal}}, \tag{3}$$

where E_{ri} is the current energy of node i and

$$E_{rtotal} = \sum_{i=1}^{n} E_{ri}. \tag{4}$$

When the cluster set-up phase is triggered, each cluster head will send the residual energy information of all cluster members to the sink, and the sink node will calculate and broadcast the total energy of the network E_{rtotal} to all nodes. We assume that the CH advertisement phase is limited to a time interval of T time units and the sensor node i announces its candidacy within a radius of R at a time instance T_{ri}:

$$T_{ri} = T(1 - P_{ri}) + k_i. \tag{5}$$

Here, k_i is a random time unit that is introduced to reduce the collision possibility of among sensor node advertisements, and $P_{ri} \in [0, 1]$ represents the probability of being electing the CH for node i among all nodes in its neighboring circle in terms of its residual energy. Each sensor elects itself to be a cluster head at the beginning of the round r (which starts at time t) with a different probability. Hence, from (5), the node with the highest residual energy will have the biggest probability of being elected as a CH in a given neighborhood. Those sensor nodes that receive an advertisement message from any other sensor node will abandon their quest to become a CH and join the corresponding cluster. Obviously, only one node can be chosen as the CH in one cluster for this round. Thus, if there are n nodes in the cluster, we have

$$E(CH) = \sum_{i=1}^{n} P_{ri} = 1. \tag{6}$$

We will not elaborate on the cluster head election. For example, in HEED, the cluster heads are elected based on the residual energy of nodes and node connection degree. The major difference of these cluster head selection protocols lies in the information exchange between the cluster head candidate and cluster members. Once the cluster protocol is determined, the energy consumption for cluster head election and data transmission will be fixed regardless whether the energy-driven or time-driven CH rotation strategy is adopted, which only influences the time when we change the CH rotation strategy. Therefore, our proposed hybrid cluster head rotation strategy can be applied to various contention-based clusters protocols so long as the head rotation strategy is adopted.

4. Energy Consumption Analysis for One Cluster Rotation

In this section, we will analyze the energy consumption of in contention-based cluster algorithm. By analyzing the energy consumption ratio between data gathering and cluster head selection in one CH round for both time-driven and energy-driven cluster head rotation strategies, we will study more efficient cluster head rotation methods.

4.1. Energy Consumption for Cluster Set-Up Phase. Once the nodes have elected themselves to be CHs using the probabilities in (3), the CH nodes must let all the other nodes within their communication range know that they have chosen this role for the current round. To achieve this purpose, each CH node broadcasts an advertisement message (ADV) using a nonpersistent carrier-sense multiple access (CSMA) MAC protocol [24]. This message contains the necessary clustering information such as the node's ID, a frame header that distinguishes this message as an announcement message and so forth. Noncluster head nodes determine their cluster heads in this round in accordance with the priority and strength of the received advertisement signal from cluster heads.

After every node has joined its own cluster, the CH calculates its TDMA schedule and broadcasts it to its cluster members. Then, the cluster set-up phase is finished and the entire network is divided into many clusters. Then the steady-state phase begins, in which the nodes collect data periodically. Noncluster head nodes send their data to their CH in the allotted time slot according to the TDMA schedule. The CH uses a data fusion algorithm to merge the received data and then send it to the sink. Next, we will analyze the energy consumption used for cluster head election in cluster set-up phase and data transmission in steady-state phase.

According to (3), in round r of cluster head set-up phase, the probability of one node being successfully selected as a cluster head within a time slot can be calculated as follows:

$$P_{r,s} = \sum_{i=1}^{n} P_{ri} \prod_{j=1, j \neq i}^{n} \left(1 - P_{rj}\right). \tag{7}$$

Here, $P_{r,f}$ denotes the probability that no one node has been selected as cluster head within a time slot in round r of the cluster head set-up phase. There is a certain probability that no nodes broadcast any cluster head advertisement frames within a slot, and we call this probability as idle rate of time slot denoted by $P_{r,i}$:

$$P_{r,f} = 1 - P_{r,s},$$
$$P_{r,i} = \prod_{i=1}^{n} \left(1 - P_{ri}\right). \tag{8}$$

Within one cluster, the cluster head election process will terminate when a node wins the election and becomes the cluster head. The other cluster members will apply to join it. We assume that $P_r(\tau)$ is the probability that the cluster head is elected successfully in τ time slot of round r. Consider

$$P_r(\tau) = P_{r,s} P_{r,f}^{\tau-1}, \quad \tau = 1, 2, 3, \ldots. \tag{9}$$

From (9), we can calculate the average mathematical expectation for the number of time slots τ when the cluster head is elected successfully. Consider

$$E(\overline{\tau}) = \sum_{\tau=1}^{\infty} \tau P_r(\tau) = \sum_{\tau=1}^{\infty} \tau P_{r,s} P_{r,f}^{\tau-1} = \frac{1}{P_{r,s}}. \tag{10}$$

Because each candidate node in the cluster set-up phase sends a cluster head advertisement frame with probability P_{ri}, if we use F_r to indicate the average expected number of advertisement frames in each time slot of round r, it can be given by

$$E(\overline{F_r}) = \sum_{i=1}^{n} P_{ri} * 1 = 1. \tag{11}$$

According to the formula (10), (11), we can calculate the expected mathematical number of advertisement frames in the whole cluster head election process of round r as follows:

$$C(r) = \frac{1}{\sum_{i=1}^{n} P_{ri} \prod_{j=1, j \neq i}^{n} \left(1 - P_{rj}\right)}. \tag{12}$$

In fact, if $\overline{N}_{r,a}$ sensor nodes send their advertisement frames, we have

$$E(\overline{F_r}) = \overline{N}_{r,a} \left(1 - P_{r,i}\right). \tag{13}$$

In the cluster with n nodes, the remaining $n - \overline{N}_{r,a}$ nodes are responsible for receiving advertisement frames. The probability of a time slot in nonidle rate is $1 - P_{r,i}$. Therefore, we can calculate the average number of receiving cluster head announcement frame in the cluster set-up phase of round r as follows:

$$H(r) = \left(n - \overline{N}_{r,a}\right) \overline{F_r} \overline{T_r} \left(1 - P_{r,i}\right)$$
$$= \frac{n - n \prod_{i=1}^{n} \left(1 - P_{ri}\right) - 1}{\sum_{i=1}^{n} P_{ri} \prod_{j=1, j \neq i}^{n} \left(1 - P_{rj}\right)}. \tag{14}$$

According to (12) and (14), the energy consumption of cluster head election in one round can be given by

$$E_{\text{ch-select}} = C(r)\left(E_{\text{elec}}l + \varepsilon_{\text{amp}}d_{\text{CH}}^{2}l\right) + H(r)E_{\text{elec}}l. \tag{15}$$

Here, d_{CH} denotes the average distance between the cluster head and other members. The left part of expression (15) represents the energy consumption of sending cluster head frame and the right part is the energy consumption of receiving cluster head circular frame. When cluster head has been elected successfully, all cluster members will send request frames to join it. Then, the CH broadcasts the TDMA schedule among its members. It is obvious that the clusters will consume the least energy if no conflict occurs. Therefore, the lower bound energy consumption of a round in the cluster set-up phase is

$$E_{\text{ch-setup}} = E_{\text{ch-select}} + 2(n-1)\left(E_{\text{elec}}l + \varepsilon_{\text{amp}}d_{\text{CH}}^{2}l\right)$$
$$+ 2(n-1)E_{\text{elec}}l. \tag{16}$$

For the sake of simplicity, we omit the energy consumption for acknowledgement frames in data or commands transmission. This kind of packets is much smaller than the data and commands packets.

4.2. Energy Consumption for Data Transmission Phase. After the completion of set-up phase, the steady-state phase for information collection and transmission begins. For one round data collection, let d_{BS} denote the distance from CH to sink that can be estimated by CH according to signal strength received from sink, the energy consumption for CH is given by

$$E_{\text{ch}} = \left(E_{\text{elec}} + \varepsilon_{\text{amp}}d_{\text{BS}}^{\alpha}\right)l + nE_{\text{DA}}l + (n-1)E_{\text{elec}}l. \tag{17}$$

Here, the value of radio dissipation coefficient $\alpha = 2$ or 4 is determined by the distance between the transmitter and receiver according to (1). Let d_{CH} denote the average distance from cluster members to CH which can be given by $M^2/2\kappa\pi$ [5], the energy consumption for all member nodes in cluster for one round data collection is calculated as follows:

$$E_{\text{non-ch}} = (n-1)\left(E_{\text{elec}} + \varepsilon_{\text{amp}}d_{\text{CH}}^{\alpha}\right)l. \tag{18}$$

The number of data collection rounds depends on the CHs rotation method. In time-driven CH rotation, the number of data transmission rounds is predetermined at the beginning of network operation. It is related to the properties of the network such as nodes density and energy status. We will provide the method to estimate it in the following section. We assume that there are k rounds of data collection and transmission, and then the energy consumption in one steady-state phase based on time-driven CH rotation is

$$E_{\text{Time-}D_r} = k \left(E_{\text{ch}} + E_{\text{non-ch}} \right). \qquad (19)$$

However, in energy-driven CH rotation strategy, the number of data transmission rounds is a function of the remaining energy of CH node. The CH node i calculates a dynamic energy threshold λ_i based on its residual before it broadcasts its CH Candidacy. The threshold is defined by $\lambda_i = cE_{\text{res}_i}$, where $c \in [0, 1]$ is a predetermined constant and E_{res_i} is the residual energy of cluster head. When the residual energy of cluster head has dropped below this threshold, the steady-state phase will be over and new CHs rotation process is triggered. If we let $\varphi_{r,i}$ denote the number of data transmission rounds that node i severs as a CH, we can calculate the energy consumption in one steady-state phase for energy-driven cluster head rotation method as follows:

$$
\begin{aligned}
E_{\text{Energy-}D_r} &= \varphi_{r,i} \left(E_{\text{ch}} + E_{\text{non-ch}} \right) \\
&= \frac{(1 - c) E_{ri} - E_{\text{choh}}}{E_{\text{ch}}} \\
&\quad \times \left(E_{\text{ch}} + E_{\text{non-ch}} \right).
\end{aligned}
\qquad (20)
$$

Here, E_{choh} denotes the energy consumption of CH node i in cluster set-up phase. When no conflict occurs, E_{choh} includes the energy consumption for broadcasting CH candidacy, receiving requests for joining from all of its members, and broadcasting TDMA schedule among its members. Therefore, its lower bound can be given by

$$E_{\text{choh}} = 2 (n - 1) \left(E_{\text{elec}} l + \varepsilon_{\text{amp}} d_{\text{CH}}^2 l \right) + (n - 1) E_{\text{elec}} l. \qquad (21)$$

5. Hybrid Energy- and Time-Driven Cluster Head Rotation Strategy

After analyzing the energy consumption in one CH round for both time-driven and energy-driven cluster head rotation strategies, we will deduce the hybrid cluster head rotation strategy which combines the advantages of both energy-driven and time-driven methods in this section. In the cluster-based WSNs, energy consumption can be divided into two categories. The first category is the energy consumption used for topology construction and maintenance. We call it additional energy cost E_a which is mainly consumed in cluster set-up phase. The second category is the energy consumption used for data transmission and reception. We call it efficiency energy cost E_e which is mainly consumed in steady-state phase. The main purpose of the WSNs is to collect as

much useful information as possible in the monitoring area. So, the more energy is used for information collection, the better energy efficiency of cluster hierarchy protocol will be achieved. We define the energy efficiency η as the proportion of the effective energy cost in the total energy cost. Consider

$$\eta = \frac{E_e}{E_e + E_a}. \qquad (22)$$

In time-driven CH rotation strategy, we get the energy efficiency according to (15), (16), and (19):

$$
\begin{aligned}
\eta_{\text{Time-}D_r} &= \frac{E_{\text{Time-}D_r}}{E_{\text{Time-}D_r} + E_{\text{ch-setup}}} \\
&= \frac{k \left(E_{\text{ch}} + E_{\text{non-ch}} \right)}{k \left(E_{\text{ch}} + E_{\text{non-ch}} \right) + E_{\text{ch-setup}}}.
\end{aligned}
\qquad (23)
$$

In energy-driven CH rotation strategy, according to (15), (16) and (20), we have the energy efficiency:

$$
\begin{aligned}
\eta_{\text{Energy-}D_r} &= \frac{E_{\text{Energy-}D_r}}{E_{\text{Energy-}D_r} + E_{\text{ch-setup}}} \\
&= \frac{\left[(1 - c) E_{ri} - E_{\text{choh}} \right] \left(E_{\text{ch}} + E_{\text{non-ch}} \right)}{\left[(1-c) E_{ri} - E_{\text{choh}} \right] \left(E_{\text{ch}} + E_{\text{non-ch}} \right) + E_{\text{ch}} E_{\text{ch-setup}}}.
\end{aligned}
\qquad (24)
$$

In (23), E_{ch}, $E_{\text{non-ch}}$, and E_{choh} are only related to the cluster size and node density. $E_{\text{ch-setup}}$ will change little if cluster scale is under good control. That is to say, in a cluster hierarchy WSNs with nodes distribution, the parameters above can be nearly seen as almost constant. Normalizing $\eta_{\text{Time-}D_r}$, we have

$$\eta_{\text{Time-}D_r} = \frac{1}{1 + \left(\left(E_{\text{ch-setup}} \right) / \left(E_{\text{ch}} + E_{\text{non-ch}} \right) \right) * (1/k)}. \qquad (25)$$

From (25), we can see that the energy efficiency for time-driven CH rotation is only related to the steady-state phase. Once the data transmission rounds k is predetermined, $\eta_{\text{Time-}D_r}$ will be fixed. This is a significant feature of the time-driven CH rotation method, which means that constant energy efficiency can be maintained regardless of how long the network runs. Furthermore, normalizing $\eta_{\text{Energy-}D_r}$, we have

$$\eta_{\text{Energy-}D_r} = 1 \times \left(1 + \frac{E_{\text{ch}} E_{\text{ch-setup}}}{E_{\text{ch}} + E_{\text{non-ch}}} * \frac{1}{(1 - c) E_{ri} - E_{\text{choh}}} \right)^{-1}. \qquad (26)$$

In (26), we have that the restriction of $(1 - c) E_{ri} > E_{\text{choh}}$. c is a predetermined constant which depends on the topology of WSNs. The energy efficiency $\eta_{\text{Energy-}D_r}$ for energy-driven CH rotation is only related to the residual energy of cluster head node E_{ri}. The more residual energy of the cluster head has, the higher energy efficiency we can obtain. The residual energy E_{ri} will decrease gradually along with the operation of WSNs. It means that more energy will be used for frequent cluster head election and cluster topology construction when $\eta_{\text{Energy-}D_r}$ becomes lower. Network can achieve good energy efficiency if the remaining energy of CHs is abundant and will get low energy efficiency if the residual energy of CHs is inadequate. This is the major drawback of energy-driven CH rotation strategy.

We set d_{CH} and d_{BS} as 30 meters and 87 meters, respectively. The distribution density of sensor node is 0.02 and each node is assigned with 0.5 J energy. For the threshold parameter c, without the loss of generality, we adopt the value $c = 0.644$ according to the research results in [22] and let $k = 5$. Advertisement set-up packets and data packets are arranged with 256 bits in length. Then, we can get the change in the energy efficiency with the network operation rounds for energy-driven CH rotation and time-driven CH rotation in clustering WSN as showed in Figure 3. We can see that high energy efficiency can be achieved at the beginning of WSNs if energy-driven CH rotation strategy is adopted. But as the operation time of WSNs increases, the residual energy of the selected CHs will decrease accordingly, which will result in decrease in energy efficiency. When the residual energy of the cluster head declines to a certain level, the energy efficiency of the energy-driven CH rotation strategy will be lower than that of the time-driven CH rotation strategy.

In order to collect as much useful information as possible in the monitoring area and keep as higher energy efficiency as possible, we can make use of the advantages of both the energy-driven strategy and time-driven CH rotation strategy in cluster hierarchy protocol. When the nodes have abundant energy, we can adopt energy-driven CH rotation strategy to achieve good energy efficiency and avoid excessive overhead frames in time-driven CH rotation policy. When WSNs' energy declines to the extent that the energy efficiency of energy-driven CH rotation strategy is lower than that of the time-driven CH rotation strategy, the CH rotation strategy will switch to time-driven method to maintain energy efficiency and data transmission efficiency. This adaptive switch can optimize the energy efficiency of the network. The analysis results above constitute the theoretical foundation of our hybrid energy- and time-driven cluster head rotation strategy in this paper.

According to the results above, when $\eta_{\text{Energy-}D_r} \geq \eta_{\text{Time-}D_r}$, we will adopt the energy-driven CH rotation strategy to obtain better energy efficiency. The time-driven CH rotation strategy is adopted when $\eta_{\text{Energy-}D_r} < \eta_{\text{Time-}D_r}$. Furthermore, we can simplify this criterion. As indicated in Figure 3, when the energy efficiency in energy-driven and time-driven CH rotation is equal to $\eta_{\text{Energy-}D_r} = \eta_{\text{Time-}D_r}$, we have

$$\frac{1}{1 + \left(E_{\text{ch-setup}}/E_{\text{ch}} + E_{\text{non-ch}}\right) * (1/k)}$$

$$= 1 \times \left(1 + \frac{E_{\text{ch}}E_{\text{ch-setup}}}{E_{\text{ch}} + E_{\text{non-ch}}} * \frac{1}{(1-c)E_{ri} - E_{\text{choh}}}\right)^{-1}.$$

$$\tag{27}$$

From (27), we can calculate the energy of the cluster head node when CH rotation strategy needs to switch from

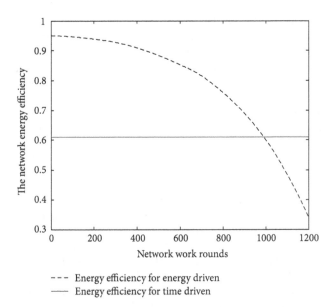

FIGURE 3: Energy efficiency in energy-driven and time-driven strategies.

energy-driven strategy to time-driven strategy. We define this energy of cluster head as critical energy value and it can be given by

$$E_{ri}^* = \frac{kE_{\text{ch}} + E_{\text{choh}}}{1 - c}. \tag{28}$$

From (28), we can see that the critical energy value of CH is only related to the intrinsic parameters of energy-driven and time-driven CH rotation. Moreover, this result proves that the hybrid CH rotation strategy does not depend on homogeneous or heterogeneous characteristics of the network and the exact cluster protocol. What is more is another important issue is to estimate the optimal data transmission rounds k for time-driven CH rotation method in (28). It is an important parameter that determines the timing for switching to the CH rotation strategy. For heterogeneous WSNs, we notice that the energy balance between sensor nodes has been greatly improved after the long time operation of the network using the energy-driven cluster head rotation strategy. It meets the network conditions for time-driven protocol to maintain high energy efficiency, and therefore, it is a good decision to switch to the time-driven cluster head rotation strategy.

In time-driven CH rotation cluster protocol, the steady-state phase should be as long as possible in order to increase energy efficiency. On the other hand, since each node's energy is limited, it will drain the energy of the CH node if the steady-state phase is too long. In [5, 18], authors have proved that if each node can be ensured to act as CH once and noncluster head node in the other rounds during network lifetime, a suboptimal network lifetime for the time-driven CH rotation cluster protocol can be achieved. Generally speaking, the sensor node with the least residual energy will die first. Let $E_{\min}$ denote the residual energy of the node with the minimum energy in WSNs when the time-driven rotation strategy is selected. To ensure that each node has enough energy to be a cluster head for one time and noncluster head sensor node for $(n-1)$ times, according to (17) and (18), we can get the following equation:

$$kE_{\text{ch}} + (n-1)\, k \frac{E_{\text{non-ch}}}{n-1} = E_{\min}. \tag{29}$$

Therefore, we can obtain the suboptimal number of data transmission rounds k when energy-driven CH rotation method is switched to time-driven method:

$$k = E_{\min} \times \Big(\big[\big(E_{\text{elec}} + \varepsilon_{\text{amp}} d_{\text{BS}}^{\alpha}\big) l + n E_{\text{DA}} l + (n-1)\, E_{\text{elec}} l\big]$$
$$+ (n-1)\big(E_{\text{elec}} + \varepsilon_{\text{amp}} d_{\text{CH}}^{\alpha}\big) l\Big)^{-1}. \tag{30}$$

We can see that the parameter k will change along with the gradual decrease of $E_{\min}$. From (28) and (30), we can calculate the corresponding k for each round of CH rotation and then get the critical energy value E_{ri}^{*}. When the residual energy of each CH $E_{ri} \geq E_{ri}^{*}$, the energy-driven CH rotation strategy will be adopted; otherwise, the time-driven CH rotation strategy will be selected.

The pseudo code of hybrid energy- and time-driven cluster head rotation strategy is presented in Algorithm 1. First, in cluster set-up phase, each node computes its P_{ri} using immediate neighbor information to run for cluster head. At the same time, the sink node computes and broadcasts parameter k to the whole network according to the Res_Energy_List that is collected and sent back by all CHs. After successful election, each CH calculates E_{ri}^{*} and compares it with its own residual energy. If CHs' residual energy is larger than E_{ri}^{*} or even equal, energy-driven CH rotation strategy is adopted; otherwise, time-driven CH rotation strategy will be used. When the network is worked based energy-driven CH rotation strategy, if the cluster head rotation is triggered, CHs will send the residual energy list Res_Energy_List of all cluster members back to the sink node. Once WSNs switch to time-driven CH rotation strategy, there is no longer any need to calculate the parameter k, and the network will operate based on time-driven CH rotation strategy until the network dies.

From Algorithm 1, we can see that the hybrid CH rotation strategy increases the message exchange of cluster protocol in cluster set-up phase. Since the cluster head selection process is message driven, we will discuss the message complexity of algorithm. We will validate that our hybrid rotation strategy does not add the complexity for all clustering protocol through the complexity analysis. When energy-driven rotation strategy is selected, at the beginning of the cluster head election phase, the sink node will broadcast system frame with parameter k included. Then κ tentative cluster heads are elected and each of them broadcasts election header frame COMPETE_HEAD_MSG. Later on, they make a decision to act as a final cluster head by broadcasting election frame FINAL_HEAD_MSG, or an ordinary node by broadcasting a quit election frame QUIT_ELECTION_MSG. They send out κ cluster heads to confirm acknowledgement CH_ADV_MSGs, and then $(N-\kappa)$ ordinary nodes transmit $(N-\kappa)$ join cluster frames JOIN_CLUSTER_MSGs. Thus, the messages add up to $N + \kappa + \kappa + \kappa + N - \kappa = 2(N + \kappa)$ in the cluster

formation stage per round, that is, $O\ (N)$. When time-driven rotation strategy is selected, the network will not select cluster head rotation strategy any longer and the message complexity is the same as that of time-driven CH rotation strategy cluster protocol. Analysis above shows that the hybrid CH rotation strategy will not increase the complexity of cluster protocol compared with single energy-driven or time-driven CH rotation strategy.

6. Simulation Results

In this section, both the numerical results and the simulation results will be presented to evaluate the performance of the hybrid energy- and time-driven cluster head rotation strategy. The simulations are performed in Matlab 7.0, and two scenarios are chosen. We will firstly discuss the influence of the threshold parameter c on network and find a suitable value for our sensor networks model. Then, we will apply our hybrid CH rotation strategy, time-driven and energy-driven CH rotation methods, respectively, to reform LEACH, which is a famous and successful cluster hierarchy protocol recently. By comparing the lifetime and valid data transmission efficiency for the three CH rotation strategies, we will prove that our hybrid CH rotation strategy truly improves the energy efficiency as well as prolongs the network lifetime in both homogeneous and heterogeneous networks. In order to conduct the experiments, proper parameters for both the sensor nodes and the network should be defined. The simulation parameters for our proposed mechanism are given in Table 1.

In the following simulation, we evaluate the three CH rotation strategies in both homogeneous and heterogeneous network. In homogeneous WSNs, 200 nodes each with 0.5 J energy are randomly dispersed in a 100×100 region with BS located at (50, 50). In heterogeneous WSNs, 200 nodes each with 0.3 J to 0.8 J energy (randomly assigned) are randomly dispersed in a 100×100 region with BS located at (50, 50).

6.1. The Analysis of Energy Threshold. As we have explained in the previous section, the energy efficiency is the standard to judge whether energy-driven and time-driven CH rotation mechanism should be selected in our hybrid CH rotation strategy. When energy-driven CH rotation is selected, the residual energy of each existing CH will determine when a network calls for a new CH selection phase. The selection phase will be triggered once the residual energy of any of CHs falls below a predetermined threshold value. This energy threshold influences the energy efficiency of energy-driven rotation method and decides when the cluster head selection policy should turn from energy-driven to time-driven mechanism. Therefore, it is vital to find out the suitable energy threshold parameter c for energy-driven CH rotation strategy based on the above network model and parameters before performance evaluation.

Figure 4 illustrates the network lifetime of LEACH based on our hybrid energy- and time-driven CH rotation strategy in homogeneous WSNs with the energy threshold parameter c increasing from 0.4 to 0.8. Figure 5 shows these results in heterogeneous WSNs. From these two figures, we can see that network lifetime will change with different threshold

---

Algorithm: Hybrid cluster head rotation mechanism

1: *Setup* ()
2: **if** Initial round then
3:        Compute P_{ri} using immediate neighbor information
4: **end if**
5: Sink computer k and broadcast CH Selection Command
6: CHs *Selection (COMPETE_HEAD_MSG, FINAL_HEAD_MSG,*
                    QUIT_ELECTION_MSG)
7: CHs *Construction (CH_ADV_MSGs, JOIN_CLUSTER_MSGs)*
8: CHs compute E_{ri}^*
9: **if** $E_{ri} \geq E_{ri}^*$
10:        {**while** ($E_{res_i} \geq cE_{ri}$)
11:            {*data_collection* ()
12:              *data_transmission* ()}
13:        CH Request BS for a CH Change
14:        CHs Sent *Res_Energy_List* to Sink
15:        **goto** 2
16:        }
17: **else goto 18**
18: Sink broadcast Switch to Time-driven CH Rotation
19: **if** Initial round then
20:        Compute P_{ri} using immediate neighbor information
21: **end if**
22: CHs *Selection* () and *Construction* ()
23 *Data_Round* = k
24: **while** (*Data_Round* > 0)
25:        {*data_collection* () and *data_transmission* ()
26:        *Data_Round* = *Data_Round*-1}
27: **else goto 19**

ALGORITHM 1: Hybrid energy- and time-driven cluster head rotation strategy.

TABLE 1: Parameters and characteristics of the network.

Parameter	Value
Network size (square)	100×100 meter
Sink location	(50, 50)
Command frame and data packet size	256 bits
Number of nodes	200
Cluster head probability	0.05
Aggregation ratio	0.1

parameters. When energy threshold is small, nodes die evenly as time passes by. When energy threshold is larger, we can see that the lifetime curve trends to right angle. Most of nodes will have a longer life and die almost simultaneously within a short time interval. When c is small, the elected cluster head node will consume most of its energy on cluster head position. After rotation, it has little residual energy and will die quickly. When c is larger, the cluster heads can still reserve some energy to act as regular nodes after fulfilling their role as cluster heads. Since noncluster head nodes consume less energy than cluster head nodes, the reserved energy can help it to last for a longer time. Nodes die almost simultaneously because all the nodes have little energy left after rotating for several times. Meanwhile, if c is larger, the CH will rotate frequently and waste lots of energy compared with sleep-listen model in steady-state phase. This result can be seen

from Figures 4 and 5. It shows that network lifetime is longer when $c = 0.6$ rather than $c = 0.7$.

In [7], the authors have proved that the optimal value c mainly varies with the distance from nodes to their CHs and with the distance from CH to sink node in a single energy-driven CH rotation. In other words, it is mainly determined by network topology structure. The network will switch to time-driven CH rotation model in the late stage of network in accordance with our hybrid rotation method. It can be seen in Figures 4 and 5 that the energy threshold parameter acquires almost the same value when the network gains the optimal lifetime no matter whether in homogeneous or heterogeneous WSNs, so long as they have the same network topology. From the simulation and analysis results above, we find that the network will achieve better lifetime when $c = 0.6$. We will adopt this threshold value in the following part. For single energy-driven CH rotation, we use the optimal value $c = 0.644$ according to the research results in [22].

6.2. Performance Comparison in Network Lifetime and Energy Efficiency. In this part, we verify the network lifetime and energy efficiency of our hybrid CH rotation strategy by LEACH cluster protocol. To estimate the lifetime of the WSNs, the metrics of First Node Dies (FNDs), Percent of the Nodes Alive (PNA), and Last Node Dies (LNDs) are always used [9, 20]. FND is useful in sparsely deployed WSNs. However, PNA is more suitable to measure the network

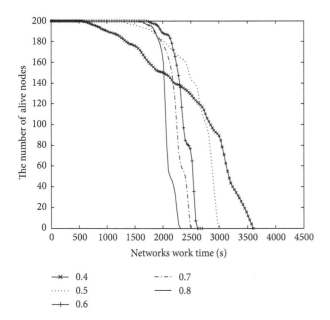

FIGURE 4: Comparison of lifetime for threshold parameter c in homogeneous WSNs.

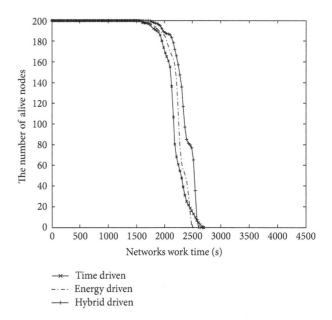

FIGURE 6: Lifetime in homogeneous WSNs for LEACH based on three rotation strategies.

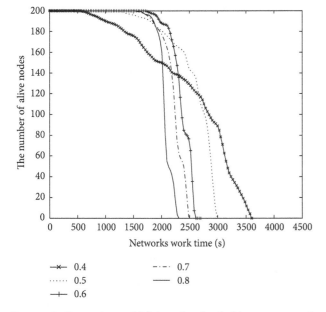

FIGURE 5: Comparison of lifetime for threshold parameter c in heterogeneous WSNs.

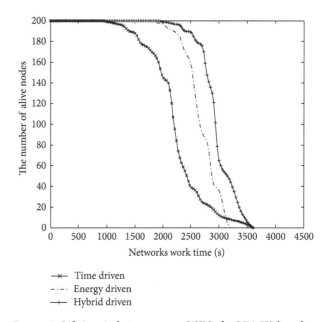

FIGURE 7: Lifetime in heterogeneous WSNs for LEACH based on three rotation strategies.

lifetime in densely deployed WSNs. LND is not suitable for practical application. Hence, in this paper, we use the FND and PNA metrics to measure performance of our CHs rotation strategy. In the case of PNA, we have assumed 95% of nodes alive in the network.

Figures 6 and 7 present the comparison of network lifetime for LEACH based on three CH rotation strategies both in homogeneous and heterogeneous WSNs. We can see that our hybrid energy- and time-driven CH rotation strategy is better than either the single energy-driven or time-driven CH rotation method both in FND and PNA. In homogeneous

network, the initial energy of each node is equal, so the time-driven cluster head rotation strategy can also achieve a better balance on energy consumption among nodes. The advantage for hybrid CH rotation strategy in the network lifetime is not obvious in FND, but there is still a lot of improvement in PNA. However, in heterogeneous network, our hybrid CH rotation approach is remarkably better than both the time-driven CH rotation strategy and the energy-driven CH rotation strategy in terms of FND and PNA. For the time-driven CH rotation strategy, the initial energy is not equal in heterogeneous WSNs and it cannot achieve the energy consumption balance among sensor nodes. On the other hand, for the energy-driven CH rotation strategy, the frequent rotation of cluster head may make all nodes always in active stage and lead to premature death in the final stage of WSNs, thus reducing the network lifetime.

The mechanism for prolonging the network lifetime by hybrid CH rotation strategy can be explained as follows. After clusters have been built successfully, the cluster head creates a TDMA schedule and tells each member node the exact time for transmission data. This allows sensor nodes to remain in the sleep model in other nodes' time slot in steady-state phase. If the node is in the sleep state, the radio and processor modules are turned off which can save considerable energy. But in cluster set-up phase, all nodes must keep active with all modules which will consume much energy especially for the radio communication module. If the energy-driven CH rotation strategy is adopted, when the nodes have abundant energy, the steady-state phase for data transmission is longer than that of time-driven CH rotation strategy, which means less cluster head frames and longer sleeps state. When the energy of nodes is scarce, if we continue to use energy-driven CH rotation method, frequent cluster head selection will happen, which will result in lots of energy waste. However, if we switch to the time-driven CH rotation strategy, frequent cluster head selection can be avoided and the network lifetime can be prolonged.

When the energy level of network is low and energy of nodes is balanced, time-driven CH rotation method can achieve higher energy efficiency than energy-driven CH rotation method. Table 2 shows the energy distribution between sensors when we switch from energy-driven CH rotation to time-driven CH rotation in heterogeneous network for LEACH. It shows that the energy of sensor nodes is quite evenly distributed among them. So, switching to time-driven CH rotation is a good choice when $\eta_{\text{Energy-}D_r} < \eta_{\text{Time-}D_r}$ and it also proves the rationality of the hybrid energy- and time-driven CH rotation strategy indirectly.

In addition to network lifetime, energy efficiency is another important performance indicator of WSNs. As replacing or recharging batteries is difficult or even impossible for sensor nodes in many cases, the cluster protocol needs to maintain high energy efficiency of networks in order to collect as much useful information as possible. According to the algorithmic details of our hybrid energy-time driven CH rotation, energy efficiency of the network is used as the criterion to select CH rotation strategy. In the next simulation test, we use the data transmission rounds that 95% of nodes are alive in the sensor network to measure and compare the energy efficiency.

Figures 8 and 9 illustrate the energy efficiency comparison among the three CH rotation strategies in both homogeneous and heterogeneous networks for LEACH. It can be seen that even though there is no big difference in network lifetime in homogeneous sensor network, our hybrid energy- and time-driven CH rotation strategy is about 1.3 times and 1.1 times more efficient in data transmission than time-driven CH rotation and energy-driven CH rotation, respectively. But in heterogeneous WSNs, the hybrid energy- and time-driven CH rotation strategy can achieve 2 times and 1.2 times

TABLE 2: Node energy distribution between sensors in heterogeneous network.

Nodes Energy Distribution (J)	When energy-driven CH rotation begins	When time-driven CH rotation begins
0-0.1	0	8
0.1-0.2	0	147
0.2-0.3	0	41
0.3-0.4	42	4
0.4-0.5	40	0
0.5-0.6	43	0
0.6-0.7	39	0
0.7-0.8	36	0

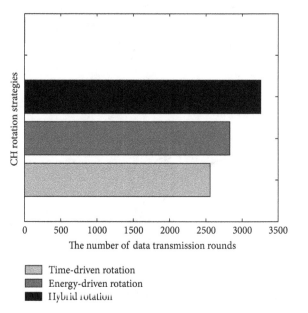

FIGURE 8: Data transmission rounds with PND for LEACH in homogeneous networks.

more efficient in data transmission than time-driven CH rotation strategy- and energy-driven CH rotation strategy, respectively. Such results are mainly attributable to the fact that time-driven CH rotation strategy does not consider the energy imbalance of nodes. Under such a circumstance, cluster head selection is triggered after a constant number of data transmission rounds no matter whether the node's energy is abundant or not, thus resulting in unnecessary energy waste. At the same time, for energy-driven CH rotation strategy, the energy efficiency will decrease sharply when the energy of network reduce to some degree. The hybrid CH rotation strategy takes full account of such a situation and can achieve good energy efficiency by selecting either energy-driven or time-driven CH rotation according to the residual energy of network in real time.

7. Conclusion

In this paper, we have proposed a hybrid energy- and time-driven CH rotation strategy for distributed wireless sensor

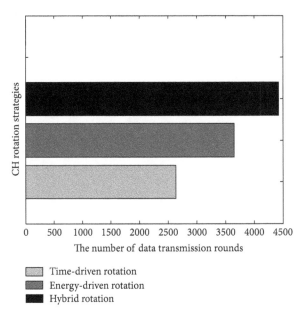

FIGURE 9: Data transmission rounds with PND for LEACH in heterogeneous networks.

networks. The main objective of our algorithm is to improve the energy efficiency and prolong the lifetime of WSNs by optimizing the CH rotation strategy in cluster hierarchy protocol. By analyzing energy consumption ratio between data gathering and cluster head selection for the time-driven cluster head rotation and energy-driven cluster head rotation, we propose the hybrid cluster head rotation strategy for WSNs, in which the CHs rotation mechanism based on time or energy will be selected according to the change of energy efficiency.

By comparing the simulation results, we find that our rotation strategy integrates the advantages of both the energy-driven CH rotation strategy and the time-driven CH rotation strategy in cluster hierarchy protocol and can enhance the energy efficiency and prolong network lifetime in both homogeneous and heterogeneous networks. As an important technology of cluster topology maintenance, our rotation strategy can be used in any cluster protocol for the topology reconstruction of the hierarchical cluster network.

The energy threshold parameter c plays an important role in our hybrid CH rotation strategy and it is mainly decided by network topology structure. In this paper, we only obtain a suitable value by simulation analysis. How to find out its optimal value in a different network topology structure for WSNs is an issue of great importance for our hybrid CH rotation strategy. We will try to find a solution that could determine the optimal value of these parameters according to different cluster topology structures in our future work.

References

[1] I. F. Akyildiz, W. Su, Y. Sankarasubramaniam, and E. Cayirci, "A survey on sensor networks," *IEEE Communications Magazine*, vol. 40, no. 8, pp. 102–105, 2002.

[2] G. Chen, C. Li, M. Ye, and J. Wu, "An unequal cluster-based routing protocol in wireless sensor networks," *Wireless Networks*, vol. 15, no. 2, pp. 193–207, 2009.

[3] D. Culler and W. Hong, "Wireless sensor networks," *Communications of the ACM*, vol. 47, no. 6, pp. 30–33, 2004.

[4] U. C. Kozat, G. Kondylis, B. Ryu, and M. K. Marina, "Virtual dynamic backbone for mobile ad hoc networks," in *Proceedings of the International Conference on Communications (ICC '01)*, pp. 250–255, Helsinki, Finland, June 2001.

[5] W. B. Heinzelman, A. P. Chandrakasan, and H. Balakrishnan, "An application-specific protocol architecture for wireless microsensor networks," *IEEE Transactions on Wireless Communications*, vol. 1, no. 4, pp. 660–670, 2002.

[6] Y. Wang, Q. Zhao, and D. Zheng, "Energy-driven adaptive clustering data collection protocol in wireless sensor networks," in *Proceedings of the International Conference on Intelligent Mechatronics and Automation*, pp. 599–604, Chengdu, China, August 2004.

[7] S. Gamwarige and E. Kulasekere, "An algorithm for energy driven cluster head rotation in a distributed wireless sensor network," in *Proceedings of the International Conference on Information and Automation (ICIA '05)*, pp. 354–359, Colombo, Sri Lanka, December 2005.

[8] Q. Zhang, D. Shao, L. Sun, and H. Huang, "A cluster head rotation based on energy consumption for wireless sensor network," *International Journal of Advancements in Computing Technology*, vol. 4, no. 11, pp. 239–247, 2012.

[9] G. Smaragdakis, I. Matta, and A. Bestavros, "SEP: a stable election protocol for clustered heterogenous wireless sensor networks," in *Proceedings of the International Workshop on SANPA*, Boston, Mass, USA, 2004.

[10] O. Younis and S. Fahmy, "HEED: a hybrid, energy-efficient, distributed clustering approach for ad hoc sensor networks," *IEEE Transactions on Mobile Computing*, vol. 3, no. 4, pp. 366–379, 2004.

[11] J. Kamimura, N. Wakamiya, and M. Murata, "Energy-efficient clustering method for data gathering in sensor networks," in *Proceedings of the 1st Workshop on Broadband Advanced Sensor Networks*, October 2004.

[12] H. Chan and A. Perrig, "ACE: an emergent algorithm for highly uniform cluster formation," in *Proceedings of the 1st European Workshop on Sensor Networks (EWSN '04)*, pp. 154–171, January 2004.

[13] C. F. Chiasserini, I. Chlamtac, P. Monti, and A. Nucci, "An energy-efficient method for nodes assignment in cluster-based ad hoc networks," *Wireless Networks*, vol. 10, no. 3, pp. 223–231, 2004.

[14] S. Bandyopadhyay and E. J. Coyle, "An energy efficient hierarchical clustering algorithm for wireless sensor networks," in *Proceedings of the 22nd IEEE Societies Annual Joint Conference of the IEEE Computer and Communications (INFOCOM '03)*, vol. 3, pp. 1713–1723, 2003.

[15] S. Bandyopadhyay and E. J. Coyle, "Minimizing communication costs in hierarchically-clustered networks of wireless sensors," *Computer Networks*, vol. 44, no. 1, pp. 1–16, 2004.

[16] T. Moscibroda and R. Wattenhofer, "Maximizing the lifetime of dominating sets," in *Proceedings of the 19th IEEE International Parallel and Distributed Processing Symposium (IPDPS '05)*, April 2005.

[17] X. Fan and Y. Song, "Improvement on LEACH protocol of wireless sensor network," in *Proceedings of the International Conference on Sensor Technologies and Applications (SENSORCOMM '07)*, pp. 260–264, Valencia, España, October 2007.

[18] R. Madan and S. Lall, "Distributed algorithms for maximum lifetime routing in wireless sensor networks," *IEEE Transactions on Wireless Communications*, vol. 5, no. 8, pp. 2185–2193, 2006.

[19] F. M. Hu, Y. H. Kim, K. T. Kim, H. Y. Youn, and C. W. Park, "Energy-based selective cluster-head rotation in wireless sensor networks," in *Proceedings of the International Conference on Advanced Infocomm Technology (ICAIT '08)*, July 2008.

[20] S. Soro and W. B. Heinzelman, "Cluster head election techniques for coverage preservation in wireless sensor networks," *Ad Hoc Networks*, vol. 7, no. 5, pp. 955–972, 2009.

[21] Y. Wu, Z. Chen, Q. Jing, and Y. C. Wang, "LENO: LEast rotation near-optimal cluster head rotation strategy in wireless sensor networks," in *Proceedings of the 21st International Conference on Advanced Information Networking and Applications (AINA '07)*, pp. 195–201, Niagara Falls, Canada, May 2007.

[22] S. Gamwarige and C. Kulasekere, "Performance analysis of the EDCR algorithm in a distributed wireless sensor network," in *Proceedings of the IFIP International Conference on Wireless and Optical Communications Networks*, Bangalore, India, April 2006.

[23] T. Rappaport, *Wireless Communications: Principles & Practice*, Prentice-Hall, Englewood Cliffs, NJ, USA, 1996.

[24] K. Pahlavan and A. Levesque, *Wireless Information Networks*, Wiley, New York, NY, USA, 1995.

9

Optimal QoM in Multichannel Wireless Networks Based on MQICA

Na Xia,[1,2] Lina Xu,[1] and Chengchun Ni[1]

[1] *School of Computer and Information, Hefei University of Technology, Hefei 230009, China*
[2] *Engineering Research Center of Safety Critical Industrial Measurement and Control Technology,*
 Ministry of Education of China, Hefei 230009, China

Correspondence should be addressed to Na Xia; xiananawo@hfut.edu.cn

Academic Editor: Xinrong Li

In wireless networks, wireless sniffers are distributed in a region to monitor the activities of users. It can be applied for fault diagnosis, resource management, and critical path analysis. Due to hardware limitations, wireless sniffers typically can only collect information on one channel at a time. Therefore, it is a key topic to optimize the channel selection for sniffers to maximize the information collected, so as to maximize the Quality of Monitoring (QoM) for wireless networks. In this paper, a Multiple-Quantum-Immune-Clone-Algorithm- (MQICA-) based solution was proposed to achieve the optimal channel allocation. The extensive simulations demonstrate that MQICA outperforms the related algorithms evidently with higher monitoring quality, lower computation complexity, and faster convergence. The practical experiment also shows the feasibility of this algorithm.

1. Introduction

With the growing application of wireless networks (e.g., WiFi, WiMax, Mesh, and WLAN), high quality management of wireless device and networks is becoming more and more important [1–3]. It has been a key point to monitor network status and performance accurately and in real time, so as to implement effective management.

Wireless monitoring is usually realized using Simple Network Management Protocol (SNMP) and base-station logs. Since they reveal detailed PHY (e.g., signal strength and spectrum density) and MAC behaviors (e.g., collision and retransmission), as well as timing information, they are essential for network diagnosis and management [4–9]. But wireless monitoring equipments are usually single-radio multichannel device [10–12]. That is to say, it has multioptional channels (In IEEE 802.11.b/g WLAN, there are 3 orthogonal channels, and in IEEE 802.11.a WLAN, there are 12 orthogonal channels). So, it is a key topic to allocate channels and other resources for these monitoring equipments to optimize the monitoring quality of entire network [13–17]. In the literature [16], it has turned out to be a NP-hard problem in user-center mode, and an effective solution for the problem will be with great significance to the performance improvement of all kinds of wireless application networks.

In this paper, we carry out the full investigation on the current wireless monitoring networks and establish a system monitoring model based on the undirected bipartite graph. Then, compared with existing algorithms, we propose an optimization solution "Multiple Quantum Immune Clone Algorithm (MQICA)" to solve the problem. Finally, the algorithm has been proved to be with good performance both in theory and experiments.

The rest of the paper is organized as follows. In Section 2, we provide a brief review of existing work on wireless monitoring. The problem formulation is presented in Section 3. The Multiple Quantum Immune Clone channel allocation algorithm (MQICA) is detailed in Section 4. Then we prove the validity of the proposed algorithm in Section 5 followed by extensive simulation experiments in Section 6. Finally, we conclude this paper with some future work in Section 7.

2. Related Work

In recent years, wireless monitoring networks have become a hot topic. The research mainly contains monitoring device, system design, fault diagnosis and so forth [4–9]. In 2004, "passive monitoring" utilizing multi-wireless sniffers was first introduced by Yeo et al. [4, 5]. He analyzed the advantages and challenges of wireless passive monitoring and preliminarily set up an application system, which fulfilled the network fault diagnosis based on time synchronization and data fusion of multisniffers. In 2005, Rodrig et al. [6] used sniffers to capture wireless communication data and analyze the performance characteristics of 802.11 WiFi network. In 2006, Cheng et al. [7] investigated a large-scale monitoring network composed of 150 sniffers and discussed the time synchronization method for distributed sniffers. In 2007, Yang and Guo et al. [8] studied the lifetime model of wireless monitoring networks and proposed to adjust the sensing and communication radius of sniffers in real time to maximize the lifetime of networks. In 2010, Liu and Cao [9] researched the relationship between the number of monitoring sniffers and false alarm rate and put forward an algorithm based on *poller-poller* structure, which can limit the false alarm rate and minimize sniffers.

It has become an important subject to optimize the channel selection of monitoring sniffers so as to improve the network monitoring quality. In 2009, Shin and Bagchi [13] researched the channel selection of sniffers in Wireless Mesh network to maximize the coverage of users. He described it as a maximum coverage problem based on *group budget constraints* [14, 15] and solved it using Greedy and Linear Programming (LP) algorithms, which achieved good performance. Based on the previous research, Chhetri et el. [16] formulated the problem of channel allocation of sniffers and proved it to be NP-hard to maximize the Quality of Monitoring (QoM) of wireless network under universal network model. Greedy and LP algorithms were employed to solve the problem. Greedy algorithm always seeks the solution with maximal current benefit during the process of resolution and misses the global optimal solution or approximate of it. Although LP algorithm can achieve better solution than others, its complexity is too high to meet the real-time optimization in dynamic wireless networks. In 2011, we applied *Gibbs Sampler* theory to address the problem and proposed a distributed channel selection algorithm for sniffers to maximize QoM of network [17]. This method utilizes the local information to select the channel with low energy but cannot achieve the global optima in most of the cases.

In [15–20], we can get an overview of much excellent work in multichannel selection of wireless network itself. In 2006, Wormsbecker and Williamson [18] studied the impact of channel selection technique on the communication performance of system and applied *soft channel reservation* technique to select channels, so as to reduce link layer data frame losses and provide higher TCP throughput. In 2007, Kanthi and Jain [19] proposed a channel selection algorithm for multiradio and multichannel mesh networks. It is based on *Spanner* conception and combined with network topology.

The experiment results showed that it can improve data throughput in communication link layer. In 2009, You et al. [20] investigated the end-to-end data transmission and the optimal allocation of channel resource in wireless cellular networks and figured it out with *stochastic quasi-gradient* method. In 2010, Hou and Huang [21] researched the channel selection problem in Cognitive Ratio networks, described it as a binary integer nonlinear optimization problem, and proposed an algorithm based on *priority order* to maximize the total channel utilization for all secondary nodes. In 2011, an interface-clustered channel assignment (ICCA) scheme was presented by Du et al. [22]. It can eliminate the collision and interference to some extent, enhance the network throughput, and reduce the transmission delay.

From what has been discussed previously, there exist great shortcomings in solution of wireless monitoring network channel allocation problems. All of these studies most focused on the wireless network itself, rather than the wireless monitoring sniffers. Existing algorithms will have high algorithm complexity, slow convergence speed, and, in most cases, it is difficult to get global optimal solution in the cases of large-scale networks or having more optional channels. Therefore, in this paper, a so-called Multiple-QICA (MQICA) algorithm, taking full advantage of the parallel characteristics of Quantum Computing (QC), is proposed. Compared with traditional Quantum Immune Clone Algorithm (QICA), MQICA possesses lots of characteristics inherited from both immune and evolution algorithms. Meanwhile, allele and Gaussian mutations are introduced in MQICA to further improve the performance of the algorithm. Extensive simulations and practical experiments demonstrate that the proposed algorithm outperforms other algorithms not only in quality of solution, but also in time efficiency.

3. Problem Description

3.1. Network Model. Consider a wireless network of m monitoring sniffers, n users, and k optional channels. $S = \{s_1, s_2, \ldots, s_m\}$ is the set of sniffers, $U = \{u_1, u_2, \ldots, u_n\}$ is the set of users, and $C = \{c_1, c_2, \ldots, c_k\}$ is the set of channels. In homogeneous networks, sniffers have the same transmission characteristics. They have the ability to read frame information and can analyze the information from users or other sniffers. But at any point in time, a sniffer can only observe transmissions over a single channel. Let p_{u_j} denote the transmission probability of a user u_j ($j = 1, 2, \ldots, n$) that works on channel $c(u_j) \in C$. These users can be a wireless router, access point or mobile phone user, and so forth. If a user sends data through a channel at time t, it will be called active user in time t.

In wireless networks, the relationship between sniffers and users can be described by an undirected bipartite graph $G = (S, U, E)$ shown in Figure 1. If u_j is in the monitoring area of s_i, there will be a connection between them, indicated by $e = (s_i, u_j)$. When s_i and u_j work on the same channel, s_i can capture the data from u_j, and then we say that u_j is covered by s_i. E represents the set of all connecting edges. If a user is outside all sniffers' monitoring area, it is excluded from G.

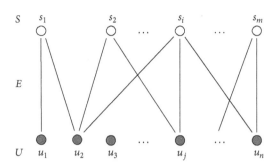

FIGURE 1: undirected bipartite graph G.

The vertex v in G is sniffer or user, namely, $v \in S \cup U$. $N(v)$ denotes the neighbors of vertex v. If the vertex is a user u_j, $N(u_j)$ means its neighbor sniffers; if the vertex is a sniffer s_i, $N(s_i)$ is the set of neighbor users of s_i. If a sniffer is inside the communication range of another sniffer, they are called adjacent sniffers. $V(s_i)$ denotes the set of adjacent sniffers of s_i, and B_{s_i} is the set of subscript of sniffers in $V(s_i)$. In this paper, we assume that the communication radius of sniffer is twice as its monitoring radius.

3.2. Problem Formulation. $\mathbf{a} : S \rightarrow C$ represents a channel selection scheme for wireless monitoring networks, and O is the set of all possible schemes. $\mathbf{a}$ can be expressed in the form of vector as follows: $\mathbf{a} = (a(s_1), a(s_2), \ldots, a(s_m))$, where $a(s_i) \in C$ is the channel selected by s_i. When s_i selects the channel $a(s_i)$, it can communicate with the neighbor users, who also work on channel $a(s_i)$. Given a channel selection scheme $\mathbf{a}$, then $S = \cup_{q=1}^{k} S_{c_q}$, $U = \cup_{q=1}^{k} U_{c_q}$, where S_{c_q} denotes the set of sniffers assigned to channel c_q, and U_{c_q} denotes the set of users working on channel c_q. Now it is able to show the relationship between all the sniffers and users working on channel c_q in the form of undirected bipartite graph $G_{c_q} = (S_{c_q}, U_{c_q}, E_{c_q})$.

Definition 1. Monitoring quality of node (MQN): when wireless monitoring network works on channel $\mathbf{a} \in O$, the monitoring quality of node s_i can be defined as follows:

$$Q_{s_i}(\mathbf{a}) = \sum_{u \in N(s_i)} p_u \cdot \frac{\mathbf{1}\left(c(u) = a(s_i)\right)}{1 + \sum_{t \in B_{s_i}} \mathbf{1}\left(c(u) = a(s_t), s_t \in N(u)\right)},$$
(1)

where $\mathbf{1}(\cdot)$ is an indicator function. It equals 1 when the condition is true and 0 otherwise. It is clear that the more neighbor users work on the same channel as s_i, the higher transmission probability these users have, and meanwhile, the less other sniffers cover these users, the higher monitoring quality s_i has. MQN reflects the number of active users available to s_i under the channel selection scheme $\mathbf{a}$. Active users are in the state of sending data.

Given a channel selection scheme $\mathbf{a}$, the Quality of Monitoring (QoM) of wireless network can be defined as follows:

$$Q(\mathbf{a}) = \sum_{s_i \in S} Q_{s_i}(\mathbf{a}).$$
(2)

So, the higher QoM is, the more active users can be monitored in the network and the higher quality of service the wireless monitoring network provides.

The problem of maximizing of QoM (MQM) can be described as follows: finding an optimal channel allocation scheme for sniffers to collect the largest amount of information transmitted by users, that is, to maximize the QoM of the network.

The channel allocation scheme will be changed according to probability during different time slot. So the maximal information collected by monitoring network in a certain period can be expressed as

$$\max \quad \sum_{\mathbf{a} \in O} Q(\mathbf{a}) \times \pi(\mathbf{a}),$$

$$\text{s.t.} \quad \pi(\mathbf{a}) \in [0, 1] \qquad (3)$$

$$\sum_{\mathbf{a} \in O} \pi(\mathbf{a}) = 1,$$

where $\pi(\mathbf{a})$ is the probability for wireless monitoring network to work on the channel allocation scheme $\mathbf{a}$.

From (3), the optimal channel allocation scheme will be got as follows:

$$\mathbf{a}^* = \arg \max Q(\mathbf{a}). \qquad (4)$$

For this complicated combination optimization problem, an effective heuristic algorithm is needed. In 2005 Jiao and Li proposed a brand new Quantum-Inspired Immune Clone Algorithm (QICA) [23]. QICA constructs antibodies in view of the superposition characteristics of quantum coding and enlarges the original population via clone operation, thus expanding the searching space and improving the performance of the algorithm when doing local search. It is very suitable for this complicated combination optimization problem because of the attributes of parallelism and provable rapid convergence. But the results in QICA are expressed in a binary form [24], which are more appropriate for solving problems in a binary encoding. Thus we need to extend it to k-resolution coding before applying the algorithm to this MQM problem in wireless monitoring network. Then, Multiple-QICA channel selection algorithm is proposed and described in detail as follows.

4. Multiple Quantum Immune Clone Channel Allocation Algorithm (MQICA)

4.1. Fundamental Definitions. To accurately describe the evolutionary process of the MQICA algorithm, the following fundamental definitions are proposed.

Definition 2 (Channel Quantum Antibody (CQA)). We define the *Channel Quantum Antibody* as the following triploid chromosome:

$$\text{CQA} \overset{\text{def}}{=} \begin{bmatrix} x_0 \cdots x_i \cdots x_{m-1} \\ \alpha_0 \cdots \alpha_i \cdots \alpha_{m-1} \\ \beta_0 \cdots \beta_i \cdots \beta_{m-1} \end{bmatrix}, \quad (5)$$

where m is called the length of the chromosome, that is, the number of the monitoring sensors. $x_i \in [0,1)$ represents channel selection scheme of the ith monitoring sensor. α_i and β_i should meet the normalization condition: $|\alpha_i|^2 + |\beta_i|^2 = 1$, where $|\alpha_i|^2$ and $|\beta_i|^2$ indicate, respectively, the nonoptimal and optimal probability of the channel selection scheme of the ith monitoring sensor. $[x_i \ \alpha_i \ \beta_i]^T$ is named as an allele of the CQA.

Definition 3 (mapping between antibody to channel). Note that in the CQA,

$$X = [x_0, x_1, \ldots, x_i, \ldots, x_{m-1}] \in R^m, \quad (6)$$

where $x_i \in [0,1)$ is a continuous real number. If it is discrete, X can be mapped into integer space that

$$\mathbf{C} = \left[c_{s_0}, c_{s_1}, \ldots, c_{s_i}, \ldots, c_{s_{m-1}} \right] \in Z^m, \quad (7)$$

where $c_{s_i} \in \{0, 1, \ldots, k-1\}$ and indicates the monitoring sensor s_i to select channel c_{s_i}. k is the total number of selectable channels in the network. The process described previously is called mapping of the CQA to channel selection scheme, briefly as antibody to channel. The *mapping relationship* is defined as follows:

$$c_{s_i} \overset{\text{mapping}}{=} \lfloor kx_i \rfloor, \quad i = 0, 1, \ldots, m-1. \quad (8)$$

Definition 4 (channel affinity). *Channel affinity* refers to the affinity degree between the CQA and the channel antigen, which is the approximate level between feasible solution and optimal solution. With the affinity value increased, the feasible solution will be much closer to the optimal one. On the contrary, the feasible solution will gradually deviate from the optimal one. *Channel affinity* is the foundation of immune selection operation.

Definition 5 (evolutionary entropy of the CQA). To measure the extent of the evolution, we introduce *evolutionary entropy* to the CQA:

$$H(X) = H(x_0, x_1, \ldots x_{m-1})$$
$$= H(x_0) + H(x_1 \mid x_0)$$

$$+ \cdots + H(x_{m-1} \mid x_0, x_1, \ldots, x_{m-2})$$
$$= \sum_{i=0}^{m-1} \left(|\alpha_i|^2 \log \frac{1}{|\alpha_i|^2} + |\beta_i|^2 \log \frac{1}{|\beta_i|^2} \right)$$
$$= -\sum_{i=0}^{m-1} \left(|\alpha_i|^2 \log |\alpha_i|^2 + |\beta_i|^2 \log |\beta_i|^2 \right)$$
$$= -2 \sum_{i=0}^{m-1} \left(|\alpha_i|^2 \log |\alpha_i| + |\beta_i|^2 \log |\beta_i| \right). \quad (9)$$

As the evolution process continues, $\alpha_i \rightarrow 0$, $\beta_i \rightarrow 0$, thus $H(X) \rightarrow 0$. So the *evolutionary entropy* can be used to describe the extent of the evolution. When the algorithm finally comes to a convergent result, the value of *evolutionary entropy* is indefinitely close to zero.

4.2. Process Design. The population is denoted as $A = \{r_1, r_2, \ldots, r_N\}$, where N indicates the scale of the population and r_i represents a CQA in it. An evolution process of the algorithm in this paper consists of three basic operations, including clone, immune genetic variation, and immune selection. Clone operation (T_c) clones each antibody and the clone scale is decided by the *channel affinity* value of the antibody. Immune genetic variation (T_m) will increase the diversity of population information. The immune selection operation (T_I) chooses from all antibodies generated by the former two operations according to their *channel affinity* and get the optimal CQA. Then compare them with the original N elite antibody r_{i0}'' [25], $i = 1, 2, \ldots, N$ in immune memory set S_m [26]. Meanwhile, it forms the new population of next generation. Thus an evolution process can be described as

$$A(t) \xrightarrow{\text{Clone Operation } (T_c)} A'(t) \xrightarrow{\text{Immune Genetic Variation } (T_m)}$$
$$A''(t) \xrightarrow{\text{Immune Selection } (T_I)} A(t+1). \quad (10)$$

After this operation, we need to do full interference cross to the new operation $A(t+1)$ and continue returning to the next, in case that the evolution still did not meet the termination conditions.

4.2.1. Cloning Operation. A self-adaptive clone operation is proposed in [23]:

$$T_c(A(t)) = \{T_c(r_1), T_c(r_2), \ldots, T_c(r_N)\}, \quad (11)$$

where $T_c(r_i) = E_i \times r_i$, $i = 1, 2, \ldots, N$ and E_i is a unit row vector with q_i columns, while q_i indicates the clone scale of the CQA and is decided by the equation as follows:

$$q_i = \left\lceil N_c \times \frac{Q(\mathbf{C}_i)}{\sum_{j=1}^N Q(\mathbf{C}_j)} \right\rceil, \quad (12)$$

where $N_c > N$. It can be concluded from (12) that if the channel affinity of a specific CQA is greater than that of the others in the population, then corresponding clone scale will be larger. Thus this clone strategy guarantees that the more excellent an antibody is, the more resource it will get, and this will obviously drive the algorithm to evolve towards the optimal solution much more quickly. Once the clone operation is completed, the population $A(t)$ is expanded to have the following form:

$$A'(t) = \left\{ A(t), A'_1(t), \ldots, A'_N(t) \right\}, \qquad (13)$$

where,

$$A'_i(t) = \left\{ r_{i1}(t), r_{i2}(t), \ldots, r_{iq_i-1}(t) \right\},$$
$$r_{ij}(t) = r_i(t), \quad j = 1, 2, \ldots, q_{i-1}. \qquad (14)$$

4.2.2. Immune Genetic Variation. MQICA algorithm implements a single-gene mutation on every triploid chromosome during the evolution. Compared with full-gene mutation, it has been proved in the literature [27] that single-gene mutation can dramatically improve the search efficiency of the algorithm. Denote r_z^t as a CQA in $A'_i(t) = \{r_{i1}(t), r_{i2}(t), \ldots, r_{iq_i-1}(t)\}$ which is generated by clone operation on the ith CQA of population $A(t)$. Choose the jth allele $\begin{bmatrix} x_{zj}^t & \alpha_{zj}^t & \beta_{zj}^t \end{bmatrix}^T$ randomly from r_z^t and perform two kinds of Gaussian mutation on it:

$$x_{zj}^{t+1,\omega} = N\left(\mu_{zj}^{t,\omega}, \left(\delta_{zj}^{t,\omega} \right)^2 \right)$$
$$= \begin{cases} x_{zj}^t + N\left(0, \left| \alpha_{zj}^t \right|^2 \right), & \omega = \alpha, \\ \dfrac{x_{\max} - x_{\min}}{2} + N\left(0, \dfrac{\left| \beta_{zj}^t \right|^2}{\chi} \right), & \omega = \beta. \end{cases} \qquad (15)$$

χ is a variable. After the Gaussian mutation, $x_{zj}^{t+1,\omega}$ might exceed the interval $[0, 1)$. To avoid it, redefine $x_{zj}^{t+1,\omega}$ as follows:

$$x_{zj}^{t+1,\omega} = \begin{cases} \dfrac{k-1}{k}, & x_{zj}^{t+1,\omega} > 1, \\ 0, & x_{zj}^{t+1,\omega} < 0, \\ N\left(\mu_{zj}^{t,\omega}, \left(\delta_{zj}^{t,\omega} \right)^2 \right), & \text{others.} \end{cases} \qquad (16)$$

Gaussian mutation consists of two operations: one performs a local search around the current solution with a variance of $\left| \alpha_{zj}^t \right|^2$, another performs a wide-range search around the mean value with a variance of $\left| \beta_{zj}^t \right|^2 / \chi$ lest the algorithm converges to a local optimal solution.

After the Gaussian mutation indicated by (15) and (16), the algorithm will calculate the *channel affinity* of the new antibody and compare it with the original one, that is, to decide which one is better between the two feasible solutions $(x_{z0}^{t+1}, \ldots, x_{zj}^{t+1,\omega}, \ldots, x_{z,m-1}^{t+1})$ and $(x_{z0}^t, \ldots, x_{zj}^t, \ldots, x_{z,q_i-1}^t)$. If the Gaussian mutation does improve the quality of the antibody, replace $x_{zj}^{t,\omega}$ with $x_{zj}^{t+1,\omega}$, and keep the probability of

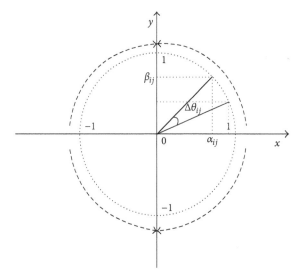

FIGURE 2: Sketch map of QRD operation.

$x_{zj}^{t,\omega}$ unchanged, that is, $\alpha_{zj}^{t+1} = \alpha_{zj}^t$, $\beta_{zj}^{t+1} = \beta_{zj}^t$. Otherwise, the Gaussian mutation has no effect and the probability indicating that the current solution is optimal should be increased. Quantum Rotation Door (QRD) is adopted to update $\left| \alpha_{zj}^t \right|^2$ and $\left| \beta_{zj}^t \right|^2$: the former will be decreased and the latter will be correspondingly increased after the rotation operation. Assume that the step size of the rotation is $\Delta\theta_{zj}^t$, the newly generated α_{zj}^{t+1} and β_{zj}^{t+1} are decided by (17)

$$\begin{bmatrix} \alpha_{zj}^{t+1} \\ \beta_{zj}^{t+1} \end{bmatrix} = \begin{bmatrix} \cos\left(\Delta\theta_{zj}^t \right) & -\sin\left(\Delta\theta_{zj}^t \right) \\ \sin\left(\Delta\theta_{zj}^t \right) & \cos\left(\Delta\theta_{zj}^t \right) \end{bmatrix} \begin{bmatrix} \alpha_{zj}^t \\ \beta_{zj}^t \end{bmatrix}. \qquad (17)$$

During the evolution, the probability of composite vector $(\alpha_{zj}^t, \beta_{zj}^t)$ will approach gradually towards y-axis, shown as in Figure 2:

(1) If $(\alpha_{zj}^t, \beta_{zj}^t)$ lies in the first or the third quadrant, an anticlockwise rotation is needed and $\Delta\theta_{zj}^t$ is positive.

(2) If $(\alpha_{zj}^t, \beta_{zj}^t)$ lies in the second or the fourth quadrant, a clockwise rotation is needed and $\Delta\theta_{zj}^t$ is negative.

(3) If $(\alpha_{zj}^t, \beta_{zj}^t)$ lies exactly on y-axis, the algorithm has converged and the current feasible solution is the optimal one.

To sum up, $\Delta\theta_{zj}^t$ is realized as follows:

$$\Delta\theta_{zj}^t = \text{sgn}\left(\alpha_{zj}^t \beta_{zj}^t \right) \Delta\theta \exp\left(-\dfrac{\left| \beta_{zj}^t \right|^2}{\left| \alpha_{zj}^t \right|^2 + N_q/N_s} \right), \qquad (18)$$

where $\text{sgn}(\cdot)$ is a sign function used to control the direction of the rotation, thus to make sure that the algorithm will finally converge to an optimal solution. $\Delta\theta$ means the maximum rotation angle in a single rotation operation. Current probability $\left| \alpha_{zj}^t \right|^2$, $\left| \beta_{zj}^t \right|^2$ as well as N_q/N_s is employed to control the rotation dimension, or that is to say, to adjust the evolutionary speed in case of precocity of an antibody: N_q represents the total number of CQAs in $A'(t)$, that is, $N_q = \sum_{i=1}^{N} q_i$ and N_s indicates how stable the current population $A(t)$ is. After every operation, including Gaussian mutation and crossover, which may update x_{ij}^t, N_s should be recalculate as follows:

$$N_s = \begin{cases} N_s + 1, & x_{ij}^{t+1} = x_{ij}^t, \ i = 1, 2, \ldots, N, \\ & j = 0, 1, \ldots, m-1, \\ 1, & x_{ij}^{t+1} \neq x_{ij}^t, \ i = 1, 2, \ldots, N, \\ & j = 0, 1, \ldots, m-1. \end{cases} \quad (19)$$

4.2.3. Immune Selecting Operation. There shall form a new population:

$$A''(t) = \left\{ A(t), A_1''(t), \ldots, A_N''(t) \right\} \quad (20)$$

after the immune genetic variation wherein

$$A_i''(t) = \left\{ r_{i1}''(t), r_{i2}''(t), \ldots, r_{iq_i-1}''(t) \right\}, \quad i = 1, 2, \ldots, N. \quad (21)$$

For each CQA in population $A''(t)$ derived from immune manipulation operation, we firstly map $X = [x_0, x_1, \ldots, x_{m-1}] \in R^m$ to channel selection scheme $\mathbf{C} = [c_{s_0}, c_{s_1}, \ldots, c_{s_{m-1}}] \in Z^m$. Then compare them with original r_{i0}'' in S_m on the basis of *channel affinity*. For all $i = 1, 2, \ldots, N$, if exists

$$\mathbf{C}_{b_i}(t) - \left\{ \mathbf{C}_{r_{ij}''}(t) \mid \max Q\left(C_{r_{ij}''} \right), j = 0, 1, 2, \ldots, q_i - 1 \right\} \quad (22)$$

making $Q(\mathbf{C}_{r_i}) < Q(\mathbf{C}_{b_i})$, $i = 1, 2, \ldots, N$, then $r_{i0}''(t + 1) = b_i(t)$, otherwise $r_{i0}''(t + 1)$ remains unchanged as $r_{i0}''(t)$. Immune selection operation selects the optimal CQA from all the antibodies generated by clone operation and immune manipulation operation as well as the immune memory set S_m to form a brand new population. After the operation is down, we can get not only new immune memory set S_m but also the new generation of CQA population $A(t + 1)$.

4.2.4. Full Interference Crossover. To make full use of the information of all CQAs in the population, thus to guarantee that new antibodies will be generated in case of antibody precocity, which may cause the algorithm converge to a local optimal solution, a full interference crossover strategy [28] is adopted in this paper. Denote the jth allele in the ith antibody before and after the crossover operation to be A_{ij} and B_{ij} respectively; the relationship between A_{ij} and B_{ij} can then be revealed as $B_{ij} = A_{[(i+j)\%N][j]}$. A simple example is shown in Tables 1(a) and 1(b) to help understand when the population scale is set to $N = 5$, and the number of the monitoring sensors and current available channels is set to $m = 8$ and $k = 5$, respectively.

TABLE 1: (a) Group information before the crossing. (b) Group information after the crossing.

(a)

NO.0:	A_{00}	A_{01}	A_{02}	A_{03}	A_{04}	A_{05}	A_{06}	A_{07}
NO.1:	A_{10}	A_{11}	A_{12}	A_{13}	A_{14}	A_{15}	A_{16}	A_{17}
NO.2:	A_{20}	A_{21}	A_{22}	A_{23}	A_{24}	A_{25}	A_{26}	A_{27}
NO.3:	A_{30}	A_{31}	A_{32}	A_{33}	A_{34}	A_{35}	A_{36}	A_{37}
NO.4:	A_{40}	A_{41}	A_{42}	A_{43}	A_{44}	A_{45}	A_{46}	A_{47}

(b)

NO.0:	A_{00}	A_{11}	A_{22}	A_{33}	A_{44}	A_{05}	A_{16}	A_{27}
NO.1:	A_{10}	A_{21}	A_{32}	A_{43}	A_{04}	A_{15}	A_{26}	A_{37}
NO.2:	A_{20}	A_{31}	A_{42}	A_{03}	A_{14}	A_{25}	A_{36}	A_{47}
NO.3:	A_{30}	A_{41}	A_{02}	A_{13}	A_{24}	A_{35}	A_{46}	A_{07}
NO.4:	A_{40}	A_{01}	A_{12}	A_{23}	A_{34}	A_{45}	A_{06}	A_{17}

4.3. Algorithm Description. Based on the discussion, the process of MQICA is described as follows.

Step 1. Set algorithm parameters and initialize population $A(0)$. Calculate the initial channel affinity of each CQA in the population, that is, the Quality of Monitoring (QoM).

Step 2. Calculate the clone scale of each CQA according to (12) and then execute clone operation. After this step, $A'(t)$ is obtained.

Step 3. Do mutation operation on $A'(t)$, and get $A''(t)$.

Step 4. Do immune selection, and those selected antibodies constitute the new population $A(t + 1)$.

Step 5. Calculate the channel affinity of each CQA in the new population as well as the evolutionary entropy of the population: if the former does not change any more and the latter tends to be close to zero infinitely or $t > t_{\max}$, the algorithm has already approximately converged, otherwise, crossover operation is applied to $A(t + 1)$ and jump to Step 2.

The pseudo code of the algorithm is also given in Pseudocode 1.

5. Performance Analysis of MQICA

We will firstly prove that MQICA, just like traditional QICA, has a dramatic ability on global optimization searching. And in next chapter, lots of experiments are given to further identify the outstanding performance of MQICA, especially on MQoM problems.

Lemma 6. *The population sequence $\{A_t, t \geq 0\}$, generated by the evolutionary process of MQICA, is a stochastic process with discrete parameters and constitutes a time homogeneous Markov chain.*

Proof. Suppose that the state space of a single CQA is Ω, $A = \{r_1, r_2, \ldots, r_N\}$ represents the population where r_i responds to

---

Input: the sniffer set $S = \{s_1, s_2, \ldots, s_m\}$, channel set
$C = \{c_1, c_2, \ldots, c_k\}$, user set
$U = \{u_1, u_2, \ldots, u_n\}$, $c\left(u_j\right)$ and p_{u_j} $(j = 1, 2, \ldots, n)$,
the iterative terminal entropy ε and the maximum iterations $t_{\max}$.
Output: the channel allocation vector **C**.

(1) $r_i(t) \leftarrow$ Generate initial population, $1 \leq i \leq N, t = 0$;
(2) Do *mappings between antibody to channel*, calculate the *evolutionary entropy* of each CQA and get $H(X_{r_i})$;
(3) $Q_i(t) \leftarrow$ function(C_{r_i});   /*compute the *channel affinity* of each antibody according to (2)*/
(4) $r_{i0}''(t) \leftarrow r_i(t)$ /*copy the original message to S_m*/
(5) **do** {
(6) $A'(t) \leftarrow A(t)$;   /* clone operation*/
(7) $A''(t) \leftarrow A'(t)$;   /*immune genetic variation*/
(8)   Update immune memory set S_m;
(9)   /*immune selection operation*/
(10) $A(t + 1) \leftarrow S_m$;
(11) $Q^* = \max(Q_i(t))$;   /*choose the max value*/
(12)   Calculate the *evolutionary entropy* update $H(X_{r_i})$;
(13)   **if** $\left((t < t_{\max}) \mid \left(\sum_{i=1}^N H\left(X_{r_i}\right) > \varepsilon\right)\right)$ **then**
(14) $t = t + 1$;
(15)   Do full interference cross and update $A(t)$;
(16)   **end;**}
(17) **while** $\left((t < t_{\max}) \mid \left(\sum_{i=1}^N H\left(X_{r_i}\right) > \varepsilon\right)\right)$;

PSEUDOCODE 1

the ith antibody in A and N is the population scale. $r_i \in \Omega$, $A \in \Omega^N$. During the evolution process, all CQAs are discrete. $X = \lfloor C/k \rfloor \in \{0, 1/k, \ldots, (k-1)/k\}$ describes the channel selection scheme. If the quantity of the CQA in population A is m, $\Omega = \{0, 1/k, \ldots, (k-1)/k\}^m \notin \phi$. So the population state space should be $|\Omega^N| = k^{Nm}$, that is, the state space during the evolution is finite. According to literature [29], denote δ to be the minimum σ-algebra generated by all cylinder set of Ω and P to be a real-value measure function defined in (Ω, δ), and thus the probability space of an CQA can be expressed as (Ω, δ, P) and the probability space of MQICA should be defined as (Ω^N, δ, P). As a result, $\{A(t), t \geq 0\}$, defined in state space (Ω, δ, P), is a stochastic sequence with discrete parameter and will change with t, the evolutionary times of our algorithm. Obviously, when the state space is replaced by (Ω^N, δ, P), the conclusion previously mentioned still holds.

Furthermore, the operations adopted in MQICA, including clone (T_c), immune gene manipulation (T_m & T_e), and immune selection (T_I), guarantee that $A(t + 1)$ is only related to $A(t)$. So $\{A(t), t \geq 0\}$ is time homogeneous Markov chain in state space (Ω^N, δ, P).

Definition 7. Denote $\mathbf{a}^* = \mathbf{C}^*$ as the optimal channel selection scheme, namely, $\mathbf{C}^* = \arg \max Q(\mathbf{a}) = \arg Q^*$, where Q^* is the QoM value corresponding to optimal channel selection scheme. MQICA will converge to global optimal solution when and only when $\lim_{t \to \infty} P(Q_t = Q^*) = 1$.

Lemma 8. *The transition probability matrix $M(T_m)$, which indicates that the probability for a CQA in clone group $A'(t)$*

changes its state from Λ^μ to Λ^λ after the MQICA mutation operation T_m, is strictly positive.

Proof. For Gaussian mutation operation G, shown in (15), assume that after the mutation $x_{zj}^{t+1} = \begin{cases} x_{zj}^{t+1,\alpha} \\ x_{zj}^{t+1,\beta} \end{cases}$, the probability for x_{zj}^t to mutate to $x_{zj}^{t+1,\alpha}$ should be

$$G\left(x_{z,j}^t, x_{z,j}^{t+1,\alpha}\right)$$
$$= \int_{x_{z,j}^t}^{x_{z,j}^{t+1,\alpha}} \left(\frac{1}{\sqrt{2\pi}\left|\alpha_{z,j}^t\right|} \cdot \exp\left(-\frac{\left(x - x_{z,j}^{t+1,\alpha}\right)^2}{\pi\left|\alpha_{z,j}^t\right|^2}\right)\right) \cdot dx$$
$$> 0.$$

$$(23)$$

By the same token, the probability for x_{zj}^t to mutate to $x_{zj}^{t+1,\beta}$ should be

$$G\left(x_{z,j}^t, x_{z,j}^{t+1,\beta}\right)$$
$$= \int_{x_{z,j}^t}^{x_{z,j}^{t+1,\beta}} \left(\frac{1}{\sqrt{2\pi}\left|\beta_{z,j}^t\right|} \cdot \exp\left(-\frac{\left(x - x_{z,j}^{t+1,\beta}\right)^2}{\pi\left|\beta_{z,j}^t\right|^2}\right)\right) \cdot dx$$
$$> 0.$$

$$(24)$$

Because these two Gaussian mutations are independent, so the probability of state transition from $\mathbf{x}_\mu$ to $\mathbf{x}_\lambda$ after this operation would be

$$
\begin{aligned}
G\left(\mathbf{x}_\mu, \mathbf{x}_\lambda\right) &= G\left(x_{z,j}^t, x_{z,j}^{t+1}\right) \\
&= G\left(x_{z,j}^t, x_{z,j}^{t+1,\alpha}\right) \cdot G\left(x_{z,j}^t, x_{z,j}^{t+1,\beta}\right) > 0.
\end{aligned}
\tag{25}
$$

When the state of α in a specific allele of an antibody is changed from a_λ to a_μ by QRD operation, the state transition probability $U(a_\mu, a_\lambda) > 0$. Thus,

$$
\begin{aligned}
m_{\mu\lambda}\left(T_m\right) &= G\left(\mathbf{x}_\mu, \mathbf{x}_\lambda\right) \times \left(1 - U\left(a_\mu, a_\lambda\right)\right) \\
&+ \left(1 - G\left(\mathbf{x}_\mu, \mathbf{x}_\lambda\right)\right) \times U\left(a_\mu, a_\lambda\right) > 0,
\end{aligned}
\tag{26}
$$

and obviously the transition probability matrix $M(T_m)$ is strictly positive.

Lemma 9. *The state transition matrix P for MQICA is a regular one.*

Proof. The state transition process of the population in Ω^N is described by the following four operations: T_c, T_m, T_I, and T_e. Denote T to be $T = T_c \cdot T_m \cdot T_I \cdot T_e$, and as a result, $r_i(t + 1) = T[r_i(t)] = T_c \cdot T_m \cdot T_I \cdot T_e[r_i(t)]$. Assume that the state of the population was transferred from Λ^μ to Λ^λ after the tth iteration, where $\Lambda^\mu, \Lambda^\lambda \subseteq \Omega^N$. So the state transition probability of MQICA is

$$
\begin{aligned}
p_{\mu\lambda}(t) &= p\{A(t+1) = Y \mid A(t) = W\} = p(Y \mid W) \\
&= \prod_{i=1}^N \left\{ p\left\{T_c\left(r_i(t)\right)\right\} \times \prod_{j=1}^{q_i-1} p\left\{T_m\left(r_{ij}(t)\right)\right\} \cdot p_m \right. \\
&\qquad \times \prod_{\eta=1}^t p\left\{T_I\left(r_{\lambda i}(t+1) = r_{\mu i}(t)\right)\right\} \\
&\qquad \left. \times p\left\{T_e\left(r_{\mu i}(t+1)\right)\right\} \cdot p_c \right\},
\end{aligned}
\tag{27}
$$

where,

$$
p\left\{T_c\left(r_i(t)\right)\right\} = \frac{Q\left(\mathbf{C}_i\right)}{\sum_{j=1}^N Q\left(\mathbf{C}_j\right)} > 0,
\tag{28}
$$

$$
p\left\{T_m\left(r_{ij}(t)\right)\right\} = m_{\mu\lambda}\left(T_m\right) \geq 0.
$$

Because the full interference cross has fixed relationships, that is, $p\{T_e(r_{\mu i}(t+1))\} = 1$, the lemma can be proved with the following three conditions.

Condition 1. When $Q(\mathbf{C}_{\mu i}) < Q(\mathbf{C}_{\lambda i})$,

$$
p\left\{T_I\left(r_{\lambda i}(t+1) = r_{\mu i}(t)\right)\right\} = 1.
\tag{29}
$$

Condition 2. When $Q(\mathbf{C}_{\mu i}) > Q(\mathbf{C}_{\lambda i})$,

$$
p\left\{T_I\left(r_{\lambda i}(t+1) = r_{\mu i}(t)\right)\right\} = 0.
\tag{30}
$$

Condition 3. When $Q(\mathbf{C}_{\mu i}) = Q(\mathbf{C}_{\lambda i})$, the evolutionary entropy of the CQA satisfies $H(X) \to 0$; in other words, the algorithm should be converged and $p_{\mu\lambda}(t) = p_{\mu\mu}(t) = 1$, and the state transition probability of MQICA can be summarized as

$$
\begin{aligned}
p_{\mu\lambda}(t) > 0, \quad &\text{s.t. } Q\left(\mathbf{C}_{\mu i}\right) \leq Q\left(\mathbf{C}_{\lambda i}\right), \\
p_{\mu\lambda}(t) = 0, \quad &\text{s.t. } Q\left(\mathbf{C}_{\mu i}\right) > Q\left(\mathbf{C}_{\lambda i}\right).
\end{aligned}
\tag{31}
$$

Obviously, $P \geq 0$ and $\exists t$ that makes $P^t > 0$. Thus P is a is regular matrix.

Lemma 10. *The Markov chain derived from MQICA is ergodic.*

Proof. Lemma 9 indicates that the state transition matrix P for MQICA is regular, and because the Markov cycle is 1, based on the basic Markov limit theorem, a unique limit $\lim_{t \to \infty} P^t = P^*$ must exist. Because $P^* > 0$, so the homogeneous Markov chain is nonzero and recurrent, thus any state in this chain would have an only limit distribution with a probability that is greater than zero regardless of how the population is initialized. As a result, MQICA can start from state i to state j within limited time; that is, when $t \to \infty$, this Markov chain could traverse the whole state space.

Lemma 11. *MQICA converges to the global optimal solution on a probability of 1.*

Proof. MQICA adopts a so-called survival of the fittest strategy, which means that the channel affinities of this Markov sequence, generated by the evolution, are monotone and will not decrease. $\Lambda^* \subseteq \Omega^N$ represents the population containing the global optimal antibody $\mathbf{r}^*$. $\mathbf{C}^*$ denotes the global optimal channel selection scheme, while Q^* denotes the global optimal channel affinity. Since the evolution process would not degenerate, Λ^* is a closed set and will be always in an attractive state, which means that for all $i \in \Lambda^*$, $\sum_{j \in \Lambda^*} p_{ij} = 1$ always holds. So once the state of the population A_t is changed to Λ^*, there would be no chance for the population to enter other state.

Based on the basic Markov limit theorem, MQICA will definitely reach state Λ^* after limited steps t_c if only the state transition matrix P is regular and the corresponding Markov chain is ergodic, which have been proved by Lemmas 9 and 10. Thus, the following equation is satisfied:

$$
\lim_{t \to \infty} P\left(Q(t) = Q_{t_c} = Q^*\right) = 1.
\tag{32}
$$

TABLE 2: Parameters setting.

N	p_m	p_c	N_c	χ	ε	t_{max}
10	0.5	0.88	15	3	10^{-5}	1000

This indicates that MQICA converges to the global optimal solution on a probability of 1.

6. Experiment Results

6.1. Simulations. In this paper, we conduct extensive experiments to validate the effectiveness of the algorithm. The program is run on a PC with Intel(R) Core(TM)2 CPU @2.40 GHz, 2 GB memory. The software platform is Windows XP. Table 2 lists the parameters of MQICA.

N is the population scales. Large N can promote the searching ability of the algorithm, meanwhile extend the running time of program. The other parameters are all set as the experiential value for MQICA applications, and the experiments result also shows the validity in this case.

From Section 5 we have known the validity of the proposed algorithm, MQICA, in solving multichannel allocation problems. Now a mass of experiment results also elaborate the effectiveness in another way. Firstly, we tentatively do three different experiments 5 times, respectively, according to the size. For small scale, $m = 3$, $k = 2$, $n = 25$; for medium scale, $m = 12$, $k = 6$, $n = 200$; for large scale, $m = 12$, $k = 9$, $n = 1000$. The experiment results are shown in Figures 3(a), 3(b), and 3(c). As can be seen from the graph, no matter how initialization is, MQICA will eventually well converge to the same optimal solution.

Secondly, in order to validate the correctness of the algorithm and eliminate the possibility of local optimal solution, we take traversal method for the small scale monitoring network. Ergodic results are shown as follows: 1.1, 1.1, 0.8, 0.767, 1.15, 1.15, 0.767, and 0.75. Obviously, MQICA can quickly find the optimal solution in small time. For medium and large scale, we both do the test fifty times. The results are expressed in Tables 3 and 4.

From Table 3, During 50-times experiment, we can see that initial channel scheme is random so the initial QoM value is not optimal. But after a certain number of iterations, the network monitoring quality has been converged to or close to the optimal value of 9.345. Similarly, Table 4 shows that the algorithm can still do a better performance for the distribution of channel options under lager networks.

Now we can easily conclude that MQICA will generate a good performance in channel allocation problems. It can be quickly uniform convergence to the optimal solution when the size of monitoring networks is small or moderate. If the scale is large; MQICA can also be better converged to the optimal or near optimal solution in most cases. These experimental results have proved the effectiveness of the proposed algorithm from various scales.

We also evaluate the performance of MQICA comparing three baseline algorithms.

TABLE 3: Result for medium scale.

ID	Q_0	Q^*	Times
1	2.439	9.345	473
2	2.536	9.345	431
3	6.304	9.345	487
4	9.003	9.345	375
5	8.604	9.345	510
6	6.966	9.345	457
7	7.444	9.171	218
8	8.046	9.345	324
9	8.667	9.345	321
10	8.856	9.345	78
11	8.871	9.345	310
12	2.122	9.345	454
13	7.164	9.345	356
14	2.439	9.345	409
15	6.304	9.345	326
16	2.536	9.345	245
17	8.667	9.345	265
18	4.350	9.345	351
19	9.345	9.345	0
20	2.122	9.345	456
21	7.164	9.345	328
22	8.604	9.345	91
23	9.003	9.345	103
24	5.438	9.345	501
25	2.536	9.171	365
26	5.473	9.345	141
27	3.180	9.345	265
28	2.439	9.345	454
29	8.992	9.345	263
30	8.646	9.003	453
31	3.857	9.345	261
32	2.122	9.345	356
33	7.444	9.345	452
34	2.597	9.345	365
35	2.122	9.345	532
36	8.367	9.345	269
37	6.304	9.345	462
38	7.146	9.345	254
39	8.171	9.345	56
40	3.200	9.345	495
41	9.003	9.345	321
42	5.251	9.345	256
43	3.062	9.345	518
44	6.304	9.345	265
45	6.996	9.345	348
46	8.046	9.345	206
47	2.536	9.345	527
48	9.345	9.345	0
49	7.164	9.345	215
50	8.171	9.345	256

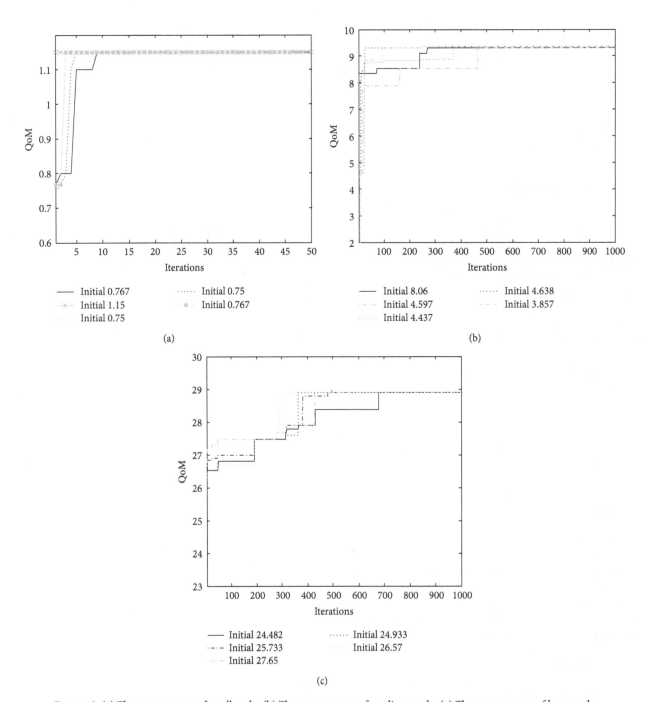

FIGURE 3: (a) The convergence of small scale. (b) The convergence of medium scale. (c) The convergence of large scale.

Greedy. Select channel for each sniffer to maximize the sum of transmission probability of its neighbor users.

Linear Programming (LP). Solve the integer programming problem from formula (4).

Gibbs Sampler. Sniffer computes the local energy of optional channels and their selection probability, then chooses one channel according to the probability.

We conducted four sets of experiments, and the number of optional channels is 2, 6, and 9, respectively. In each experiment, the four algorithms are compared in different aspects of performance. The algorithm program runs 30 times to get the average result for evaluation.

In the first set of experiment, 1000 users are distributed in $500 \times 500\,\text{m}^2$ square field as shown in Figure 4; transmission probability $p_u \in [0, 0.06]$. The field is partitioned in several regular hexagon units to construct cellular framework. Each unit center is equipped with a base station (BS) working on a certain channel and users in the unit work on the same channel as BS. Every two adjacent units are on different channels. For easy to control, 25 sniffers are deployed

TABLE 4: Results for large scale.

ID	Q_0	Q^*	Times
1	24.150	28.900	684
2	26.367	28.900	596
3	27.200	28.850	352
4	28.900	28.900	0
5	28.250	28.900	152
6	25.850	29.050	715
7	27.417	28.900	254
8	24.533	28.900	561
9	28.450	28.900	215
10	27.250	28.900	325
11	27.200	28.900	387
12	28.467	28.900	152
13	24.533	28.900	356
14	27.050	28.900	261
15	28.700	28.900	164
16	28.150	28.850	92
17	26.900	28.900	364
18	24.533	28.900	259
19	24.750	28.900	381
20	25.850	28.900	681
21	28.267	28.900	154
22	24.750	29.050	296
23	27.200	28.900	614
24	25.700	28.900	265
25	24.150	28.900	562
26	28.567	28.900	244
27	27.800	29.050	264
28	25.700	28.900	157
29	24.533	28.900	246
30	27.800	28.900	106
31	27.417	28.900	315
32	28.850	28.900	26
33	27.800	29.050	268
34	24.533	28.900	654
35	27.200	28.900	341
36	25.700	28.900	465
37	26.750	28.900	287
38	28.467	28.900	384
39	27.900	29.050	468
40	27.200	28.900	215
41	24.750	28.900	216
42	24.150	28.900	656
43	23.587	28.900	146
44	25.700	28.900	356
45	28.267	28.850	21
46	27.200	28.900	265
47	24.533	28.900	378
48	27.800	28.900	198
49	28.700	28.850	254
50	26.750	28.900	394

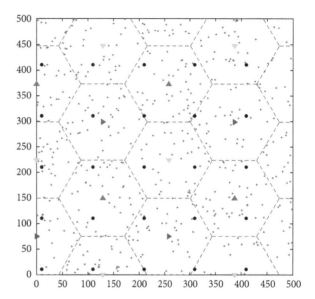

FIGURE 4: Wireless network topology Hexagonal layout with users (purple "+"), sniffers (solid dots), and base stations (isosceles triangles) of each cell (different color representing working on different channels).

uniformly in the field to form a network to monitor the communication activities of users in the field. Monitoring radius of sniffer is 120 meters and 3 optional channels (in IEEE 802.11.b/g WLAN, there are 3 orthogonal channels, the 1st, 6th, and 11th, with center frequency 2412 MHz, 2437 MHz, and 2462 MHz). MQICA, LP, Greedy, and Gibbs Sampler are applied separately to solve the optimal channel selection scheme for sniffers. The quality of solution (QoM) of the four algorithms is shown in Figure 5.

As depicted in Figure 5, after 700 iterations, the proposed MQICA algorithm converges to the extremely optimal solution (QoM = 28.975). LP algorithm takes the second place with QoM up to 28.105, while Gibbs Sampler and Greedy algorithm achieve the QoM of 27.048 and 23.893, respectively. It is shown that the Multiple Quantum Immune Clone Algorithm improves the convergence rate of other algorithm effectively and produces a better global searching ability.

Table 5 demonstrates the statistical results of the three sets of experiments. Among the four algorithms, MQICA and Gibbs Sampler both run 20 times in each set of experiments to get the average optimal solution and its QoM value. As deterministic methods, LP and Greedy just run once. From Table 5, we can see that MQICA outperforms LP in three sets of experiments and evidently better than Gibbs Sampler and Greedy. Furthermore, MQICA converges fast, with shorter running time than Gibbs Sample.

6.2. Practical Network Experiment. In this section, we evaluate the proposed MQICA algorithm by practical network experiment based on campus wireless network (IEEE 802.11.b WLAN). 21 WiFi sniffers were deployed in a building to collect the user information from 1 pm to 6 pm (over 5 hours).

TABLE 5: Statistical results of three sets of experiments.

Experiment no.	MQICA		Gibbs sampler		LP		Greedy	
	Average optimal QoM	Running time/s (1000 iter.)	Average optimal QoM	Running time/s (1000 iter.)	QoM	Running time/s (1 iter.)	QoM	Running time/s (1 iter.)
1 (2 channels)	27.338	10.616	26.052	28.938	27.105	0.562	22.872	0.093
2 (6 channels)	26.760	11.695	26.261	30.953	26.484	0.812	23.363	0.109
3 (9 channels)	26.263	11.759	26.140	35.031	26.088	0.934	23.481	0.119

TABLE 6: Parameters setting.

Active probability	0~0.01	0.01~0.02	0.02~0.04
Number of users	578	15	29

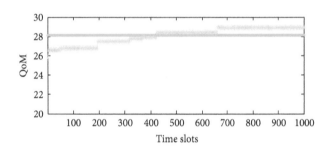

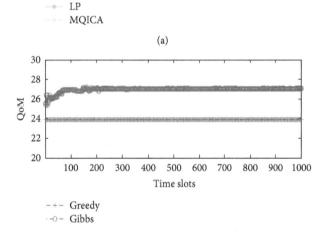

(a)

(b)

FIGURE 5: Performance comparison of the four algorithms in the first set of experiments (3 optional channels).

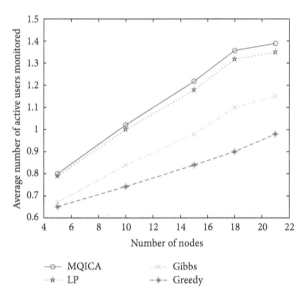

FIGURE 6: QoM of campus wireless network with different number of sniffers.

monitored active users) is growing up with the increment of sniffers (from 5 to 21). Except the experiment with 21 sniffers, the other sets of experiments were conducted repeatedly with different sniffers selected randomly from the 21 sniffers, and the statistical average value of QoM was recorded and shown in Figure 6. Since the average activity probability is 0.0026, the largest number of active users is less than 1.7 during every time slot. By comparing with LP, Gibbs Sampler, and Greedy, the proposed MQICA exhibits its superiority and feasibility in the practical network environment.

7. Conclusion

In this paper, we investigate the channel allocation for sniffers to maximize the Quality of Monitoring (QoM) for wireless monitoring networks, which is proved to be NP-hard. A Multiple-Quantum-Immune-Clone-based channel selection algorithm (MQICA) is put forward to solve the problem. By theoretical proof and extensive experiments, we demonstrate that MQICA can solve the channel allocation problem effectively, and outperform related algorithms evidently with fast convergence. As an ongoing work, we are reducing the computation complexity and proving the convergence performance of algorithm in theory.

Each sniffer captured approximately 320,000 MAC frames. Totally 622 users were monitored working on 3 orthogonal channels. The number of users in 1st, 2nd, and 3rd channels is 349, 118, and 155, respectively. The activity probabilities (active probability of a user is computed as the percentage of the user's active time in a unit time.) of these users were recorded in Table 6. It is shown that the activity probabilities of most users are less than 1%. The average activity probability is 0.0026.

Figure 6 depicted the QoM of network with different number of sniffers. It is clear that the QoM (the number of

Acknowledgments

This work is funded by the National Science Foundation of USA (CNS-0832089), the National Natural Science Fund of China (61100211 and 61003307), and the Postdoctoral Science Foundation of China (20110490084 and 2012T50569).

References

[1] J. Zander, S. L. Kim, and M. Almgren, *Radio Resource Management for Wireless Networks*, Artech House, Norwood, Mass, USA, 2001.

[2] L. M. Correia, D. Zeller, O. Blume et al., "Challenges and enabling technologies for energy aware mobile radio networks," *IEEE Communications Magazine*, vol. 48, no. 11, pp. 66–72, 2010.

[3] Y. Liu, K. Liu, and M. Li, "Passive diagnosis for wireless sensor networks," *IEEE/ACM Transactions on Networking*, vol. 18, no. 4, pp. 1132–1144, 2010.

[4] J. Yeo, M. Youssef, and A. Agrawala, "A framework for wireless LAN monitoring and its applications," in *Proceedings of the 3rd ACM Workshop on Wireless Security (WiSe '04)*, pp. 70–79, ACM, New York, NY, USA, October 2004.

[5] J. Yeo, M. Youssef, T. Henderson, and A. Agrawala, "An accurate technique for measuring the wireless side of wireless networks," in *Proceeding of the Workshop on Wireless Traffic Measurements and Modeling (WiTMeMo '05)*, pp. 13–18, USENIX Association, Berkeley, Calif, USA, 2005.

[6] M. Rodrig, C. Reis, R. Mahajan, D. Wetherall, and J. Zahorjan, "Measurement-based characterization of 802.11 in a hotspot setting," in *Proceedings of the ACM SIGCOMM Workshop on Experimental Approaches to Wireless Network Design and Analysis*, pp. 5–10, New York, NY, USA, August 2005.

[7] Y. C. Cheng, J. Bellardo, P. Benkö, A. C. Snoeren, G. M. Voelker, and S. Savage, "Solving the puzzle of enterprise 802.11 analysis," in *Proceedings of the Conference on Applications, Technologies, Architectures, and Protocols for Computer Communications (SIGCOMM '06)*, pp. 39–50, ACM, New York, NY, USA, 2006.

[8] W. G. Yang, T. D. Guo, and T. Zhao, "Optimal lifetime model and it's solution of a heterogeneous surveillance sensor network," *Chinese Journal of Computers*, vol. 30, no. 4, pp. 532–538, 2007.

[9] C. Liu and G. Cao, "Distributed monitoring and aggregation in wireless sensor networks," in *Proceedings of the 29th Conference on Information Communications (INFOCOM '10)*, pp. 1–9, IEEE Press, Piscataway, NJ, USA, 2010.

[10] J. Jin, B. Zhao, and H. Zhou, "DLDCA: a distributed link-weighted and distance-constrained channel assignment for single-radio multi-channel wireless mesh networks," in *Proceedings of the International Conference on Wireless Communications and Signal Processing (WCSP '09)*, pp. 1–5, Nanjing, China, November 2009.

[11] C. E. A. Campbell, K. K. Loo, and R. Comley, "A new MAC solution for multi-channel single radio in wireless sensor networks," in *Proceedings of the 7th International Symposium on Wireless Communication Systems (ISWCS '10)*, pp. 907–911, York, UK, September 2010.

[12] Z. Zhang and X. Yu, "A simple single radio multi-channel protocol for wireless mesh networks," in *Proceedings of the 2nd International Conference on Future Computer and Communication (ICFCC '10)*, pp. V3-441–V3-445, Wuhan, China, May 2010.

[13] D. H. Shin and S. Bagchi, "Optimal monitoring in multi-channel multi-radio wireless mesh networks," in *Proceedings of the 10th ACM International Symposium on Mobile Ad Hoc Networking and Computing (MobiHoc '09)*, pp. 229–238, MobiHoc, New Orleans, La, USA, May 2009.

[14] B. J. Kim and K. K. Leung, "Frequency assignment for IEEE 802.11 wireless networks," in *Proceedings of the 58th IEEE Vehicular Technology Conference (VTC '03)*, pp. 1422–1426, Orlando, Fla, USA, October 2003.

[15] C. Chekuri and A. Kumar, "Maximum coverage problem with group budget constraints and applications," in *Proceedings of the International Workshop on Approximation Algorithms for Combinatorial Optimization Problems*, pp. 72–83, APPROX, Cambridge, Mass, USA, 2004.

[16] A. Chhetri, H. Nguyen, G. Scalosub, and R. Zheng, "On quality of monitoring for multi-channel wireless infrastructure networks," in *Proceedings of the 11th ACM International Symposium on Mobile Ad Hoc Networking and Computing (MobiHoc '10)*, pp. 111–120, MobiHoc, Chicago, Ill, USA, September 2010.

[17] P. Arora, N. Xia, and R. Zheng, "A gibbs sampler approach for optimal distributed monitoring of multi-channel wireless networks," in *Proceedings of IEEE GLOBECOM*, pp. 1–6, IEEE Communication Society Press, 2011.

[18] I. Wormsbecker and C. Williamson, "On channel selection strategies for multi-channel MAC protocols in wireless ad hoc networks," in *Proceedings of the IEEE International Conference on Wireless and Mobile Computing, Networking and Communications (WiMob '06)*, pp. 212–220, IEEE Computer Society, Washington, DC, USA, June 2006.

[19] C. N. Kanthi and B. N. Jain, "Spanner based distributed channel assignment in wireless mesh networks," in *Proceedings of the 2nd International Conference on Communication System Software and Middleware and Workshops (COMSWARE '07)*, pp. 1–10, COMSWARE, Bangalore, India, January 2007.

[20] L. You, P. Wu, M. Song, J. Song, and Y. Zhang, "Dynamic control and resource allocation in wireless-infrastructured distributed cellular networks with OFDMA," in *Proceedings of the 38th International Conference on Parallel Processing Workshops (ICPPW '09)*, pp. 337–343, Vienna, Austria, September 2009.

[21] F. Hou and J. Huang, "Dynamic channel selection in cognitive radio network with channel heterogeneity," in *Proceedings of the 53rd IEEE Global Communications Conference (GLOBECOM '10)*, pp. 6–12, Miami, Fla, USA, December 2010.

[22] Z. G. Du, P. L. Hong, W. Y. Zhou, and K. P. Xue, "ICCA: Interface-clustered channel assignment in multi-radio wireless mesh networks," *Chinese Journal of Electronics*, vol. 39, no. 3, pp. 723–726, 2011.

[23] L. Jiao and Y. Li, "Quantum-inspired immune clonal optimization," in *Proceedings of the International Conference on Neural Networks and Brain Proceedings (ICNNB '05)*, pp. 461–466, Beijing, China, October 2005.

[24] Y. Y. Li and L. C. Jiao, "Quantum-inspired immune clonal algorithm for SAT problem," *Chinese Journal of Computers*, vol. 30, no. 2, pp. 176–183, 2007.

[25] K. A. de Jong, *An analysis of the behavior of a class of genetic adaptive systems [Ph.D. thesis]*, University of Michigan, 1975.

[26] Y. Yu and C. Z. Hou, "A clonal selection algorithm by using learning operator," in *Proceedings of International Conference on Machine Learning and Cybernetics*, pp. 2924–2929, August 2004.

[27] X. Z. Wang and S. Y. Yu, "Improved evolution strategies for high-dimensional optimization," *Control Theory and Applications*, vol. 23, no. 1, pp. 148–151, 2006.

[28] A. Narayanan and M. Moore, "Quantum-inspired genetic algo-
rithms," in *Proceedings of the IEEE International Conference on
Evolutionary Computation (ICEC '96)*, pp. 61–66, Nogaya, Japan,
May 1996.

[29] W. X. Zhang and Y. Liang, *The Mathematical Basis of Genetic
Algorithm*, Press of Xi'an Jiaotong University, 2000.

10

A Data Transmission Scheme Based on Time-Evolving Meeting Probability for Opportunistic Social Network

Fu Xiao,[1,2,3] **Guoxia Sun,**[1] **Jia Xu,**[1,2,3] **Lingyun Jiang,**[1,2,3] **and Ruchuan Wang**[1,2,3]

[1] *College of Computer, Nanjing University of Posts and Telecommunications, Nanjing, Jiangsu 210003, China*
[2] *Jiangsu High Technology Research Key Laboratory for Wireless Sensor Networks, Nanjing, Jiangsu 210003, China*
[3] *Key Lab of Broadband Wireless Communication and Sensor Network Technology (Nanjing University of Posts and Telecommunications), Ministry of Education Jiangsu Province, Nanjing, Jiangsu 210003, China*

Correspondence should be addressed to Fu Xiao; xiaof@njupt.edu.cn

Academic Editor: Shukui Zhang

With its widespread application prospects, opportunistic social network attracts more and more attention. Efficient data transmission strategy is one of the most important issues to ensure its applications. As is well known, most of nodes in opportunistic social network are human-carried devices, so encounters between nodes are predictable when considering the law of human activities. To the best of our knowledge, existing data transmission solutions are less accurate in the prediction of node encounters due to their lack of consideration of the dynamism of users' behavior. To address this problem, a novel data transmission solution, based on time-evolving meeting probability for opportunistic social network, called TEMP is introduced, and corresponding copy management strategy is given to reduce the message redundancy. Simulation results based on real human traces show that TEMP achieves a good compromise in terms of delivery probability and overhead ratio.

1. Introduction

Driven by the emergence and application of large number of mobile devices, which are characterized with low-cost, powerful, and short-range communication capabilities, wireless ad hoc network has acquired rapid development. With further research, people started to pay attention to the mobile ad hoc networks, especially those whose communication equipments are deployed on the moving object, such as wildlife tracking network [1], vehicle network [2], and pocket switched network [3]. Traditional communication mode is no longer applicable in these practical application scenarios, due to the regular disruption caused by the sparse deployment, quick movement, and strict constraint both on storage and energy of nodes. Opportunistic network [4], which achieves data transmission via node mobility, appeared in such a situation. As a more natural ad hoc network style, opportunistic network transfers messages through a storage-carry-forward hop-by-hope strategy.

To achieve reliable data transmission for opportunistic network, multicopy technique is usually adopted when the real-time path cannot be guaranteed, for instance, EPIDEMIC [5] and PROPHET [6]; in other words, there are multiple copies of the same message in the network. This will cause data redundancy which affects the network performance. Therefore, efficient data transmission strategy requires effective copy management strategy. In a typical opportunistic network, nodes move randomly and quickly; nevertheless, for opportunistic social network, the mobility of nodes is controlled by human social activities, and the encounters between nodes are more stable and regular, so we can use the history activities of nodes to predict the encounter of nodes in the future in opportunistic network as paper [7] elaborated.

Combined with the characteristic of the opportunistic network as well as the need of copy management, a data transmission based on node time-evolving meet probability which consists of message forwarding and management is proposed in this paper. Message forwarding is divided into three steps: find the periodic neighbor of the destination node, find the appropriate time slot for forwarding, and forward the message to the node which has higher meet probability with the destination in the right slot. There are two cases for the message management: multicopy strategy is adopted to establish quick contact with the destination in the first step of message forwarding, and for the last two steps message is forwarded in a single copy way to reduce network overhead.

The rest of this paper is structured as follows. Section 1 briefly analyses the related work and our work is elaborated in Section 2. Section 3 presents the simulation and the evaluation and future work of this paper is presented in Section 4.

2. Related Works

A variety of data transmission strategies for opportunistic social network communication is proposed. LABLE [8] proposed by Hui and Crowcroft is the earliest work; the authors think that nodes that belong to the same community have higher encounter opportunity, and they assume that each node has a label to identify their communities; the message is forwarded to the destination directly or by the relay nodes that belong to the same community with the destination. It is inefficient unless the source node can be met directly with the node that is in the same community with destination node. On the basis of LABLE, a community-based data transmission strategy, called Bubble Rap, is proposed in paper [3]. Bubble Rap relied on community and centrality; each node has a local centrality that describes the popularity of the node with its local community and a global centrality across the whole network; it first bubbles the message up based on the global centrality, until the message reaches a node which is in the same local community as destination. The related community detection algorithms, SIMPLE, k-CLIQUE, and MODULARITY are given in paper [9]. Node similarity is defined in [10] to describe the neighborhood relationship between nodes, according to the history of node encounter. Based on the neighborhood relationship, a distributed community detection algorithm is given, as well as a community-based epidemic forwarding. Based on the literature [10], a new social pressure metric (SPM) is introduced in [11] to accurately detect the quality of friendship; this approach considers both direct friendship and indirect friendship to construct its community. It can help to make smarter decisions. Nevertheless, the calculation of metric needs the whole contact information which may be unrealistic for opportunistic network.

All the above work is community-based data transmission strategy. It generates considerable network traffic for community information maintenance overhead. Moreover, most community detection algorithm may lead to the formation of monotonically increasing cluster due to lack of time information; that is, more and more nodes are added to the community with time elapsed, but the outdated nodes cannot be removed from the community timely. On the other hand, community detection takes a long time and brings a "slow start" problem to the network. In summary, community-based data transmission strategy makes good use of community feature of opportunistic social network, but it requires

an efficient community detecting algorithm to improve the performance.

At the same time, researchers also proposed a series of data transmission strategy based on node meeting opportunity predicting. PROPHET is a kind of multicopy transmission strategy that can be applied to the opportunistic social network. In the protocol, each node maintains its own transmission probability to the destination and message is forwarded to the node which has a greater meet probability with destination when two nodes meet. There is a "lag" problem when forecasting the encounter probability; furthermore, the excessive copy of the message causes larger overhead. A novel strategy based on node sociability is given in [12]; the key idea is that of assigning to each node a time-varying scalar parameter which captures its social behavior in terms of frequency and types of encounters, and then node forwards message only to the most social nodes. In [13] Mei et al. found that people with similar interests tend to meet more often and then proposed SANE, a social-aware and stateless routing for opportunistic social network; the interest profile of an individual is represented as a k-dimensional vector. The cosine similarity is defined to express the interest similarity between two nodes; a message should be forward to nodes whose interest similar to destination. PeopleRank [14] ranks the node according to the node importance using a similar algorithm as PageRank; node forwards message to destination or a more important node. The author of dLife [15] believes that opportunistic social network should consider the dynamism of users' behavior resulting from their daily routines; each node has two functions: TECD that captures the evolution of social interaction among pairs of users in the same daily period of time over consecutive days; and TECDi that captures the node's importance. The message is forwarded to the encounter if its TECD to destination is bigger than that of the carrier, or its TECDi is higher than that of the carrier when the relationship to destination is unknown. And the literature [16] explored how much delay has to be tolerated for the message delivery from the source to the destination.

3. The TEMP Strategy

3.1. Problem Description. In a typical opportunistic network, node mobiles follow the same pattern (such as random model), so nodes are very similar in terms of data transfer. However, nodes in opportunistic network are mainly human-carried devices whose mobility is controlled by people; therefore, node mobility is distinct, but their encounter is more regular and stable. As described in [15], nodes have different encounter relationship with different nodes at different time periods of the same cycle because of its daily routines. As shown in Figure 1, A has 5 directly meeting nodes, B, C, D, E, and F, if two nodes meet each other in the related time slot, there is a line between them, and the number of encounters is represented by value w on the line. In summary, nodes have similar encounter relation within the same time slot in different cycles but different encounter relation at different time frames of the same cycle; these features should be considered when designing data transmission strategy.

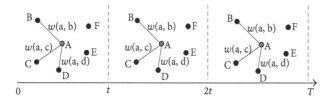

FIGURE 1: The contact information of A at different time slots within the same cycle.

M(B, C)   M(A, B) M(A, C)   M(B, C)

t1   t2   t3   t4

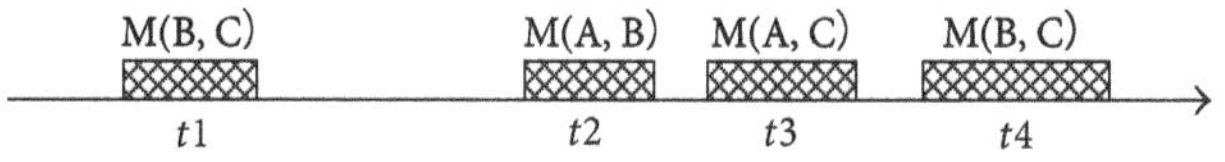

FIGURE 2: A common scenario of node contact for illustration of the lag problem.

FIGURE 3: Sketch for illustrating the problem of dLife.

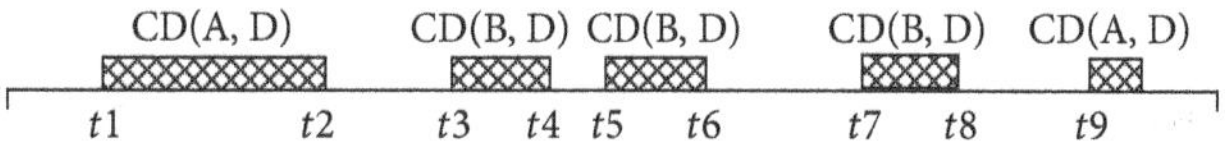

CD(A, D)   CD(B, D) CD(B, D)   CD(B, D) CD(A, D)

t1   t2   t3 t4 t5 t6   t7 t8 t9

FIGURE 4: Sketch for elaborating node's contact information.

Next, we will first analyze the deficiencies of the existing typical solutions and then present our solution, TEMP forwarding strategy.

3.2. Problem Analysis of Existing Solutions.
PROPHET may be first thought of when we try to reflect node time-varying meet probability; in PROPHET the update method mainly includes the increase and decay in the probability. The probability increases according to formula (1) when A meets B and decays in time as formula (2):

$$P_{(A,B)} = P_{(A,B)old} + (1 - P_{(A,B)old}) \times P_{init}, \quad (1)$$

$$P_{(A,B)} = P_{(A,B)old} \times \gamma^k. \quad (2)$$

There is a reaction lag problem in this update method for the prediction of node meeting probability. Consider a common situation shown in Figure 2, at time $t3$; for node B and C, their meet probability decays to a small value after $t3 - t1$, but the probability of A and B increases recently because they meet a while back, then there is $P(A, B) > P(C, B)$ according to PROPHET. Therefore when node A and C encounter at $t3$, C forwards the message, whose destination is B, to A. However we find that it is node C meets node B instead of A in the near future. The message is forwarded toward an incorrect direction just because of the lag problem.

To describe the dynamic probability of contact between nodes, dLife uses TECD and TECDi, two time-varying parameters. First it acquired the average contact length of nodes for each time slot; then for a certain time slot, the meeting probability of two nodes is calculated by the weighted average contact length, with each weighed by a certain coefficient. The main problem of dLife is shown in Figure 3; according to dLife we have TECD(A, D) > TECD(A, C) when C meets D in the first sample slot, so if C has message destination for A, dLife will forward the message to D; however, later we will find that C has more opportunity to meet A in the rest of time slot, so message should be still carried by C. For opportunistic social network, the contact number of nodes is limited, and the more often nodes met before, the less chance they will meet in the future for a certain time slot. Note that, this is different with different cycles; it

is universally thought that nodes have chance to meet each other, if they met often in the previous cycles.

3.3. Our Solutions.
The research results in [7] show that nodes encounter each other with periodic regularity, and node's contact information of last cycle can be used to predict node's meet probability for the next cycle. At the same time dLife pointed out that nodes have different contact relationships for different time slots within the same cycle. Based on the above facts, we make the following assumptions: nodes have varying encounter relationships during different time slots of the same cycle, but for the same time slot in different cycles, node's encounter is relatively stable.

3.3.1. Node's Encounter Probability at Time t within Slot i.
First, if the encounter interval of any two nodes is available, the time length between t and the time that node meets destination is acquired; the shorter the length is, the more suitable the node is chosen as the relay node, so we can use formula (3) to represent the meeting probability:

$$P(t)_{(A,B)m} \propto \frac{1}{(d_{(A,B)m} - (t - t_{(A,B)m-1}))} \quad (3)$$

t is the current time, $t_{(A,B)m-1}$ represents the number $m - 1$ meeting time of A and B, and the time interval between number $m - 1$ and number m meeting time of node A and B is $d_{(A,B)m}$. But it is unrealistic to predict the exact time that any two nodes meet at an opportunistic network, even if the information can be obtained; it needs high storage overhead to store this information. Next we will give an approximate solution which is computational and has low storage cost.

We can obtain the contact duration of any two nodes in an arbitrary time slot according to the history information. For a specific time slot i, the contact duration of A and B is relatively stable, which is used to estimate the meet probability by dLife. To make a better prediction, the number and sequence of node's encounter also should be considered. For example, as shown in Figure 4, the shadow rectangles represent the contact duration, the total contact duration of A and B is TCD(A, B), and then we have TCD(A, D) > TCD(B, D). However, for the probability of node's encounter, we should have $P(A, D) > P(B, D)$ before time $t1$, $P(B, D) > P(A, D)$ during $t2$ to $t3$ and $P(A, D) > P(B, D)$ between $t8$ and $t9$.

Based on the above analysis, the method of calculation of node's encounter probability at any time t within the slot i is given as formula (4)

$$P_i(t)_{(A,B)} \propto \left(\text{TCD}(A, B)_i - \text{CD}(t)_{(A,B)}\right) \qquad (4)$$

$\text{CD}(t)_{(A,B)}$ is the contact duration of A and B before time t within slot i, and their total contact duration in slot i is $\text{TCD}(A,B)_i$; take the deviation into consideration; if $\text{CD}(t)_{(A,B)} > \text{TCD}(A,B)_i$, $P_i(t)_{(A,B)}$ is set 0. $\text{TCD}(A,B)_i$ is calculated based on the average contact duration in slot i of history cycles, as formula (5), j is the number of historical cycles, and $\text{CD}(A, B)$ represents the contact duration of A and B in slot i of cycle k as follows:

$$\text{TCD}(A, B)_i = \frac{\sum_{k=1}^{j} \text{CD}(A, B)_{k,i}}{\sum_{k=1}^{j} k}. \qquad (5)$$

3.3.2. Message Forwarding Strategy. TEMP divides a node's active cycle into multiple sampling slots according to node's day-to-day itinerary form. Each node maintains its own contact information of each slot. If two nodes can meet directly, they are neighbor node for each other. A's neighbor node set in slot i is $N_i(A)$, and the total neighbor of A in the entire cycle is $N(A) = \cup N_i(A)$. TEMP forwarding strategy mainly comprises three stages: (1) find the periodic neighbor of the destination node; (2) find the appropriate time slot for forwarding; (3) forward the message to the node which has higher meet probability with the destination in the right slot. Next we will explain the three stages in detail.

(1) Find the periodic neighbor of the destination node.

If the destination node of message does not belong to the neighbor set of the message carrier, the message needs to be forwarded to nodes which have neighbor relationship with the destination as soon as possible. That is, the message carrier node A meets with B, if B satisfies the condition:

$$\frac{(|N(B) \setminus N(A)|)}{|N(B)|} \geq \lambda. \qquad (6)$$

A forwards the message to B, λ is an adjustable parameter, and it is set to 1 in order to reduce the message redundancy in this paper). Messages are forwarded by this way until they reach a node that has neighbor relationship with the destination. Then the message forwarding moves into the second stage.

(2) Find the appropriate time slot for forwarding.

The main purpose of this stage is to find the most recent time slot that the message can be delivered. We define the distance between slot i and j as $\text{dis}(i, j)$, which is calculated according to formula (7) as follows:

$$\text{dis}(i, j) = \begin{cases} j - i & j \geq i \\ j + S - i & j < i \end{cases} \qquad (7)$$

S is the number of the time slot in a cycle. Note that, $\text{dis}(i, j)$ is different from $\text{dis}(j, i)$. Assume the destination of message is D. After the previous stage, the message's current carrier A must have neighbor relationship with D; that is, D belongs to

A's neighbor collection of a certain time slot i, $D \in N_i(A)$. when A meets with B at slot k, if there exist $D \in N_i(B)$ and $\text{dis}(k, i) > \text{dis}(k, j)$, A forwards the message to B. And so it goes on, until the most recent delivery time slot arrives. Then message forwarding goes to step 3.

(3) Forward the message to the node which has higher meet probability with the destination in the right slot.

Message forwarding reaches this stage; it means that the message current carrier can meet with the message's destination D at the current slot i. So if the message's carrier A meets B at time t, if the condition $P_i(t)_{(B,D)} > P_i(t)_{(A,D)}$ is met, A forwards the message to B.

3.3.3. Copy Management. Copy management aims to reduce the message redundancy and the network load. Copy management includes the following two aspects.

(1) In the message diffusion stage, namely, the first step of the forwarding policy, the destination's information is unavailable. In this condition, the message is forwarded based on multicopy strategy; that is, the message carrier still save a copy of the message after it forwards the message to another node. The goal here is to establish contact with destination as soon as possible by the multicopy strategy.

(2) In the last two steps of message forwarding, message carrier has established contact with the destination, so the message is forwarded in a single copy way. The carrier deletes the message once it forwards the message to an appropriate node to reduce the redundancy.

4. Simulation and Evaluation

4.1. Simulation Settings. We develop the TEMP on the DTN simulation platform, ONE1.4.1 [17], developed by the Helsinki University, and also give the performance evolution based on the simulation results. The experimental scenario is based on real human movement trajectory data sets, Cambridge Traces [18]. In order to evaluate the performance of each algorithm, we generate 5000 messages in advance using createCreates.pl, a Perl script of ONE. The source and destination of message are randomly selected, and the message size is evenly distributed between 10 KB and 100 KB. Table 1 shows the main parameters of the simulation.

To evaluate the performance of TEMP, we will compare it to dLife and PROPHET in terms of delivery rate, overhead ratio, and network delay and discuss the results.

4.2. Effect of TTL. In this experiment message buffer size is set to 2 MB. In Figure 5, we can see that the delivery ratio of each protocol develops with the increasing of TTL. dLife and PROPHET achieve high delivery ratio when TTL is less than 1 day, but once the TTL is greater than 1 day, the delivery ratio of TEMP improves significantly and eventually much higher than the other two protocols. In the implementation of TEMP, node's activity cycle is set to 1 day, so when the message TTL is less than 1 day, the performance of TEMP is poor. At the same time, we note that while node's activity cycle in dLife is

TABLE 1: Default parameter value.

Parameter	Value
Simulation time	990000 s
Update interval	60 s
Number of messages	5000
Message size	10 kB–100 kB
Message TTL	2 day
Buffer size	2 MB
Transmit speed	11 Mbps
ProphetRouter.secondsInTimeUnit	10 s
ProphetRouter.p_init	0.75
ProphetRouter.beta	0.25
ProphetRouter.gamma	0.98
Dlife.numberofslot	24
λ	1

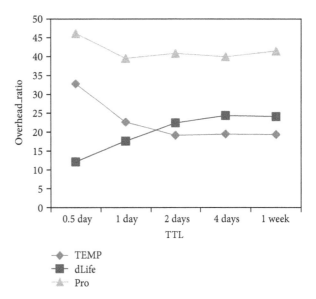

FIGURE 6: Overhead ratios under varying TTL.

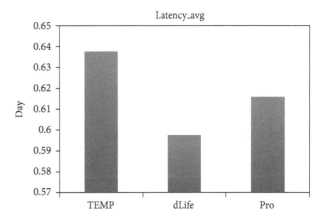

FIGURE 7: Average network delays.

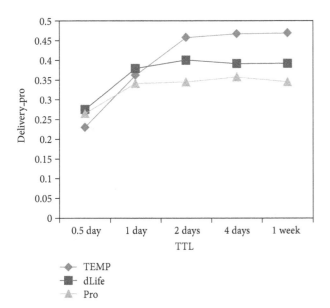

FIGURE 5: Delivery ratios under varying TTL.

also set to 1 day, it achieves better performance than TEMP when message TTL is less than 1 day. The reason is that dLife uses the weighted sum of node's contact duration of every slot to calculate TECD and TECDi, and the coefficient of each slot is very close to each other which makes dLife more likely to use the total contact duration to predict node's encounter probability. In a word, it makes little sense to divide the slot for dLife.

The definition of overhead ratio in Figure 6 adopts ONE's default value; that is, overhead_ratio = (relayed-delivered)/delivered. Figure 6 shows that compared with ROPHET TEMP and dLife can reduce the overhead ratio significantly. When message TTL is less than about 1 day, the message forwarding mainly uses multicopy strategy for TEMP, so the overhead ratio of TEMP is much higher than dLife, but it decreases with the addition of message TTL and remains stable finally.

We also observed the delay of each protocol when the TTL changes. In the experiments, we found that when the TTL increases, the delay of each protocol changes slightly. So we use the average of network delay in different TTL settings for evaluation and plot them in Figure 7. We find that even though the average delay of TEMP is higher than that of dLife and PROPHET, the difference among them is less than 0.04 day (about an hour) which is acceptable in opportunistic network.

4.3. Effect of Buffer Size. We studied the effect of buffer size on the performance in this part; TTL value is set to 2 days. The results of the experiment are showed in Figures 8–13.

The plot shows that TEMP outperforms all the other forwarding schemes on delivery ratio. In normal conditions, the usage of multicopy strategy can improve message delivery ratio. However, network resources, such as storage, energy, are limited in opportunistic social network; a large number of message copies bring huge resource consumption which will reduce network performance and bring high overhead

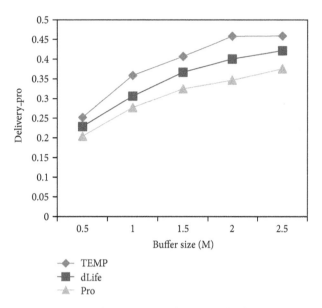

FIGURE 8: Delivery ratios under varying buffer sizes.

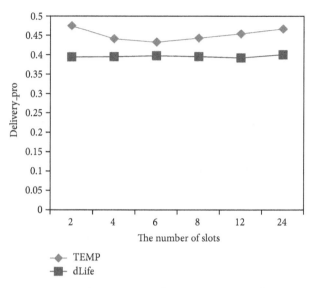

FIGURE 11: Delivery ratios under varying number of slots.

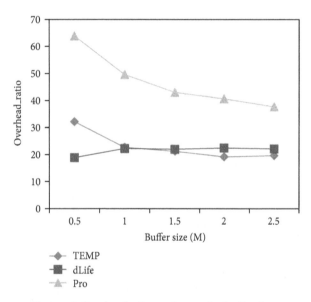

FIGURE 9: Overhead ratios under varying buffer sizes.

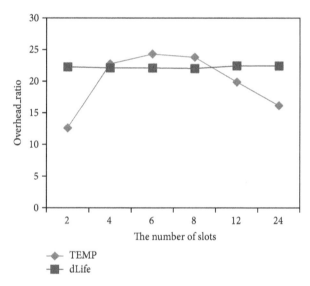

FIGURE 12: Overhead ratios under varying number of slots.

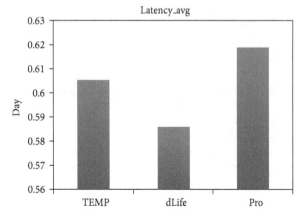

FIGURE 10: Average network delays.

ratio as is shown in Figure 9; therefore, the delivery ratio of dLife and PROPHET is poor. Moreover, the "lag problem" of PROPHET further decreases the delivery ratio.

Figure 10 shows the average delay of the three forwarding schemes under different buffer sizes. dLife takes node's global importance into consideration and uses TECDi (similar to PageRank algorithm) to make message forwarding decision, so it achieves the best performance on delay. Note again, the calculation of a node's importance metric TECDi relied on the prior obtaining of its neighbor's importance which is very complex. TEMP only uses node's local information and avoids this disadvantage. Overall, the difference of delay, less than 0.03 day (about 0.72 hour), among them is very slightly for opportunistic social network with delay tolerance capacity.

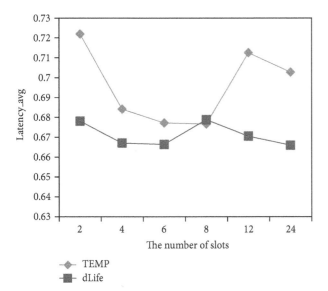

FIGURE 13: Average delays under varying number of slots.

4.4. Analysis of Time Slot Division. In paper [15], the author pointed out that dLife achieved the best performance when the cycle was divided into 24 time slots. In all experiments above, we used 24 time slots in the implementation of dLife. But for TEMP, we adopt 4 time slots, it should be noted that this division is not optimal for TEMP, and we adopted 4 time slots because we take the two main periods, namely, 6:00 am–12:00am and 12:00 pm–18:00 pm, of human activities into consideration. In fact, the division of time cycle should be based on a large number of observations, but in this paper we divided the time cycle into multiple slots of equal length for convenience. In the following parts, we talk about the effect of time slot division on TEMP and dLife.

The curves in Figure 11 show that the delivery ratio performance of TEMP is always higher than that of dLife under different time cycle divisions. From all the three figures above, that is, Figures 11, 12, and 13, we can find that the performance of dLife changes slightly. This further proves that it makes little sense for dLife to divide time slot although its original intention is to reflect node's different encounter relationship by dividing time slot. Compared to dLife, TEMP is more sensitive to slot division which makes it more suitable for opportunistic social network that node's activities are obviously different during different time slots.

5. Conclusion and Future Work

In this paper, we propose a data transmission strategy, called TEMP, for opportunistic social network. It consists of message forwarding and copy management strategy. Simulation results show that TEMP is more efficient in terms of delivery ratio and overhead ratio. Simultaneously it is more suitable for the scene in which node's activities show a significant difference during different time slots. It is well known that the community is a very important feature of opportunistic social network, but the existing community detection algorithm is nonadaptive and complex. Thus, in the future work, we aim

to study a computable and self-adaptive community detection algorithm to assist the message forwarding. Such as, we can use GPS or RFID to locate the community that the node is currently in; of course, the community is a geo-community, but for offline network, node's mobility preference is always associated with the geographic information.

Acknowledgments

This work is sponsored by National Natural Science Foundation of China (61003236, 61170065, 61100199), Scientific & Technological Support Project of Jiangsu (BE2012755), Scientific Research & Industry Promotion Project for Higher Education Institutions (JHB2012-7), and a Project funded by Priority Academic Program Development of Jiangsu Higher Education Institutions (Information and Communication, YX002001).

References

[1] P. Juang, H. Oki, Y. Wang, M. Martonosi, L.-S. Peh, and D. Rubenstein, "Energy-efficient computing for wildlife tracking: design tradeoffs and early experiences with ZebraNet," in *Proceedings of the 10th International Conference on Architectural Support for Programming Languages and Operating Systems*, pp. 96–107, October 2002.

[2] U. G. Acer, P. Giaccone, D. Hay, G. Neglia, and S. Tarapiah, "Timely data delivery in a realistic bus network," *IEEE Transactions on Vehicular Technology*, vol. 61, no. 3, pp. 1251–1265, 2012.

[3] P. Hui, J. Crowcroft, and E. Yoneki, "BUBBLE Rap: social-based forwarding in delay-tolerant networks," *IEEE Transactions on Mobile Computing*, vol. 10, no. 11, pp. 1576–1589, 2011.

[4] Y.-P. Xiong, L.-M. Sun, J.-W. Niu, and Y. Liu, "Opportunistic networks," *Journal of Software*, vol. 20, no. 1, pp. 124–137, 2009.

[5] A. Vahdat and D. Becker, "Epidemic routing for partially connected ad hoc networks," Tech. Rep. CS-2000-06, Duke University, 2000.

[6] L. Anders and D. Avri, "Probabilistic routing in intermittently connected networks," *ACM Mobile Computing and Communications Review*, vol. 7, no. 3, pp. 19–20, 2003.

[7] N. Eagle and A. S. Pentland, "Eigenbehaviors: identifying structure in routine," *Behavioral Ecology and Sociobiology*, vol. 63, no. 7, pp. 1057–1066, 2009.

[8] P. Hui and J. Crowcroft, "How small labels create big improvements," in *Proceedings of the 5th Annual IEEE International Conference on Pervasive Computing and Communications Workshops*, pp. 65–70, Washington, DC, USA, March 2007.

[9] P. Hui, E. Yoneki, S. Y. Chan, and J. Crowcroft, "Distributed community detection in delay tolerant networks," in *Proceedings of the 2nd ACM International Workshop on Mobility in the Evolving Internet Architecture (MobiArch '07)*, Article no. 7, New York, NY, USA, August 2007.

[10] F. Li and J. Wu, "LocalCom: a community-based epidemic forwarding scheme in disruption-tolerant networks," in *Proceedings of the 6th Annual IEEE Communications Society Conference on Sensor, Mesh and Ad Hoc Communications and Networks (SECON '09)*, Rome, Italy, June 2009.

[11] E. Bulut and B. K. Szymanski, "Friendship based routing in delay tolerant mobile social networks," in *Proceedings of the 53rd IEEE Global Communications Conference (GLOBECOM '10)*, Troy, NY, USA, December 2010.

[12] F. Fabbri and R. Verdone, "A sociability-based routing scheme for delay-tolerant networks," *EURASIP Journal on Wireless Communications and Networking*, vol. 2011, Article ID 251408, 13 pages, 2011.

[13] A. Mei, G. Morabito, P. Santi, and J. Stefa, "Social-aware stateless forwarding in pocket switched networks," in *Proceedings of the IEEE International Conference on Computer Communications (INFOCOM '11)*, pp. 251–255, Shanghai, China, April 2011.

[14] A. Mtibaa, M. May, C. Diot, and M. Ammar, "PeopleRank: social opportunistic forwarding," in *Proceedings of the IEEE International Conference on Computer Communications (INFO-COM '10)*, San Diego, Calif, USA, March 2010.

[15] W. Moreira, P. Mendes, and S. Sargento, "Opportunistic routing based on daily routines," in *IEEE International Symposium on a World of Wireless, Mobile and Multimedia Networks*, pp. 1–6, 2012.

[16] Y. Zhu, H. Zhang, and Q. Ji, "How much delay has to be tolerated in a mobile social network," *International Journal of Distributed Sensor Networks*, vol. 2013, Article ID 358120, 8 pages, 2013.

[17] The ONE 1.4.1 [EB/OL], Nokia Research Center, Helsinki, Finland, 2010, http://www.netlab.tkk.fi/tutkimus/dtn/theone/.

[18] J. Scott and R. Gass, "Crawdad trace cambridge/haggle (v.2006-09-15)," 2006, http://crawdad.cs.dartmouth.edu/cambridge/haggle/imote/content.

11

Distributed and Fault-Tolerant Routing for Borel Cayley Graphs

Junghun Ryu,[1] Eric Noel,[2] and K. Wendy Tang[1]

[1] *Department of Electrical & Computer Engineering, Stony Brook University, SUNY, Stony Brook, NY 11794-2350, USA*
[2] *AT&T Labs, USA*

Correspondence should be addressed to K. Wendy Tang, wendy.tang@stonybrook.edu

Academic Editor: Yanmin Zhu

We explore the use of a pseudorandom graph family, Borel Cayley graph family, as the network topology with thousands of nodes operating in a packet switching environment. BCGs are known to be an efficient topology in interconnection networks because of their small diameters, short average path lengths, and low-degree connections. However, the application of BCGs is hindered by a lack of size flexibility and fault-tolerant routing. We propose a fault-tolerant routing algorithm for BCGs. Our algorithm exploits the vertex-transitivity property of Borel Cayley graphs and relies on extra information to reflect topology change. Our results show that the proposed method supports good reachability and a small End-to-End delay under various link failures scenarios.

1. Introduction

Various graph-based interconnection networks have been applied to wavelength division multiplexed optical networks [1, 2], distributed parallel computation [3], distributed control [4], satellite constellations [5], chip design [6–9], and wireless sensor networks [10, 11]. In peer-to-peer overlay network schemes, various structure graphs are investigated compared to unstructured P2P overlay network [12]. For the example of structured P2P, k ring lattice is used in Chord [13] and de Bruijn graph is used in Koorde and Distance Halving [14, 15]. Also there are theoretic analyses to apply de Bruin and Cayley graphs to P2P [16, 17].

Deterministic characteristics for connections between nodes in structured graphs allow theoretical analysis and guarantee global properties such as a diameter and average path length [18]. Also graph-based networks can have symmetry, hierarchy, connectivity, and hamiltonicity, which are desired properties comparing random graph-based networks [17, 19].

Borel Cayley graphs (BCGs) have been shown to be efficient candidates for interconnection networks [20]. BCGs are known to have small diameters, average path lengths, and low-degree constant connections. The degree-diameter problem has been investigated in the contexts of interconnection networks [21, 22], wavelength division multiplexed optical networks [23], and VLSI layout design [24]. Also, BCGs are symmetric graphs, a property that enables distributed routing [25]. With consensus protocol [26], distributed node to node message exchange rule to drive nodes to an agreement for a quantity of interest, BCG showed better performance than mesh, torus, and small world networks [27]. Even though BCGs have such favorable properties, there are practical limitations in applying BCGs to networks. One of them is the lack of fault-tolerant routing algorithms: existing BCG routing algorithms do not account for node or communication link failures. Researchers have studied fault-tolerant routing on mesh, toroidal mesh, and de Bruijn graphs [28–30].

In this paper, we present a fault-tolerant routing algorithm for BCG, which accounts for communication link failures. For fault-tolerant routing, the routing tables of nodes are updated distributively in response to link failures. We quantify the performance of the routing algorithm by considering packet reachability and average hop count for different levels of communication link failures. Our simulation results show our proposed method to improve delivery performance by 20% to 350%. We also show packet congestion by proposed algorithms according to packet generation rate. We assume that contention is solved by the MAC layer. Thus, we abstract this case as a graph with point-to-point links and transform the problem into a graph.

This paper is organized as follows. Section 2 reviews basic concepts and definitions for BCGs and related terminology. Section 3 presents our network model and compares BCGs with other known graph topologies. Section 4 presents the data structures used by our proposed routing algorithm for BCGs. Section 5 describes behaviors of the proposed routing algorithm. Section 6 presents simulation results to estimate reachability and the average hop count of our proposed routing algorithm. Conclusions are presented in Section 7.

2. Preliminaries

In the following, we provide a definition of Cayley graphs, Borel subgroup, and Borel Cayley graphs.

Definition 1 (Cayley graph [20]). A graph $C = \mathbb{C}(V, G)$ is a Cayley graph with vertex set V such that if two nodes $v_1, v_2 \in V$ are adjacent then $v_1 = v_2 * g$ for some $g \in G$, where $(V, *)$ is a finite group and $G \subset V \setminus \{I\}$. G is called the generator set of the graph and I is the identity element of the finite group $(V, *)$.

The definition of a Cayley Graph requires vertices to be elements of a group but does not specify a particular group.

Definition 2 (Borel subgroup). If V is a Borel subgroup of general linear 2×2 matrices set, then

$$V = \left\{ \begin{pmatrix} x & y \\ 0 & 1 \end{pmatrix} : x = a^t (\text{mod } p), y \in Z_p, t \in Z_k \right\}, \tag{1}$$

where a is a fixed parameter $a \in Z_p \setminus \{0, 1\}$, p is prime, and k is the order of a. That is, k is the smallest positive integer such that $a^k = 1 \ (\text{mod } p)$.

Definition 3 (Borel Cayley graph (BCG) [20]). Let V be a Borel subgroup and let G be a generator set such that $G \subseteq V \setminus \{I\}$, then $B = \mathcal{B}(V, G)$ is a Borel Cayley graph with vertices 2×2 matrix elements of V. There exists a directed edge from v to u if only only if $u = v * g$, where $u \neq v \in V$, $g \in G$ and $*$ is the modulo-p multiplication chosen as a group operation.

Definition 4 (GCR [20]). A graph R is a generalized chordal ring (GCR) if nodes of R can be labeled with integers modulo number of nodes N, and there exists a divisor q of N such that node i is connected to node j if and only if node $i + q$ (mod N) is connected to node $j + q$ (mod N).

The connection rules of elements are defined by connection constants. Based on Definition 4, connection constants for i and $i + q$ are identical. When the graph is four regular, there are four connection constants. For example, Figure 1 shows a degree 4 GCR with 21 nodes and $q = 3$ classes. For

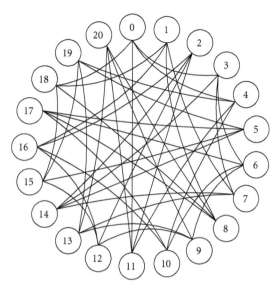

FIGURE 1: A Borel Cayley graph in the GCR representation with $p = 7, a = 2, k = 3, t_1 = 0, t_2 = 1, y_1 = 1$, and $y_2 = 1$.

$V = 0, 1, 2, \ldots, 20$ and any $i \in V$, the connection rules can be define as

if $i(\text{mod} 3) =$

$$\begin{cases} \text{"0"} : i \text{ is connected to } i + 3, i - 3, i + 4, i - 10 \quad (\text{mod} 21) \\ \\ \text{"1"} : i \text{ is connected to } i + 6, i - 6, i + 7, i - 4 \quad (\text{mod} 21) \\ \\ \text{"2"} : i \text{ is connected to } i + 9, i - 9, i - 7, i + 10 \quad (\text{mod} 21). \end{cases} \tag{2}$$

Proposition 5. For any finite Cayley graph with vertex set V and any $T \in V$ such that $T^m = I$, there exists a GCR representation of C with divisor $q = N/m$, where I is the identity element.

The proof of these propositions is given in [20] and not repeated here. T is referred to as the transform element. a_i are class representing elements.

For simplicity of the GCR representation, we chose T and a_i as follows [20]:

$$T = \begin{pmatrix} 1 & 1 \\ 0 & 1 \end{pmatrix}, \qquad a_i = \begin{pmatrix} a & 0 \\ 0 & 1 \end{pmatrix}^i. \tag{3}$$

Any vertex $v \in V$ is represented with T and a_i as follows [20]:

$$v = T^j * a_i = \begin{pmatrix} 1 & j \\ 0 & 1 \end{pmatrix} \begin{pmatrix} a^i & 0 \\ 0 & 1 \end{pmatrix} = \begin{pmatrix} a^i & j \\ 0 & 1 \end{pmatrix}. \tag{4}$$

BCGs are defined over a group of matrices. The systematic representation of BCGs from the group domain to the integer domain is useful for routing because nodes are defined in the integer domain and the integer domain provides a systematic

For a degree-4 Borel Cayley graph in the GCR representation with $T = \begin{pmatrix} 1 & 1 \\ 0 & 1 \end{pmatrix}$ and $a_i = \begin{pmatrix} a^i & 0 \\ 0 & 1 \end{pmatrix}$,

we have $q = k$ classes, where $a^k = 1 \pmod p$. Assume the generators to be g_1, g_2, g_1^{-1} and g_2^{-1}, where

$$g_1 = \begin{pmatrix} a^{t_1} & y_1 \\ 0 & 1 \end{pmatrix}, \qquad g_2 = \begin{pmatrix} a^{t_2} & y_2 \\ 0 & 1 \end{pmatrix}.$$

Given the source $i = m_1 q + c_1$ and the destination $j = m_2 q + c_2$.

While $(i \neq j)$

    Step 1: Identify new destination,

$$j' = \langle a^{q-c_1}(m_2 - m_1) \rangle_p q + \langle c_2 - c_1 \rangle_q,$$

    where $\langle \, \rangle_p$ signifies the operation within the bracket $\langle \, \rangle$ is modulo p.

    Step 2: From row j' of a precalculated routing table, determine which link to take.

    Step 3: Identify new source, $i' = mq + c$ and

        $m = y_1, c = t_1$, if link g_1 was chosen

        $m = y_2, c = t_2$, if link g_2 was chosen

        $m = p - \langle a^{q-t_1} y_1 \rangle, c = q - t_1$, if link g_1^{-1} was chosen

        $m = p - \langle a^{q-t_2} y_2 \rangle, c = q - t_2$, if link g_2^{-1} was chosen

    Step 4: $i = i'$ and $j = j'$

ALGORITHM 1: Vertex-transitive routing algorithm for Borel Cayley graphs.

description of connections. The node ID representation in GCR ($ID_g(v)$) is denoted as follows [20]:

$$ID_g(v) = q * j + i, \qquad (5)$$

where q is the parameter k in Definition 2.

Symmetry or vertex transitivity is a preferable attribute for an efficient interconnection network topology. Informally, a symmetric or vertex-transitive graph looks the same from any node. This property allows to use an identical routing table at every node. Mathematically, this implies that for any two nodes a and b in the graph there exists an automorphism of the graph that maps a to b. This property is very useful for practical implementation of interconnection networks. Most of the well-known interconnection graphs, such as the toroidal mesh, hypercube, and cube-connected cycle, exhibit this property.

Proposition 6. *All Cayley graphs are vertex transitive [20].*

Every Cayley graphs can be represented with integer node labels through a transformation into a generalized chordal ring topology. However, generally speaking, GCR graphs are not fully symmetric. In [20], the authors provide a framework for the formulation of the complete symmetry (or vertex transitivity) of Cayley graphs in the integer domain of GCR representations.

Proposition 7. *Assume a Borel Cayley graph in the GCR representation with transform element $T = \begin{pmatrix} 1 & 1 \\ 0 & 1 \end{pmatrix}$ and representing elements of each class i as $a_i = \begin{pmatrix} a^i & 0 \\ 0 & 1 \end{pmatrix}$. Let $i = m_1 q + c_1, j = m_2 q + c_2$, and $i' = m'q + c'$. If i is connected to j with a sequence of generators, then i' is connected to j' with the same sequence of generators, where $j' = \langle m' + a^{\langle c'-c_1 \rangle_q}(m_2 - m_1) \rangle_p q + \langle c' - c_1 + c + 2 \rangle_q$ [25].*

Algorithm 1 shows Vertex-transitive routing (VT routing) algorithm that exploits the inherent symmetry of Cayley graphs and uses the identical routing table at any node [25].

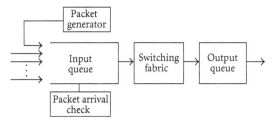

FIGURE 2: Node model.

3. Topology Comparison

3.1. Network Model. A network that consists of a set of nodes is connected by full duplex point-to-point links. The node model is depicted in Figure 2. Each node consists of an input queue for transit messages (Rx), a packet generator, a switching fabric, and an output queue. Modules inside a node are connected by zero delay links. It takes a single time unit for a packet to move from an output queue to an input queue. Time is slotted and synchronized so that all nodes receive and transmit packets simultaneously.

An input queue is FIFO served. In each time slot, the input queue accepts up to the number of packets, the degree of a node in the same time slot. Depending on the model, the input buffer size ranges from one to infinity. The output buffer size is one. The packet arrival module removes packets from the input queue if the current node is the destination node. The switching fabric determines the next node of the packet taken from the input queue by a routing algorithm. Every node in the network can be a source, a destination, or a relay. We assume that nodes generate information at a constant average rate of R packets per time slot (Packet generator).

Three traffic patterns are considered in this paper: All-to-All traffic pattern (Pattern 0), All-to-one traffic pattern (Pattern 1), and All-to-M traffic pattern (Pattern 2). In Pattern 0, all nodes are the source and destination nodes, which

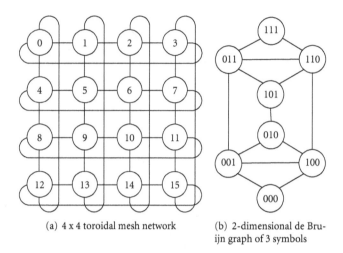

(a) 4 x 4 toroidal mesh network   (b) 2-dimensional de Bru-
                                          ijn graph of 3 symbols

FIGURE 3: Toroidal mesh network and de Bruijn graph.

```
(1)  procedure Routing Algorithm For UDB (cur, dst)    ▷cur: the current node, dst: the destination node
(2)      i ⟵ match_fwd(cur, dst)
(3)      j ⟵ match_bwd(cur, dst)
(4)      if i < j then
(5)          using FP sent to the particular left neighbor
(6)      else if i = j then
(7)          randomly using FP or BP
(8)      else
(9)          using BP sent to the particular right neighbor
(10)     end if
(11) end procedure
```

ALGORITHM 2: Undirected de Bruijn graph routing algorithm.

generate packets to uniformly randomly selected destination node. The probability of any source node communicating to any destination node in the network is constant and equal to $1/n$ where n is the number of destination nodes. In Pattern 1, nodes send packets to node 0, the only destination node. That is, the one node (sink) gathers the information generated by all other nodes in the network [31]. In Pattern 2, nodes send packets to a group of nodes, 5% of the total nodes in this case. This network model depicts a situation arising in integrated devices. Nodes located on the borders can be connected to high-capacity transmission lines.

3.2. Topologies. Toroidal mesh networks and de Bruijn graphs are popular topologies for interconnection networks [1, 5, 16]. In the following, we provide a definition for toroidal mesh networks and de Bruijn graphs. Then we show simulation results comparing Borel Cayley graphs with the aforementioned traffic patterns.

3.2.1. Toroidal Mesh Network. Figure 3(a) shows a toroidal mesh network (torus) which consists of R rows by C columns. When a node is represented by $rC + c$, neighboring nodes are defined as follows: $((r-1) \bmod R)C + c$, $rC + (c - 1) \bmod C$, $((r+1) \bmod R)C + c$, and $rC + (c + 1) \bmod C$. We

use a Greedy row-first routing algorithm on the torus mesh network. If a packet is not in the destination column, then the packet is routed along the row towards the destination column. Otherwise the packet is routed along the column toward the destination node [32].

3.2.2. De Bruijn. The undirected de Bruijn graph (UDB) has $N = d^k$ nodes of degree $2d$ [1]. We use binary de Bruijn graphs $DG(2, k)$ of $N = 2^k$ nodes. A node of the network with binary address $a_{k-1}a_{k-2} \cdots a_1 a_0$ has neighbors: $a_{k-2}a_{k-3} \cdots a_0 a_{k-1}$, $a_{k-2}a_{k-3} \cdots a_0 \bar{a}_{k-1}$, $a_0 a_{k-1} \cdots a_2 a_1$, and $\bar{a}_0 a_{k-1} \cdots a_2 a_1$. Figure 3(b) shows an undirected de Bruijn graph for $k = 3$ and $d = 2$ where self-loops are removed.

Algorithm 2 corresponds to the routing algorithm for UDB. The routing algorithm consists of transmitting a packet to either its left or right neighbors [33]. Algorithm 2 defines the Forward Path (FP) as the path taken by a packet when a left neighbor is chosen as the next node and the Backward Path (BP) when a right neighbor is chosen. From de Bruijn graph's properties, it is easy to calculate the number of hops that it needs to reach the destination using FP or BP. This is done by matching the postfix portion of the source address with the prefix portion of the destination address.

The more digits are matched; the shorter is the path between source and destination. For example, in Figure 3(b), assume node 011 needs to transmit a packet to node 110. Since 11 is the postfix of the source and the prefix of the destination, node 011 will reach node 110 in one hop. In [33], it defined *match_fwd(cur, dst)* to be an operation which returns the number of hops required to reach the destination along a FP. Similarly, *match_bwd(cur, dst)* returns the number of hops along a BP.

3.2.3. Performance Comparison. The parameters for the mesh networks we used for performance comparison are described in Table 1. BCG and Torus are degree 4 graphs. Most nodes of UDB have degree 4 except the few nodes, with self-loops. Table 2 shows our benchmark mesh networks topological properties such as the diameter and the average path length. The diameter is the greatest distance between any two nodes. The average path length is the average number of edges between all possible node pairs. Constrained by degree 4, BCG has the smallest diameter and the shortest average path length.

We also considered the performance of our network models. We used two metrics for comparison: (a) End-to-End delay and (b) reachability. We define End-to-End delay as the time required by packets to travel from a source to a destination and the reachability as the number of packets reaching destination over the number of generated packets. When running our simulations, we used the three types of traffic patterns presented in 3.1. We set the input buffer length to infinite, 5, and 10. Our simulation running time is 100000 ticks.

Figure 4 shows End-to-End delay (ETE delay) as a function of packet generation rate for our three traffic patterns. BCG exhibits the smallest End-to-End delay across all traffic patterns. Each network shows that End-to-End delay increases rapidly above a certain traffic generation rate called *traffic congestion point*. An efficient network topology should consider both End-to-End delay and network saturation. BCG shows a small End-to-End delay and a more robust traffic congestion point than UDB and Torus.

When a buffer at each node is finite, packets can be overflowed for large packet generation rates and thus reachability is not achieved as 100%. Figures 5 and 6 show reachabilities with buffer length 10 and 5, respectively. Reachability with finite buffer decreases above certain packet generation rate. Decreasing reachability packet generation rate of BCG is larger than others even though they have almost the same number of nodes and edges. UDB and Torus show similar reachabilities with traffic pattern 1 because End-to-End delays of traffic pattern 1 increase rapidly together at the similar packet generation rate.

4. Data Structure of Exhaustive Routing

A conventional routing algorithm for Borel Cayley graphs, Vertex-transitive routing, exploits the graphs vertex-transitive property. That property allows to use an identical routing table in every node. The routing table is created

TABLE 1: Mesh networks parameters.

	N	Parameters
BCG	1081	$P = 47, k = 23, a = 2, t_1 = 1, t_2 = 7, y_1 = 1, y_2 = 1$
Torus	1088	$R = 32, C = 34$
UDB	1024	$d = 2, k = 10$

TABLE 2: Static Property.

	AVG. path length	Diameter
BCG	5.54	7
Torus	16.52	33
UDB	6.77	10

for node 0 only; and for other nodes to use that table, a simple node ID translation is applied to the destination node ID. The Vertex-transitive routing algorithm guarantees the shortest path between any source-destination pair. However, Vertex-transitive routing only applies to a static network and cannot account for node/link failures. The goal of our proposed routing algorithm (Exhaustive routing) is to route messages in the presence of link failures.

Exhaustive routing has two phases. In Phase 1, packets are routed through the shortest path according to the Static Routing Table. If there is a link failure making the shortest path unavailable, a Dynamic Routing Table for Type 1 packets is updated and other shortest paths (following the Static Routing Table) will be used. However, when all shortest paths from the BCG are disconnected, there can still be a path between the source and destination. In that case, Phase 2 of Exhaustive routing is used.

Phase 2 exploits the path length information in the Static Routing Table to search for possible routes besides the shortest paths from BCG. A Dynamic Routing Table for Type 2 packets is created to indicate "next best" paths as well as any unusable link due to failures. Basically, in Phase 2, packets are routed according to the path length information and update unusable links in the Dynamic Routing Table.

We define two types of routing tables according to whether or not the table changes in response to link failures: (a) a Static Routing Table and (b) a Dynamic Routing Table. The following provides a more detailed description of the two types of routing tables.

4.1. Static Routing Table. The Static Routing Table is precalculated and identical across all nodes. The Static Routing Table is defined for a reference source node, node 0. Each time a message needs to be routed from a node different than node 0. So the destination ID is mapped from absolute ID (Global ID of the destination in a network) to relative ID (ID of the destination in the view of the current node regarded as a reference node) as follows, referring to Algorithm 1:

$$j' = \langle a^{q-c_1}(m_2 - m_1) \rangle_p q + \langle c_2 - c_1 \rangle_q, \qquad (6)$$

where the current node's absolute ID is $m_1 q + c_1$, the destination node's absolute ID is $m_2 q + c_2$, and j' is the relative destination ID. We denote the absolute ID of node

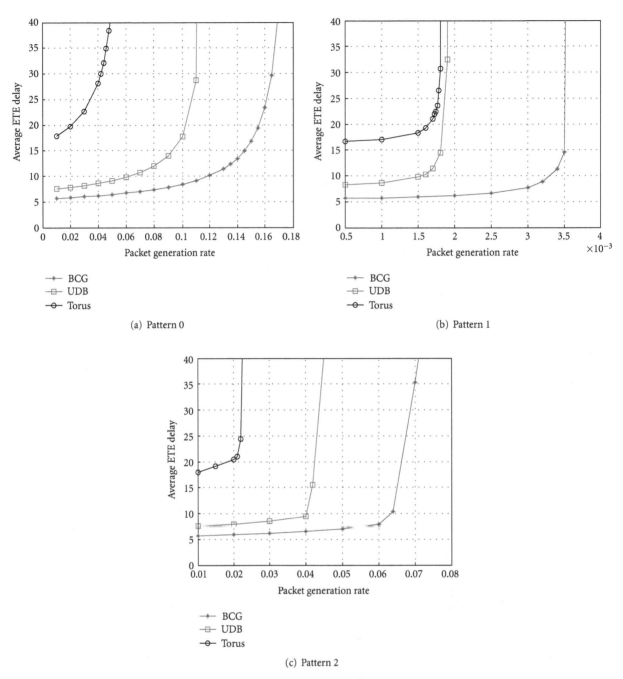

FIGURE 4: End-to-End delay with infinite buffer.

u by $a\text{ID}(u)$ and the relative ID of node u at node v by $r\text{ID}(u, v)$. Row indexes of Static Routing Table are relative IDs.

The number of rows in the Static Routing Table is the number of nodes minus one and the number of columns is the number of generators (nodal degree). In Figure 7(a), a number 1 in the routing table for Vertex-transitive routing indicates the shortest path through that generator link. For instance, for the relative destination ID 4, the shortest path at node u is through generator g_2.

The Static Routing Table for Exhaustive routing (SRTBL) includes the shortest path lengths to destination through an indicated generator. The shortest path lengths are calculated from Dijkstra's algorithm [34]. The first row of the Vertex-transitive routing table in Figure 7(a) shows an entry of 1 in the generator g_1^{-1} cell. On the other hand, in the first row of SRTBL in Figure 7(b), the shortest path is though generator g_1^{-1} and is two hops away from destination. If we choose the generator g_2 not g_1^{-1}, it would take four hops to reach destination. We denote the routing data to node v from node u by $\text{SRTBL}(r\text{ID}(v, u))$ and the hop count through generator g from node u to node v by $\text{SRTBL}(r\text{ID}(v, u), g)$. For example, $\text{SRTBL}(r\text{ID}(3, 0)) = (1, 3, 3, 3)$ and $\text{SRTBL}(r\text{ID}(3, 0), g_2) = 3$.

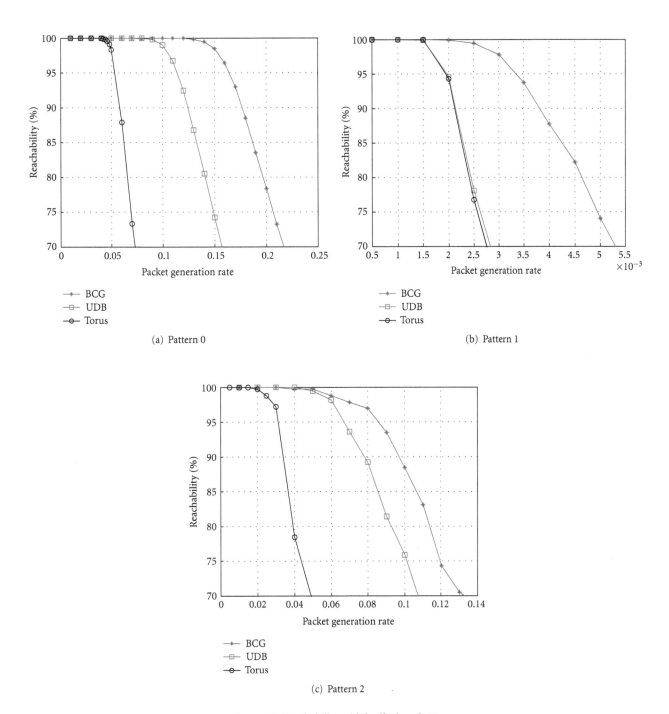

(a) Pattern 0

(b) Pattern 1

(c) Pattern 2

FIGURE 5: Reachability with buffer length 10.

4.2. Dynamic Routing Table.

The Dynamic Routing Table (DRTBL) is generated or updated based on route availability. From the contents of a received packet, a node can determine whether or not certain shortest path links are no longer available. We will explain how to determine when links are no longer available in Section 5. DRTBL is generated for each destination node, hence the size of DRTBL will vary. For example, node u detects that the g_2 link for node v is no longer available. If there is no DRTBL for node v, node u generates a new DRTBL for node v. Otherwise, it sets the g_2 link to zero in existing DRTBL for node v. DRTBLs

are unique at each node. So the relative ID is no longer needed. The index of DRTBL is the absolute ID. We denote routing data for node v at node u by $\mathrm{DRTBL}(aID(v), aID(u))$ and data indicated by generator g for node v at node u by $\mathrm{DRTBL}(aID(v), aID(u), g)$.

The Exhaustive routing algorithm has two phases during which Type 1 and Type 2 packets are forwarded in the first phase and the second phase, respectively. We denote DRTBL for Type 1 packets by D1RTBL and DRTBL for Type 2 packets by D2RTBL. Table 3 summarizes routing tables for Exhaustive routing.

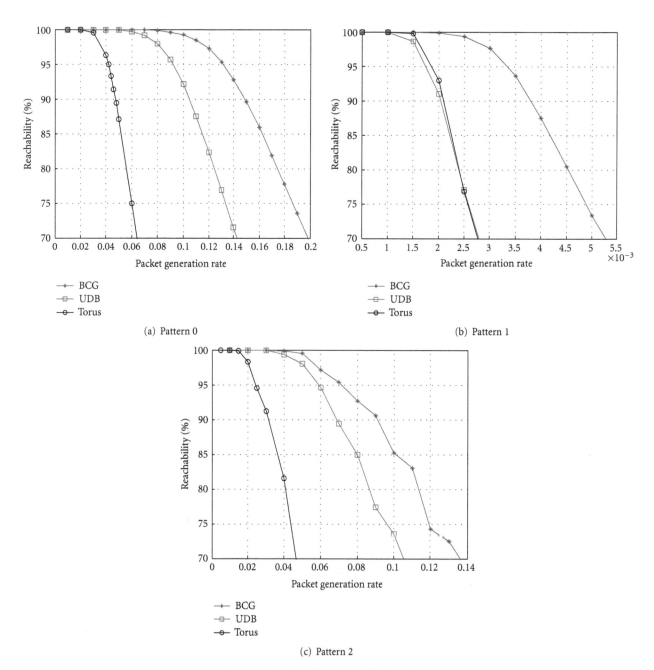

FIGURE 6: Reachability with buffer length 5.

5. Phases of Exhaustive Routing

5.1. Phase 1. Phase 1 of Exhaustive routing exploits all the shortest paths extracted from BCG with SRTLB and D1RTBL.

5.1.1. Forwarding Rule of Phase 1. In Phase 1 of Exhaustive routing, the goal of forwarding a packet is to identify links corresponding to the shortest paths for the destination in SRTBL. Then packets are forwarded to a randomly selected link among the identified shortest path links. When a node can no longer forward a packet using the SRTBL, the shortest path links are disconnected, and the node forwards the

packet to the previous node using the packet's Path history. Path history is an ordered list of nodes traversed by the packet being routed. The Path history is included in the Packet frame as follows:

Packet frame

$$= \{\text{Source}, \text{Destination}, \text{Packet Type}, \text{Path history}\}.$$
$$(7)$$

5.1.2. Generating Dynamic Routing Table of Phase 1. Once a node receives a packet, it uses the Path history of the packet to determine whether or not the packet is a returned packet. If the node ID is found at the position

	g_1	g_1^{-1}	g_2	g_2^{-1}
1	0	1	0	0
2	0	0	0	1
3	1	0	0	0
4	0	0	1	0
5	1	1	1	0

	g_1	g_1^{-1}	g_2	g_2^{-1}
1	3	2	4	4
2	3	4	3	2
3	1	3	3	3
4	3	3	1	2
5	3	3	3	4

(a) Routing table for Vertextransitive routing

(b) Static Routing Table for Exhaustive routing

FIGURE 7: Original vertex-transitive routing table and Static Routing Table of BCG in Figure 1. Note that some parts of routing tables are omitted for brevity.

TABLE 3: Summary of routing tables for Exhaustive routing.

SRTBL	Precalculated
	Data are not changed
	Data are path lengths via generator
	For Phase 1 and Phase 2
D1RTBL	Generated dynamically
D2RTBL	Data are bits indicating the available links
	Data are updated when node/link failures occur
D1RTBL	For Phase 1
	Initialized with data indicating shortest path links
D2RTBL	For Phase 2
	Initialized with data indicating all links are to be explored

before the last in the Path history, the received packet is a returned packet. When a node receives a returned packet, its D1RTBL is generated or updated. The SRTBL consists of path lengths via each generator. The links in SRTBL with smallest cell for a given rID are used. For example, in Figure 7(b), when node a determines the packet whose destination is node b ($rID(b, a)$ = 5) is a returned packet via generator g_1; it generates the D1RTBL for node b. we get $D1RTBL(aID(b))$ = $(1, 1, 1, 0)$ since the smallest number is 3 in the $SRTBL(rID(b, a)$ = 5) = $(3, 3, 3, 4)$. It sets the entry indicated by generator g_1 to zero. Finally, node a has $D1RTBL(aID(b))$ = $(0, 1, 1, 0)$.

The generator link used by a returned packet is set to zero in the D1RTBL. Upon receiving a returned packet, if another shortest path exits (D1RTBL entry for the destination is 1), the node forwards the packet to a node indicated by the generator link. Otherwise the node removes the last node ID from the Path history and forwards the packet to the previous node. If the packet goes back all the way to the source node and the source node does not have any shortest path to the destination from D1RTBL, the node changes the packet type from Type 1 to Type 2. Phase 1 of Exhaustive

routing supports routing delivery as long as there is at least one shortest path extracted from BCG. Algorithm 3 shows Phase 1 of our Exhaustive routing algorithm.

5.2. *Phase 2.* Table generation rules and packet forwarding rules for Type 1 and Type 2 packets are different. A Type 1 packet returns to source when there is no shortest path within D1RTBL. Then the source node changes the packet type from Type 1 to Type 2. The Type 2 packet is forwarded via a communication link having the smallest value in the SRTBL when a node does not have a D2RTBL of the destination.

A packet gets stuck at a node having no available shortest path in Phase 1. In Phase 2, the node receiving Type 2 packet updates or generates a D2RTBL of the destination node. The D2RTBL is initialized to 1 at all edges when generated. Type 2 packets directly refer to all path lengths information from the SRTBL. The node chooses the link having the smallest path length in SRTBL and an entry of one in the corresponding D2RTBL. When no outgoing link can be identified, a node forwards the packet back to the previous node in the Path history. From this, Exhaustive routing exploits more routes to destination. This mechanism improves the reachability exploiting more available paths to destination. Figure 8 shows our Exhaustive routing algorithm flow.

The phase 2 of Exhaustive routing can have loops as shown in Figure 9. Assume node s sends a packet to node d via a. The packet reaches to node e via c but the communication link is disconnected. Then except the incoming link, the packet is forwarded to node f. The packet follows in a circle like $a \rightarrow b \rightarrow c \rightarrow e \rightarrow f \rightarrow h \rightarrow a \rightarrow b$. To prevent loops, Phase 2 uses a different method to check whether a packet is a returned packet. In the case of Phase 1, a node checks whether the previous node of the last node in the Path history is itself. However, in the case of Phase 2 of Exhaustive routing, the node checks all the Path history node IDs. Then node a is a returned packet referring to the Path history (s, a, b, c, e, f, h). Node a sets to zero at the generator

```
(1)  procedure Packet forwarding (pkt)
(2)    if pkt.dst = curID then                        ▷ pkt.dst: destination of packet
(3)        Packet delivery is successful              ▷ curID: node ID of current node
(4)        Return
(5)    end if
(6)    if pkt.dst is a returned packet Table then
(7)        Update Dynamic Routing Table              ▷ Case: node in path history
(8)    end if
(9)    if pkt.dst Dynamic Routing Table then
(10)       if There is an available link in row of destination in Dynamic Routing Table then
(11)           Forward the packet to randomly selected available generator link in Dynamic Routing Table
(12)           Return
(13)       else if pkt.src = curID then
(14)           Change a type of pkt from Type 1 to Type 2      ▷ There is no available shortest path from BCG
(15)           Go to Phase 2 of Exhaustive routing
(16)       else
(17)           Update Path history and forward the packet to the previous node
(18)       end if
(19)   else if Row of destination in Static Routing Table then
(20)       Forward the packet to randomly selected available generator link, which has the smallest path length within the
       same row, in Static Routing Table
(21)       Return
(22)   end if
(23) end procedure
```

ALGORITHM 3: Phase 1 of Exhaustive routing.

link to node b in D2RTBL(d, a). The generator to h also sets to zero through the same method. Finally, node a delivers the packet via node m with Path history (s, a).

6. Simulation

We have designed simulators and performed experiments to evaluate our proposed fault-tolerant routing algorithm. We simulated BCG networks with $N = 1081$ (N is the number of nodes). We list the parameter values for BCGs used in Table 1. Parameters p and a determine N and BCG parameter k. Parameters t_1 and y_1 were used to construct the first generator. Parameters t_2 and y_2 were used to construct the second generator. Using two different generators and their inverse generators, we construct undirected degree 4 BCGs. We arbitrary chose parameters ts and ys for generators.

6.1. Static Property Performance. First, we simulated network disconnection by edge eliminations on BCG. We randomly select edges to be eliminated. For each simulated case, we generated 100 networks. The BCG is originally a connected graph. When we eliminate some edges, the network can consist of multiple network components (components are not connected each other). We measured packet delivery performance to the largest component only if the largest component has over 95% of the total nodes. Figure 10 shows the percentage of connected graphs among the 100 network samples for each edge elimination rate. From those results, we simulated BCG ranging from 5% to 35% elimination of edges.

We showed two metrics for comparison of proposed routing algorithms: (a) routability and (b) the average hop count. We define the routability as the number of reachable source and destination pairs among all pairs of nodes in the largest component of a network and the average hop count as the average number of nodes traversed by a packet between its source and destination. In this subsection, the simulator does not generate a packet before the previous sent packet is dropped by a routing algorithm or reached to the destination (only one packet exists in the network), which helps to measure the routing algorithm performance regardless of packet congestion and buffer length.

We compared Exhaustive routing with Exhaustive routing with only Phase 1 routing (Phase 1 routing) and vertex-transitive routing (VT routing). Results of the Exhaustive routing are acquired after dynamic routing tables are stabilized. For comparison purpose, in our implementation of the original VT routing, a random optimal link is chosen in cases where multiple optimal links exist. When there is no available link, the packet is discarded.

6.1.1. Routability. Figure 11 shows routability of BCG with 1081 nodes after eliminating edges. Phase 1 routing shows larger routability than Vertex-transitive routing because Phase 1 routing exploits all shortest paths between source and destination. Exhaustive routing shows the largest routability.

6.1.2. Average Hop Count. Figure 12 shows the average hop counts of BCG with 1081 nodes with 35% edge elimination. Comparing the average hop counts of our proposed

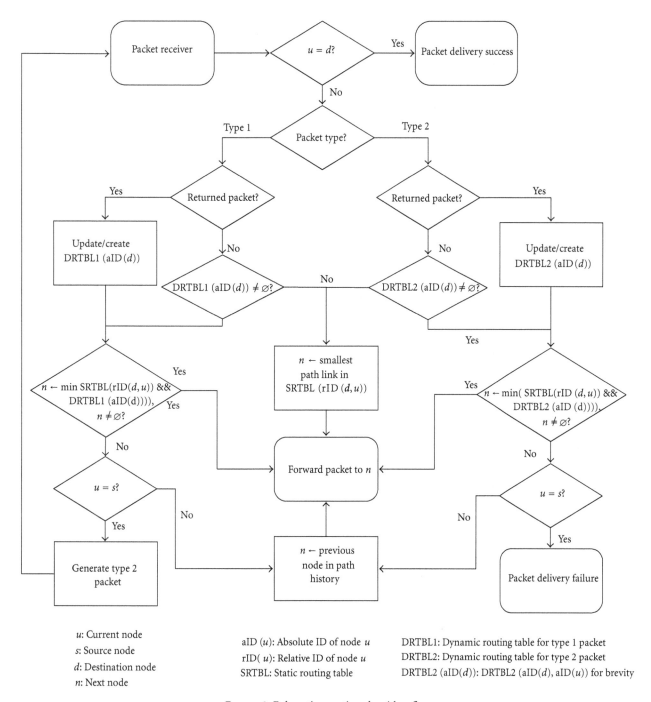

FIGURE 8: Exhaustive routing algorithm flow.

algorithms is unfair when routability is not the same. For example, one routing algorithm supports packet delivery to only nodes within a short distance from their sources and another routing algorithm supports packet delivery to all the nodes. In this case, average hop count of the second algorithm is larger than the former. So we compared only average hop count of Exhaustive routing with the results of Optimal routing in which the shortest path from the current network between the source and destination node is used. When a packet is not delivered to the destination, we exclude it from the average hop count.

6.1.3. Distribution of Hop Counts. We investigated frequency of hop counts when nodes are eliminated. Figure 13 shows hop counts distribution. The histogram of hop counts exhibits a right-skewed distribution with a high frequency of short hop counts.

6.2. Dynamic Property Performance. We show dynamic properties of our routing algorithms, which means measuring performance when multiple packets are flowing simultaneously in the network, as opposed to the case of static properties. In this case, packet generation rate and buffer

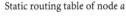

Static routing table of node a

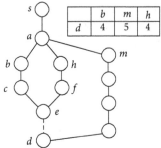

FIGURE 9: Network to illustrate a loop of Exhaustive routing. The dot line between nodes indicates that the communication is disconnected.

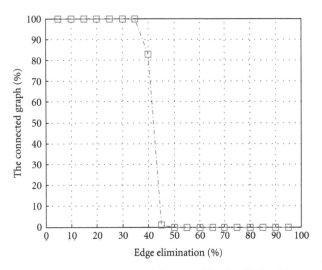

FIGURE 10: Connected graph in case with edge elimination.

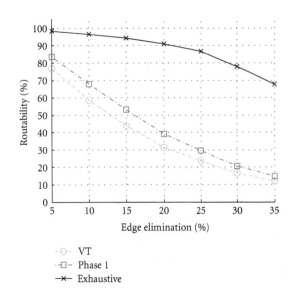

FIGURE 11: Routability with 1081 BCG after edges are eliminated.

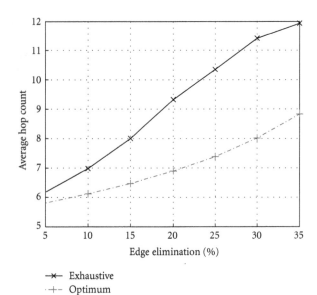

FIGURE 12: Average hop count with 1081 BCG after edges are eliminated.

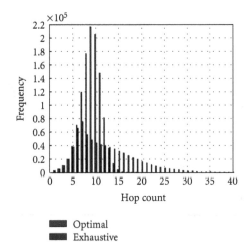

FIGURE 13: Hop count distribution of BCG with 1081 nodes after 35% edge elimination. Note that hop counts exceeding 40 are not shown for brevity.

length are important parameters. We used the network model described in Section 3 and removed a randomly chosen edge each time unit according to the edge failure rate. Simulation running time is 1000000 ticks that is ten times longer than previous one because more time is needed to observe the effects of link failures. The evaluation was done in terms of the reachability according to packet generation rate, edge failure rate, and buffer length.

Table 4 shows reachability, the average ETE delay, and average occupied buffer length with infinite buffer and 0.0005 edge failure rate. Exhaustive routing produced the highest reachability but also the longest End-to-End delay. End-to-End delay does not consider nonreached packets.

Figure 14 shows reachability as a function of packet generation rate from 0.05 to 0.25. With 0.05 packet generation

TABLE 4: Routing comparison with infinite buffer, 0.05 packet generation rate, and 0.0005 edge failure rate.

	Reachability	ETE delay	Buffer length
VT	56.97%	6.14	0.23
Phase 1	60.7175%	6.23	0.19
Exhaustive	92.75%	9.19	0.43

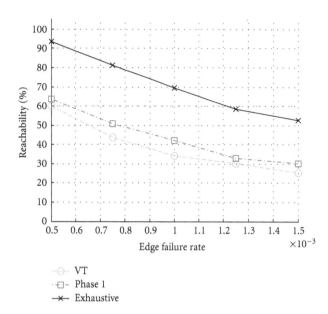

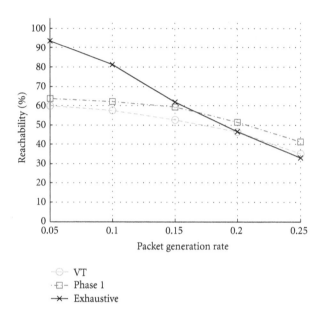

FIGURE 14: Comparison of fault-tolerant routing reachability with buffer length 5 and 0.0005 edge failure rate according to packet generation rate.

FIGURE 15: Comparison of fault-tolerant routing reachability with buffer length 5 and 0.05 packet generation rate according to edge failure rate.

rate, Exhaustive routing produced 56% and 47% better reachability than VT routing and Phase 1, respectively. However, as packet generation rate increases, the performance becomes similar because of network capacity and overflowed packets. With 0.25 packet generation rate, Phase 1 routing shows 26% better reachability than Exhaustive routing because Exhaustive routing has a longer average hop count to support higher reachability in static analysis. It increases occupied buffer length and packets are dropped. Phase 1 routing shows better reachability than VT routing even at high packet generation rate. Phase 1 routing does not try to send packets by Dynamic Routing Table when there is no shortest path extracted from BCG. So packets guaranteed shortest path length existing in the network. Also, the occupied buffer length of Phase 1 is smaller than one of VT.

We investigated reachability in response to edge failure rate with 0.05 packet generation rate as shown in Figure 15. We changed edge failure rate, which means that frequent of edge failure changes and the number of fault edges is changed at the end of simulation. The total edge number of a degree-4 BCG with 1081 nodes is 2162 and at the edge failure rate of 0.0005, 0.00075, 0.001, 0.00125, and 0.0015, the expected number of eliminated edges at the end of simulation are 500, 750, 1000, 1250, and 1500, respectively. Regardless of edge

failure rate, Exhaustive routing shows 50% to 100% better reachability. Reachabilities of VT routing, Phase 1 routing, and Exhaustive routing are decreased by 42%, 47%, and 56%, respectively, as edge failure rate increases from 0.0005 to 0.0015.

7. Conclusions

In networks, communication failures are possible scenarios. The existing vertex-transitive routing for Borel Cayley graphs, described in Section 2, cannot efficiently tolerate node/link failures. We proposed a fault-tolerant routing algorithm, the "Exhaustive routing," that uses an identical routing table at each node and exploits multiple shortest paths.

Exhaustive routing has two phases. In Phase 1, packets are routed through the shortest path existing in the Borel Cayley graph. When all shortest paths from the BCG are disconnected, Phase 2 of Exhaustive routing is used to exploit possible paths besides the shortest paths in the Borel Cayley graph. Through simulation, we found that the proposed Exhaustive routing showed 20% to 350% better routability than that of the vertex-transitive routing with various amount of link failures. Regarding the average hop count, Exhaustive routing showed just 30% longer than the Optimal routing. We also showed good network topology properties of Borel Cayley graph comparing with torus and de Bruijn graphs with various traffic patterns.

When we consider simultaneous multiple packets flowing, Exhaustive routing showed over 50% better reachability with certain packet generation rate. However, with high packet generation rate, Phase 1 routing showed better reachability because it sends packets along the guaranteed shortest paths of the original Borel Cayley graph. In summary,

Exhaustive routing has good reachability and small average hop counts. Our proposed fault-tolerant routing algorithm makes it possible for Borel Cayley graphs to be deployed in realistic network scenarios.

Acknowledgments

The authors are partially supported by the National Science Foundation under Grants nos. CNS 0829656 and IIP 0917956. Any opinions, findings, and conclusions or recommendations expressed in this paper are those of the authors and do not necessarily reflect the views of the National Science Foundation.

References

[1] K. N. Sivarajan and R. Ramaswami, "Lightwave networks based on de Bruijn graphs," *IEEE/ACM Transactions on Networking*, vol. 2, no. 1, pp. 70–79, 1994.

[2] K. Zhu and B. Mukherjee, "Traffic grooming in an optical WDM mesh network," *IEEE Journal on Selected Areas in Communications*, vol. 20, no. 1, pp. 122–133, 2002.

[3] R. Duncan, "Survey of parallel computer architectures," *Computer*, vol. 23, no. 2, pp. 5–16, 1990.

[4] R. D'Andrea and G. E. Dullerud, "Distributed control design for spatially interconnected systems," *IEEE Transactions on Automatic Control*, vol. 48, no. 9, pp. 1478–1495, 2003.

[5] J. Sun and E. Modiano, "Capacity provisioning and failure recovery for Low Earth Orbit satellite constellation," *International Journal of Satellite Communications and Networking*, vol. 21, no. 3, pp. 259–284, 2003.

[6] T. Bjerregaard and S. Mahadevan, "A survey of research and practices of network-on-chip," *ACM Computing Surveys*, vol. 38, no. 1, pp. 71–121, 2006.

[7] H. Moussa, A. Baghdadi, and M. Jézéquel, "Binary de Bruijn interconnection network for a flexible LDPC/turbo decoder," in *Proceedings of the IEEE International Symposium on Circuits and Systems (ISCAS '08)*, pp. 97–100, May 2008.

[8] A. El Gamal, "Trends in CMOS image sensor technology and design," in *Proceedings of the IEEE International Devices Meeting (IEDM '02)*, pp. 805–808, December 2002.

[9] M. Mirza-Aghatabar, S. Koohi, S. Hessabi, and M. Pedram, "An empirical investigation of mesh and torus NoC topologies under different routing algorithms and traffic models," in *Proceedings of the 10th Euromicro Conference on Digital System Design Architectures, Methods and Tools (DSD '07)*, pp. 19–26, IEEE Computer Society, Washington, DC, USA, August 2007.

[10] E. Noel and W. Tang, "Novel sensor MAC protocol applied to cayley and manhattan street networks with cross bow MICA2," in *Proceedings of the 3rd Annual IEEE Communications Society on Sensor and Ad Hoc Communications and Networks (SECON '06)*, vol. 2, pp. 626–631, September 2006.

[11] A. A. Taleb, J. Mathew, and D. K. Pradhan, "Fault diagnosis in multi layered De Bruijn based architectures for sensor networks," in *Proceedings of the 8th IEEE International Conference on Pervasive Computing and Communications Workshops (PERCOM '10)*, pp. 456–461, April 2010.

[12] E. K. Lua, J. Crowcroft, M. Pias, R. Sharma, and S. Lim, "A survey and comparison of peer-to-peer overlay network schemes," *IEEE Communications Surveys & Tutorials*, vol. 7, no. 2, pp. 72–793, 2005.

[13] I. Stoica, R. Morris, D. Karger, M. F. Kaashoek, and H. Balakrishnan, "Chord: a scalable peer-to-peer lookup service for internet applications," in *Proceedings of the conference on Applications, Technologies, Architectures, and Protocols for Computers Communications (ACM SIGCOMM '01)*, pp. 149–160, ACM, New York, NY, USA, August 2001.

[14] M. F. Kaashoek and D. R. Karger, "Koorde: a simple degree-optimal distributed hash table," in *Proceedings of the International Peer-to-Peer Symposium (IPTPS '03)*, 2003.

[15] M. Naor and U. Wieder, "Novel architectures for P2P applications: the continuous-discrete approach," *ACM Transactions on Algorithms*, vol. 3, no. 3, article 34, 2007.

[16] D. Loguinov, J. Casas, and X. Wang, "Graph-theoretic analysis of structured peer-to-peer systems: routing distances and fault resilience," *IEEE/ACM Transactions on Networking*, vol. 13, no. 5, pp. 1107–1120, 2005.

[17] C. Qu, W. Nejdl, and M. Kriesell, "Cayley dhts—a group-theoretic framework for analyzing dhts based on cayley graphs," in *Proceedings of the International Symposium on Parallel and Distributed Processing and Applications (ISPA '04)*, Springer, 2004.

[18] G. Barrenetxea, B. Berefull-Lozano, and M. Vetterli, "Lattice networks: capacity limits, optimal routing, and queueing behavior," *IEEE/ACM Transactions on Networking*, vol. 14, no. 3, pp. 492–505, 2006.

[19] S. B. Akers and B. Krishnamurthy, "Group-theoretic model for symmetric interconnection networks," *IEEE Transactions on Computers*, vol. 38, pp. 555–566, 1992.

[20] K. W. Tang and B. W. Arden, "Representations of borel cayley graphs," *SIAM Journal on Discrete Mathematics*, vol. 6, pp. 655–676, 1993.

[21] J. C. Bermond, C. Delorme, and J. J. Quisquater, "Strategies for interconnection networks: some methods from graph theory," *Journal of Parallel and Distributed Computing*, vol. 3, no. 4, pp. 433–449, 1986.

[22] M. Miller and J. Siran, "Moore graphs and beyond: a survey of the degree/diameter problem," *Electronic Journal of Combinatorics*, vol. 14, 2009.

[23] G. Panchapakesan and A. Sengupta, "On a lightwave network topology using Kautz digraphs," *IEEE Transactions on Computers*, vol. 48, no. 10, pp. 1131–1137, 1999.

[24] J. Díaz, J. Petit, and M. Serna, "A survey of graph layout problems," *ACM Computing Surveys*, vol. 34, no. 3, pp. 313–356, 2002.

[25] K. W. Tang and B. W. Arden, "Vertex-transitivity and routing for Cayley graphs in GCR representations," in *Proceedings of the ACM/SIGAPP Symposium on Applied Computing (SAC '92)*, pp. 1180–1187, ACM, New York, NY, USA, March 1992.

[26] R. Olfati-Saber and R. M. Murray, "Consensus problems in networks of agents with switching topology and time-delays," *IEEE Transactions on Automatic Control*, vol. 49, no. 9, pp. 1520–1533, 2004.

[27] J. Yu, E. Noel, and K. W. Tang, "A graph theoretic approach to ultrafast information distribution: borel Cayley graph resizing algorithm," *Computer Communications*, vol. 33, no. 17, pp. 2093–2104, 2010.

[28] J. W. Mao and C. B. Yang, "Shortest path routing and fault-tolerant routing on de Bruijn networks," *Networks*, vol. 35, no. 3, pp. 207–215, 2000.

[29] C. T. Ho and L. Stockmeyer, "A new approach to fault-tolerant wormhole routing for mesh-connected parallel computers," *IEEE Transactions on Computers*, vol. 53, no. 4, pp. 427–438, 2004.

[30] R. V. Boppana and S. Chalasani, "Fault-tolerant wormhole routing algorithms for mesh networks," *IEEE Transactions on Computers*, vol. 44, no. 7, pp. 848–864, 1995.

[31] C. Intanagonwiwat, R. Govindan, D. Estrin, J. Heidemann, and F. Silva, "Directed diffusion for wireless sensor networking," *IEEE/ACM Transactions on Networking*, vol. 11, no. 1, pp. 2–16, 2003.

[32] B. Parhami, *Introduction to Parallel Processing: Algorithms and Architectures*, Kluwer Academic, Norwell, Mass, USA, 1999.

[33] Z. Feng and O. W. Yang, "Routing algorithms in the bidirectional de Bruijn graph metropolitan area networks," in *Proceedings of the Military Communications Conference (MILCOM '94)*, vol. 3, pp. 957–961, IEEE, October 1994.

[34] E. W. Dijkstra, "A note on two problems in connexion with graphs," *Numerische Mathematik*, vol. 1, no. 1, pp. 269–271, 1959.

12

Stair Scheduling for Data Collection in Wireless Sensor Networks

Jinbiao Chen,[1] Yongcai Wang,[1] Yuexuan Wang,[1] and Changjian Hu[2]

[1] *Institute for Interdisciplinary Information Sciences (IIIS), Tsinghua University, Beijing 100084, China*
[2] *NEC Laboratories, Beijing, China*

Correspondence should be addressed to Yongcai Wang; wangyc@tsinghua.edu.cn

Academic Editor: Liusheng Huang

Spatially organized clusters are basic structure for large-scale wireless sensor networks. A cluster is generally composed by a large amount of energy-limited low-tier nodes (LNs), which are managed by a powerful cluster head (CH). The low-tier nodes that are close to the cluster head generally become bottlenecks in data collection applications. Energy efficient scheduling is important for the low-tier sensors to be longevous while guaranteeing reliable communication. In this paper, based on three aspects of performance considerations including network longevity, multihop communication reliability, and sensing system cost minimization, we propose a stair duty-cycle scheduling method for the low-tier sensors. It is designed to make the LNs in the same cluster sleep cooperatively for most of the time and wake up in assigned sequence for multihop communication. Stair scheduling cannot only improve the energy efficiency of the network but also guarantee high communication reliability and low transmission delay. Efficiency of the proposed stair scheduling is verified by analysis and intensive simulations. The results show that the performances of stair scheduling are much better than that of random scheduling algorithms.

1. Introduction

Large-scale sensor networks are attracting great research interests, because they are promising in various applications such as precision agriculture and environment monitoring [1]. In order to cover the broad area of interest where information should be monitored, such a sensor network often contains thousands or tens of thousands of small and energy limited sensors. If these sensors are directly managed by the base station, the network will suffer large communication overhead, energy inefficiency problems, and unreliability multihop communication problems. Clustering scheme was proposed by researchers to organize the sensors into two-tiered structure [2]. In the higher tier, some energy-rich sensors are deployed as backbones to organize the energy-limited sensors within their geographic neighborhood to form clusters. In the lower tier, the energy-limited sensors capture, encode, and transmit relevant information of the designated area to the cluster head (CH). Since the CHs are rich in resources, the system performances are mainly determined by the lower tier nodes (LNs.)

Sleeping and scheduling technique is the main solution to conserve energy of the LNs. As reported in INSIGHT [3], an LN works in "sleep" state in terms of radio OFF, sensor OFF, and with HPL management can save energy up to two magnitudes than the basic "listen" state. This suggests putting LNs into sleep state for most of the time and only wake them up in periodical short slot for data capturing and transmitting. But because the LNs do not serve in sleep state, this leads to an LN scheduling problem for both energy saving and QOS preserving.

Many single-hop LN scheduling schemes were proposed. In single-hop cluster, every LN transmits data directly to the CH. The LNs need not forward messages from other nodes, so they can turn to the sleep state independently to save energy [3, 4]. In [4], high density LNs are deployed in each cluster, and a linear-distance-based scheduling has been used to define the sleep schedule of the LNs. In [5], small portion of LNs are scheduled to be activated among redundant deployed SNs for coverage preserving. In [6], LNs are scheduled based on analytical hierarchy process which considers residual energy, sensing coverage overlapping, and so forth. However, single-hop cluster is limited in scale. Many expensive CHs will be needed to cover a broad land.

Multi-hop cluster in which LNs transmit data along a multi-hop route towards the CH is proposed by the researchers of [7, 8], which has better scalability and is more cost-efficient. But the LN scheduling problem becomes difficult in a multi-hop scenario. The LNs can no longer sleep independently, because if a relay node turns to sleep, the multi-hop route which it serves will be shut down. To support multi-hop communication, joint LN scheduling becomes necessary. In [9], distributed data gathering scheduling in multihop sensor networks was proposed by using greedy algorithm to extract a rooted spanning tree. Their work focuses on routing. It did not address jointly scheduling problem for reliable communication. In [8], hops-based sleep scheduling algorithm was proposed to assign different active probabilities to different hop LNs to balance the energy consumption. In [10], localized probabilistic routing algorithm was proposed for optimizing network lifetime. However, in their studies, the communication was assumed to happen round by round. How the LNs are jointly scheduled for multi-hop communication was not explicitly discussed.

We propose a stair scheduling method in this paper. Its basic idea is to schedule the LNs in one cluster to sleep and work cooperatively to conserve energy as well as to support multi-hop communication. With this purpose, in stair scheduling, we act as follows.

(1) We propose "Stair Scheduling" to control the working slots of the LNs based on the level-based routing tree [8]. The cluster is divided into levels, and a child node in the ith level always transmits data to a parent in the $(i-1)$th level. The child always activates and sleeps one slot earlier than its parent. Each slot contains m slices, and an LN randomly selects one slice to transmit data in its active transmission slot for collision avoidance.

(2) hop-by-hop time synchronization is proposed to avoid time drifting and make the "Stair Scheduling" work in a fully distributed manner.

(3) Average function hop-by-hop data aggregation is proposed to further enhance the energy saving as well as to balance the energy consumption.

We further analyze the energy and communication reliability models of the joint scheduled cluster with respect to the cluster size and LN parameters. The results are applied to optimize the design of the network to choose a suitable number of CHs for system cost minimization. Simulation results verify the energy efficiency and communication reliability of stair scheduling and further show that it is more efficient and applicable than traditional single-hop random scheduling (SRS) and multi-hop random scheduling (MRS).

The rest of this paper is organized as follows. In Section 2, we describe the system model and formulate the problem. In Section 3, we develop the stair scheduling algorithm. Section 4 presents the energy and reliability models of the joint scheduled cluster and the network optimization results using stair scheduling. Section 5 summarizes the simulation

results and the paper is concluded in Section 6, with remarks and future work discussions.

2. System Model and Problem Formulation

2.1. Assumption and Network Model. The basic assumptions and network model are outlined as follows.

(i) We consider two-tiered sensor network, which contains low-tier energy-limited nodes (LNs) and high-tier cluster heads (CHs). The LNs are not redundant. They are deployed in an economic way for exact land coverage. Each node is responsible for the monitoring of its own vicinity. They capture and transmit data periodically. The sampling frequency is denoted as U.

(ii) The CHs do not sense data but receive and aggregate raw data from LNs and report the result to the base station. The CH has enough energy and is never considered to be a bottleneck.

(iii) The cluster area is in circular shape with radius R and centered by the CH. LNs are evenly distributed in the cluster area. All the LNs have the same sensing range r_s, maximum transmission range r_c, and the initial energy E, and we assume $r_c = 2r_s$.

(iv) Each LN generates l-bit data in a period and transmits the data towards the CH using a level-base routing tree [8, 11]. Symmetry link is assumed in data forwarding that if A can hear B, then B can hear A.

2.2. Problem Formulation. We consider large-scale sensor monitoring system, such as habitat or agriculture monitoring. In these systems, application requires that each LN reports its vicinity's information U times per hour. This prohibits an LN from sleeping for an arbitrary long time. Every LN must be active periodically. Since only CH reports results to the base station, the sampling frequency of LNs should be the same with the reporting frequency of the CH. Therefore, U is denoted as the *sampling frequency* of the cluster, and the *sampling period* is $T = 1/U$.

For an LN, each sampling period can be further divided into *task slots*. In each task slot, the LN can choose to sleep, sense, process data, receive message, or transmit message. We omit sensing and data processing time. Therefore, in a task slot, the LN either sleeps, receives, nor transmits message. We suppose that each slot is equal in length and denote the slot length by T_m. Each sample period is therefore divided into $M = T/T_m$ task slots. The joint scheduling problem becomes slot state assignment problem with joint consideration of the system performance. Formally, in a sample period, the ith LN has slots $\mathbb{S}^i = \{S_1, S_2, \ldots, S_M\}$, and the task of scheduling is to determine the state of each slot.

If a cluster has N LNs, each sampling period contains M task slots, each slot can be assigned v states, and the solution space of the joint scheduling problem will be v^{MN}. We can see that it encounters a combination explosion problem with respect to v, M, and N. In addition, because an LN is commonly not aware of other LNs' status, the joint scheduling problem is challenging.

But a heuristic is that, for energy saving and in order to support multi-hop communication, the LNs in one cluster should sleep for most of the time and should have some overlaps in their active time slots to exchange message. In view of this, we propose a multi-hop joint scheduling (stair scheduling) algorithm. The details will be given in the next section.

3. Multihop Joint Scheduling

3.1. Overview of Stair Scheduling. The basic idea of stair scheduling is to schedule the LNs in one cluster to sleep and work cooperatively to conserve energy as well as to support multi-hop communication. The design of joint scheduling basically contains three schemes as follows.

(1) "Stair scheduling" is proposed to assign every LN three continuous active slots in a sample period: "R-Slot" to listen to child nodes, "T-Slot" to sense and forward data, and "Syn-Slot" to synchronize time. A child node will be always activated one slot earlier than its parent, so that its forwarding can be heard by its parent. Therefore, most energy is conserved by sleeping and reliable multi-hop communication is supported. For collision avoidance, every task slot is further designed to contain m slices. The length of each slice is equal to the atomic data transmission time, which is denoted by t. So the slot length $T_m = mt$. In "T-slot" an LN randomly selects one slice to transmit data for collision avoidance.

(2) A hop-by-hop time synchronization scheme is proposed to avoid sensor time drifting and make stair scheduling work in fully distributed manner. Due to "Stair scheduling," when a parent LN forwarding its message in its "T-Slot," for the symmetric link, its children will hear this broadcasting in their "Syn-Slot." The children synchronize time with the parent. When the hop-by-hop synchronization reaches the CH, the whole link is synchronized and "Stair scheduling" can work distributedly.

(3) Average-function-based hop-by-hop data aggregation is proposed to further enhance energy saving and to balance the energy consumption.

The detailed design of the proposed stair scheduling is as follows.

3.2. Stair Scheduling. "Stair scheduling" is to assign active task slots to LNs based on the hop counts of the LNs. It is initialized by the CH and is continually maintained by the LNs themselves during the data collection process.

3.2.1. Premise for Stair Scheduling. The level-based energy-balance routing (LEB) tree [8] and time synchronization among LNs and CH should be achieved at the cluster formation phase. The level-based energy-balance routing tree [8] is different from the shortest-path tree. Sensors are divided into levels based on the average hop progress, which can be easily

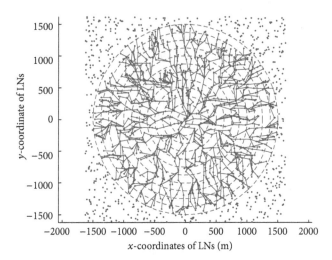

FIGURE 1: Level-based energy-balance multihop communication in a cluster.

obtained by flooding during the initialization phase [2, 12]. In LEB, for energy balance, a flag is assigned to each LNs, which is initially set to 0 and is changed to 1 once it acts as a relay for any other sensors. So when the node in the ith level finds its closest neighbor in the $(i-1)$th level and has flag = 1, it will try to select the second closest neighbor in the $(i-1)$th level as the relay. If it happens that all the neighbors in the $(i-1)$th level have flag = 1, the sensor in the ith level will randomly choose a neighbor in the $(i-1)$th level as the relay node.

After initialization of LEB, the CH is aware of the levels of all the LNs and all the links in its cluster. Figure 1 shows a graph illustration of the CH's knowledge after LEB construction in a cluster. The square in the center is the CH and the surrounding points are LNs. The dashed circle is the levels.

3.2.2. Stair Scheduling Scheme. If the largest level is n, and the sample period of each LN is divided into M task slots, the "stair scheduling" works as follows.

(1) For an ith level of the LN, it will sleep from its 1st to $(n-i-1)$th slots and will activate at the $(n-i)$th slot. The active status will last three slots, and then the LN turns to sleep, till the end of the sample period. Among the three active slots, we have the following.

(i) The first slot is used to receive messages from the child LN in the $(i+1)$th level. We call it "R-Slot."

(ii) The second slot is used to sense local area and forward message to a parent node in the $(i-1)$th level. We call it "T-Slot."

(iii) The third active slot is used to synchronize time between the parent node and this node. Since the link is symmetry, when the parent node relays the message towards CH, the broadcasting will be overheard by this child. The overheard message is processed to synchronize time between the parent and this node. We call this slot "Syn-Slot."

For communication collision avoidance, each slot is designed to contain m slices. In "T-Slot," the LN randomly selects one slice for data transmission. Carrier sense and retransmission scheme is not used in stair scheduling.

(2) A special case will appear for the level n LNs. Since they do not relay other LNs' message, they only assign their first two slots to be active.

(i) The first slot is a "T-Slot" to sense local area and transmit message.

(ii) The second slot is used to synchronize time with a parent node in the $(n - 1)$th level, which is a "Syn-Slot."

Figure 2 shows a graph illustration of the task slot assignments for LNs in the different levels. We can see two features of "stair scheduling" as follows.

(1) The active task slots of LNs form a stair shape with respect to the hop count; that is, a child LN will be activated one slot earlier than its parent.

(2) For LNs in two neighboring levels, they have two overlapped active slots. The "T-Slot" of the child overlaps with the "R-Slot" of the parent. This establishes the link for data transmission. The "Syn-Slot" of the child overlaps with the "T-Slot" of the parent. This establishes the hop-by-hop time synchronization.

3.3. Time Synchronization.

Time synchronization plays an important role in stair scheduling. It is carried out during two phases: initialization phase and run-time hop-by-hop time synchronization.

In the initialization phase, time synchronization is carried out by Flooding Time Synchronization Protocol (FTSP) [13]. This is done simultaneously with the setting up of the LEB routing tree. Initially, all the LNs are active and their timers are not synchronized. The CH periodically broadcasts m CH messages for both time synchronization and LEB routing tree. The message generation time $t_{0,j}$ is broadcasted in each message, where j is the message index. When an LN receives the CH message, it uses the MAC-layer time-stamping to measure the packet forwarding delay. With the recorded delays of the previous hops, the LNs in the ith hop adjust their clock to

$$t_{i,j} = t_{0,j} + \sum_{k=1}^{i-1} s_{k,j}, \tag{1}$$

where $s_{k,j}$ is the delay at the kth hop. Since m CH messages are broadcasted periodically each LN will obtain a sequence of synchronized time $\{t_{i,1}, \ldots, t_{i,m}\}$. Linear regression is used to achieve high accuracy of the clock synchronization [13].

In the running phase, time synchronization is done hop-by-hop to avoid clock drifting. In "T-slot," LN broadcasts sensing data together with its local time. This broadcasting will be heard by its child nodes due to the symmetry link. These child nodes use the MAC-layer time stamping to record the processing delay and adjust their clock to the clock of their parents. With this hop-by-hop scheme, children synchronize

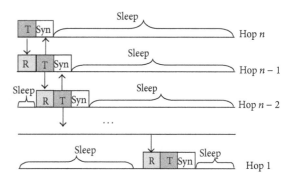

FIGURE 2: Joint active task slot scheduling with the "stair scheduling" method.

clock with their parents, and the process repeats until the CH is reached as the last parent. Hence the clocks of the whole cluster can be continuously synchronized. And based on this, all LNs can maintain the "stair scheduling" in a fully distributed manner.

3.4. Hop-by-Hop Data Aggregation.

In addition to stair scheduling, we adopt hop-by-hop data aggregation to enhance energy saving. For data collection with reverse shortest-path tree, the ideal data aggregation will be chain-based hop-by-hop data aggregation as discussed in PEGASIS [14]. However, such chain-based data aggregation poses high requirement to the scheduling of node transmission. Any child node should transmit earlier than its parent sensor; otherwise, redundant packet will be generated and additional energy will be consumed [15]. However, the authors of [14] have not discussed the details of the transmission scheduling.

The "stair scheduling" of stair scheduling provides fine solution to such chain-based hop-by-hop data aggregation, because in stair scheduling any child sensor will transmit data one slot earlier than its parent sensor. To implement hop-by-hop data aggregation, for an LN node, in R-Slot, it listens to messages from its child nodes. The data is extracted from the messages and is stored. In T-Slot, the LN senses its vicinity. The local readings will be merged with the stored data, and the results will be forwarded towards CH. We propose *average function* in data aggregation. If the size of the received data is l_r and the size of the local sensed data is l_s, using *average function*, the size of the merged data to be forwarded will be $l_f = \max\{l_r, l_s\}$. The energy performance of stair scheduling using average aggregation functions will be analyzed and evaluated in Sections 4 and 5.

4. Performance Analysis of Stair Scheduling for Network Optimization

In this section, we analyze the multi-hop reliability and energy consumption model of stair scheduling with respect to the cluster parameters. The model will be applied to optimize the tier-structure design of the sensor network.

4.1. Basic Analysis. We consider large-scale sensor systems, where sensors are not redundantly deployed for the cost consideration. Each sensor is responsible for the monitoring of its own vicinity. The sampling frequency U is commonly very low, for example, two samples per hour, and so forth.

For the monitoring completeness, there must be enough LNs deployed in the field to provide full land coverage. Based on the result of 1-coverage [16] analysis that calculates the probability of any point covered by at least one LN, the density of LN deployment can be derived as

$$\lambda = -\frac{\log(1 - P_{1\text{-cover}})}{\pi r_s^2}, \qquad (2)$$

where $P_{1\text{-cover}}$ is the desired 1-coverage probability. Since CHs do not sense data, whatever the cluster size chosen, for coverage preserving, the required LN density is λ. When CHs are deployed, the LNs are organized into clusters, and the number of LNs in each cluster can be calculated as $N = \lambda \pi R^2$. The following performance analysis and simulations are all carried out in such a coverage preserving scenario.

A simple but effective energy consumption model for sensor operations is assumed in this paper [1, 8, 17]. To transmit l-bits data over distance d, the sender will expend energy as

$$E_{TX}(l, d) = l * E_{\text{elec}} + l * \epsilon_{\text{amp}} * d^\gamma, \qquad (3)$$

where E_{elec} is the unit and ϵ_{amp} is the amplifier energy. γ is the path loss factor, usually $2 < \gamma < 4$, and here we assume $\gamma = 2$. The energy expended by a receiver depends only on the length of the data and can be expressed as

$$E_{RX}(l) = l * E_{\text{elec}}. \qquad (4)$$

Therefore, the key issue of energy consumption model of stair scheduling counts the transmission and reception times of a sensor in a sample period. In [8], the average hop progress of the sensor network r_h was derived as

$$r_h = \sqrt{3}\lambda \int_0^{r_c} x^2 e^{(\pi/3)\lambda(x^2 - r_c^2)} dx, \qquad (5)$$

where r_c is the sensor's maximum transmission range and λ is the density of the sensors. The result divides the circular shape cluster into $n = R/r_c$ levels and verifies that sensors in the ith level have the most probability to reach CH by i hops. With this result, due to the uniform sensor distribution, the average number of sensor nodes in each level is

$$N_i = \pi \lambda (2i - 1) r_h^2, \qquad (6)$$

where $i = 1, \ldots, n$. We assume that cluster radius R can be divided exactly by r_h.

According to the uniform distribution, an outer level will have more sensors than an inner level. So the average number of children for a sensor in level i is

$$C_i = \frac{N_{i+1}}{N_i}. \qquad (7)$$

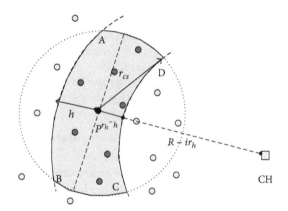

FIGURE 3: The interference region.

4.2. Multihop Communication Reliability. With "stair scheduling," for an arbitrary LN, if its "T-slot" comes, it randomly selects a slice within the m slices of the "T-slot" to transmit data. If two LNs share the same parent and select the same slice to transmit data, their messages will collide, and the transmissions will fail. Although the link can be enhanced by retransmission schemes, and so forth [18], we focus more on the performance of the basic stair scheduling and leave the enhanced methods to future work.

We suppose that an LN node C in the ith level tries to transmit. For the "stair scheduling" of stair scheduling, only the LNs in the same level share the same parent of C may collide C's transmission. Recall that the parent node found children nodes by broadcasting with radius r_c in the initialization phase. The "coparent circle" of C is therefore a circle centered at its parent node, and with radius r_c. We suppose that C's parent is node P, which locates in the $(i-1)$th level. Figure 3 shows the scenario. In the figure, the region of the ith level is ring centered at CH and with inner radius $(i - 1)r_h$ and outer radius ir_h. The "interference region" is the region indicated by ABCD, which is the overlapped area of the "coparent circle" and the ith level ring.

4.2.1. Lower Bound of Transmission Reliability. Because even two LNs are within the "interference region," they may have different parents and their transmissions may not collide. So based on the following assumptions, we will get a lower bound of the transmission reliability. The assumption is as follows: "if two LNs are within interference region of each other and transmit data in the same time slice, their transmissions will collide." The lower bound will help us to understand the worst case of the transmission reliability of stair scheduling to direct cluster design. We can see that the area of the "interference region" is a function of i and h, where h is the distance from P to the inner border of the ith level ring. We denote the area by $S_c(i, h)$. Since LNs are uniformly deployed, the probability that there are k LNs within S_c is $p(k, S_c) = ((\lambda S_c)^k/k!)e^{-\lambda S_c}$. If all the other $k - 1$ LNs select different slices from C's transmission slice, C's transmission will success. This probability is

$$p(i,h) = \sum_{k=0}^{\infty}\left(1-\frac{1}{m}\right)^{k-1}\frac{(\lambda S_c(i,h))^k}{k!}e^{-\lambda S_c(i,h)}$$

$$= \frac{m}{m-1}e^{-\lambda S_c(i,h)/m}, \tag{8}$$

where λ is node density and m is the number of slices. We can see that $p(i,h)$ is a monotone decreasing function of $S_c(i,h)$. If we can find an upper bound for $S_c(i,h)$, we will get the lower bound of $p(i,h)$.

We firstly consider the case $r_c < (i-1)r_h$, where the "co-parent" radius is smaller than the inner radius of the ring. This is corresponding to the case when C locates in some outer levels in which $i > 1 + r_c/r_h$. Since $r_c < 2r_h$ [8], this is corresponding to the case when $i \geq 3$.

It is easy to give an upper bound to $S_c(i,h)$ for this case, because the parent node P should locate in the $(i-1)$th level. As shown in Figure 4, when it locates on the inner border of the ith level, the "co-parent circle" and the ith level ring will form the maximum overlapped area, which is indicated by EFGH. It is easy to verify that the area of EFGH is an upper bound of $S_c(i,h)$. We denote this upper bound interference area as $S_{\mathrm{up}}(i)$ as follows:

$$S_{\mathrm{up}}(i) = \frac{2r_c^2}{\pi(\beta-\theta)} + \frac{2\alpha(ir_h)^2}{\pi}$$

$$- r_c(i-1)r_h\sin\beta - \frac{2\gamma((i-1)r_h)^2}{\pi} \tag{9}$$

$$+ r_c((i-1)r_h)\sin\theta$$

$$\geq S_c(i,h), \quad \forall h \in [0, r_h],$$

where

$$\alpha = \arccos\frac{(ir_h)^2 - r_c^2 + ((i-1)r_h)^2}{2i(i-1)r_h^2},$$

$$\beta = \arccos\frac{((i-1)r_h)^2 + r_c^2 - (ir_h)^2}{2(i-1)r_hr_c}, \tag{10}$$

$$\theta = \arccos\frac{((i-1)r_h)^2 + r_c^2 - (ir_h)^2}{2(i-1)r_hr_c},$$

$$\gamma = \pi - 2\theta.$$

Now we consider the cases when $i = 1$ or $i = 2$. When $i = 1$, the LNs transmit directly to CH. The maximum "interference area" will be $S_{\mathrm{up}}(i) = \pi r_h^2$. When $i = 2$, the upper bound of the "interference area" will be $S_{\mathrm{up}}(i) = \pi r_c^2 - r_h^2$, as illustrated in Figure 5.

Therefore, we got the lower bound of the expected communication reliability of the ith hop as

$$\underline{P(i)} = \frac{m}{m-1}e^{-\lambda S_{\mathrm{up}}(i)/m} \leq P(i). \tag{11}$$

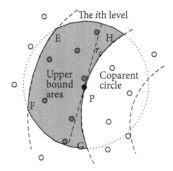

FIGURE 4: Upper bound when $i \geq 3$.

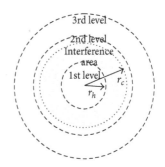

FIGURE 5: Upper bound of $S_c(i,h)$ when $i = 2$.

Therefore, the lower bound of the multi-hop communication reliability when a message is forwarded from the level $i + j$ to the level i is

$$\underline{P(i+j,i)} = \prod_{k=i+1}^{i+j} P(i+k). \tag{12}$$

With the parameter settings in Table 1, where $P_{1\text{-cover}} = 0.99$, $n = 12$ and $r_c = 200$, the lower-bound of the hop-by-hop communication reliability and the lower bound of the multi-hop communication reliability are shown in Figure 6. We can see basically the following

(i) The lower bound varies with i. The lower bound increases as i decreases from 12 to 3. This is because the interference region becomes smaller as the level decreases. $\underline{P(i)}$ is small in the first and second levels, because, in such cases, the LNs are close. The number of LNs in the interference region becomes larger.

(ii) The multi-hop communication reliability decreases with the increasing of the forwarding hops. This gives us hints that in designing cluster, we should limit the number of forwarding hops.

4.3. Energy Consumption Model of Stair Scheduling. After analyzing the communication reliability in each hop, we derive the energy model for LNs in different hops. We assume that when two messages collides the energy for message transmission and reception will be consumed.

For an LN in the outmost nth level, it transmits its sensed data to its parent in its "T-Slot" and receives a time

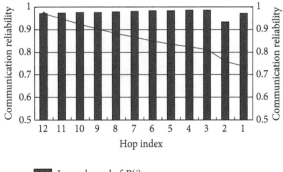

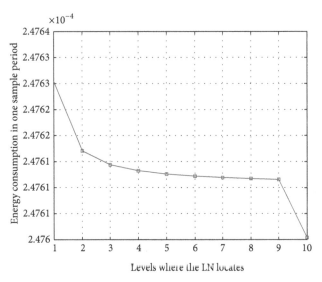

FIGURE 6: The lower bound of $P(i)$ and the multihop reliability derived using the lower bound of $P(i)$.

FIGURE 7: Energy consumption in one sample period where LNs locate in different levels.

synchronization message from this parent in the "Syn-Slot." Its energy consumption in one sample period is

$$E(e_n) = l * E_{\text{elec}} + l * \epsilon_{\text{amp}} * (r_h)^\gamma + l * E_{\text{elec}}. \tag{13}$$

For an LN in the ith level, it receives data in "R-Slot" from its children. In "T-Slot," it senses local area and transmits the aggregated data to its parent. Since the received message is l-bits, and the local generated data is l-bits, the aggregated data with also be l-bits due to the average aggregation function. Then, in its "R-Slot," it receives a time synchronization message from this parent. Its energy consumption in one sample period is

$$E(e_i) = \left(2 + \frac{N_{i+1}}{N_i}\right) * l * E_{\text{elec}} + l * \epsilon_{\text{amp}} * (r_h)^\gamma. \tag{14}$$

The comparison of the energy consumption for LNs in different levels is shown in Figure 7, with parameter settings in Table 1. We can see the following.

TABLE 1: Setting of parameters.

Parameter	Value
E_{elec}	10^{-10}
l	100 (bits)
r_s	100 (m)
$P_{1\text{-cover}}$	0.999
ϵ_{amp}	10^{-10}
γ	2
r_c	200 (m)
n	10

(1) LN in the first level has the highest energy consumption rate, and LN in the outmost level has the lowest energy consumption rate. This is due to that the first level has the fewest number of sensors, so they averagely have the heaviest burden to relay data. But the outmost LNs need not to relay data at all.

(2) The difference among energy consumption rates is very small. The difference between energy consumption of the first level LNs and the tenth level LNs is only $(2.4763 - 2.476)/2.476 = 0.012\%$. This balance owes to the "stair scheduling" and "average aggregation function" of stair scheduling. By "stair scheduling," LNs in different levels activate for almost the same amount of slots. By average aggregation, different levels of LNs receive and forward nearly similar amount of data.

With the energy consumption model of stair scheduling, we can further analyze the energy consumption of the cluster and apply the analysis result to optimize the design of the tier structure.

4.4. Optimize the Design of Tier Structure. We can use the derived performances of stair scheduling to optimize the design of cluster. This is a typical multiple objectives optimization problem.

The controllable variable is the number of levels: n, which indeed determines the size of cluster. If a cluster has n levels, the size of one cluster is $\pi * (nr_h)^2$.

The constraint is that the cluster area should cover the full sensing field. For using the minimal number of clusters to cover the sensing field, the cell CH distribution [19] will be optimal. Suppose the area of sensing field is S, and the required number of CHs is

$$n_{\text{CH}} = \frac{2 * \pi}{3\sqrt{3}}. \tag{15}$$

The energy metric is to minimize the energy consumption of the first level, since it is the bottleneck of the lifetime of the cluster. So $m_1 = E(e_1)$.

The communication reliability metric is to maximize the reliability to forward a message from level n to level 1 as follows:

$$m_2 = \underline{P(n, 1)} = \prod_{k=1}^{n-1} \underline{P(k)}. \tag{16}$$

The cost metric is to minimize the deployment cost of the sensors. Since the number of LNs is fixed by coverage preserving requirement. The cost is determined by the number of CHs, that is to minimize $m_3 = n_{CH} * cost$.

By assigning weights to different metrics, we can arrive at an optimized design of n by performance trading off as

$$n = \arg\min_{n} \left(w_1 m_1 - w_2 m_2 + w_3 m_3 \right), \tag{17}$$

where w_1, w_2, and w_3 are user assigned positive weights. Discussion of the cluster optimization will be out of the scope of this paper. We leave it to future work. We simply choose $n = 10$ in the following evaluations.

5. Performance Evaluation

5.1. Simulation Settings. We build a discrete event simulator using MATLAB 7.0 to evaluate the performances of stair scheduling. We compare the performances of the proposed stair scheduling with traditional single-hop randomized sleeping scheduling (SRS) [3] and multi-hop random sleeping scheduling (MRS). The results shown in Figures 9–13 are the means of 100 independent runs. In each simulation run, we generate a certain number of LN nodes and randomly place them in a rectangle sensing area with size $5000 * 5000\,(\text{m}^2)$. The number of nodes is determined by the node density, which is calculated by (2) by varying the 1-coverage probability from 0.9 to 0.99. Each LN captures data and reports data to CH. The sensing radius of LN is $r_s = 100$ meters and the communication radius $r_c = 200$ meters. The sample period of LN is half an hour $T = 1800{,}000$ ms and the time slice to finish a transmission event is fixed at $t = 9$ ms. The length of the task slot is $T_m = mt$, where m varies in the range of $(10, 100)$.

SRS uses single-hop cluster in which every LN directly transmits data to CH. The number of clusters is decided based on the constraint of cluster coverage [19]. In each cluster, the LNs are independently scheduled, with active probability $p_{RSS} = T_m/T$. Transmission will succeed if two transmissions do not collide.

Stair scheduling and MRS uses the same size of clusters and they both use LEB routing and divide the cluster into the same n levels. In MRS, LNs in each level are scheduled independently to capture, transmit, and forward data. When an LN in the ith level is activated, it broadcasts message towards level $i - 1$. If the message reaches its parent LN in the level $i - 1$, the transmission will succeed; otherwise, the transmission in this hop will fail. For the fairness of SRS, stair scheduling, and MRS, we set the average active duration in one period to be the same $p_{SRS} = p_{MRS} = T_m/T$. LNs in SRS, MRS, and stair scheduling share the same parameters and the same energy coefficients.

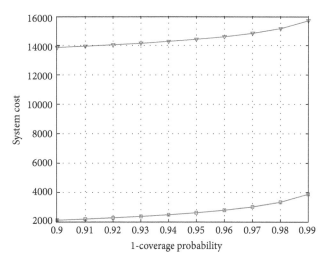

FIGURE 8: System cost as a function of 1-coverage probability for SRS, stair scheduling, and MRS.

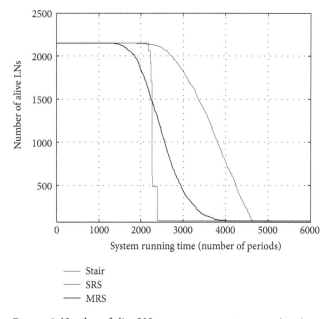

FIGURE 9: Number of alive LN sensors versus system running time.

5.2. Simulation Results

5.2.1. System Cost. We focus on the energy and communication reliability performances with the joint consideration of the system cost.

The system cost means the total cost of deployed LNs and CHs. We suppose that the cost of one CH node is 50 times of the cost of an LN. In SRS, the radius of the cluster is the same with the communication radius of LN. In MRS and stair scheduling, the radius of the cluster is fixed at 10 times of the average hop progress.

Figure 8 shows the influence of node density on the system cost performance. When the required 1-coverage

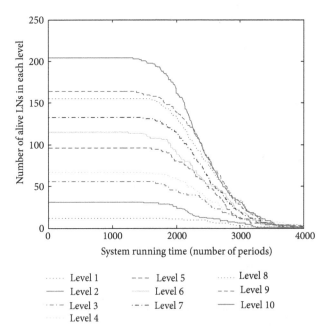

FIGURE 10: Alive LNs in each level versus system running time in MRS.

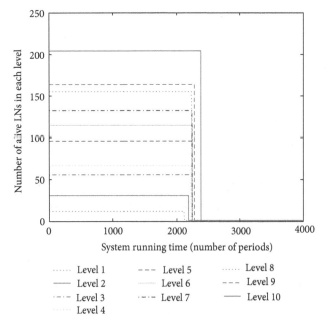

FIGURE 11: Alive LNs in each level versus system running time in stair scheduling.

probability varies from 0.9 to 0.99, the corresponding node density varies from $0.73 * 10^{-4}$ to $0.1466 * 10^{-3}$. The corresponding system cost to cover the sensing field using SRS, stair scheduling, and MRS is plotted in Figure 8. We set the cost of one LN to one unit. We can see that the system cost of SRS is nearly seven times larger than the cost of stair scheduling and MRS. The cost of stair scheduling and MRS is the same since they use the same cluster structures.

5.2.2. Energy Performance. Figure 9 shows the number of alive LNs in the network as a function of system running time. The results show the following.

(i) Basically, SRS has better LN lifetime performance. This is not a surprise because in SRS, each LN only senses and transmits local data. They do not relay other sensors message.

(ii) The difference between SRS and stair scheduling and MRS is not very large. This owes to the average function hop-by-hop data aggregation method that we used in stair scheduling and MRS. With it, LNs in stair scheduling and MRS transfer a similar amount of data in each hop.

Figures 10 and 11 further show the number of alive LNs in each level of the cluster for MRS and stair scheduling. We can see the following

(1) Basically, the energy is almost evenly consumed. Most LNs in stair scheduling and MRS can work for more than 2000 periods. In both MRS and stair scheduling, the LNs in the outmost level live the longest time and the LNs in the first level consume energy more quickly. This coincides with our analysis that LNs in the inner levels will have higher burden with message forwarding.

(2) The curves of stair scheduling are much steeper than the curves of MRS. This means that LNs in different levels consume energy more evenly in stair scheduling than that in MRS. It will help LNs work together for longer time without performance degradation. The reason is due to the active slot control of the "stair scheduling."

5.2.3. Communication Reliability. For communication reliability evaluation, to concentrate on the performance of transmission scheduling, we do not consider the path loss coefficient. In SRS, communication will fail only when more than one LN start data transmission to the same CH in the same time slot. In MRS, communication may fail due to two cases. (1) When a child node transmits data, its parent node is sleeping and is not aware of the transmission. (2) Multiple children transmit data to the same parent in the same time slot. In stair scheduling, communication will fail when more than one LN start data transmission to the same CH in the same time slot. Figure 12 compares the communication reliability of SRS, stair scheduling, and MRS in different levels. Cluster using SRS only has one level and each LN directly transmits to CH. We can see that the communication reliability is very high. Clusters using stair scheduling and MRS have multiple levels. The communication reliability of MRS is very low, because the child and parent are not jointly scheduled. The probability that a child and its parent are active together is very small. The reliability of stair scheduling is much better than that of MRS, because children and parents are jointly scheduled. When a child transmits data, his parent is active and is waiting for its transmission.

Figure 13 compares the multi-hop communication reliability. The communication reliability of stair scheduling is

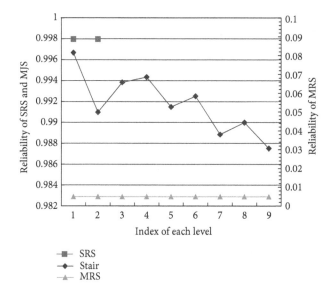

FIGURE 12: Communication reliability in each level.

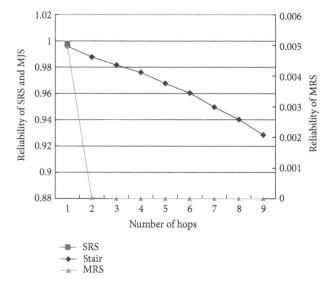

FIGURE 13: Multi-hop communication reliability versus number of hops.

still larger than 0.9 after nine hops. But the communication reliability of MRS is lower than 0.001 after only two hops. The results further confirm that joint scheduling is necessary in multi-hop clusters and stair scheduling provides satisfactory communication reliability.

5.2.4. Performance Summary. With the above simulation results, we can see that stair scheduling is more applicable for large-scale sensor networks than SRS and MRS. Although SRS has good energy and reliability performances, its main drawback is the high cost for deployment of large amount of CHs. The main drawback of MRS is the low reliability in multi-hop communication. The proposed stair scheduling on one hand has good energy performance and on the other

hand can provide satisfactory multi-hop communication reliability.

6. Conclusion

In this paper, we have proposed a stair scheduling method for data collection in tiered large-scale sensor network. The hop-by-hop time synchronization and data aggregation are proposed to make sensors in one cluster sleep and work cooperatively to conserve energy as well as to support multi-hop communication.

Particularly, in "Stair Scheduling," Child node in the ith level always activates and sleeps one slot earlier than its parent, so that LNs in each level can sleep for most of the time and can forward data reliably. Hop-by-hop time synchronization is proposed to avoid time drifting and make the "Stair Scheduling" work in a fully distributed manner. Simulation results have verified that the proposed stair scheduling provides efficient energy and communication reliability performances, which makes it more applicable than MRS and SRS. In future work, we will study the link reliability by introducing enhanced mechanisms of communication collision avoidance and the cluster optimization methods.

Acknowledgment

This work was supported in part by the National Natural Science Foundation of China under Grants 61202360, 61073174, and 61033001.

References

[1] Y. Wang and Y. Wang, *Distributed Storage and Parallel Processing in Large-Scale Wireless Sensor Networks*, vol. 20 of *High Performance Computing: From Grids and Clouds to Exascale*, IOS Press, 2011.

[2] M. Medidi and Y. Zhou, "Extending lifetime with differential duty cycles in wireless sensor networks," in *Proceedings of the 50th Annual IEEE Global Telecommunications Conference (GLOBECOM '07)*, pp. 1033–1037, November 2007.

[3] M. Demirbas, K. Y. Chow, and C. S. Wan, "INSIGHT: internet-sensor integration for habitat monitoring," in *Proceedings of the International Symposium on a World of Wireless, Mobile and Multimedia Networks (WoWMoM '06)*, pp. 553–558, IEEE Computer Society, June 2006.

[4] J. Deng, Y. S. Han, W. B. Heinzelman, and P. K. Varshney, "Scheduling sleeping nodes in high density cluster-based sensor networks," *Mobile Networks and Applications*, vol. 10, no. 6, pp. 825–835, 2005.

[5] D. Tian and N. D. Georganas, "A coverage-preserving node scheduling scheme for large wireless sensor networks," in *Proceedings of the 1st ACM International Workshop on Wireless Sensor Networks and Applications*, pp. 32–41, ACM, September 2002.

[6] X. Wu, J. Cho, B. dAuriol, and S. Lee, "Sleep nodes scheduling in Cluster-Based heterogeneous sensor networks using AHP," in *Embedded Software and Systems*, Y. Lee, H. Kim, J. Kim, Y. Park, L. Yang, and S. Kim, Eds., vol. 4523 of *Lecture Notes in Computer Science*, pp. 437–444, Springer, Berlin, Germany, 2007.

[7] J. Paek, B. Greenstein, O. Gnawali et al., "The tenet architecture for tiered sensor networks," *ACM Transactions on Sensor Networks*, vol. 6, no. 4, article 34, 2010.

[8] Y. Wang, Y. Wang, H. Tan, and F. C. M. Lau, "Maximizing network lifetime online by localized probabilistic load balancing," in *Proceedings of the 10th International Conference on Ad-hoc, Mobile, and Wireless Networks (ADHOC-NOW '11)*, pp. 332–345, Springer, 2011.

[9] S. Bhattacharjee and N. Das, "Distributed data gathering scheduling in multihop wireless sensor networks for improved lifetime," in *Proceedings of the International Conference on Computing: Theory and Applications (ICCTA '07)*, pp. 46–50, IEEE Computer Society, March 2007.

[10] Y. Wang, D. Wang, W. Fu, and D. P. Agrawal, "Hops-based sleep scheduling algorithm for enhancing lifetime of wireless sensor networks," in *Proceedings of the IEEE International Conference on Mobile Ad Hoc and Sensor Sysetems (MASS '06)*, pp. 709–714, October 2006.

[11] W. Pak, J. G. Choi, and S. Bahk, "Tier based anycast to achieve maximum lifetime by duty cycle control in wireless sensor networks," in *Proceedings of the International Wireless Communications and Mobile Computing Conference (IWCMC '08)*, pp. 123–128, August 2008.

[12] I. Caragiannis, C. Kaklamanis, and P. Kanellopoulos, "New results for Energy-Efficient broadcasting in wireless networks," in *Proceedings of the 13th International Symposium on Algorithms and Computation (ISAAC '02)*, pp. 332–343, Springer, 2002.

[13] M. Maroti, B. Kusy, G. Simon, and A. Ledeczi, "Robust multihop time synchronization in sensor networks," in *Proceedings of the International Conference on Wireless Networks (ICWN '04)*, pp. 454–460, June 2004.

[14] S. Lindsey and C. Raghavendra, "PEGASIS: power-efficient gathering in sensor information systems," in *Proceedings of the IEEE Aerospace Conference Proceedings*, vol. 3, pp. 3-1125–3-1130, 2002.

[15] S. Commuri and V. Tadigotla, "Dynamic data aggregation in wireless sensor networks," in *Proceedings of the IEEE 22nd International Symposium on Intelligent Control (ISIC '07)*, pp. 1–6, October 2007.

[16] C. Wu and Y. Chung, "Heterogeneous wireless sensor network deployment and topology control based on irregular sensor model," in *Proceedings of the 2nd International Conference on Advances in Grid and Pervasive Computing (GPC '07)*, pp. 78–88, Springer, 2007.

[17] L. Zhao, X. Hong, and Q. Liang, "Energy-efficient self-organization for wireless sensor networks: a fully distributed approach," in *Proceedings of the IEEE Global Telecommunications Conference (GLOBECOM '04)*, pp. 2728–2732, December 2004.

[18] J. Yuan, Z. Li, W. Yu, and B. Li, "A cross-layer optimization framework for multicast in multi-hop wireless networks," in *Proceedings of the 1st International Conference on Wireless Internet (WICON '05)*, pp. 47–54, July 2005.

[19] Y. Wang, D. Han, Q. Zhao, X. Guan, and D. Zheng, "Clusters partition and sensors configuration for target tracking in wireless sensor networks," in *Proceedings of the 1st International Conference on Embedded Software and Systems (ICESS '05)*, pp. 333–338, Springer, 2005.

13

Circular Collaborative Beamforming for Improved Radiation Beampattern in WSN

N. N. Nik Abd Malik, M. Esa, S. K. Syed Yusof, S. A. Hamzah, and M. K. H. Ismail

UTM MIMOS CoE Telecommunication Technology, Faculty of Electrical Engineering, Universiti Teknologi Malaysia, 81310 Johor Bahru, Johor, Malaysia

Correspondence should be addressed to N. N. Nik Abd Malik; noordini@fke.utm.my

Academic Editor: Adnan Kavak

This paper presents a novel collaborative beamforming (CB) method of wireless sensor network (WSN) by organizing sensor node location in a circular arrangement. Appropriate selection of active CB nodes and cluster is needed each time to perform CB. The nodes are modeled in circular array location in order to consider it as a circular antenna array (CAA). This newly proposed circular collaborative beamforming (CCB) is further presented to solve two different objectives, that is, sidelobe level (SLL) suppression and first null beamwidth (FNBW). Analyses obtained are compared to those from previous work. The findings demonstrate a better CB performance of intelligent capability, and the difference is shown in normalized power characteristic.

1. Introduction

Inside WSN environment, collaborative beamforming (CB) can be beneficial in increasing signal to noise ratio (SNR), thus boosting the energy efficiency of the system. In contrast with direct transmission transmitter-receiver or hop-by-hop transmission, CB spreads the energy consumption over multiple transmitters and improves the signal strength at the receiver [1]. Therefore, the CB nodes need less energy for data transmission, thus balance the energy consumptions, and desirably extend the network lifetime.

Works supporting sensor network in the literature, which utilizes wireless array, including [2–4] investigated usefulness of method and implementation schemes of a transmission array. Gaussian probability density function (pdf) is utilized to model the spatial distribution of sensor nodes in a cluster of WSNs [2] by proposing node selection algorithm [5]. The impact of Gaussian pdf as the spatial distribution is explored on the beampattern characteristic and compared with similar case when uniform pdf is used in [6]. The algorithm is developed to control the sidelobes by searching over different node combinations [7]. Ahmed and Vorobyov consider the

random nodes deployed in Gaussian pdf, while the proposed work considers the uniform random nodes distribution.

In spite of the significant contributions from previous literatures on CB, none of the works offer a CB by implementing circular antenna array (CAA). To the best of the authors' knowledge, this is the first work dealing with this problem. In this paper, the circular array technique is specially designed for WSNs with intelligent capability. The conventional uniform circular antenna array (UCA) may not be directly applied in WSN as it requires the exact location of elements in circular arrangement, a requirement that does not conform with random distribution nature of sensor nodes. Therefore, this is the main challenge of adapting this CAA into the context of WSN environment.

This paper presents a novel method of optimizing sensor node location in a circular arrangement. In this problem, the appropriate selection of active CB nodes and cluster is needed at each time to perform CB in WSN. The nodes are modeled in circular array location in order to consider it as a CAA. In the preliminary version of this work [8], it is shown that the linear sensor nodes array (LSNA) is able to achieve a desirable adaptive beampattern with narrow main lobe and acceptable sidelobes level (SLL). Novel concept is offered with regard to intelligently optimizing and locating the selected sensor nodes to participate and form an array of sensor nodes. The concept is extended here through an alternate approach which employs hybrid least-square speedy particle swarm optimization-based circular collaborative beamforming (HLPSO-based CCB). The earlier work is reported in [9]. The biologically-inspired algorithm of particle swarm optimization (PSO) algorithm is improved and utilized to select the optimum nodes to participate in CB. The objective is to keep the main advantages of the standard PSO, such as simple implementation, low algorithmic complexity, and few control parameters, while maintaining the performance. Therefore, the proposed HLPSO characteristics are particularly attractive for WSNs since the computational resources such as memory and energy are limited.

The main idea in the proposed method is the desired objectives of radiation beampattern with minimum SLL and controllable size of FNBW. The proposed intelligent method of HLPSO-based CCB for determining optimum location of sensor node is proved superior to alternate techniques in terms of the normalized power gain with desired objectives. Up to date, an intelligent approach to determine optimum sensor nodes location to participate in wireless array network by employing bioinspired algorithm has not been reported or published so far by other authors.

2. The Network and Geometrical Array Model

2.1. The Network Model. WSN consists of a large number of sensor nodes in random deployment, which are wirelessly connected. The nodes are self-organized and are in connection with a controlling station as described in [10]. Each sensor node's location is determined using location discovery techniques [11] and is reported back to the controller. The central processor in a controlling station has detailed knowledge of each sensor node's location. It is also capable of selecting the appropriate manager node (MN), thus active cluster (AC) as per user requirement. Each sensing node, S_z is able to sense the environment and collect its own data. The selected MN gathers the data from the sensing nodes and then multicasts a final data packet to all the selected collaborative sensor nodes, that is, active CB nodes. The data from these sensing nodes are aggregated at the MN and only the needed information will be multicast. The active CB nodes will collaboratively transmit the same data in a synchronous manner. These active CB nodes, which perform as a CAA, have the possibility to form a narrow highly directive beam to the intended target point, where the receivers may be placed in order to collect all the transmitted data sent by collaborative nodes.

2.2. The Geometrical Array Model. The collaborative array antenna radiates power in all directions; hence, the simulation work should be in 3-dimensional scope. It is assumed that all sensor nodes are located on a 3-dimensional x-y-z plane. Consider a 3-dimensional characteristic of N-element CAA placed at the x-y-z plane. Assume $z = 0$; therefore the

plane is visualized to run parallel to the earth's surface. The array factor (AF) of the CAA [12] is given by

$$\mathrm{AF}(\theta, \phi) = \sum_{n=1}^{N} e^{j[\kappa r_n \sin\theta \cos(\phi - \phi_n) + \alpha_n]},$$

$$\alpha_n = -\kappa r_n \sin\theta_0 \cos(\phi_0 - \phi_n),$$

$$r_n = \sqrt{(x_n)^2 + (y_n)^2}, \tag{1}$$

$$\phi_n = \tan^{-1}\left(\frac{y_n}{x_n}\right),$$

where N, κ, θ, ϕ, x_n, and y_n are the number of elements, wavenumber $\kappa = 2\pi/\lambda$, elevation angle, azimuth angle, x-coordinate, and y-coordinate (x_n, y_n) of the nth element, respectively. θ_0 and ϕ_0 are the maximum radiation angles. The normalized power gain, G_{norm}, in decibel is as stated in

$$G_{\mathrm{norm}}(\theta, \phi)_{\mathrm{dB}} = 10\log_{10}\left[\frac{|\mathrm{AF}(\theta, \phi)|^2}{\max|\mathrm{AF}(\theta, \phi)|^2}\right]. \tag{2}$$

3. Hybrid Least-Square Speedy Particle Swarm Optimization (HLPSO)

PSO is applied to determine the optimum distance location of the nodes, which performs the highest performance as refer to objective scopes. Some improvements have been adopted in original PSO [13] in order to overcome the weaknesses and to adapt the algorithm inside WSNs environment. The novel HLPSO is proposed by integrating two novel mechanisms, that is, constraint boundaries variables and particle's position and velocity reinitialization. Moreover, the least-square approximation algorithm (LS) is integrated into it to improve the effectiveness and the capabilities of PSO in CCB application.

3.1. Global Constraint Boundaries Variables. Two sets of global constraint boundaries variables for lower boundary L and upper boundary U for different position particles, d_{s1} and d_{sn} ($n = 2, 3, \ldots, N$), are adopted and represented as

$$L_1 \leq d_{s1} < U_1,$$

$$L_N \leq d_{sn} < U_N. \tag{3}$$

These two boundaries are applied to restrict d_{s1} and d_{sn} to stay inside the solution space. Additionally, maximum upper limit and minimum lower limit are also assimilated inside this proposed HLPSO, that is, U_{max} and L_{min}, respectively. These two limits are determined before the computation of the objective function, *of*, in order to enhance the diversity of the particle's searching abilities to be more global and freedom. Thus, it is expressed as

$$
d_{s1} = \begin{cases} d_{s1} = L_1 \xrightarrow{\text{yields}} of\left(L_1\right), & \text{if } d_{s1} > U_{\max}, \\ d_{s1} = d_{s1} \xrightarrow{\text{yields}} of\left(d_{s1}\right), & \text{if } L_{\min} \leq d_{s1} < U_{\max}, \\ d_{s1} = L_1 \xrightarrow{\text{yields}} of\left(L_1\right), & \text{if } d_{s1} \leq L_{\min}, \end{cases}
$$

$$
d_{sn} = \begin{cases} d_{sn} = L_N \xrightarrow{\text{yields}} of\left(L_N\right), & \text{if } d_{sn} > U_{\max}, \\ d_{sn} = d_{sn} \xrightarrow{\text{yields}} of\left(d_{sn}\right), & \text{if } L_{\min} \leq d_{sn} < U_{\max}, \\ d_{sn} = L_N \xrightarrow{\text{yields}} of\left(L_N\right), & \text{if } d_{sn} \leq L_{\min}. \end{cases}
\tag{4}
$$

3.2. Particle's Position and Velocity Reinitialization. The random numbers of particle position d_{sn} can be a factor of the particle's tendency to leave the initially defined search space. Therefore, a modification based on the absorbing wall conditions by [14] is implemented in this algorithm. In order to control the movement of particle from flying outside the border of the search space, the velocity v_{sn} is zeroed whenever the particle d_{sn} goes over the boundaries U_N and L_N. However, the particle d_{sn} is then pulled back inside the search space by reinitializing it as random numbers r generated from the values of $[L_{\min}, U_{\max}]$. The objective of this reinitialization of d_{sn} is to prevent the particle from being stuck in local optima scenario where the particle is trapped and inhibited to search for a better solution. By introducing the reinitialization, a more flexible and comprehensive searching can be done by the particle with noted limitations, as expressed by

$$
v_{sn} = \begin{cases} v_{sn} = 0 \longrightarrow d_{sn} = r\left[L_{\min}, U_{\max}\right], & \text{if } d_{sn} > U_N, \\ v_{sn} = v_{sn}, & \text{if } L_N \leq d_{sn} < U_N, \\ v_{sn} = 0 \longrightarrow d_{sn} = r\left[L_{\min}, U_{\max}\right], & \text{if } d_{sn} \leq L_N. \end{cases}
\tag{5}
$$

By using (5), the particle movement may be triggered again so that it has the highest probability to search for the optimum global best. In addition, the particle position is also forced to stay inside the upper boundary U and lower boundary L as denoted by following equations:

$$
d_{s1} = \begin{cases} d_{s1} = U_1, & \text{if } d_{sn} > U_1, \\ d_{s1} = d_{s1}, & \text{if } L_1 \leq d_{sn} < U_1, \\ d_{sn} = L_1, & \text{if } d_{sn} \leq L_1, \end{cases}
$$

$$
d_{sn} = \begin{cases} d_{sn} = U_N, & \text{if } d_{sn} > U_N, \\ d_{sn} = d_{sn}, & \text{if } L_N \leq d_{sn} < U_N, \\ d_{sn} = L_N, & \text{if } d_{sn} \leq L_N. \end{cases}
\tag{6}
$$

The integration of the LS approximation algorithm in this HLPSO is required so that the desired radiation beampattern performance can be closely approximated to the desired beampattern results. Due to the random spatial positioning of

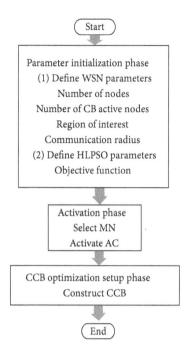

FIGURE 1: Flow chart for HLPSO-based CCB.

nodes, LS algorithm provides the ability to alter and create a radiation beampattern by introducing weights on each node. The determination of the weights allows elimination of the effect of random nodes position errors in WSNs. The effect of weights can be removed through equalization.

3.3. Hybrid Least-Square Particle Swarm Optimization-Based Circular Collaborative Beamforming (HLPSO-Based CCB). The proposed network model of HLPSO-based CCB consists of a random deployment of Z stationary sensor nodes inside the region of interest of $\Lambda\,\text{m}^2$, which are organized in a different cluster. Each node is denoted in Cartesian coordinates of (x_k, y_k) with k representing the number of nodes. Each cluster has an MN designated as the leader, which manages in searching and selecting only the participating CB active nodes to form the HLPSO-based CCB in circular arrangement. The MN also acts as the centre of the CCB, but it is not participating in the CAA construction. Therefore, MN organizes a subset of its cluster nodes into a distributed CCB, $M_n = (m_1, m_2, \ldots, m_N)$ coordinating their transmissions to direct the main beam towards the receivers.

There are three phases in HLPSO-based CCB: parameter initialization, activation, and optimization setup phases. The flow chart for the three phases of HLPSO-based CCB has been shown in Figure 1. A description of each follows.

3.3.1. Parameter Initialization Phase. The initial parameters for WSNs environment are listed in Table 1.

The proposed HLPSO manages to search for the optimum element distance of CCB and deal with the desired objectives. The desired parameters for HLPSO are illustrated in Table 2. These parameters are initialized by referring to the desired objectives of the organization scheme.

TABLE 1: Parameters and values of 8-node CCB.

Parameters	Symbol	Values
Number of all nodes	Z	900 nodes
Area of interest	Λ	$900\,\text{m}^2$
Density	ρ	$1\,\text{node/m}^2$
Manager node	$\text{MN}\,(x_{\text{MN}}, y_{\text{MN}})$	(14.51, 20.91)
Area of active cluster	X	$123\,\text{m}^2$
Nodes inside active cluster	Z_S	119
UCA radius	r^{UCA}	$2.5464\,\text{m}$
CCB radius	r^{CCB}	$2.9421\,\text{m}$

TABLE 2: List of parameters used in HLPSO implementation.

Parameters	Symbol	Value
Number of particles	S	30
Dimension of particles	N	8
Iterations	It	500–1000
Range of particles	D	0 to $2\lambda_O$
Upper boundary for d_n	U_N	$2.2\lambda_O$
Lower boundary for d_n	L_N	$0.1\lambda_O$
Maximum upper limit	$U_{\max}$	$0.1\lambda_O$
Maximum lower limit	$L_{\min}$	$2.5\lambda_O$
Velocity	V	0 to 0.2
Learning factors	$c_1 = c_2$	2.0
Maximum weight	$\omega_{\max}$	0.9
Minimum weight	$\omega_{\min}$	0.4

3.3.2. Activation Phase. MN with coordinates of $(x_{\text{MN}}, y_{\text{MN}})$ is activated which has the most neighbor nodes within its communication radius, C. Then, the AC area, $X\text{m}^2$, is determined by referring to the MN as the centre of the X. The total number of nodes, Z_S, within X is activated.

3.3.3. CCB Optimization Setup Phase. The procedures needed to formulate this CCB optimization setup scheme are described as follows.

Step 1. Construct the virtual circle with C radius by referring to MN as the center of the circle.

Step 2. Establish HLPSO algorithm to optimize the sensor node location.

Step 2(a). Initialize HLPSO parameters.

Step 2(b). Generate random initial location, d_{sn}, $[d_{sn}] = [d_{s1}, d_{s2}, d_{s3}, \ldots, d_{sN}]$ and velocity, v_{sn}, $[v_{sn}] = [v_{s1}, v_{s2}, v_{s3}, \ldots, v_{sN}]$ for each particle, where N and s are the dimensional problem and number of particles, respectively.

Step 2(c). Calculate the objective function, that is, of, where of_{SLL} is the objective function of SLL minimization term as defined in

$$of_{\text{SLL}}\left(\theta_{\text{SLL}}\right) = \sum_{\text{SLL}_1=1}^{\text{MaxSL}} \left|\text{AF}\left(\theta_{\text{SLL}_1}\right)\right|_{\text{dB}} + \sum_{\text{MinSL}}^{\text{SLL}_2=181} \left|\text{AF}\left(\theta_{\text{SLL}_2}\right)\right|_{\text{dB}}, \tag{7}$$

where θ_{SLL_1} and θ_{SLL_2} are the angles, where the SLL is minimized in the lower band (from $\theta_{\text{SLL}_1=1}$ to $\theta_{\text{SLL}_1=\text{MaxSL}}$) and in the upper band (from $\theta_{\text{SLL}_2=\text{MinSL}}$ to $\theta_{\text{SLL}_2=181}$), respectively. of_{bw} is the objective function FNBW term as defined in

$$of_{\text{bw}}\left(\theta_{\text{bw}}\right) = \sum_{\text{bw}=\text{bw}1}^{\text{bw}2} \left|\text{AF}\left(\theta_{\text{bw}}\right)\right|_{\text{dB}}, \tag{8}$$

where θ_{bw} is the angle of desired FNBW; that is, FNBW = $\theta_{\text{bw}2} - \theta_{\text{bw}1}$ which is the range of angles of the major lobe.

Step 2(d). Determine the previous best location, *pbest*, $P = [p_s] = [p_1, p_2, p_3, \ldots, p_S]$. Set $of(p_s)$ value to be equal to $of(d_{sn})$.

Step 2(e). Determine the global best position, $G = [g_n] = [g_1, g_2, g_3, \ldots, g_N]$. Set $g_n = \min(p_s)$ or $g_n = \text{optimum}(p_s)$.

Step 2(f). Update v_{sn}:

$$v_{sn}\left(\tau + 1\right) = \omega v_{sn}\left(\tau\right) + c_1 r_1 \left[p_s\left(\tau + 1\right) - x_{sn}\left(\tau\right)\right] + c_2 r_2 \left[g_n\left(\tau + 1\right) - x_{sn}\left(\tau\right)\right], \tag{9}$$

where c_1 and c_2 are acceleration constants and r_1 and r_2 are uniformly distributed numbers in $[0, 1]$. $\tau + 1$ and τ refer to the time index of the current and previous iterations. ω is the inertial weight factor. Then, limit V using (5).

Step 2(g). Update d_{sn}:

$$d_{sn}\left(\tau + 1\right) = d_{sn}\left(\tau\right) + v_{sn}\left(\tau + 1\right) \tag{10}$$

and limit D of the particles by using (6).

Step 2(h). Update *pbest* as follows.

If $of(d_{sn})$ is better than $of(p_s)$, then update p_s and store $d_{sn}(p_s)$.

Step 2(i). Update *gbest* as follows.

If $of(p_s)$ is better than $of(g_n)$, then update g_n and store $d_{sn}(g_n)$.

Step 2(j). If the maximum iteration number is met, terminate the algorithm, otherwise, proceed to Step 2(c).

Step 3. Construct CAA by using the distance result d_{sn} from the HLPSO algorithm. The constructed CAA is assumed with N-node with spacing distance of d_{sn}. The sensor node location of x- and y-coordinates, $B_n(x_n^B, y_n^B)$, is referring to the values of d_{sn}.

Step 3(a). Calculate the radius, r^d, from d_{sn} by using

$$r^d = \frac{\sum_{n=1}^{N} d_{sn}}{2\pi}. \tag{11}$$

Step 3(b). Calculate phase ϕ_n for every d_{sn} ($n = 1, 2, \ldots, N$). These r^d and ϕ_n values are the polar coordinates of HLPSO optimized location of sensor nodes, $B_n(r^d, \phi_n)$. The ϕ_n is calculated using

$$\phi_n = \frac{\left(2\pi \sum_{n=1}^{N} d_{sn}\right)}{\sum_{n=1}^{N} d_{sn}}. \tag{12}$$

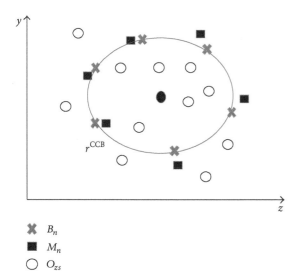

FIGURE 2: Locations of B_n, O_{zs}, and M_n with radius of r^{CCB}.

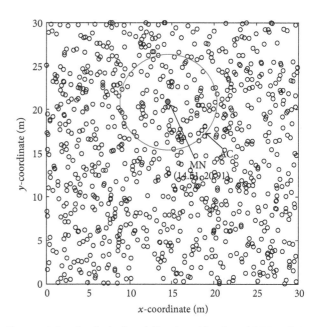

FIGURE 3: Randomly deployed Z nodes with selected MN and AC.

Step 3(c). Convert the polar coordinates $B_n(r^d, \phi_n)$, to the Cartesian coordinates, $B_n(x_n^B, y_n^B)$ by using

$$x_n^B = \left(r^d \cos \phi_n\right) + x_{MN},$$
$$y_n^B = \left(r^d \sin \phi_n\right) + y_{MN}, \tag{13}$$

where (x_{MN}, y_{MN}) are the coordinates of MN.

The construction of this optimum CAA is illustrated in Figure 2. The MN is located at the centre of B_n; however MN does not participate in this CAA. Virtual circle for B_n is constructed with a radius of r^{CCB}.

Step 3(d). Determine the normalized gain, G_{norm}^B, by using (2).

Step 4. Start searching CCB nodes.

Step 4(a). Select the minimum Euclidean distance, d_n^{min}, between $B_n(x_n^B, y_n^B)$ and the nearest node inside AC, $O_{zs}(x_{zs}^O, y_{zs}^O)$,

$$\min\left\{\sqrt{\left[(x_n^B - x_{zs}^O)^2 + (y_n^B - y_{zs}^O)^2\right]}\right\} = d_n^{min} \tag{14}$$

with $zs = 1, 2, \ldots, ZS$ nodes inside AC.

Step 4(b). Choose the O_{zs} which has d_n^{min} with coordinates (x_{zs}^O, y_{zs}^O)

Step 4(c). Activate O_{zs} and appoint it as an optimum CCB. CCB is represented as $M_n(x_n^M, y_n^M)$, $M_n \in O_{zs}$. The mapping process is illustrated in Figure 2.

Step 4(d). This set of optimal CCB will be performed collaboratively as an N-element distributed CAA.

Step 5. Determine normalized gain, G_{norm}^{CCB}, of final CCB using (2).

Step 6. Change radius of both r^{UCA} for UCA and r^{CCB} for CCB, with both depending on the desired size of beamwidth.

Step 6(a). Return to Step 1 for different virtual circles.

Step 6(b). Compare the radiation beampattern performance results for different r values.

Step 7. Select the best solution.

The final solution from the proposed CCB is to select the active nodes to perform CB. The intelligent feature in this proposed algorithm is how the algorithm managed to select the best team of active nodes to accomplish CB with user desired requirements. Examples of such requirements are the desired radiation beampattern with minimum SLL and expected size of FNBW. Results are then validated with UCA [12] and circular sensor node array (CSA) as evidence of the effectiveness. Active nodes of CSA are selected based on the UCA, which has the nearest location to nodes of UCA. In CSA optimization setup phase, Step 2 of establishing HLPSO is not included because the distance between nodes d_{sn} of CSA are directly from the distance between nodes of UCA.

4. Results and Analysis

The computed optimization results in radiation beampatterns are analyzed in different cases of N-node CCB with different objectives. The validation performances are demonstrated between CCB and corresponding results obtained from the CSA and conventional UCA [12].

Figure 3 illustrates the simulation scenario for 8-node CCB in MATLAB environment. It shows the random deployment of Z nodes inside the area of interest, that is, Λ, with selected MN. Initially, Z nodes are in a sleep mode. The red

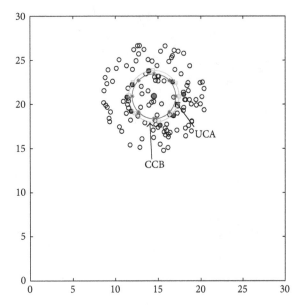

FIGURE 4: Virtual circles (a) blue depicts UCA and (b) green depicts CCB, and nodes (c) blue stars depict A_n, (d) green squares depict B_n, (e) blue circles depict R_n, and (f) square magentas depict M_n.

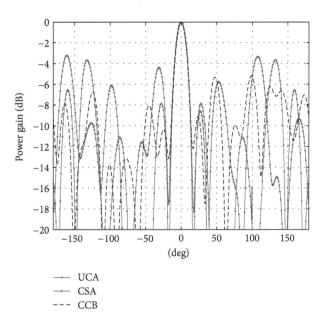

FIGURE 6: Radiation beampattern of 8-node CCB with SLL minimization.

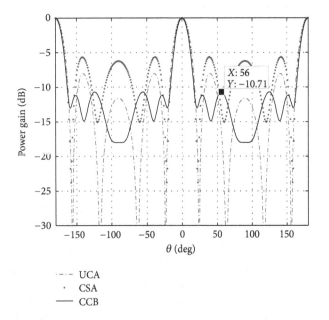

FIGURE 5: Radiation beampattern of 8-node CCB with SLL minimization.

circle marks the AC area, that is, X, with MN at the center of the AC. Figure 4 only highlights the nodes inside the AC. These Z_S nodes are in an idle mode, waiting for any instructions from MN or the center controller. Green circle is a virtual circle with r^{CCB}. Green squares denote coordinates for HLPSO-based nodes, $B_n(x_n^B, y_n^B)$, while square magentas denote CCB active nodes, $M_n(x_n^M, y_n^M)$. The CSA active nodes, R_n, are represented by light blue circles.

Table 3 lists the x- and y-coordinates for B_n and M_n for $n = 1, 2, \dots, 8$ nodes. The Euclidean distance errors

ε_n between HLPSO-based nodes B_n and the proposed CCB active nodes M_n are also demonstrated in the same table. The sum average for all distances for 8-node CCB is calculated as 0.4021.

4.1. Sidelobe Level (SLL) Suppression. In the proposed CCB, SLL can be successfully suppressed to increase the received power at the receivers and to avoid interference from other interrupting access points or clusters or prevent these access points or clusters from recovering the transmitted signal. Figure 5 demonstrates the computed normalized gain for 8-node CCB at x-z plane ($\phi = 0°$). It is observed that, for 360° radiation beampattern, the main beam gain exists at two different angles, that is, 0° and 180°. The maximum SLL obtained is low which is only −10.71 dB, while the maximum SLLs of UCA and CSA are approximately −8.03 dB and −5.63 dB, respectively.

The optimization then considers a circular array with FNBW of 38° with the main beam angle pointing towards $\theta_0 = 0°$. Figure 6 shows the computed radiation beampatterns for y-z plane ($\phi = 90°$), magenta curve for UCA with fixed spacing of $\lambda/2$ between elements, and blue curve for CSA, whereas black curve was proposed for CCB by using HLPSO. It can be clearly observed that the SLL suppression of CCB is generally better than that obtained from both UCA and CSA. All the minor lobes have been successfully minimized with the highest peak SLL to be approximately −5.20 dB compared to the maximum SLL of UCA and CSA of −3.66 dB and −3.21 dB, respectively. The two high lobes at −132° and 132° which exist in UCA have been greatly suppressed in this newly proposed CCB by considerable amount of 4 dB and 2 dB, respectively. At y-z plane, only one main beam exists in CCB for 360° radiation beampattern. These showed that the weakness of LSNA [8] which generates two main beams in 360° radiation beampattern is improved with CCB.

TABLE 3: Coordinates of B_n and M_n with difference Euclidean distances, ε_n.

n	x_n^B	y_n^B	x_n^M	y_n^M	$\varepsilon_n = \sqrt{(x_n^M - x_n^B)^2 + (y_n^M - y_n^B)^2}$
1	17.0	22.4	16.7	22.6	0.3374
2	14.4	23.9	13.9	23.8	0.5204
3	12.0	22.5	12.0	22.2	0.3117
4	11.6	21.1	11.4	20.8	0.3362
5	12.3	19.0	11.9	19.2	0.4503
6	15.1	18.0	15.2	17.6	0.4337
7	16.7	18.9	16.8	18.7	0.2445
8	17.5	20.9	18.0	21.1	0.5828
					$\sum_{n=1}^{8} \varepsilon_n / 8 = 0.4021$

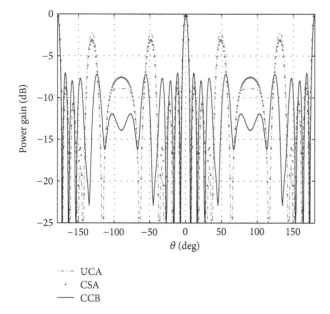

FIGURE 7: Radiation beampattern of 12-node CCB with SLL minimization.

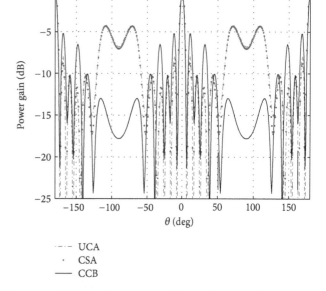

FIGURE 8: Radiation beampattern of 16-node CCB with SLL minimization.

The next case considers 12-node CCB. It demonstrates the different effects on the radiation beampattern performance with different arrangements of the node location. It can be seen from Figure 7 that the conventional UCA exhibits relatively high SLL at $-131°$, $-49°$, $49°$, and $131°$, which is similar to CSA. The maximum SLL of CCB shows degradation, that is, decrease of 5.02 dB, compared to the maximum SLL of UCA (i.e., -2.19 dB at $49°$).

16-node CCB is then considered. It can be observed from Figure 8 that the highest peak SLL of approximately -4.32 dB exists at $-109°$, $-71°$, $71°$, and $109°$ for both UCA and CSA. However, CCB managed to greatly minimize the SLL until -14.30 dB at the respective angles. As the number of CB active nodes increases, it not only can increase the gain but also narrows the FNBW as desired. In this case of 16-node ICSA, the FNBW is only $14°$.

Three cases are analyzed with different numbers of CCB nodes as shown in Table 4. From the results, it is noted that this newly proposed CCB can overcome the undesired increment of the SLLs in UCA and CSA by intelligently optimizing the participating CB active nodes.

4.2. Controllable First Null Beamwidth (FNBW).
An advantage of CCB over UCA and CSA is that the CCB has the capability to adjust the desired amount of FNBW. It is essential to control FNBW in order to decrease the energy consumption. The size of FNBW is needed to be narrower for data transmission to focus the radiation to the attempted destination. In contrast, the size for FNBW is needed to be wider for direction-finding applications.

It reveals the different effects on the size of FNBW performance with the different arrangements of the node location. The radiation patterns of 8-node CCB are plotted in Figure 9. It illustrates a smaller radius of CCB with $r = 1.0312$, resulting in a wider FNBW of approximately $64°$ compared to Figure 10 with $r = 4.098$. It can be seen that the 8-node CCB intelligently accomplishes any desired size of FNBW, either wider or narrower, by optimizing the active

TABLE 4: Percentage improvement of SLL performance for CCB in different cases.

Case	N	N-node CCB		N-node CSA		N-element UCA		Improvement (%)
		SLL (dB)	FNBW (°)	SLL (dB)	FNBW (°)	SLL (dB)	FNBW (°)	
1	8	−5.2	38	−3.21	38	−3.66	38	61.99
	8	−10.71	46	−5.63	46	−8.03	46	90.23
2	12	−7.04	16	−3.07	16	−2.19	16	129.32
3	16	−14.03	14	−4.32	14	−4.32	14	224.77

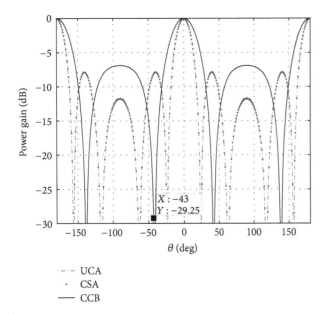

FIGURE 9: Radiation beampattern of 8-node CCB with wider FNBW.

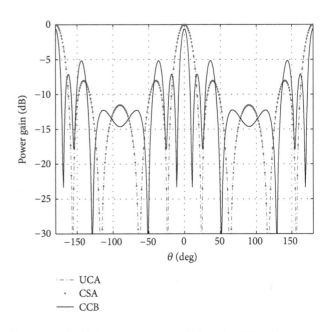

FIGURE 10: Radiation beampattern of 8-node CCB with narrow FNBW.

CB nodes selection. Both CSA and UCA exemplify a similar performance with $r = 1.9098$. The trade-off performance between SLL and FNBW is obviously illustrated. All the minor SLLs have increased throughout the elevation angles. The SLL increases with adaptive FNBW, both CCB and FNBW of 86° and 22°, generate a higher SLL compared to UCA and CSA.

Next case considers 12-node CCB with $r = 5.9761$ to optimize the size of FNBW. The radiation patterns are depicted in Figure 11. It is observed that the FNBW of the optimized 12-node CCB is wider (i.e., 44°) than that of 12-node CSA (i.e., 30°). Additionally, all the minor SLLs have decreased throughout the elevation angles at approximately only −11.51 dB. The subsequent array considered is also a 12-node CCB but with smaller radius of $r = 1.6932$. It shows a larger FNBW (i.e., 50°) as compared to CSA (i.e., 16°) as shown in Figure 12.

It can be observed that a good performance of radiation pattern is obtained from CCB as compared to the previous CSA. It is also shown that different radii contribute to different performances of CCB. In addition, it is noted that the 12-node CCB with FNBW of 50° maintains low SLL throughout the angles that is less than −7.483 dB. Therefore, it is proven that, by implementing the objective function together with CCB, the desired FNBW

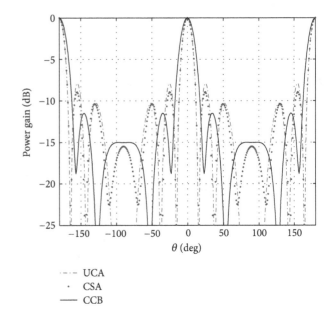

FIGURE 11: Radiation beampattern of 12-node CCB with narrow FNBW.

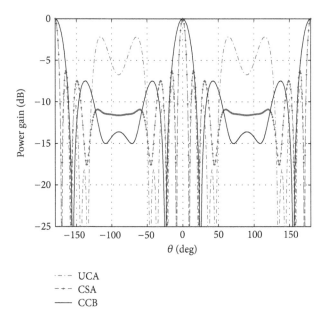

[2] K. Yao, R. E. Hudson, C. W. Reed, D. Chen, and F. Lorenzelli, "Blind beamforming on a randomly distributed sensor array system," *IEEE Journal on Selected Areas in Communications*, vol. 16, no. 8, pp. 1555–1566, 1998.

[3] M. F. A. Ahmed and S. A. Vorobyov, "Beampattern random behavior in wireless sensor networks with Gaussian distributed sensor nodes," in *Proceedings of the IEEE Canadian Conference on Electrical and Computer Engineering (CCECE '08)*, pp. 257–260, May 2008.

[4] Z. Han and H. V. Poor, "Lifetime improvement of wireless sensor networks by collaborative beamforming and cooperative transmission," in *Proceedings of the IEEE International Conference on Communications (ICC' 07)*, pp. 3954–3958, June 2007.

[5] M. F. A. Ahmed and S. A. Vorobyov, "Node selection for side-lobe control in collaborative beamforming for wireless sensor networks," in *Proceedings of the IEEE 10th Workshop on Signal Processing Advances in Wireless Communications (SPAWC '09)*, pp. 519–523, June 2009.

[6] H. Ochiai, P. Mitran, H. V. Poor, and V. Tarokh, "Collaborative beamforming for distributed wireless ad hoc sensor networks," *IEEE Transactions on Signal Processing*, vol. 53, no. 11, pp. 4110–4124, 2005.

FIGURE 12: Radiation beampattern of 12-node CCB with wide FNBW.

[7] M. F. A. Ahmed and S. A. Vorobyov, "Sidelobe control in collaborative beamforming via node selection," *IEEE Transactions on Signal Processing*, vol. 58, no. 12, pp. 6168–6180, 2010.

[8] N. N. N. A. Malik, M. Esa, S. K. S. Yusof, and S. A. Hamzah, "Optimization of adaptive linear sensor node array in wireless sensor network," in *Proceedings of the Asia-Pacific Microwave Conference (APMC '10)*, pp. 2336–2339, Singapore, December 2009.

can be controlled that simultaneously improved the SLL suppression.

[9] N. N. N. A. Malik, M. Esa, S. K. S. Yusof, and S. A. Hamzah, "Optimization of linear sensor node array for wireless sensor networks using Particle Swarm Optimization," in *Proceedings of the Asia-Pacific Microwave Conference (APMC '10)*, pp. 1316–1319, December 2010.

5. Conclusion

The problem of array beamforming is the presence of error beampattern caused by random sensor position errors. The proposed CCB can effectively improve reliability, capacity, and coverage by intelligently adjusting the shape of the beam patterns under different constraints, either by suppressing the SLL or managing the size of FNBW as per desired usage. The proposed CCB has the ability to select the active CB nodes and dynamically control the radiation beampattern to enhance the reception while minimizing the interferences using the proposed HLPSO-based CCB algorithms. The radiation beampattern expression of the proposed CCB is obtained, and it is further proved. Different properties of the radiation beampattern have been successfully analyzed and proven.

[10] P. Vincent, M. Tummala, and J. McEachen, "A new method for distributing power usage across a sensor network," *Ad Hoc Networks*, vol. 6, no. 8, pp. 1258–1280, 2008.

[11] M. Batson, J. McEachen, and M. Tummala, "Enhanced collection methodology for distributed wireless antenna systems," in *Proceedings of the IEEE International Conference on System of Systems Engineering (SOSE '07)*, April 2007.

[12] C. A. Balanis, *Antenna Theory: Analysis and Design*, Wiley, New York, NY, USA, 3rd edition, 2005.

[13] J. Kennedy and R. Eberhart, "Particle swarm optimization," in *Proceedings of the 1995 IEEE International Conference on Neural Networks*, pp. 1942–1948, December 1995.

Acknowledgments

The work is supported by Universiti Teknologi Malaysia and Ministry of Education Malaysia, RUG vote PY/2012/01578 and FRGS vote 4F039.

[14] Z. Zaharis, D. Kampitaki, A. Papastergiou, A. Hatzigaidas, P. Lazaridis, and M. Spasos, "Optimal design of a linear antenna array using particle swarm optimization," in *Proceedings of the 5th WSEAS International Conference on Data Networks, Communications and Computers*, pp. 69–74, Bucharest, Romania, October 2006.

References

[1] J. Feng, Y. Nimmagadda, Y. H. Lu, B. Jung, D. Peroulis, and Y. C. Hu, "Analysis of energy consumption on data sharing in beamforming for wireless sensor networks," in *Proceedings of the 19th International Conference on Computer Communications and Networks (ICCCN '10)*, pp. 1–6, August 2010.

14

Adaptive Deployment Scheme for Mobile Relays in Substitution Networks

Karen Miranda, Enrico Natalizio, and Tahiry Razafindralambo

Inria Lille-Nord Europe, FUN Research Team, 40 avenue Halley, 59650 Villeneuve d'Ascq, France

Correspondence should be addressed to Karen Miranda, karen.miranda@inria.fr

Academic Editor: Hannes Frey

We present how the mobility of routers impacts the performance of a wireless substitution network. To that end, we simulate a scenario where a wireless router moves between three static nodes, a source and two destinations of UDP traffic. Specifically, our goal is to *deploy* or *redeploy* the mobile relays so that application-level requirements, such as data delivery or latency, are met. Our proposal for a mobile relay achieves these goals by using an adaptive approach to self-adjust their position based on local information. We obtain results on the performance of end-to-end delay, jitter, loss percentage, and throughput under such mobility pattern for the mobile relay. We show how the proposed solution is able to adapt to topology changes and to the evolution of the network characteristics through the usage of limited neighborhood knowledge.

1. Introduction

Problem Description. It is critical to design efficient algorithms to support ubiquitous services in networked environments. This is due to the fact that wireless technologies are evolving into the next generation, so an increasing number of users will enjoy ubiquitous access. Some of the main challenges include a fairly complex node placement/deployment problem without prior knowledge of the optimal network topology or optimal mobile routers locations.

Previous work has focused on deployment and placement of mobile devices (e.g., robots) for area coverage [1–5]. In our work, the goal is to deploy a set of wireless mobile devices between classical network routers to restore the connectivity without prior knowledge of the optimal placement of the devices. Additionally, most efforts to date use local area networks, ad hoc networks, wireless sensor networks, and mesh networks for several different purposes, such as community and neighborhood networking, transportation systems, networking for developing countries, connection of isolated locations, spontaneous networking, and disaster recovery [6]. In these papers, the spontaneous networking approach is used for specific cases, such as hurricanes, earthquakes, fiber optic cable cuts, flash crowds, or in presence of weak connectivity. Instead, in this paper, we consider the use of controlled mobility provided to wireless routers to restore or improve network connectivity. We assume that mobile relays have *self-organization*, *self-optimization*, and *self-healing* capabilities in order to allow a flexible, scalable, and resilient deployment. Hence, the main issue in this context is how to *deploy* or *redeploy* the wireless mobile relays in order to keep the network services running.

Contributions. (1) We introduce different adaptive strategies for the deployment/redeployment of wireless mobile relays. (2) Our solution is localized, scalable, and adaptive. (3) We show that our scheme outperforms the static approach.

Paper Organization. The remainder of this paper is structured as follows. In Section 2, we state the problem, introduce some motivating applications, and state our assumptions, followed in Section 3 by the description of our solution, the simulation model, and the performance metrics. In Section 4, we evaluate the proposed scheme through extensive simulations and discuss the experimental results. Finally, Section 5 concludes this work and presents future developments.

2. Some Background

Spontaneous networking, or public service networking, is used in specific cases such as hurricanes, earthquakes, fiber optic cable cuts, flash crowds, or in presence of weak connectivity, the network not only must be deployed in a short period of time, but also must have capabilities as self-organization, self-optimization, and self-healing [7]. This type of networks is called rapidly deployable network (RDN).

We consider a substitution network (SN) as a kind of RDN. An SN is a temporary wireless network created to help the base network to keep providing services. This substitution network must be rapidly deployed to quickly adapt to network topology changes and to ensure the network connectivity [8].

A specific example of an application of an SN is the contractor's mistake in the Sydney's Business District [9]. In 2009, some contractors cut through 10,000 of Telstra company copper wires and 8 fiber optic cables by mistake. This caused over 12,000 business and residential customers without phone, mobile, or Internet services for several days. The cost to Telstra of this mistake was AU$1 million just to repair the wires, plus the compensation cost for the affected customers and a demand by the Australian government. Finally, it took Telstra about a week to replace the cables and restore the service.

Another example is after a natural or man-made disaster, such as earthquakes or terrorist attacks, when the communications networks are not destroyed but congested. In September 11, 2001, the radio network used by the Emergency Medical Service was saturated by panicked operator transmitting unnecessary information [10].

2.1. Related Work. In the last years, many schemes and solutions have been proposed to improve network performance by placing wireless relays in specific positions [11, 12]. The most common objectives are energy consumption and coverage as presented in [4, 13–17]. However, these solutions are not suitable to substitution networks because they depend on a preplaned deployment.

Evans et al. introduced in 1999 the concept of a rapidly deployable network [18]. The main idea is to deploy a network infrastructure *in promptu* to provide communication services for military applications. After this work, several deployment schemes have been proposed in the literature not only for military communications but also for emergency communications.

In order to address the deployment problem, a relay-based approach is presented in [19–21]. In most of these proposals, the first responders, for example, firemen or policemen, carry a personal mobile radio and small relays. Then, the first responders must drop these devices while exploring the emergency zone in order to maintain the connectivity with the central command thus creating a multihop network. Each mobile radio exchanges control information with the closest relay to decide when to drop a new small relay. So, the main focus is to propose a deployment decision process that maximizes the network performance.

Bao and Lee present a method to rapid deploy an ad hoc backbone for spontaneous networks with no preplanning [19]. The authors present a collaborative deployment algorithm, which takes into account physical or link quality measurements such as signal-noise ratio and packet loss rate. The algorithm measures the link quality through control messages added to the control packet header of the ad hoc routing protocol. They assume that each device can notice the different type of its neighbors, that is, if the neighbor is a mobile device or a relay, and also they keep track of each relay deployed.

Later, Souryal et al. present an algorithm for NIST real-time deployment of mesh networks project [21]. The authors propose an algorithm based on a quick evaluation of the physical layer performed by the mobile radio. In a nutshell, the mobile radio establishes one-hop communication by constantly broadcasting probe packets to previous relays, when some relays in the range respond with a probe ACK packet, the mobile radio measures the RSS through ACK reception, if the RSS value falls below a given threshold level, then a new relay must be dropped.

Nevertheless, the concept of static relays has changed, for example, the LANdroids project launched by the Defense Advanced Research Projects Agency, DARPA. The goal is to propose an RDN for battlefield based on mesh networks composed of small mobile relays. Based on this call, a spreadable connected autonomic network (SCAN) is presented in [22]. SCAN is a mobile network that automatically maintains its own connectivity by moving constantly its nodes. The authors present the SCAN algorithm capable to deal with environments where the predeployment mapping is expensive or infeasible without any previous information of the environment. This protocol proposes an online distributed process where each node uses two-hop radius knowledge of the network topology and each of them determines when to stop its motion if the decision criterion indicates risk of dividing or disconnecting the network.

2.2. Key Points. We propose to deploy a network composed of a fleet of dirigible wireless mobile routers for public service. In order to fully adapt to the current conditions, the mobile routers should move or redeploy on demand. This means that, not only the edges of the net may move but also the core or part of the core. One of the deployment issues is in which direction move the router to avoid disconnection or degradation of the quality of service (QoS).

The deployment of a network composed of a fleet of dirigible wireless mobile routers (named from now on as *substitution network*) can be useful in case of multiple link failures as in natural disasters, weak connectivity, fiber optic cable cuts, or flash crowds.

In this work, we focus on a typical use case of substitution networks as presented in [8]. In this scenario, the substitution network aims at helping a base network to restore and maintain some of the basic services available before the failure. Thus, a fleet of mobile relays is self-deployed to compose a substitution network together with the base network. Thereby, we evaluate an adaptive positioning scheme to increase the network depending on the driving applications.

Our basic idea is that, during the network lifetime, each wireless mobile device of the substitution network determines a new position by using the feedback on the link quality coming from its neighbors.

We assume that two nodes are "neighbors" when they are within the communication range of each other. Likewise, we assume that some of the devices are fixed, that traffic needs to be transferred between two fixed devices, and that wireless devices dynamically move in the scenario and act as relays, regardless the routing protocol. Besides, we assume that each device is aware of its own position by using GPS or any other localization system, so as to allow nodes to use controlled mobility. More ever, as with many link layer protocols, we assume that each node is equipped with a timer and an 802.11 wireless card, and it has an identifier that is unique in the network (MAC address).

In this paper, we use the term "broadcast" for message propagation in a device's neighborhood. As well as, we call "link parameter" a measure of link quality between a mobile device and each of its neighbors, for example, signal-noise ratio (SNR), received signal strength (RSS), round-trip-time (RTT), and transmission rate (TR).

Based on the assumptions above, we propose a solution to deploy/redeploy intermediate mobile relays, that is,

(1) localized: every decision taken by the mobile relay is based only on close neighbors (i.e., one-hop neighbors) and local link information. The mobile routers take advantage of probe packets to exchange information about their surrounding links status, and drive their positioning;

(2) scalable: as a consequence of the previous property, our solution is scalable on the network size and the mobility strategy of the surrounding wireless mobile routers;

(3) adaptive: the algorithm ensures that the connectivity quality is permanently monitored based on close neighbors and local link information. As a consequence, the proposed placement scheme is adaptive to topology changes and to the evolution of the network characteristics.

3. Proposed Scheme

Briefly, the major steps of the algorithm that runs in each node independently are the following: (1) measurement of the "link parameter" (2) computation of the new position and (3) movement towards the computed position. Each of these steps is described.

No prior knowledge of the optimal mobile device locations is assumed to be available at nodes. Our algorithm uses close neighbors and local links information to allow nodes to position themselves. Each relay runs the algorithm regularly and measures the link parameters.

3.1. Detailed Operation

3.1.1. Measure Link Parameters. In order to measure link parameters, we use an intrusive method. The wireless mobile device regularly (every t seconds) broadcasts *probe request* packets containing a sequence number and the *id* or MAC address of the wireless mobile device. Each node receiving *probe request* replies with a *probe reply message* by using unicast transmission and including information such as its id, its position, and any local information regarding the link parameters. We use an intrusive method to get up-to-date information regarding link parameters but also to get a consistent and fair view of each link in the surroundings of a mobile device. An additional advantage of using broadcasting of *probe request* packets is that we can avoid the clock synchronization problem between devices.

It is important to notice that the probe packets, request and reply, have a higher access priority than other packets. Specifically, when a probe packet is generated, it will be put at the head of line in the link layer queue. However, these packets cannot preempt a scheduled transmission at the MAC layer. Note also that since the mobile routers are only used as relays, they are able only to exchange protocol stack information up to network layer. Thus, they cannot use application or transport layer measures directly or indirectly related with the "link parameter" currently measured.

3.1.2. Compute New Position. Each node computes its new position based on the surrounding link parameters every $k \times t$ seconds, where k is the number of probe packets, to ensure that enough measures are used to get consistent statistics on the link parameter. The wireless mobile device stores the received value and the measurements obtained through the probe reply. A sliding window is used to compute the statistics, and a FIFO policy is used to remove older values of the link parameters.

The wireless mobile device compares the values of the link parameter received from the next and the previous hop, X_{next} and X_{prev}. For example, when the considered parameter is the round-trip time ($X = $ RTT), if $X_{next} > X_{prev}$, then the wireless device will move toward the next node. The degree of the inequality changes according to the link parameter considered. In this case, we assume that RTT is somehow related to the distance between nodes. In case of multiple flows passing through the same device, the wireless mobile device will move towards the node i with the maximum RTT. The link parameter measurements are averaged and used to compute the new position. The mobile device can use measurements from different layers. We consider RTT as a network layer metric, TR as the rate at which a packet is sent, as a link layer metric, and the SNR and the RSS as physical layer metrics.

3.1.3. Move to New Position. In this step, each wireless device moves forward on the computed direction for a distance d. This stepwise choice is arbitrary and it would be easier to relate the traveled distance d to the link parameter value. However, we chose this stepwise movement to be

(i) **Message formats:**
    ProbeRequest messages: Identifier *src*;
    ProbeReply messages: Identifier*src, dst*;
(ii) **Parameter:**
    double ProbePeriod, SendTime, RTT;
    int   *k*, Move;
PartI—Link parameters *n*:
(1) set TIMER to expire in time ProbePeriod;
(2) **while** (1) **do**
(3)   **if** (TIMER ≤ 0) **then**
(4)   Send ProbeRequest Message;
(5)   SendTime = NOW;
(6)   set TIMER to expire in time ProbePeriod;
(7)   **end if**
(8) **end while**
(9) **while** (1) **do**
(10)   Upon reception of a ProbeReply
(11)   RTT = NOW − SendTime;
(12)   Store RTT in a table with the ProbeReply sender;
(13) **end while**
Part II—Compute new position and move:
(1) set TIMER to expire in time $k \times$ ProbePeriod;
(2) **while** (1) **do**
(3)   **if** (TIMER ≤ 0) **then**
(4)   Compute link parameter for Next and Prev hops;
(5)   **if** ($RTT_{next} > RTT_{prev}$) **then**
(6)   Move towards the Next hop;
(7)   **else if** ($RTT_{next} < RTT_{prev}$) **then**
(8)   Move towards the Prev hop;
(9)   **else**
(10)   Do not move;
(11)   **end if**
(12)   set TIMER to expire in time $k \times$ ProbePeriod;
(13)   **end if**
(14) **end while**

ALGORITHM 1: APA (adaptive positioning algorithm).

more realistic since in real environments, some geographical positions cannot be considered as a suitable position due to potential obstacles, for example, a wireless mobile device cannot cross a vehicles road.

Based on the link parameter measurements, the mobile device tries to equalize the metrics for both the previous node and the next node. The study of this tradeoff is left as a future work. It is important to notice here that we assume a correlation between link parameters and position due to wireless channel impairments or fading effects, for example.

The protocol version of the proposed scheme, named APA for (adaptive positioning algorithm), is given in Algorithm 1.

3.2. Topology and Simulation Description. We implement APA by using the NS 2.29 [23] network simulator with patches that reflect real wireless propagation, real wireless physical layer, and the adaptive autorate fallback (AARF) mechanism for 802.11b [24]. AARF adapts the transmission rates depending on the network conditions, in order to increase link reliability. Rather than using a fixed threshold,

AARF adapts such threshold following binary exponential backoff. We also extend the simulator by adding a realistic channel propagation and error model, as proposed in [25], by adding the effect of interference and different thermal noises to compute the signal to noise plus interference ratio (SINR) and accounting for different bit error rate (BER) to SINR curves for the various codings employed. We use the DSR protocol for our simulations in order to account with an initial routing solution. As we mentioned before, APA is not tied to any routing protocol in particular, so it is designed to work with any routing protocol. Table 1 shows all the parameters used in our simulations.

Below, we present an experimental performance evaluation of APA under different network metrics such as *throughput, delay,* and *jitter.* They are defined as follows:

(i) average throughput (TH). The average throughput of a data transfer is: F/T *bits/sec,* where F is the number of bits transferred every second to the final destination;

TABLE 1: Simulation parameters.

	Propagation	Two ray ground
	Error model	Real
	Antennas gain	$G_t = G_r = 1$
Physical	Antennas height	$h_t = h_r = 1\,\text{m}$
	Min received power	$P_{r-\text{thresh}} = 6.3\,\text{nW}$
	Mobile router energy	50 J
	Communication range	240 m
	802.11b	Standard compliant
MAC	Basic rate	2 Mbps
	Auto rate fallback	1, 2, 5.5, 11 Mbps
LL	Queue size	50 pkts
	Policy	Drop tail
Routing	Static	Dijkstra
	Routing traffic	None
Transport and application	Flow	CBR/UDP
	Packet size	1052B
Statistics	Number of simples	$k = 10$
	Broadcast period	$t = U(0.1)$
Mobility	Movement step	$d = 2\,\text{m}$

FIGURE 1: Simple evaluation scenario.

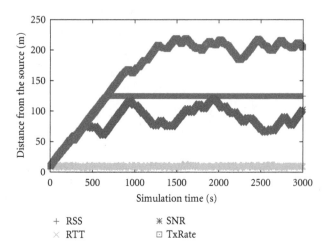

FIGURE 2: Placement evolution with APA comparison (RSS, RTT, SNR, and TxRate).

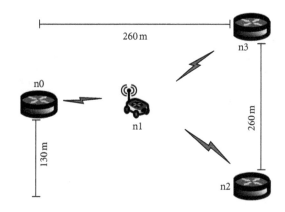

FIGURE 3: Evaluation scenario with one source and two different destinations.

(ii) average end-to-end delay (D). This is the total average time for a packet to travel from source to destination;

(iii) average jitter (J). We compute the jitter as the measure of the variability over time of the packet latency across a network; as known, jitter is a function of the delay;

(iv) loss percentage (L). The loss percentage is equal to $((l-T)/l) \times 100$, where l is the total number of packets arriving at the receiver during the simulation time, and T is the total number of packets.

At the transport layer, we transmit UDP traffic with a packet size of 1000 B. We also vary the average transmission rate with steps of 10, 50, 200, 300, 600, 1000 kbps for each set of simulations. Each simulation runs for a period of 2000 seconds.

4. Results

We start by simulating a simple scenario with a source and a destination node that communicate through one wireless mobile relay (Figure 1). In this topology, the destination

node is placed 250 meters far from the source node. At the beginning of the simulation, the relay node is placed 10 meters far from the source node. Thus, the relay starts moving by using our APA algorithm.

Thus, we evaluate the convergence of our proposal with each link parameter, RSS, RTT, SNR, and TxRate. We use the topology illustrated in Figure 1, with UDP traffic with a packet size of 512 B during 3,000 seconds. The resulting movements are depicted in Figure 2, the relay moves between the source and the destination trying to position itself by equalizing each of the mentioned parameters. We observe that, by using RSS as input for our scheme, the relay reaches exactly the middle position (i.e., 125 meters from the source) after less than one third of the simulation, and it remains in that position for the rest of the simulation time. Besides, when the relay uses the RTT, SNR, and TxRate as input, it keeps moving without reaching a fixed position.

Accordingly, we evaluate the network performance changing the number of flows and destinations. We use the topology depicted in Figure 3, where we present a source

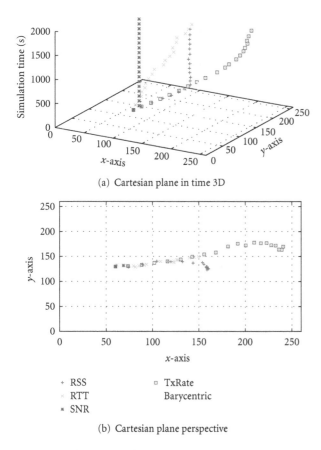

(a) Cartesian plane in time 3D

(b) Cartesian plane perspective

+ RSS   □ TxRate
× RTT   Barycentric
∗ SNR

FIGURE 4: Deployment evolution in time (RSS, RTT, SNR, TxRate, and Barycentric), contrasting the relay placement as function of time.

(n0) and two destinations (n2, n3) out of range. So, we use a relay (n1) to connect the source and the destinations. At the beginning of the simulation, the relay (n1) is placed 60 meters far from the source node (n0) on the straight line that connects the source node from the middle position between the receiver nodes (n2 and n3). For all the simulations, we consider transmitting UDP packets with a size of 1000 B, and we vary the transmission rate as we described in the previous section.

We compare the performance of each link parameter versus the performance of a fixed node. The fixed node is positioned on the barycenter of the given topology, that is, 173 meters far from the source node on the straight line that connects the source node from the middle position between the receiver nodes.

We present in Figure 4, the positioning evolution of the relay by using APA. This figure presents two views of the evolution, Figure 4(a) is a 3D view showing the movement on the Cartesian plane with the time on the z-axis. We observe that, when the relay uses SNR as the equalizing parameter, it stops moving after 200 seconds, by using RSS, it stops moving after 1500 seconds, whereas by using RTT and TxRate, it continues moving until the end of the simulation. The movement trace is depicted in Figure 4(b). Here, we

observe that by using TxRate, the relay goes close to n3. We also observe that only the RTT parameter reaches the point that is closer to the barycenter, and the RTT-based scheme improves its performance in this scenario compared with the simple scenario presented before.

In the following simulation campaigns, we transmit two UDP flows starting at the same time. The source node (n0) transmits Flow 1 to destination node 1 (n2) and Flow 2 to the destination node 2 (n3). In Figure 5, we show the average end-to-end delay and the average jitter comparison for each flow. The performance for these two parameters, when the mobile relay is positioned on the barycenter, is constant. We see also that for a transmission rate under 600 kbps, the mobile relay obtains low values for both delay and jitter.

Figure 6 shows the results for throughput and the packet loss. We can see that when the relay is positioned on the barycenter, as the transmission rate increases, the results are constant and outperform those obtained by using the mobile relay. Besides, as the transmission rate increases, the packet loss grows. For both metrics, the RTT parameter performs better than the RTT, SNR, and TxRate parameters.

However, these results do not reflect the performance during the simulation time. This is important because, as we can see in Figure 7, the mobile relay in some moments improves the throughput values obtained with the static relay. We have to recall that the mobile relay starts moving from a position 60 meters far from the source node, which is worse than the barycenter in terms of network performance; but, when using our algorithm, the mobile relay improves its position and its performance on the fly.

5. Conclusion

In this paper, we have presented a scheme based on different link parameters for substitution networks that operates in environments where connectivity guarantee is an issue.

We have introduced a suite of algorithm strategies to control the placement of wireless mobile devices. In particular, we have focused on networks where the source and the destination nodes of UDP traffic are connected through multihop communications performed by wireless mobile devices that act as relays. Specifically, our goal has been to *deploy* or *redeploy* the wireless mobile devices so that application-level requirements, such as data delivery or latency, are met. The APA algorithm we have proposed achieves these goals by using a localized and adaptive approach that determines the optimal positions of mobile relays in terms of delay, jitter, loss percentage, and throughput. Our simulation results show the importance of the placement of wireless mobile relay nodes to increase the performance at the application level. Finally, we compared our solution with the optimal theoretical placement, which is the barycenter.

Our future work will focus on determining theoretically the optimal placement of the relay nodes in order to increase quality of service and quality of experience.

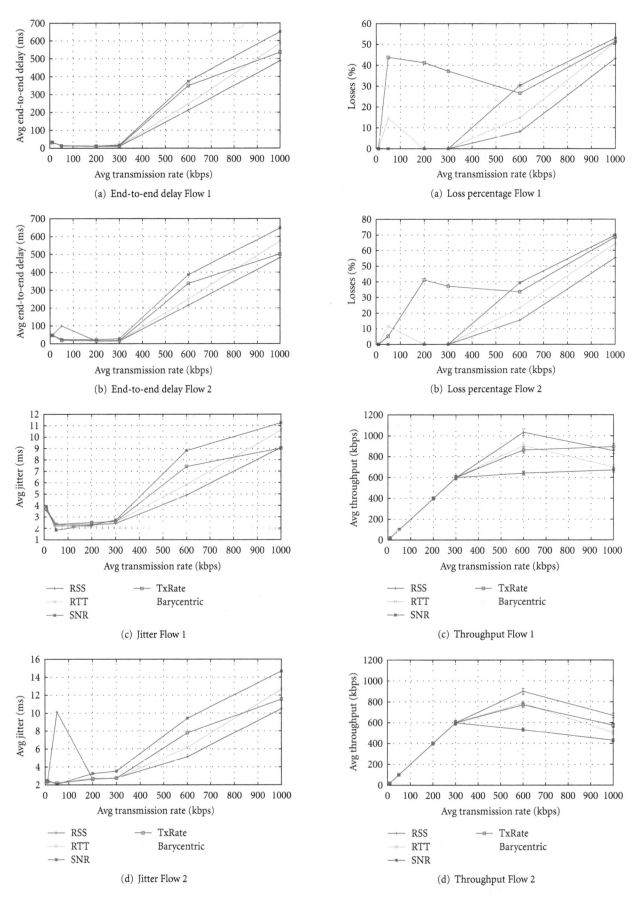

FIGURE 5: End-to-end delay and jitter comparison.

FIGURE 6: Throughput and packet loss percentage comparison.

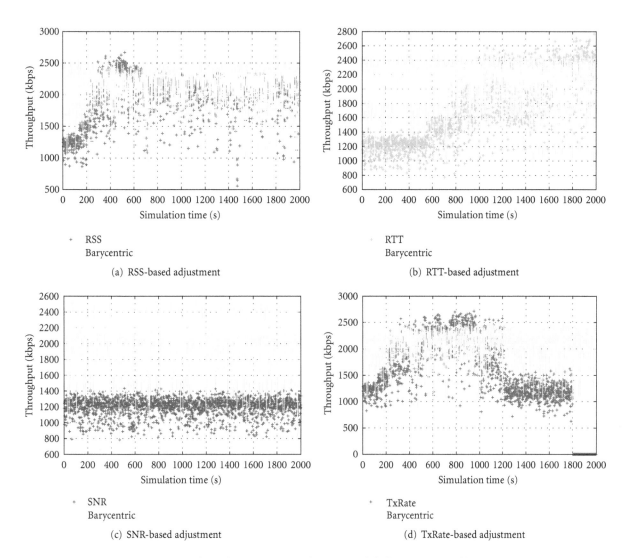

FIGURE 7: Instant throughput comparison between each link parameter and barycentric.

Acknowledgments

This work is partially supported by the French National Research Agency (ANR) under the VERSO RESCUE project (ANR-10-VERS-003) and by the Inria ARC MISSION grant.

References

[1] M. A. Batalin and G. S. Sukhatme, "Coverage, exploration and deployment by a mobile robot and communication network," *Telecommunication Systems*, vol. 26, no. 2–4, pp. 181–196, 2004.

[2] I. Chatzigiannakis, A. Kinalis, and S. Nikoletseas, "Sink mobility protocols for data collection in wireless sensor networks," in *Proceedings of the ACM International Workshop on Mobility Management and Wireless Access (MobiWAC '06)*, pp. 52–59, Terromolinos, Malaga, Spain, October 2006.

[3] W. Wang, V. Srinivasan, and K.-C. Chua, "Trade-offs between mobility and density for coverage in wireless sensor networks," in *Proceedings of the 13th Annual ACM International*

Conference on Mobile Computing and Networking (MobiCom' 07), pp. 39–50, Montréal, Québec, Canada, 2007.

[4] E. Natalizio, V. Loscri, and E. Viterbo, "Optimal placement of wireless nodes for maximizing path lifetime," *IEEE Communications Letters*, vol. 12, no. 5, pp. 362–364, 2008.

[5] T. Razafindralambo and D. Simplot-Ryl, "Connectivity preservation and coverage schemes for wireless sensor networks," *IEEE Transactions on Automatic Control*, vol. 56, no. 10, Article ID 5977008, pp. 2418–2428, 2011.

[6] W. Allen, A. Martin, and A. Rangarajan, "Designing and deploying a rural ad-hoc community mesh network testbed," in *Proceedings of the IEEE Conference on Local Computer Networks (LCN '05)*, pp. 740–743, Sydney, Australia, November 2005.

[7] R. Bruno, M. Conti, and E. Gregori, "Mesh networks: commodity multihop ad hoc networks," *IEEE Communications Magazine*, vol. 43, no. 3, pp. 123–131, 2005.

[8] T. Razafindralambo, T. Begin, M. Dias De Amorim, I. G. Lassous, N. Mitton, and D. Simplot-Ryl, "Promoting quality of service in substitution networks with controlled mobility," in *Proceedings of the 10th International Conference on Ad-Hoc, Mobile, and Wireless Networks (ADHOC-NOW '11)*, pp. 248–261, Paderborn, Germany, 2011.

[9] R. Charette, "Cable cut in Sydney's central business district,"
     in *Risk Factor blog IEEE Spectrum*, 2009, http://spectrum.ieee
     .org/riskfactor/computing/it/cable-cut-in-sydneys-central-
     business-district.

[10] A. M. Townsend and M. L. Moss, "Telecommunications in-
     frastructure in disasters: preparing cities for crisis communi-
     cations," Tech. Rep., Center for Catastrophe Preparedness and
     Response, 2005.

[11] S. Commuri and M. K. Watfa, "Coverage strategies in wireless
     sensor networks," *International Journal of Distributed Sensor
     Networks*, vol. 2, no. 4, pp. 333–353, 2006.

[12] R.-H. Zhang, Z.-P. Jia, and X.-S. Xu, "Nodes deployment
     mechanism based on energy efficiency in wireless sensor net-
     works," *International Journal of Distributed Sensor Networks*,
     vol. 5, no. 1, p. 99, 2009.

[13] J. Carle and D. Simplot-Ryl, "Energy-efficient area monitoring
     for sensor networks," *Computer*, vol. 37, no. 2, pp. 40–46, 2004.

[14] D. Simplot-Ryl, I. Stojmenovic, and J. Wu, "Energy-efficient
     backbone construction, broadcasting, and area coverage in
     sensor networks," in *Handbook of Sensor Networks: Algorithms
     and Architecture*, John Wiley & Sons, 2005.

[15] K. T. Phan, R. Fan, H. Jiang, S. A. Vorobyov, and C. Tellam-
     bura, "Network lifetime maximization with node admission
     in wireless multimedia sensor networks," *IEEE Transactions on
     Vehicular Technology*, vol. 58, no. 7, pp. 3640–3646, 2009.

[16] J. Zhang and T. M. Lok, "Cooperative protocols for multiple-
     source multiple-relay wireless networks," *International Journal
     of Sensor Networks*, vol. 4, no. 4, pp. 209–219, 2008.

[17] A. Bari, D. Teng, R. Ahmed, and A. Jaekel, "Relay node place-
     ment with energy and buffer constraints in wireless sensor
     networks using mobile data collector," *International Journal of
     Sensor Networks*, vol. 8, no. 3-4, pp. 147–159, 2010.

[18] J. B. Evans, G. J. Minden, K. S. Shanmugan et al., "Rapidly
     deployable radio network," *IEEE Journal on Selected Areas in
     Communications*, vol. 17, no. 4, pp. 689–703, 1999.

[19] J. Q. Bao and W. C. Lee, "Rapid deployment of wireless ad hoc
     backbone networks for public safety incident management,"
     in *Proceedings of the 50th Annual IEEE Global Telecom-
     munications Conference (GLOBECOM '07)*, pp. 1217–1221,
     November 2007.

[20] A. Wolff, S. Subik, and C. Wietfeld, "Performance analysis
     of highly available ad hoc surveillance networks based on
     Dropped Units," in *Proceedings of the IEEE International Con-
     ference on Technologies for Homeland Security (HST '08)*, pp.
     123–128, Boston, Mass, USA, May 2008.

[21] M. R. Souryal, A. Wapf, and N. Moayeri, "Rapidly-deployable
     mesh network testbed," in *Proceedings of the IEEE Global
     Telecommunications Conference (GLOBECOM '09)*, pp. 1–6,
     December 2009.

[22] J. Reich, V. Misra, D. Rubenstein, and G. Zussman, "Con-
     nectivity maintenance in mobile wireless networks via con-
     strained mobility," in *Proceedings of the IEEE INFOCOM*, pp.
     927–935, April 2011.

[23] Network simulator v.2, http://isi.edu/nsnam/ns/.

[24] M. Lacage, M. H. Manshaei, and T. Turletti, "IEEE 802.11
     rate adaptation: a practical approach," in *Proceedings of the
     7th ACM Symposium on Modeling, Analysis and Simulation of
     Wireless and Mobile Systems*, pp. 126–134, October 2004.

[25] J. Del Prado Pavon and S. Choi, "Link adaptation strategy
     for IEEE 802.11 WLAN via received signal strength measure-
     ment," in *Proceedings of the International Conference on Com-
     munications (ICC '03)*, pp. 1108–1113, Anchorage, Alaska,
     USA, May 2003.

15

Adaptive Message Rate Control of Infrastructured DSRC Vehicle Networks for Coexisting Road Safety and Non-Safety Applications

Wenyang Guan,[1] Jianhua He,[2] Chao Ma,[1] Zuoyin Tang,[2] and Yue Li[1]

[1] *College of Engineering, Swansea University, Swansea SA2 8PP, UK*
[2] *School of Engineering and Applied Science, Aston University, Birmingham B4 7ET, UK*

Correspondence should be addressed to Chao Ma, mac1@aston.ac.uk

Academic Editor: Lin Bai

Intelligent transport system (ITS) has large potentials on road safety applications as well as nonsafety applications. One of the big challenges for ITS is on the reliable and cost-effective vehicle communications due to the large quantity of vehicles, high mobility, and bursty traffic from the safety and non-safety applications. In this paper, we investigate the use of dedicated short-range communications (DSRC) for coexisting safety and non-safety applications over infrastructured vehicle networks. The main objective of this work is to improve the scalability of communications for vehicles networks, ensure QoS for safety applications, and leave as much as possible bandwidth for non-safety applications. A two-level adaptive control scheme is proposed to find appropriate message rate and control channel interval for safety applications. Simulation results demonstrated that this adaptive method outperforms the fixed control method under varying number of vehicles.

1. Introduction

Intelligent transport system (ITS) has received wide interests since the last decade due to its huge potentials on traffic safety applications, business logistics, route planning, entertainment, and many other applications. However, one of the big challenges for ITS is on the vehicle machine to machine communications. Due to the large quantity of vehicles, high mobility, and bursty traffic from the safety and nonsafety applications, the traditional cellular networks can not provide cost effective and real-time communications for large-scale ITS applications, especially for safety applications. On the other hand, among the broad ITS applications, road traffic safety applications have been a subject of worldwide concern. It has been extensively studied to actively prevent accidents or passively minimize the consequences of accidents. Driven by advances in wireless communications and mobile networking, collaborative safety applications (CSAs) enabled by vehicular communications are widely considered to be key for the success of future road safety [1]. Vehicle to vehicle (V2V) and vehicle to infrastructure (V2I) communications can enable exchange of vehicle information and proactive warning of potential hazards for collaborative

safe application, such as emergency stops, merging traffic, vehicles in a driver's blind spot, imminent collision, and driving assistant messages that related to safety driving.

Among direct V2V communication technologies, dedicated short-range communications (DSRC) is a strong candidate for CSA. Compared to cellular networks, it can provide very high data transfer rates at low cost in circumstances where minimal communication latency and isolated relatively small communication zones are important. DSRC technology is robust and can be built into large-scale vehicles [2–4]. The US Federal Communications Commission (FCC) has allocated 75 MHz of spectrum in the 5.9 GHz band for DSRC [5]. DSRC standards are currently being developed by organizations including the IEEE [6] and the Society of Automobile Engineers (SAE). IEEE is specifying a wireless access in vehicular environment (WAVE) for DSRC to provide seamless, interoperable V2V, and vehicle to roadside unit (RSU) (V2R) communication services [6]. SAE is defining a standard message set and data dictionary for DSRC-based vehicle safety applications. The US National Highway Traffic Safety Administration (NHTSA) has undertaken several projects to test vehicle safety applications performance by simulation and field experiments.

To reduce system costs, both road safety applications and non-safety applications are likely to be deployed over multiple DSRC channels. According to the specified multichannel operations, time-division multiplexing is used for the DSRC devices to monitor the control channel (CCH) for safety information and service channels (SCH) for non-safety applications. All the DSRC devices need to monitor CCH at the CCH intervals. One big challenge for the coexisting safety and non-safety application is how to effectively ensure QoS for safety applications while leave as much as bandwidth for non-safety applications. Safety applications have higher priority and they have stringent requirements for reliable real-time message delivery, as excessive message delays or message loss hinders the effectiveness of CSA and can even cause unexpected negative consequences. However, the QoS requirements are hard to be met by the random channel access specified in the IEEE 802.11 DCF [7–10]. On the other hand, the non-safety applications should not get as much bandwidth as possible to provide efficient non-safety services. For the safety applications, their QoS perceived are affected by a wide range of factors, such as resource provisioning and congestion control. In this paper, we consider two major types of safety applications: event-driven safety applications (ESA) and periodic safety applications (PSA). Their QoS can be differentiated by channel access schemes and message rate control schemes. ESA is designed to be used for emergency scenarios. It creates and broadcast messages if accidents happened or are emerging. PSA is designed for announcing existence of a vehicle and broadcast non-emergent messages. PSA messages are periodically generated and broadcasted to help build mutual awareness and implement some simple CSAs [1]. Compared to PSA messages, ESA messages have higher priority to inform or make a caution to the following vehicles with global positioning system (GPS) information included.

With the challenges on the development of coexisting safety and non-safety applications over DSRC-based vehicle networks, it is important to improve the utilization of the limited spectrum resources for DSRC networks, while meeting the QoS requirements for the road safety applications. In this paper, we propose an adaptive control scheme to avoid network congestion and provide good QoS for safety applications. The objectives are to provide high-availability and low-latency channel for high-priority, ESA messages and maximize channel utilization for low priority PSA messages and non-safety applications. To facilitate the adaptive control of the DSRC networks, we use an off-line simulation based approach to find out the best possible configurations of CCH interval, safety message rate, and channel access parameters for given combinations of safety QoS requirements and the number of vehicles. Here we assume each vehicle in the network is equipped with a DSRC radio. A utility function is proposed to take the QoS requirements of safety applications into account and solve the multiple objectives optimization problem for the coexisting safety and non-safety applications. The identified configurations are then adaptively used online by a roadside access point (AP) for both CCH interval control and channel access control. We focus on the broadcast-based safety applications in this paper.

In the literature, Wang and Hassan [11] investigated the impact of CCH interval on the QoS of single safety application and channel availability for non-safety applications. However, the service differentiated channel access and congestion control are not considered in [11]. The authors have studied adaptive message rate control for DSRC vehicle networks, in which safety message rate is controlled in a distributed manner by the vehicles in freeways [10]. In this paper, the focus is on a road intersection where an access pointer (AP) is deployed for centralized network control. A distributed message rate control method for ad hoc vehicle networks is proposed for single safety application in [12]. A centralized message rate control in road intersections is studied for two differentiated safety application in [13]. However, it is noted that all the above works have not considered the impact and adaptive configuration of CCH interval.

The remaining of this paper is organized as follows. We briefly introduce the background knowledge on DSRC and 802.11p Standard in Section 2. Section 3 presents the design of the adaptive congestion control method. Numerical results are presented in Section 4. Finally, we make a conclusion in Section 5.

2. Background

2.1. DSRC Standard Activities. For economic concerns, DSRC is expected to provide both road safety and commercial services. The overall WAVE architecture developed by IEEE for DSRC includes IEEE 802.11p (MAC and PHY standards) and IEEE Std 1609.1 to 1609.4. At the MAC layer, IEEE 802.11p is based on IEEE 802.11e, which has been augmented with QoS support. IEEE 802.11e can provide multiple priorities to different applications by differentiating DCF-based channel access parameters [7]. At the physical layer, 802.11p is the same as 802.11a except that 802.11p is operated with 10 MHz bandwidth instead of 20 MHz for 802.11a. More details on the 802.11 channel access schemes is referred to in [7].

Multichannel operation is specified in IEEE Std 1609.4. In the multichannel framework, a control channel (CCH) is to be used exclusively for road safety messages and service announcements, while the other channels are service channels (SCH). It is required that all WAVE devices need to monitor CCH at regular intervals. To account for the devices that can not simultaneously monitor CCH and SCH, synchronization procedure has been proposed to coordinate the channel using time-division multiplexing [14]. A synchronization interval comprises a CCH interval, a SCH interval, and two guard intervals.

2.2. Channel Access in 802.11p Standard. For each Access Category (AC), an enhanced distributed coordination access (EDCA) process will be started to contend for transmission opportunities (TXOPs) using a set of distinct EDCA parameters, including arbitration interframe space (AIFS) instead of DIFS in DCF. AIFS(AC) is determined by AIFS(AC) = SIFS + AIFSN(AC), where AIFSN(AC) is an integer indication of the number of slots that a station belonging to AC should defer before either invoking a backoff or starting a

Adaptive Message Rate Control of Infrastructured DSRC Vehicle Networks for Coexisting Road Safety and
Non-Safety Applications

167

TABLE 1: Default EDCA parameter set.

AC	Example	CWmin	AIFSN
AC0	BK	a CWmin	9
AC1	Best effort (BE)	a CWmin	6
AC2	Video	(a CWmin + 1)/2 − 1	3
AC3	Voice	(a CWmin + 1)/4 − 1	2

transmission after a SIFS duration. AC values of 0, 1, 2, and 3 present background, best effort, video, and voice, as shown in Table 1, respectively.

3. Adaptive Control Scheme

In this section, we present a two-level adaptive control scheme for the coexisting safety and non-safety applications. For the safety applications, we consider both emergency and routine safety applications. We take a road intersection as an example network scenario where a fixed roadside AP has the full control of setting for the CCH interval and other system parameters. In the first level, the time allocated to the CCH and the SCH is controlled and adapted according to traffic loads in a relatively long-time scale. In the second level, adaptive congestion control is applied to the CCH in a relatively short-time scale. The objectives of the design are to ensure QoS of high priority ESA messages while maximizing channel utilization for low priority PSA messages and non-safety applications. The reason to maximize channel utilization for low priority PSA messages is that low priority PSA applications which coexist with ESA application over the DSRC control channel are also important for CSA. For example, periodically broadcasted PSA messages which include vehicle positions enable mutual awareness.

There are two major parts included in the adaptive control scheme. The first part is an offline procedure to find out the optimal configurations of CCH interval, message rate, and backoff exponent (BE) for a set of QoS requirements and given number of vehicles. These optimal configurations are then applied in the second part where the roadside AP requests the vehicles to update the configurations according to the QoS requirements and an estimated number of vehicles in the road intersection.

It is noted that in addition to the control of CCH interval and message rate, a MAC layer blocking mechanism is used by all the vehicles for safety applications [10]. The MAC layer blocking mechanism is used to immediately block low priority PSA messages by a vehicle if it detects that the channel is busy for longer than a channel busy threshold in any CCH interval. The proposed adaptive control scheme is implemented in a centralized manner. This is different from traditional network congestion control protocols such as TCP and TFRC protocols, which control only the packet transmission rate and are implemented in a distributed approach at the transport layer. The proposed method is also different from distributed rate adaptation method proposed in [10] as the AP can fully control the system configurations for the vehicles in the road intersection.

3.1. Offline Determination of Optimal Configurations. To facilitate the adaptive control, we use an offline simulation-based approach to find out the best possible configurations of CCH interval, safety message rate, and channel access parameters for given combinations of and safety QoS requirements (e.g., message successful probability and message delivery delay) and the number of vehicles.

Here offline simulation approach means determination of optimal configurations by simulation of a system that is not in operation, which is contrast to the approach that may be used to adaptively find the proper configurations from the real system in operation. A simulator is developed for this purpose. Although it is possible to use analytical models to determine the optimal configurations, we believe the analytical models may not be efficient to take into account the complex system operations and parameters, such as unsaturated traffic load, MAC layer backoff, and blocking.

A challenge on the determination of optimal configuration is the multiple objectives optimization for the whole vehicle network, namely, provisioning of high available channel for ESA messages and high channel utilization for PSA messages, and leaving more channel time to non-safety applications. For example, a low PSA message rate will present higher channel availability to ESA messages but at the cost of less transmitted PSA messages. To tackle the multiple objective optimization problem, we use a utility function to find out the combination of BE, message rate, and the minimal CCH interval which can satisfied the specific QoS. In the proposed utility function, the performance metrics of message success probability, average transmit delay, and transmit rate are taken into account. It is noted that there could be alternative utility functions defined for the multiple objective optimization problem. Investigation of alternative utility functions is left for our future work.

Let P_e and P_p denote message success probability for ESA messages and PSA messages, respectively. Let D_e and D_p denote message delivery delay for ESA messages and PSA messages, respectively. Let R_e and R_p denote the average number of successfully received ESA messages and PSA messages by one vehicle in one second, respectively. We can have the following proposed utility function (denoted by Θ):

$$
\begin{aligned}
\Theta = R_e + \left(P_{s,e} - P_{\text{thr},e}\right)^+ + \left(D_{\text{thr},e} - D_e\right)^+ \\
+ R_p + \left(P_{s,p} - P_{\text{thr},p}\right)^+ + \left(D_{\text{thr},p} - D_p\right)^+,
\end{aligned}
\tag{1}
$$

where $P_{\text{thr},e}$ and $P_{\text{thr},p}$ are preset thresholds for the message success probability of ESA and PSA messages, respectively. $D_{\text{thr},e}$ and $D_{\text{thr},p}$ are preset thresholds for delivery delay of ESA and PSA messages, respectively.

The threshold function $(x)^+$ used in the utility function is expressed by

$$
\begin{aligned}
(x)^+ = 0, \quad \text{if } x \leq 0, \\
(x)^+ = 1, \quad \text{if } x > 0.
\end{aligned}
\tag{2}
$$

The reason that the threshold function is used is that for some given QoS requirements on the ESA and PSA applications, we want to maintain a message success

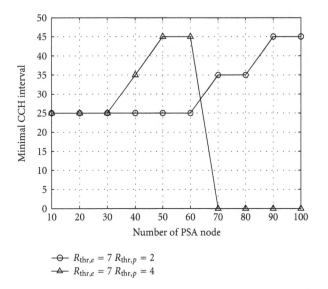

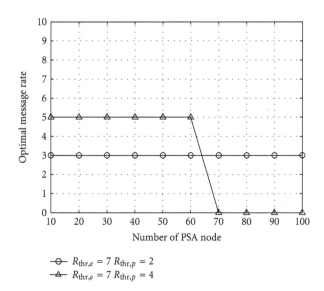

FIGURE 1: Minimal CCH interval satisfying the preset QoS requirements with $R_{thr,p} = 2$ and 4.

FIGURE 3: Optimal message rate against the number of PSA vehicles with $R_{thr,p} = 2$ and 4.

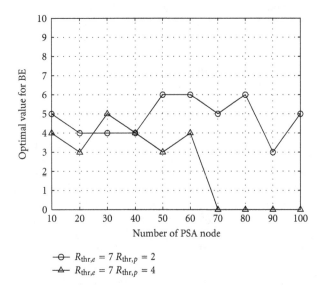

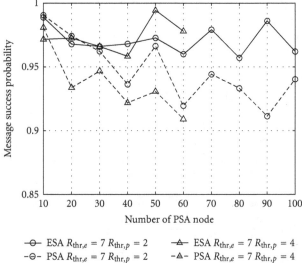

FIGURE 2: Optimal BE against the number of PSA vehicles with $R_{thr,p} = 2$ and 4.

FIGURE 4: Message success probability against the number of PSA vehicles with $R_{thr,p} = 2$ and 4.

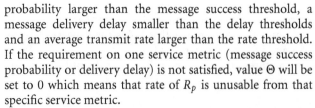

probability larger than the message success threshold, a message delivery delay smaller than the delay thresholds and an average transmit rate larger than the rate threshold. If the requirement on one service metric (message success probability or delivery delay) is not satisfied, value Θ will be set to 0 which means that rate of R_p is unusable from that specific service metric.

With the preset parameters, we can determine a configuration table which gives the minimal CCH interval and the optimal configuration of message rate, and BE which meet given QoS requirements with various number of vehicles in the network. Note that the determination of the optimal configurations is only needed at the roadside AP.

3.2. Online Adaptation of Configurations. In this procedure, the AP applies the findings from the offline procedure on the minimal CCH interval and the optimal configurations of message rate for PSA applications. The procedure operates as follows. Firstly, the AP estimates the number of vehicles (N_{est}) at the road intersection for every T_{est} seconds through the received PSA messages, which are broadcasted by the vehicles at the road intersection. In this paper, we set $T_{est} = 60$. According to the estimated number of vehicles and the preset QoS requirements, the AP looks up the configuration table to get the minimal CCH interval and the optimal configurations of message rate and BE. The value of CCH interval and the optimal configuration is then broadcasted

Adaptive Message Rate Control of Infrastructured DSRC Vehicle Networks for Coexisting Road Safety and Non-Safety Applications

169

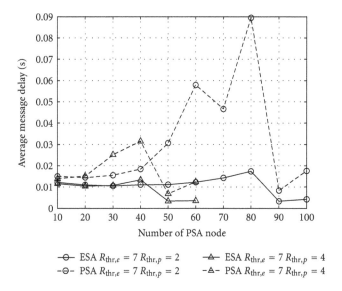

FIGURE 5: Message delivery delay against the number of PSA vehicles with $R_{\text{thr},p} = 2$ and 4.

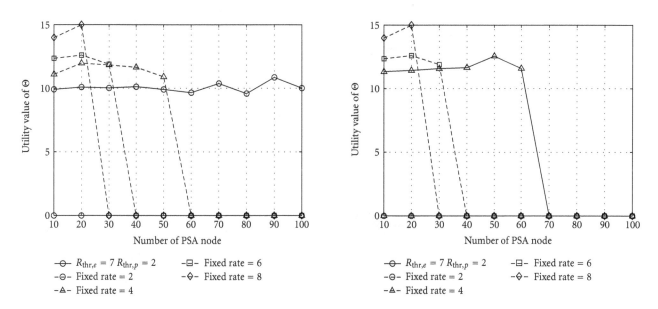

FIGURE 6: Utility Θ of adaptive control and Type I FCS for $R_{\text{thr},p} = 2$.

FIGURE 7: Utility Θ of adaptive control and Type I FCS for $R_{\text{thr},p} = 4$.

in ESA messages by the AP at different time scales (every TS_{CCH} seconds for CCH interval broadcast and every TS_{rate} for message rate broadcast) to the vehicles at the intersection. In default, TS_{CCH} is set to 300 seconds and TS_{rate} is set to 30 seconds. Vehicles received the AP configuration instructions update their configurations accordingly. In addition, the AP keeps monitoring the safety applications QoS performances during the system operations. If the perceived QoS performances are better than the required, the CCH interval is increased with a step of 10 ms to improve the QoS performances for safety applications. In reverse the CCH interval is reduced with the same step if the QoS performances are poor than the QoS requirements.

4. Numerical Result

We have built a discrete event-driven simulator to evaluate the performance of the adaptive control scheme for DSRC vehicle networks. All vehicles are located with uniform distribution along the roads at a junction and a roadside; AP is located at the center of the junction. We assume a single hop ad hoc network in which each vehicle can hear transmissions from other vehicles. For simplicity, we assume there are two classes of vehicles in the network. The first class of vehicles transmit only ESA messages while the second class of vehicles transmit only PSA messages. Message block event at MAC layer is triggered to provide high available bandwidth for ESA messages with a MAC blocking threshold of 70%

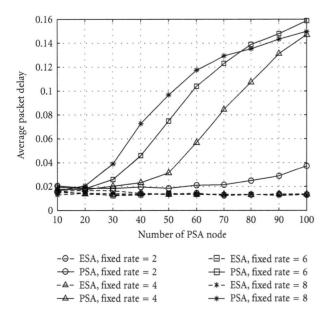

FIGURE 8: Message delay of Type I FCS.

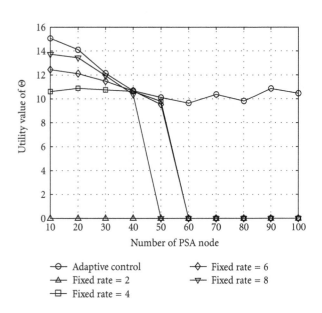

FIGURE 10: Utility Θ of adaptive control and Type II FCS for $R_{\text{thr},p} = 2$.

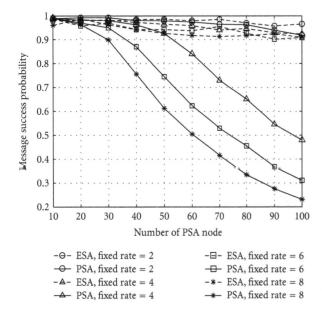

FIGURE 9: Message success probability of Type I FCS.

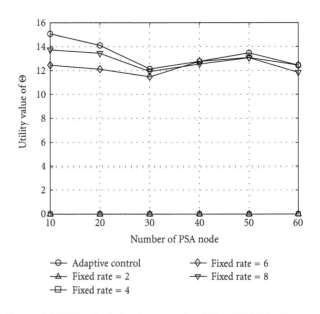

FIGURE 11: Utility Θ of adaptive control and Type II FCS for $R_{\text{thr},p} = 4$.

in a single SI. Performance for MAC blocking thresholds of 50% and 90% is also investigated in the simulations. For simplicity, we assume that there are three first-class vehicles, which periodically send eight ESA messages per second. All safety messages have the same length of 250 bytes and are broadcasted at the rate of 3 Mbps. An ideal channel is assumed where a message can be successfully received if no collision happens.

We have used the following configurations for the thresholds in the proposed utility function: $R_e = 7$, R_p ranging from 2 to 8, $P_{\text{thr},e} = 0.9$, $P_{\text{thr},p} = 0.9$, $D_{\text{thr},e} = 0.02$, and $D_{\text{thr},p} = 0.1$. The CCH interval is configurable in the set

$[15, 25, 35, 45]$ ms, which corresponds to 30%, 50%, 70%, and 90% of a 50 ms synchronization interval (SI), respectively.

With the above parameter configurations, we obtained the optimal configuration of message rate, BE, and CCH interval length. The minimal CCH interval length satisfying the preset QoS requirements and the corresponding optimal configurations of BE and message rate is plotted against the number of vehicles in Figures 1, 2, and 3, respectively. The preset QoS requirements are with message success probability $P_{\text{thr},p} = 0.9$ and message rate $R_{\text{thr},e} = 7$, $R_{\text{thr},p} = 2$ and 4.

Adaptive Message Rate Control of Infrastructured DSRC Vehicle Networks for Coexisting Road Safety and
Non-Safety Applications

171

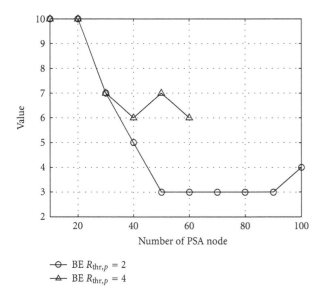

FIGURE 12: Optimal message rate of adaptive control scheme.

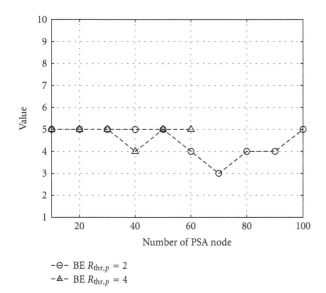

FIGURE 13: Optimal BE of adaptive control scheme.

It can be observed from Figure 3 that message rate must be at least 5 messages per second to satisfy the QoS requirement $R_{\text{thr},p} = 4$. However, the minimal CCH interval length is increased to 45 ms with 60 vehicles and $R_{\text{thr},p} = 4$. With more than 60 vehicles in the network, none combination of CCH interval and message rate can satisfy the QoS requirement. In these cases, message rate, BE, and CCH interval length are plotted as 0 in the figures.

Figures 4 and 5 present the performances of message success probability and delivery delay under the QoS requirement of $R_{\text{thr},p} = 2$, and 4. It can be seen that the combination of BE, rate, and CCH interval length selected by the offline procedure performs well in QoS provisioning, that is, ESA messages delay is lower than 20 ms, message success probability for both ESA and PSA is over than 90% as required.

We plot the utility value Θ for QoS requirement of $R_{\text{thr},p} = 2$ and 4 in Figures 6 and 7. For performance comparison, we plot the results obtained for a type fixed control scheme (called Type I FCS) in which the CCH interval and message rate are fixed irrespective of the dynamic traffic loads. For the Type I FCS we set BE to 4 and CCH interval length to 35 ms. Several fixed message rates are selected for comparison. It is observed from the figures that the adaptive control scheme can achieve larger utility than the Type I FCS in most of the cases. And more importantly the adaptive control scheme can use much smaller CCH interval length to satisfy safety applications QoS, which means non-safety applications are left with more channel time. In Figures 8 and 9, we plot the corresponding average message delay and success probability of ESA and PSA messages for Type I FCS.

Next we compare the performance of the adaptive control scheme with that of another type of fixed control scheme (called Type II FCS), which uses the CCH interval length identified in the adaptive control scheme but uses fixed message rate for PSA. The utility values of the adaptive control scheme and the Type II FCS are plotted in Figures 10 and 11 for the QoS requirements of $R_{\text{thr},p} = 2$ and 4, respectively. We can see from Figures 10 and 11 that although Type II FCS can leave the same amount of channel time to non-safety applications as the adaptive control scheme, it has much smaller utility values than the adaptive control scheme due to the use of fixed message rates in the FCS. The optimal message rate and BE for PSA are plotted in Figures 12 and 13, respectively.

It can be observed from Figure 12 that with less vehicles in the network, message rate can reach as high as 10, and still meet the QoS requirement, and BE maintains stable relatively. With the number of vehicle increasing, message rate is as low as 3, and BE becomes unstable when $R_{\text{thr},p} = 2$, while none of any combinations can meet the QoS requirement when $R_{\text{thr},p} = 4$.

5. Conclusion

In this paper, we investigated a system control issue faced by the coexisting safety and non-safety application deployed over DSRC vehicle networks. A two-levels adaptive control scheme was proposed with one level on CCH interval control and the other level on message rate and channel access control. The objective is to ensure QoS requirements for safety applications while leaving as much bandwidth as possible for non-safety applications. An offline procedure is used to determine the optimal configurations of CCH interval, safety message rate, and channel access parameters. A utility function is proposed to solve the multiobjectives optimization problem and take the safety application QoS into account. The identified configurations are applied online by the roadside AP according to the estimated number of vehicles. Results demonstrate that the adaptive control scheme significantly improves system performances over the fixed control scheme with changing number of vehicles and QoS requirements from the road safety applications.

Acknowledgments

The work is supported by the UK Engineering and Physical Sciences Research Council (EPSRC) with Grant Reference no. *EP/I010157/1* and the National Natural Science Foundation of China (NSFC) under the Grant no. 61103177.

References

[1] Vehicle Safety Communications Project, "Vehicle safety communications project," Final Report, CAMP IVI Light Vehicle Enabling Research Program DOT HS 810 591, 2006.

[2] J. Zhu and S. Roy, "MAC for dedicated short range communications in intelligent transport system," *IEEE Communications Magazine*, vol. 41, no. 12, pp. 60–67, 2003.

[3] S. Biswas, R. Tatchikou, and F. Dion, "Vehicle-to-vehicle wireless communication protocols for enhancing highway traffic safety," *IEEE Communications Magazine*, vol. 44, no. 1, pp. 74–82, 2006.

[4] D. Jiang, V. Taliwal, A. Meier, W. Holfelder, and R. Herrtwich, "Design of 5.9 GHz DSRC-based vehicular safety communication," *IEEE Wireless Communications*, vol. 13, no. 5, pp. 36–43, 2006.

[5] Federal Communications Commission, FCC Report and Order FCC 03-324, 2004.

[6] IEEE 802, *Amendment For Wireless Access For the Vehicular Environment (WAVE)*, 2010.

[7] IEEE Std 802, *Wireless LAN Medium Access Control (MAC) enhancements for Quality of Service (QoS)*, 2005.

[8] J. Yin, T. Elbatt, G. Yeung et al., "Performance evaluation of safety applications over DSRC vehicular ad hoc networks," in *Proceedings of the 1st ACM VANET International Workshop on Vehicular Ad Hoc Networks*, pp. 1–9, October 2004.

[9] J. He, Z. Tang, T. O'Farrell, and T. M. Chen, "Performance analysis of DSRC priority mechanism for road safety applications in vehicular networks," *Wireless Communications and Mobile Computing*, vol. 11, no. 7, pp. 980–990, 2011.

[10] J. He, H. H. Chen, T. M. Chen, and W. Cheng, "Adaptive congestion control for DSRC vehicle networks," *IEEE Communications Letters*, vol. 14, no. 2, pp. 127–129, 2010.

[11] Z. Wang and M. Hassan, "How much of dsrc is available for non-safety use?" in *Proceedings of the 5th ACM VANET International Workshop on VehiculAr Inter-NETworking*, pp. 23–29, September 2008.

[12] M. Torrent-Moreno, J. Mittag, P. Santi, and H. Hartenstein, "Vehicle-to-vehicle communication: fair transmit power control for safety-critical information," *IEEE Transactions on Vehicular Technology*, vol. 58, no. 7, pp. 3684–3703, 2009.

[13] W. Guan and J. He, "Adaptive congestion control of DSRC vehicle networks for collaborative road safety applications," in *IEEE Workshop on Wireless Local Area Networks (WLN '11)*, 2011.

[14] IEEE Std 1609, *IEEE Trial-Use Standard For Wireless Access in Vehicular Environments (WAVE) Multi-Channel Operation*, 2006.

16

Holes Detection in Anisotropic Sensornets: Topological Methods

Wei Wei,[1] Xiao-Lin Yang,[2] Pei-Yi Shen,[3] and Bin Zhou[4]

[1] *School of Computer Science and Engineering, Xi'an University of Technology, Xi'an 710048, China*
[2] *College of Management Science, Chengdu University of Technology, Chengdu 610059, China*
[3] *National School of Software, Xidian University, Xi'an 710071, China*
[4] *College of Science, Xi'an University of Science and Technology, Xi'an 710054, China*

Correspondence should be addressed to Xiao-Lin Yang, yangxlcdut@gmail.com

Academic Editor: Chuan Foh

Wireless sensor networks (WSNs) are tightly linked with the practical environment in which the sensors are deployed. Sensor positioning is a pivotal part of main location-dependent applications that utilize sensornets. The global topology of the network is important to both sensor network applications and the implementation of networking functionalities. This paper studies the topology discovery with an emphasis on boundary recognition in a sensor network. A large mass of sensor nodes are supposed to scatter in a geometric region, with nearby nodes communicating with each other directly. This paper is thus designed to detect the holes in the topological architecture of sensornets only by connectivity information. Existent edges determination methods hold the high costs as assumptions. Without the help of a large amount of uniformly deployed seed nodes, those schemes fail in anisotropic WSNs with possible holes. To address this issue, we propose a solution, named PPA based on Poincare-Perelman Theorem, to judge whether there are holes in WSNs-monitored areas. Our solution can properly detect holes on the topological surfaces and connect them into meaningful boundary cycles. The judging method has also been rigorously proved to be appropriate for continuous geometric domains as well as discrete domains. Extensive simulations have been shown that the algorithm even enables networks with low density to produce good results.

1. Introduction and Motivation

Sensornets are appearing as promising techniques for pervasive data exchange and information sharing. Sensornets are tightly linked with the geometric environment in which they are deployed. Detecting topological holes is a very important task in wireless sensor networks [1]. In many crucial safe-related scenarios, such as earthwork construction and mine exploitation cases, we need to determine whether topological holes in space topological structure exist, thus, we can send the urgent warning for users so as to prevent the disasters that happen suddenly and have enough time to deal with the accidents in time. Many existing countermeasures usually do strong assumptions. As we know, all of mathematical theorems have their own used field. That is to say, before we use these mathematical methods to solve the practical problems, we need to proof at least explain that these mathmatic ways can be used in the specialized domain.

Simultaneously, those current methods either enquire customerized hardware devices or have strong assumptions on the network environment, leading to low efficiency and applicability. In this work, we fundamentally analyze the detecting mind of space holes issue by topology methodology and by observing the inevitable topology deviations introduced by holes. We generalize the definition of space holes in practical scenarios and propose a topological approach. Mathmatical proof and simulation results show that our approach can detect and locate various holes and relies solely on topological information of the network. To the best of our knowledge, we try our best to make the first attempt towards a purely topological approach to detect holes distributedly without any rigorous requirements and assumptions. At the same time, we also solve the applied domain problem of mathmaitical theorem by removing the theoretical barriers to finish it. Our approach achieves superior performance and applicability with the least limitations.

On one hand, sensor network applications for example environment monitoring and data collection demand wealthy coverage over the region of interest. On the other hand, the global topology of a WSN has a great influence on the design of basic networking functionalities, for example, point-to-point routing and data collecting mechanisms. In this paper we study the problem of discovering the global geometry of the sensornets field, especially, inspecting sensor nodes on the boundaries (both inner and outer boundaries). The standpoint we take is to regard the sensornet as a discrete sampling of the underlying geometric environment. This is inspired by the fact that sensornets are to offer dense monitoring of the potential space. Therefore, the shape of the sensor field, that is, the boundaries, indicates significant characters of the underlying environment. These boundaries usually have physical correspondences, such as a building floor plan, a map of a transit network, topography changes, and barriers (skyscrapers, subsidence areas, etc). Holes can also map to events that are being monitored by the sensornet. If we consider the sensors with readings above a threshold to be "invalid", then the hole borders are essentially isocontours of the landscape of the property of interest.

Cases include the identification of regions with overheated sensors or abnormal chemical contamination. Holes are also important indicators of the universal health of a sensornet, for example insufficient coverage and connectivity. The detection of holes divulges groups of destroyed sensors because of physical destruction or power consumption, where additional sensor deployment is demanded. Besides the real scenario mentioned above, understanding the global geometry and topology of the sensor field is of great importance in the design of basic networking operations. For example, in the sensor deployment problem, if we are desirous to spread some mobile sensors in an unknown region formed by static sensor nodes, knowing the border of the region permits us to guarantee that newly added sensors are deployed only in the expected region.

A number of networking protocols also exploit geometric intuitions for simplicity and scalability, for instance geographical greedy forwarding [2, 3]. Such algorithms based on local greedy advances may fail at local minima if the sensor networks have nontrivial topology. Backup methods, for instance face, routing on a explanate subgraph, can assist packets avoid local minima, but build high traffic on hole boundaries, and eventually destroy the network lifetime [2, 3]. This artificial product is not amazing because any algorithm with a strong geometrical application, for example geographical forwarding, ought to stick to the genuine shape of the sensor field. Currently, there are lots of routing schemes that address explicitly the importance of topological properties and propose routing with virtual coordinates that are adaptive to the inner geometric features [4, 5]. The construction of these virtual coordinate systems needs the identification of topological features. We focus on developing a judgment method that detects hole boundaries based on the Poincare Conjecture theory.

The rest of this paper is organized as follows. We first give a brief overview of this scheme in Section 2. And then, we present the PPA design principle in a continuous domain and

offer the solid and complete theoretical proof to describe how the traditional and continuous topological theory (Poincare-Perelman Theorem) can be suitably (appropriately) applied to discrete and practical scenarios. As a result, we utilize the Poincare-Perelman Theorem to judge (determine) whether there are existing holes in real topological spaces. Namely, the constructing topological structure of continuous deployment of sensors over the Euclidean plane can also be used to justify whether holes in practical applications exist. We can efficiently detect holes danger and therefore send alert notice in real and safe field applications. In Section 3, we perform the problem formulation and holes detection in discrete environments. Section 4 extends the discussion into the practical discrete context. Section 5 evaluates the proposed scheme through comprehensive simulations and compares it with state of the art-area-based approaches localization schemes. We conclude the work in Section 5.

2. Prior Works

A lot of methods have been presented to judge sensor locations in WSNs. A universal overview of the state-of-the-art localization schemes is available in [6].

Existing researches on edges recognition can be separated into three classifications: geometric, statistical, and topological methods. Geometric methods that were proposed by Fang et al. [1] for boundary detection use geographical location information. This method assumes that the sensor nodes can sense their geographical locations and that the communication graph follows the UDG (Unit Disk Graph) assumption, when two nodes are connected by an edge if and only if their interval is at most 1. The description of holes in [1] is closely interrelated with geographical forwarding so that a packet can only get stuck at a node of hole edges. Fang et al. also presented a simple algorithm that greedily sweeps along hole boundaries and eventually discovers boundary cycles. Statistical methods for boundary detection usually make assumptions about the probability distribution of the sensor deployment. Fekete et al. [7] proposed a border detection algorithm for sensors (uniformly) randomly deployed inside a geometric region. The primary idea is that boundaries nodes have much lower average degrees than nodes in the "interior" of the network. Statistical arguments cause an appropriate degree threshold to differentiate border nodes. An statistical way is to calculate the "restricted stress centrality" of a vertex v, which measures the quantity of shortest paths going through v with a bounded length [7]. Nodes in the interior tend to have a higher centrality than nodes on the boundary. With a sufficient nodes density, the centrality of the nodes holds dual features so that it can be used to detect boundaries. The dominating weak points of these two algorithms are the idealized request on sensor deployment and density: the mean density needs to be 100 at least. In real scenario, the sensors are not as dense and they are unnecessarily arranged uniformly and randomly. There are also topological methods to prime deficient sensor coverage and holes. Ghrist and Muhammad [8] presented an algorithm that detects holes via homology with no knowledge of sensor locations; on the contrary, the algorithm is centralized, with assumptions that both the sensing range and communication range are disks with radii carefully tuned. Kröller et al. [9] presented an algorithm by probing for combinatorial structures called flowers and augmented cycles. They make less restrictive assumptions on the problem setup, modeling the communication graph by a quasi UDG, with nodes p and q demonstrably linked by an edge if $d(p,q) \leq \sqrt{2}/2$ and not connected if $d(p,q) > 1$. The success of this algorithm critically depends on the identification of at least one flower structure, which might not often be the case specially in a sparse network. For a real scenario, Funke [10] developed a simple heuristic with only connectivity information. The essential idea is to build iso contours with hop count from a root node and identify where the contours are broken. Under the unit-disk graph assumption and adequate sensor density, the algorithm outputs nodes marked as border with certain guarantees. Definitely, for each node of the geometry boundary, the algorithm enables to mark a corresponding sensor node within distance 4.8, and each node marked as boundary is within distance 2.8 from the actual geometry boundary [11]. The simplicity of the algorithm is appealing; however, the algorithm only identifies nodes that are near the boundaries but does not show how they are connected in a meaningful way. The density requirement of the algorithm is also rather high; so as to obtain good results, the average degree generally needs to be at least 16.

From mathematics aspect, the Poincare Conjecture [12] is a theorem about the specification of the three-dimensional sphere among three-dimensional manifolds. Original conjectured is proposed by Henri Poincare, the claim considers a space that locally resembles ordinary three-dimensional space but is connected, finite in size, and lacks any boundary (a closed three-dimensional manifold). The Poincare Conjecture states that if each loop in such a space can be continuously tightened to a point, then it must be a three-dimensional sphere. An similar result has been proved in higher dimensions. (Some related content is partially referred to the Wikipedia information).

2.1. Definitions of Manifold.
A manifold is a space made by conglutinating together pieces of Euclidean space, which is called charts. For example you could take two-dimensional disks and bend them around two hemispheres and then stick them together to form a two-dimensional sphere. (See also in Figure 1(d)).

A torus (the surface of a donut) can be established utilizing a rectangular diagram as shown in this image. The colored parallelograms explain how a pattern on the associated surface would arise in case the edges were once again disconnected. (See also in Figures 1(b) and 1(c)). A pair of solid balls can made a three-dimensional sphere. It should be required to discern every point of the first ball boundary with the corresponding point of the second one. Other kinds of manifolds can be established by the mimetic ways.

2.2. Explanations of Homeomorphic.
Generally, two shapes are homeomorphic if one of these shapes can be transformed

(a) A loop can be contracted to a point without leaving the sphere surface

(b) Gradual Construction of a torus based on a rectangle

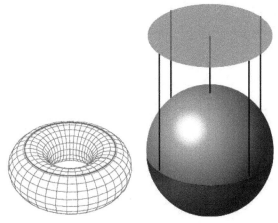

(c) Any chromatic loops cannot be contracted to a point without leaving the torus surface

(d) Hemispheres mapped to a Whole Sphere

FIGURE 1: Diagram of manifold.

into the other without pause or discontinuity. A homeomorphism is a function of continuous domain that maps points of one object into another.

Two spaces are regarded as homeomorphic if a homeomorphism between them exists. Such as, a two-dimensional sphere is homeomorphic to the surface of a cube; homoplastically, a three-dimensional sphere is homeomorphic to the three-dimensional boundary of a four-dimensional hypercube. In the above-mentioned primary concepts, they can aid to comprehend the specification of the Poincare-Perelman Theorem: the Poincare-Perelman Theorem says that a three-dimensional manifold which is compact, has no boundary and is simply connected must be homeomorphic to a three dimensional-sphere. The original phrasing was as follows: consider a compact three dimensional manifold V without boundary. Is it possible that the fundamental group of V could be trivial, even though V is not homeomorphic to the three-dimensional sphere? This centurial challenging problem is proofed by Grigori Perelman [12] in 2006.

Here is the standard form of the conjecture: every simply connected, closed tridimensional manifold is homeomorphic to the triaxial sphere. Therefore, a centralized method of collecting all of the information to a central server is not feasible for large sensor networks.

2.3. Preliminaries. Materials for topology theory. The following definitions in topology theory can be found in [13].

Topology. Let X be a set. $\mathcal{T} \subseteq 2^X$ is called a topology on X if (1) $\varnothing, X \in \mathcal{T}$; (2) if $A, B \in \mathcal{I}$, then $A \cap B \in \mathcal{T}$; (3) if $\{A_i \mid i \in I\} \subseteq \mathcal{T}$, then $\bigcup_i A_i \in \mathcal{T}$. The pair $(X, \mathcal{T})$ is called a topological space. The members of $\mathcal{T}$ are called open sets. If Y is a subset of X, then $\mathcal{T} \mid Y = \{U \cap Y \mid U \in \mathcal{T}\}$ is a topology on Y and called the induced topology of $(X, \mathcal{T})$. A bijection $f : (X_1, \mathcal{T}_1) \to (X_2, \mathcal{T}_2)$ between two topological spaces is called a homeomorphism if $B \in \mathcal{T}_2$ iff $f^{-1}(B) \in \mathcal{T}_1$ for any $B \subseteq X_2$. In this case, $(X_1, \mathcal{T}_1)$ and $(X_2, \mathcal{T}_2)$ are said to be homeomorphic to each other.

Dense Set. Let $(X, \mathcal{T})$ be a topological space and $C \subseteq X$. A point $x \in X$ is called a cluster of C if $U \cap C \neq \varnothing$ any $U \in \mathcal{T}$ with $x \in U$. Denote C^- as the set of all cluster of C, called the closure of C. The set C is called a closed set if $C = C^-$. A set is called a clopen set if it is simultaneously open and closed. A set C is called dense of $(X, \mathcal{T})$ if $C^- = X$. Dense set is an important and useful concept in topology. For example, every continuous map from a dense set of a topological space to another topological space can be extended onto the whole topological space. Thus dense sets in a topological space may share some same topological properties as the whole topological space, for example the connectedness as Theorem 1 shows.

Partition. The specification of partition £ for a set X, a family of subsets $\{X_i \mid i \in I\}$ is called a partition of X, if $\bigcup_i X_i = X$ and $X_i \cap X_j = \varnothing$ for all $i, j \in I$ with $i \neq j$.

2.4. Our Contributions. We develop a practical and efficient determination solution for boundary detection in sensor networks, using only the communication graph and not making unrealistic assumptions. We do not assume any location information, angular information, or distance information. More importantly, we do not request that the communication graph obeys the unit disk graph model or the quasi-unit disk graph model. Actual communication ranges are not circular disks and are often quite irregularly shaped [14]. Algorithms that depend on the unit disk graph model fail in practice (e.g., the extraction of a planar subgraph by the relative neighborhood graph or Gabriel graph [15].

Our PPA method also readily provides other topological and geometric information, such as the number of holes (genus), the nearest hole to any given sensor, and the sensor field's medial axis (the collection of nodes with at least two closest boundary nodes), which is useful for virtual coordinate systems for load-balanced routing [4]. Simulation results show that our algorithm correctly determines useful borders for sensor networks with rational node density (average degree 10 and above) and distribution (e.g., uniform). The algorithm also works well for nonuniform distributions. The algorithm is efficient. The entire procedure involves only

three network flooding procedures and greedy shrinkage of paths or cycles. Further, as a theoretical ensure, we prove that for a continuous geometric space bounded by polygonal obstacles, the case in which node density approaches infinity, the algorithm correctly discovers all of the boundaries. More definitely, we investigate the fact that a legitimate multihop sensor network deployed on the surface of a geometric terrain, (even possibly including irregular boundaries, inner obstacles, or even on a non-2D plain) PPA solution is able to accurately estimate the node-to-node distances and calculate node locations with only 3 seeds, thus increasing system scalability and usage as well as lowering hardware costs. In addition, PPA does not presume the superior communication capability of seeds, that is, with much larger radio range than those of the ordinary nodes [16].

Due to all mentioned above assumptions based on UDG graph model and its basis on the symptom of packing number, it is thus inaccurate under non-UDG graphs. Indeed, there are still no perfect symptoms found to establish an all-round method in the resource-limited sensornets. Our design is originated from the perspective of topological observation and is based on the theory of Poincare Conjecture, our solution is orthogonal to existing approaches and takes a step towards relaxing these assumptions and expanding the applicability of methods.

3. Problem Formulation and Holes Detection

The definition has been given under the constraints of the UDG communication graph model, which has been proven far from practical in many analytical and experimental works. Second, the distance-based definition in Euclidean space naturally binds the hole features with external geometric environments and thus neglects the inherent topological impacts introduced by holes. We hereby present a more general and fundamental definition of the hole based only on network topologies and aim to present the inherent characteristics of holes. According to the Poincare-Perelman Theorem, in the three dimensions space, the donut topology is homeomorphous to the coffee cup topology (see also Figure 2(b)). As shown in Figure 2(a), since these two topologies are not equivalent (namely, not homeomorphism), we can determine that the holes in the monitored areas based on the Poincare-Perelman Theorem exist (see also Figures 2(a) and 2(b)). Since these two topologies are not equivalent (namely, not homeomorphism), we can determine that the holes in the monitored areas based on the Poincare-Perelman Theorem exist.

In real scenario, we will treat the multihole condition. But in this proposed solution, we currently do not differentiate the numbers of holes. In future work, we will discuss and deal with this condition.

Owing to constructing the network topological structure of monitored areas, in given the surface S, we first select an arbitrary point in S as the root and run a continuous Dijkstra shortest path algorithm [17, 18] to construct the topology structure (manifold) of monitored areas. As shown in Figure 3(a) and Figure 3. Consequently, we can determine whether any closed and simply connected manifold is

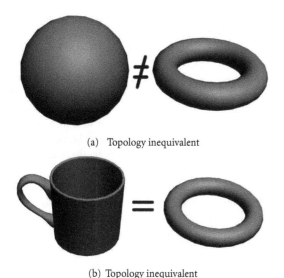

(a) Topology inequivalent

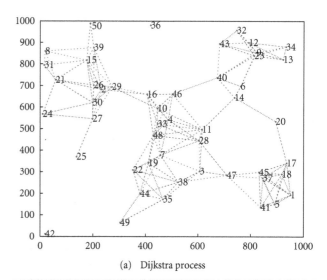

(a) Dijkstra process

(b) Topology inequivalent

FIGURE 2: Diagram of manifold.

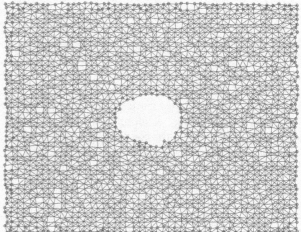

(b) Hole detection process

FIGURE 3: Diagram of hole boundary construction.

homeomorphic to the three dimensions sphere. If it is not homeomorphic to the three dimensions sphere. It refers to there is/are hole(s) in the monitored areas. (See also in Figure 3(b)).

3.1. Holes Detection in Discrete Environments. We have characterized the impact of holes and described the principles of holes detection under continuous settings in the previous section. In a real multihop network, however, nodes are deployed discretely on the field. In this section, we focus on solving the mapping question from the discrete domain to continuous geometric domain. Since the theory of Poincare-Perelman Theorem belongs to the judgement of continuous geometric domain, we need to proof the correctness and applicability of this topological judgement. By means of the following solid proof, we can transfer the discrete topological space to the continuous geometric domains. Namely, we utilize the partial discrete topology structure to substitute the whole continuous geometric topology. As a result, we can apply the theory of Poincare-Perelman Theorem to judge the existence of holes in the monitored areas by WSNs.

Let $\mathcal{T}$ be a topology on a set X and $Y \subseteq X$. Then $\mathcal{T} \mid Y = \{U \cap Y \mid U \in \mathcal{T}\}$ is a topology on Y, called the induced topology on Y and in this case $(Y, \mathcal{T} \mid Y)$ is always called a subspace of $(X, \mathcal{T})$ and $\mathcal{T}$ an extension of $\mathcal{T} \mid Y$ from Y to X. We confirm that these two topological spaces $(X, \mathcal{T})$ and $(Y, \mathcal{T} \mid Y)$ have the same topological properties. In a topological space X, a subset U is called dense if $U^- = X$, where U^- is the closure of U in $(X, \mathcal{T})$. A topological space $(X, \mathcal{T})$ is called connected if there exists no clopen (simultaneously closed and open) subset except empty and whole set X.

Theorem 1. *Suppose that $(Y, \mathcal{T}_1)$ is a dense subspace $(X, \mathcal{T}_2)$, then $(Y, \mathcal{T}_1)$ is connected if and only if $(X, \mathcal{T}_2)$ is connected.*

Proof. Suppose that $(Y, \mathcal{T}_1)$ is connected. If $(X, \mathcal{T}_2)$ is not connected, then there exists a clopen set U in $(X, \mathcal{T}_2)$ and $U \notin \{X, \varnothing\}$. Put $V = U \cap Y$, we have that V is a clopen set in $(Y, \mathcal{T}_1)$, which implies that $V = Y$ and $Y \subseteq U$ (obviously, $V \neq \varnothing$). Since Y is dense in $(X, \mathcal{T}_1)$, we have $X = Y^- \subseteq U^- = U$, which contradicts to $U \neq X$. Conversely, suppose that $(X, \mathcal{T}_2)$ is connected. If $(Y, \mathcal{T}_1)$ is not connected, then it contains a clopen set V which is neither Y nor $\varnothing$. For this V, there exist a clopen set U in $(X, \mathcal{T}_2)$ such that $V = U \cap Y$. In order to induce a contradiction, we only need to show that $U \neq X$. If $U = X$, then $V = U \cap Y = Y$, which is another contradiction to $V \neq Y$. The proof is complete.

Remark 2. If a topological space $(X, \mathcal{T})$ is n-connected topological space ($n \geq 2$), then $(X, \mathcal{T})$ can exactly be separated into $n - 1$ connected subspace $\{(X_i, \mathcal{T} \mid X_i) \mid i = 1, 2, \ldots, n - 1\}$ such that $\{X_i \mid i = 1, 2, \ldots, n - 1\}$ is a partition of X. By Theorem 1, if $(Y, \mathcal{T}_1)$ is a dense subspace $(X, \mathcal{T}_2)$, then $(Y, \mathcal{T}_1)$ is n-connected if and only if $(X, \mathcal{T}_2)$ is n-connected. As mentioned in the above Remark, the definition of concept partition for a set X, a family of subsets $\{X_i \mid i \in I\}$ is called a partition of X, if $\bigcup_i X_i = X$ and $X_i \cap X_j = \varnothing$ for all $i, j \in I$ with $i \neq j$.

The following verdict is usually held for any set that satisfies the requirement of the theory. Whatever the set is finite or infinite. We assume that a certain area deployed the WSNs. This area can be considered as a smooth curve equipped with the traditional Euclidean topology, the set of all sensors equipped with their own topology can be considered as a subspace of the former one. Furthermore, we assume that the set of all sensors is dense in this area.

We assume that the whole sensor nodes set, which completely cover the monitored area, constructs a dense set. A dense set is the monitored area which is abundantly and completely covered by the large quantities of sensor nodes. Therefore, the network topology can be continuously expanded to the monitored area. Specially, some part of sensornets can be destroyed by some accidents so that it will lead to form a hole in the architecture of topology. As a result, there exists a hole in the corresponding practical area. The sensornets corresponding geometric structure is a universal Euclid topology, particularly, if a hole in this monitoring area exists. If and only if the topology of sensornets is sub dense space of area topology space. Furthermore, If and only if the geometric topology of monitored area is connected completely, consequently, the constructing topology of sensornets is interconnected. Simultaneously, if and only if there exists holes in the geometric topology of monitored area, as a result, there exists holes in the constructing topology of sensornets.

Thus detecting whether there are holes existing in sensornets topology is equivalent to detecting whether there are holes in the monitored area.

Steps. Symbolic Interpretation. Area S, $\mathcal{T}$ is the Euclidean topology of S. The set C denotes the sensornets while C_1 denotes the efficient sensornets. Precondition: set C is dense in $(S, \mathcal{T})$.

(1) Let S_1 be the closure of C_1 on $(S, \mathcal{T})$. If it exists holes, then $S1 \subseteq S$. (2) Obtaining $\mathcal{T}_1$ while the topology $\mathcal{T}$ of S is constrained in the S_1. Therefore, $(S_1, \mathcal{T}_1)$ is a subspace of $(S, \mathcal{T})$. (3) In the above mentioned, S_1 is continuous set. Consequently, we can depend on the Poincare Conjecture theory to determine whether there are holes that existed in monitoring area. If there are holes in the topology structure of $(S_1, \mathcal{T}_1)$, then there are holes in the topology structure of C. The above-mentioned theory can guarantee this determination.

3.2. Topological Boundary Recognition. Suppose a large number of sensor nodes are scattered in a geometric region with nearby nodes communicating with each other directly. Our goal is to discover the nodes on the boundary of the sensor field, using only local connectivity information. We propose a solution that identifies boundary cycles for the sensor field. For compact 2-dimensional surfaces without boundary, if every loop can be continuously tightened to a point, then

the surface is topologically homeomorphic to a 2 spheres, usually just called a sphere. The Poincare Conjecture asserts that the same is true for 3-dimensional surfaces. (See also in Figure 1(a)). Practically, for obtaining the topology of monitored areas, we firstly use the Dijkstra Shortest Path algorithm [17] to construct the topology (manifold) of monitored areas. Consequently, we can determine whether any closed and simply connected manifold is homeomorphic to the three dimensions sphere. If it is not homeomorphic to the three dimensions sphere, it refers to there is/are hole(s) in the monitored areas (see also Figure 3(b)).

In the following, we first outline the Dijkstra Shortest Path algorithm and then explain each step in detail.

Algorithm allows the node at which we are starting to be called the initial node. Let the distance of node Y be the distance from the initial node to Y. Dijkstra's algorithm that allocates some initial distance values and will try to increase them step-by-step. Assign to every node a distance value. Set it to zero for our initial sensor node and to infinity for all other nodes. Mark all nodes as unvisited. Set initial sensor node as current. For current node, consider all its unvisited neighbors and calculate their distance (from the initial node). For instance, if current node (A) has distance of 6, and an edge connecting it with another node (B) is 2, the distance to B through A will be $6 + 2 = 8$. If this distance is less than the previously recorded distance (infinity in the beginning, zero for the initial node), overwrite the distance. When we are done considering all neighbors of the current node, mark it as visited. A visited node will not be checked ever again; its distance recorded now is final and minimal. If all nodes have been visited, finish. Otherwise, set the unvisited node with the smallest distance (from the initial node) as the next "current node". Suppose you want to find the shortest path between two intersections on a map, a starting point and a destination. To accomplish this, you could highlight the streets (tracing the streets with a marker) in a certain order, until you have a route highlighted from the starting point to the destination. The order is conceptually simple: at each iteration, create a set of intersections consisting of every unmarked intersection that is directly connected to a marked intersection, and this will be your set of considered intersections. From that set of considered intersections, find the closest intersection to the destination (this is the "greedy" part, as described above) and highlight it and mark that street to that intersection, draw an arrow with the direction, then repeat. In each stage mark just one new intersection. As getting to the destination, follow the arrows backwards. There will be only one path back against the arrows, the shortest one. The basic idea is to detect the existence of holes by judging whether if the existing topology is equivalent to sphere in the three-dimension space. Based on the mentioned above, we can construct a topology of monitored areas. Intuitively, it is very hard to determine the existence of holes by the two-topology structure. We assume our method can obtain the whole monitored topology, and then we can compare this obtained topology with sphere topology. Finally, we can determine whether holes in the monitored area exist.

4. Simulations

We performed extensive simulations in various scenarios, with the goal to evaluate the performance of the algorithm with respect to the network topology, node density and distribution, so on. We particularly note that our method works well even in cases of very low average degree, such as less than 10, or even as low as 10 in some models. Its ability is also similar to average degree 20 condition. Degree 6 has been shown to be optimal for mobile networks [19]. For each figure in this part, we assume a root node in the upper left corner and middle to illustrate the communication range of the sensor field.

4.1. Random Distribution of Sensors. In this experiment, we first assume that the network connectivity and link quality are good enough. In terms of a uniform distribution, we randomly deploy 1600 nodes in a square region with one hole. The average degree of the graph is discriminated by regulating the communication radius. As expected, Figures 4(a) and 4(b) show the results of our method. We can efficiently judge the hole existing in the monitored area. Connectivity is necessary for computing the shortest path tree. Practically, this low-degree graph with insufficient connectivity is the major troubling issue for prior boundary detection methods. Since our method only requires the communication graph, we can use several simple policies to raise artificially the average degree. For a disconnected network, we use the largest connected component of the graph to build our shortest path tree. Then we artificially enlarge the communication radius by taking two/three hops neighbors as fake one-hop neighbors. According to this means, the connectivity of the graph will be made better, and the results will be improved correspondingly by this simple strategy. The result using three hops neighbors has fewer incorrectly marked extremal nodes, and the final judgement is in good result except that the boundary cycle is not very tense. This is understandable since we make the communication range artificially larger, so that more nodes could be equivalently to distribute on the boundary now. Therefore, based on our solution, we can efficiently find holes in the supervised area.

4.2. Grid with Random Perturbation. In this simulation, we put about 1600 nodes on a grid and then perturbed each point by a random shift. Especially, for each original grid node we create two random numbers modulo the length and the width of each block of the grid and use these two small numbers to perturb the positions of the nodes. This distribution may be a good approximation of manual deployments of sensors; it also gives an alternative means of modeling "uniform" distributions, while avoiding clusters and holes that can arise from the usual continuous uniform distribution or Poisson process. As the theoretic verification considering, our method generates very good results, while average degree of graphs is ten or more.

4.3. Low Density, Sparse Graphs. In the experiments, we spread sensor nodes in a square region with one hole. In order to guarantee good connectivity, the nodes are distributed on a randomly perturbed grid. Our experiments show that if we amend the communication radius and decrease the density of nodes, our solution is performed very well, even for low density or sparse condition, as long as the average degree is at about ten or more. See also Figure 4(c).

5. Conclusion and Discussion

We devote our most efforts to explore the application of Poincare Conjecture to resolve the holes detection of safety-monitored areas in WSNs. Based on the theoretic specification, we can judge whether there are holes in the detected area. Because the detected network topology is not homeomorphous to the three dimensions sphere, it can be confirmed to have holes in the detected topology architecture. Therefore, we can accomplish the detecting holes purposes. The proposed new detection solution enables us to find holes in the continuous case, in discrete sensors networks several implementation issues arise. First, even for a given homotopy type, there needs not be a unique shortest path between two nodes. Thus, the boundary topology discovered by our solution, as shown in the simulations, may not tightly surround the real boundaries. Currently, we have two approaches to improve it. One is to make use of the fact that the nodes with lower degree are more likely to be on the boundary; thus, we implemented a preferential scheme for low-degree nodes when computing shortest paths. Another approach is to use an iterative method to find more extremal nodes and then refine the topology; this can also help to address the issue that several extremal points may have the same positions because we use hop counts to approximate true distances. Second, deciding the correct orderings of the extremal nodes requires some care. In the continuous case, extremal nodes project to their nearest node. In the discrete case, since we employ hop counts to approximate the true distance, it is possible that different extremal points are mapped to the same position on the inner boundary, obscuring their ordering. Again, by using an iterative procedure, we delete all the extremal nodes with duplicate positions except one and then iteratively find more extremal points and refine the boundary gradually. In real scenarios, the sensor nodes often know some partial location information or relative angular information. Such positional information can help to improve the performance of our holes detection solution, for example, when we utilize the shortest path algorithm to construct the topology of monitored areas. If the nodes have knowledge of a general arctic direction, it is easier to distinguish the extremal nodes in the interior and exterior of rough boundary. Also, if we have estimated distance or other rough localization information, other than pure hop count, the procedure to find shortest paths will become more reliable. Finally, our method discussed until now assumes a sensor field with holes. We remark that the case with no holes can be solved as well.

Finally, our method discussed until now assumes a sensor field with holes. We remark that the case with no holes can be solved as well. If a network topology is equivalent to

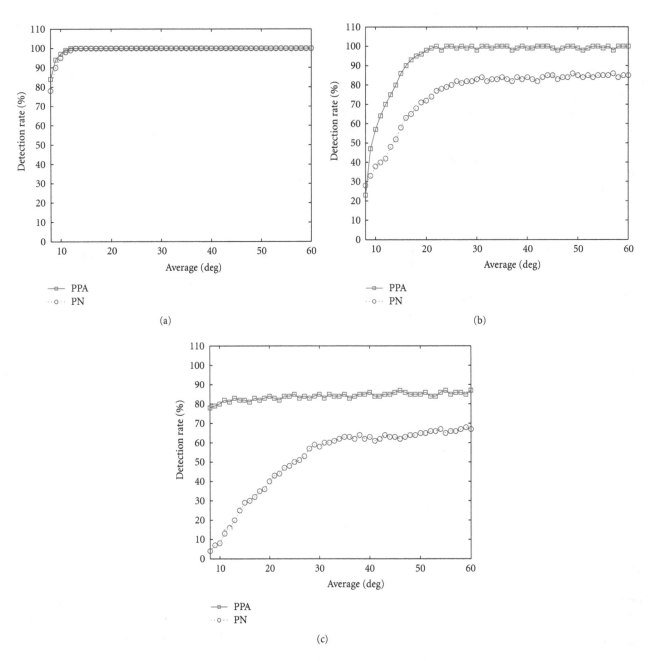

FIGURE 4: Percent Detected against various node density.

(homeomorphous) the three dimensions sphere, then it have no holes on the monitored areas based on the proofed of Poincare Conjecture, vice versa.

6. Conclusion

In this paper, a novel CT reconstruction model is proposed based on the approximate inverse where the kernel of the FDK method is derived and is used to complete the reconstruction. In order to eliminate the imposed ring artifacts, the kernel is truncated with proper radius. Reconstruction results show that the compact support FDK kernel reconstruction model can suppress the ring artifacts. The proposed reconstruction model preserves the simplicity of the FDK reconstruction method and also provides an alternative to realize the approximate inverse method for circular trajectory. And when the kernel of an algorithm is modified, the corresponding reconstruction formula is also modified accordingly. And this give us another way to improve the existing reconstruction methods.

Acknowledgments

The authors would like to thank the anonymous reviewers for their constructive feedback and valuable input. Thanks are due for the supports to our program from the TI, the

XILINX, and the Software School of Xidian University. This program is partially supported by NSFC (Grant no. 61072105, 61007011) and also supported by the Open Projects Program of National Laboratory of Pattern Recognition. The project is also partially supported by Natural Science Basic Research Plan in Shaanxi Province of China (Program no. 2010JM8005) and Scientific Research Program Funded by Shaanxi Provincial Education Department (Program no. 11JK0504).

References

[1] Q. Fang, J. Gao, and L. J. Guibas, "Locating and bypassing holes in sensor networks," *Mobile Networks and Applications*, vol. 11, no. 2, pp. 187–200, 2006.

[2] P. Bose, P. Morin, I. Stojmenović, and J. Urrutia, "Routing with guaranteed delivery in ad hoc wireless networks," *Wireless Networks*, vol. 7, no. 6, pp. 609–616, 2001.

[3] B. Karp and H. T. Kung, "GPSR: greedy Perimeter Stateless Routing for wireless networks," in *Proceedings of the 6th Annual International Conference on Mobile Computing and Networking (MOBICOM '00)*, pp. 243–254, August 2000.

[4] J. Bruck, J. Gao, and A. Jiang, "MAP: medial axis based geometric routing in sensor networks," in *Proceedings of the 11th Annual International Conference on Mobile Computing and Networking (MobiCom '05)*, pp. 88–102, September 2005.

[5] Q. Fang, J. Gao, L. J. Guibas, V. De Silva, and L. Zhang, "GLIDER: Gradient Landmark-Based Distributed Routing for sensor networks," in *Proceedings of the 24th Conference of the IEEE Communication Society (INFOCOM '05)*, pp. 339–350, March 2005.

[6] J. Hightower and G. Borriello, "Location systems for ubiquitous computing," *Computer*, vol. 34, no. 8, pp. 57–66, 2001.

[7] S. P. Fekete, A. Kröller, D. Pfisterer, S. Fischer, and C. Buschmann, "Neighborhood-based topology recognition in sensor networks," *Lecture Notes in Computer Science*, vol. 3121, pp. 123–136, 2004.

[8] R. Ghrist and A. Muhammad, "Coverage and hole-detection in sensor networks via homology," in *Proceedings of the 4th International Symposium on Information Processing in Sensor Networks (IPSN '05)*, pp. 254–260, April 2005.

[9] A. Kröller, S. P. Fekete, D. Pfisterer, and S. Fischer, "Deterministic boundary recognition and topology extraction for large sensor networks," in *Proceedings of the 17th Annual ACM-SIAM Symposium on Discrete Algorithms*, pp. 1000–1009, January 2006.

[10] S. Funke, "Topological hole detection in wireless sensor networks and its applications," in *Proceedings of the Joint Workshop on Foundations of Mobile Computing*, pp. 44–53, 2005.

[11] S. Funke and C. Klein, "Hole detection or: 'how much geometry hides in connectivity?'," in *Proceedings of the 22nd Annual Symposium on Computational Geometry (SCG '06)*, pp. 377–385, June 2006.

[12] Poincare and Jules Henri, *The American Heritage Dictionary of the English Language*, Houghton Mifflin Company, Boston, Mass, USA, 4th edition, 2000.

[13] J. L. Kelly, *General Topology*, D. Van Nostrand, Princeton, NJ, USA, 1955.

[14] D. Ganesan, B. Krishnamachari, A. Woo, D. Culler, D. Estrin, and S. Wicker, "Complex behavior at scale: an experimental study of low-power wireless sensor networks," Tech. Rep. UCLA/CSD-TR 02-0013, UCLA, 2002.

[15] Y. J. Kim, R. Govindan, B. Karp, and S. Shenker, "Geographic routing made practical," in *Proceedings of the 2nd USENIX/ACM Symposium Networked System Design and Implementation*, pp. 217–230, 2005.

[16] T. He, C. Huang, B. M. Blum, J. A. Stankovic, and T. Abdelzaher, "Range-Free Localization Schemes for Large Scale Sensor Networks," in *Proceedings of the 9th Annual International Conference on Mobile Computing and Networking (MobiCom '03)*, pp. 81–95, September 2003.

[17] E. W. Dijkstra, "A note on two problems in connexion with graphs," *Numerische Mathematik*, vol. 1, no. 1, pp. 269–271, 1959.

[18] F. Li, J. Luo, C. Zhang, S. Xin, and Y. He, "UNFOLD: uniform fast on-line boundary detection for dynamic 3D wireless sensor networks," in *Proceedings of the 12th ACM International Symposium on Mobile Ad Hoc Networking and Computing (MobiHoc'11)*, pp. 141–152, 2011.

[19] E. M. Royer, P. M. Melliar-Smith, and L. E. Moser, "An analysis of the optimum node density for ad hoc mobile networks," in *International Conference on Communications (ICC '01)*, pp. 857–861, June 2000.

17

Hardware Architecture Design for WSN Runtime Extension

Ángel Asensio, Rubén Blasco, Álvaro Marco, and Roberto Casas

Institute of Engineering Research (I3A) of the University of Zaragoza, 50018 Zaragoza, Spain

Correspondence should be addressed to Roberto Casas; rcasas@unizar.es

Academic Editor: Ling Wang

Internet of Things imposes demanding requirements on wireless sensor networks as key players in context awareness procurement. Temporal and spatial ubiquities are one of the essential features that meet technology boundaries in terms of energy management. Limited energy availability makes anywhere and anytime sensing a challenging task that forces sensor nodes to wisely use every bit of available power. One of the earliest and most determining decisions in the electronic design stage is the choice of the silicon building blocks that will conform hardware architecture. Designers have to choose between dual architectures (based on a low-power microcontroller controlling a radio module) and single architectures (based on a system on chip). This decision, together with finite state machine design and application firmware, is crucial to minimize power consumption while maintaining expected sensor node performance. This paper provides keys for energy analysis of wireless sensor node architecture according to the specific requirements of any application. It thoroughly analyzes pros and cons of dual and single architectures providing designers with the basis to select the most efficient for each application. It also provides helpful considerations for optimal sensing-system design, analyzing how different strategies for sensor measuring and data exchanging affect node energy consumption.

1. Introduction

Internet of Things (IoT) applications and scenarios are very heterogeneous: environmental monitoring in large areas [1], people monitoring in their own homes [2], or industrial environments [3] are some examples. This derives different requirements regarding network architecture and sensing nodes design [4]. According to Merriam-Webster dictionary, ubiquity is defined as the capacity of presence everywhere and in many places simultaneously. Sensors are today needed in different scenarios, and in all of them it is desirable that they be operative everywhere and every time they are required; for this reason, it is said that future sensors must be ubiquitous. It has two faces: spatial ubiquity—which inherently forces wireless communications and absence of wired power sources—and temporal ubiquity—which implies availability along functioning time (maximum energy autonomy) and also availability at any given time. Whichever the case, it leads to the common need of installation's runtime maximization and consequently minimization of energy demanded by sensing nodes [5]. There are many options to power wireless sensor nodes [6], but a real installation usually poses severe

limitations: there is not unlimited power source available, energy from the environment is scarce and not enough for continuous running (e.g., indoors), maintenance of sensors is problematic (e.g., physically hard to reach to change batteries or expensive), and so forth. Thus, is critical to minimize node's power consumption while maintaining application's required quality of service. It is well known that power consumption has a high impact over quality of service offer by a WSN and its lifetime [3–5, 7]; the paper is centered on its analysis.

Depending on the deployment scenario, sensor duties will vary: data sensing, processing, aggregation, forwarding, sending, and so forth. In this paper we focus on a common case in many IoT applications: a sensor node periodically samples (every t_{SAMPLE}) one or more sensors (temperature, humidity, light, presence, chemical concentration, etc.), and then it performs some data processing and reports the readings to the network every t_{REPORT}.

Standard IEEE 1451 describes a set of open, common, network-independent communication interfaces for connecting transducers (sensors or actuators) to microprocessors, instrumentation systems, and control/field networks [8].

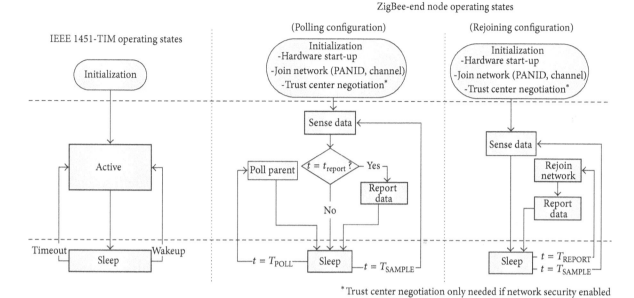

FIGURE 1: Finite state machine that defines a sensing node attending to IEEE 1451 and ZigBee standards.

IEEE 1451 introduces the concept of a transducer interface module (TIM) as a module that contains the interface, signal conditioning, analog-to-digital and/or digital-to-analog conversion, and, in many cases, the transducer. The specification defines a generic finite state machine (FSM) in Figure 1 that describes the operation of sensing nodes—TIMs—with three different operational states: initialization, active, and sleep [9].

IEEE 1451 is not restricted to any communication technology, and thus FSM definition is generic and leaves to each standard the specification of the substates needed. There are many WSN protocols available [10], and we select ZigBee for the study as it is a mature wireless standard for sensor networks, worldwide accepted, and with many hardware manufacturers available. The methodology described could be easily applied to any other standard. According to the standard specification [11], FSM states are defined as follows (Figure 1).

(1) *Initialization State.* Besides hardware startup (oscillator warmup, peripheral initialization, etc.), the ZigBee node has to initialize the network which means to check its network parameters (PANID—personal area network identifier—and channel mask), and if previously not joined to any network then scan the radio channels to discover available networks, join to a specific network, announce itself in the network, and, if the network has security enabled, wait to be authenticated by the Trust Center and for successful acquisition of the network key.

(2) *Active State.* Minimum tasks defined are polling its parent (to check if there are messages pending for the node), responding to any device discovery or service discovery operations requested, periodically requesting the Trust Center to update its network key (if security is enabled), processing device announce messages from other nodes, rejoining the network if disconnected for any reason, searching for alternative parent in order to optimize recovery latency and reliability, and so forth. Besides these network tasks, the node will also manage the sensors it might has, process and send sensor data, and so forth.

(3) *Sleep State.* It generically does not have any network or sensor and process duty assigned. This state is devoted to power electronics down to the maximum and to wait until there is any task to do switching to active state.

Temporal ubiquity of a wireless sensor node might suppose that communication with node must be guaranteed with a minimal latency time. This is commonly implemented following two different strategies that ensure lowest power of a wireless node: stay connected doing periodical network polls to receive incoming messages or leave the network and periodically reconnect. According to ZigBee specification, this is implemented following two different strategies shown in Figure 1.

(i) Polling configuration indicates that sensor node never leaves the network and periodically polls its "parent" (another node in the network that holds its messages while it sleeps).

(ii) Rejoining configuration indicates that sensor node leaves the network between reporting periods.

Both strategies are considered in ZigBee standard but no one is always more convenient than the other; while the first strategy guarantees that the node will receive messages from the network every time it polls, the second strategy reduces radio power consumption between reports to the minimum.

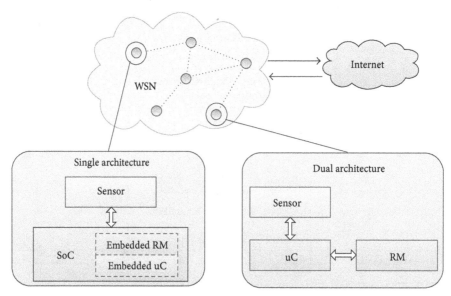

FIGURE 2: Sensor node's single and dual hardware architecture.

Energy required to retrieve and send data from the sensor to its destination must be as small as possible and its optimization needs from a multidisciplinary knowledge are improved electronic stages, network management optimization, cooperative tasking, or other alternatives [12]. It should be approached from a combined perspective [13] that merges network, (spatial distribution of network nodes [14], medium access control [15], routing [16], etc.) and node design considerations. Hardware [17] and firmware [18] design of the sensing node is crucial and it is usually done in a superficial way, just looking at the power requirements of the different hardware blocks and optimizing firmware [19].

This paper analyses energy issues associated with the different design alternatives. The next section shows main hardware architectures used to build a wireless sensor: single and dual. Then, based on the implementation of the previously described finite state machine, a mathematical model of energy consumption is defined. The energetic impact derived from hardware architecture and runtime pattern is presented in Section 4. Finally, several considerations about how design strategies impact over energy consumption and performance comparison of different WSN platforms are shown.

2. Hardware Architecture

The building blocks of a sensor node are power management, sensor, communication, and control and/or processing. Wireless communications are the power hungriest part in a node [20]; nevertheless, its impact in overall energy demand can be reduced as these systems optimize its use to the maximum. On the contrary, power consumption of the sensor is often lower compared to communications, but it can have larger influence on the overall system performance depending on how the node performs the measuring process (sampling rate, signal conditioning, data acquisition, etc.) [21]. As a consequence, hardware architecture of node is

critical when implementing a real application and electronic designers must decide between two different architectures.

(1) Dual architecture is composed of a microcontroller (uC) that runs the application and control and a radio module (RM) that implements wireless communication. Depending on the radio module, it can just be a transceiver implementing the lowest ISO/OSI layers of a standard (e.g., TI's CC2420 [22], that is, IEEE 802.15.4 compliant) or implementing a specific wireless standard to the application level (e.g., Ember's EM260 network coprocessor implementing ZigBee stack). Both cases share in common the RM that is not programmed, but is just configured or controlled through Universal Asynchronous Receiver/Transmitter (UART), Serial Peripheral Interface (SPI), or Inter-Integrated Circuit (I^2C) protocols [23] using a set of commands provided by the manufacturer.

(2) Single architecture is composed of a system-on-chip (SoC) embedding a radio module and a programmable microcontroller. In this case, the hardware manufacturer provides wireless standard compliance through an API and/or development environment that the programmer uses and implements the application and downloads it to the SoC. (e.g., Ember's 35x with EmberZNet Pro [24] or TI's CC2530 [25] with Z-Stack).

As seen in Figure 2, both architectures can be used to implement a low power consumption end node. Hardware manufacturers are clearly pointing to single architectures in order to maximize energy efficiency, reduce complexity, easily design, and so forth. Nevertheless, is this always true?, under which conditions?, is the strategy of splitting tasks between two low power microcontrollers more convenient in terms of energy efficiency? [26]. In order to answer

TABLE 1: Power modes per silicon blocks (uC, RM, and SoC).

	Power mode 0 (PM$_0$)	Power mode 1 (PM$_1$)	Power mode 2 (PM$_2$)	Power mode 3 (PM$_3$)
Microcontroller	Deep sleep (low power timer running)	Low power (slow oscillator, peripherals interrupts on)	High power (fast oscillator)	Not applicable
Radio module	Deep sleep or powered off	Not applicable	Not applicable	Radio on
System on chip	Deep sleep (low power timer running)	Not applicable	Internal uC high power and radio off	Internal uC active and radio on

these questions, in the following sections we compare both architectures analyzing the energy consumption related to each state first theoretically (Section 3) and then with two real implementations.

3. Runtime Energy Consumption Analysis

Energy monitoring during design and commissioning of a wireless sensor network is challenging. Real measurement in specific nodes is possible [27]; nevertheless, WSN characteristics make it difficult to set nodal energy meters all over the network. Thus, it is common to use tools based on nodes' and networks' models that simulate hardware [28], data traffic [29], and associated energy consumption. As it is of key importance to understand the origin of every nanoamp in order to achieve the lowest power consumption [30] and due to the fact that there are no models that consider the architectures described, in the following we study in depth the energy associated with each substate and transition of the sensing node's FSM described in Figure 1.

Minimization of energy consumption is a tradeoff between strategy chosen, application times between events (t_{SAMPLE}, t_{REPORT}, and t_{POLL}), and hardware architecture. According to this, many authors propose different energy models, most of them differentiating between four silicon modules: microprocessor, transceiver, sensor, and power supply [31]. In this study, as we aim to compare the hardware architectures discussed in previous section, it is not needed to consider sensor and power supply models because both will equally affect the energy balance; for example, whichever sensor(s) we use, they will output a digital serial communication interface (e.g., SPI and I^{2}C) or an analog signal that will be, respectively, digitalized by the uC or the SoC.

The estimation of the power consumption of a sensor node is normally based on determination of each of the operation modes of the sensor [32]. These modes are highly influenced by the communication protocol and system hardware. In Table 1, we specify all the power modes in which a node will work.

Table 2 specifies the power mode in which the hardware (uC, RM, and SoC) of the sensor will be in order to work according to poll configuration scheme in Figure 1. (We use poll configuration as it is the most complex scenario and rejoin configuration eliminates "poll parent" state, and the PM$_0$ of the RM will be reduced, while PM$_{0 \rightarrow x}$ will increase.) Energy necessary to switch between power modes is not negligible, especially when going from low power to high power [33], thus it is also indicated in Table 2.

Energy consumed in a given state "x" will be the sum of its "m" substates calculated as

$$E_x = V \times \sum_{j=0}^{m} \int_0^{t_j} i_j(t)\,dt = V \times \sum_{j=0}^{m} Q_j, \qquad (1)$$

where V is the voltage supply and the second term is the integral of the current consumed i_j and during the time t_j the substate lasts.

Attending to the substates and considering the information that can be measured and extracted from hardware datasheets and application notes, the charge demanded by each state is defined in Table 3, where $I_{UC,RM,SoC_{0,1,2,3}}$ is the current consumed by uC, RM, and SoC in power modes 0, 1, 2, and 3 respectively, $Q_{UC,RM,SoC_{0,1,2,3 \rightarrow 0,1,2,3}}$ is the charge drained by uC, RM, and SoC in transitions between corresponding power modes, $t_{UC_{0,1 \rightarrow 1,2,3}}$ is the time needed by uC to change from modes 0 and 1 to 1 and 2, respectively, $Q_{RM,SoC_{INIT,REPORT,POLL}}$ is the charge drained by RM and SoC in network initialization, data report, and parent poll, $t_{RM,SoC_{INIT,REJOIN,REPORT,POLL}}$ is the time needed by RM and SoC in respective network process, t_{SENSOR} is the time needed by the sensing entities to sensor a valid measure in their outputs, $I_{UC,SoC_{ACQ}}$ is the current needed by uC and SOC for data acquisition from the sensing entities, for example, A/D conversion, $t_{UC,SoC_{ACQ}}$ is the time needed by uC and SOC for data acquisition from the sensing entities, for example, A/D conversion, $I_{UC,RM_{SCI}}$ is the current needed by uC and RM for data communication via serial communication interface, $t_{SCI_{REPORT,POLL,POLL\_ANSW}}$, is the times needed to communicate between RM and uC via serial communication interface, and t_{SLEEP} is the time in sleep mode.

As we aim to compare both architectures, many simplifications are possible.

(i) Terms related to network operations ($Q_{RM,SoC_{INIT,SEND,POLL}}$) and power state change ($Q_{RM,SoC_{0,1,2,3 \rightarrow 0,1,2,3}}$) are equivalent in terms of energy consumption for RM and SoC. (This assumption can be considered as RM and SoC from the same manufacturer share the same radiofrequency hardware, for example, Texas Instruments' CC2520 transceiver and CC2530 SoC or Ember's EM357 coprocessor and EM357 SoC.)

(ii) Charge needed for network initialization is only consumed once and it is negligible compared to the charge needed by other states and consequently to the charge of the battery (below 0,05% with a 1000 mAh battery).

TABLE 2: Power modes in each substate of a normal operating cycle of a sensing node.

States	Substates	Dual architecture		Single architecture
		UC	RM	SoC
Init network	Scan channels	PM_0	PM_3	PM_3
	Discover networks	PM_0	PM_3	PM_3
	Join network	PM_0	PM_3	PM_3
	Announce node in network	PM_0	PM_3	PM_3
Sense data	Change power mode	$PM_{0\to1}$	PM_0	$PM_{0\to2}$
	Activate sensor and wait for data ready	PM_1	PM_0	PM_2
	Acquire data	PM_1	PM_0	PM_2
Report data	Change power mode	$PM_{0\to2}$	$PM_{0\to2}$	$PM_{0\to2}$
	Exchange "report_data" command (RM → uC)	PM_2	PM_3	—
	Change power mode	$PM_{2\to0}$	$PM_{2\to3}$	$PM_{2\to3}$
	Rejoin network (if not polling periodically)	PM_0	PM_3	PM_3
	Send data to the network	PM_0	PM_3	PM_3
Poll parent	Change power mode	$PM_{0\to2}$	$PM_{0\to2}$	$PM_{0\to2}$
	Exchange Poll event (uC → RM)	PM_2	PM_2	—
	Change power mode	$PM_{2\to1}$	$PM_{2\to3}$	$PM_{2\to3}$
	Poll parent in the network	PM_1	PM_3	PM_3
	Change power mode	$PM_{1\to2}$	$PM_{3\to2}$	—
	Exchange "poll response" (RM → uC)	PM_2	PM_2	—
Sleep	Change power mode	$PM_{x\to0}$	$PM_{x\to0}$	$PM_{x\to0}$
	Sleep	PM_0	PM_0	PM_0

TABLE 3: Consumption in each substate of a normal operating cycle of a sensing node.

States	Substates	Dual architecture	Single architecture
Init network	Scan channels		
	Discover networks	$I_{UC_0} \times t_{INIT} + Q_{RM_{INIT}}$	$Q_{SoC_{INIT}}$
	Join network		
	Announce node in network		
Sense data	Change power mode	$Q_{UC_{0\to1}} + I_{RM_0} \times t_{UC_{0\to1}}$	$Q_{SoC_{0\to2}}$
	Activate sensor and wait for data ready	$(I_{UC_1} + I_{RM_0}) \times t_{SENSOR}$	$I_{SoC_2} \times t_{SENSOR}$
	Acquire data	$(I_{UC_1} + I_{UC_{ACQ}} + I_{RM_0}) \times t_{UC_{ACQ}}$	$(I_{SoC_2} + I_{SoC_{ACQ}}) \times t_{SoC_{ACQ}}$
	Change power mode	$Q_{UC_{1\to0}}$	$Q_{SoC_{2\to0}}$
Report data	Change power mode	$Q_{UC_{0\to2}} + Q_{RM_{0\to2}}$	$Q_{SoC_{0\to2}}$
	Exchange "report_data" command (RM → UC)	$(I_{UC_2} + I_{UC_{SCI}} + I_{RM_2} + I_{RM_{SCI}}) \times t_{SCI_{REPORT}}$	0
	Change power mode	$Q_{UC_{2\to0}} + Q_{RM_{2\to3}}$	$Q_{SoC_{2\to3}}$
	Send data to the network (rejoin if needed)	$(I_{UC_0} \times t_{REPORT}) + Q_{RM_{REJOIN}} + Q_{RM_{REPORT}}$	$Q_{SoC_{REJOIN}} + Q_{SoC_{REPORT}}$
	Change power mode	$Q_{RM_{3\to0}}$	$Q_{SoC_{3\to0}}$
Poll parent	Change power mode	$Q_{UC_{0\to2}} + Q_{RM_{0\to2}}$	$Q_{SoC_{0\to2}}$
	Exchange Poll event (UC → RM)	$(I_{UC_2} + I_{UC_{SCI}} + I_{RM_2} + I_{RM_{SCI}}) \times t_{SCI_{POLL}}$	0
	Change power mode	$Q_{UC_{2\to1}} + Q_{RM_{2\to3}}$	$Q_{SoC_{2\to3}}$
	Poll parent in the network	$(I_{UC_1} \times t_{POLL}) + Q_{RM_{POLL}}$	$Q_{SoC_{POLL}}$
	Change power mode	$Q_{UC_{1\to2}} + Q_{RM_{3\to2}}$	$Q_{SoC_{3\to0}}$
	Exchange "poll response" (RM → UC)	$(I_{UC_2} + I_{UC_{SCI}} + I_{RM_2} + I_{RM_{SCI}}) \times t_{SCI_{POLL\_ANSW}}$	0
	Change power mode	$Q_{UC_{2\to0}} + Q_{RM_{2\to0}}$	
Sleep	Sleep	$(I_{UC_0} + I_{RM_0}) \times t_{SLEEP}$	$I_{SoC_0} \times t_{SLEEP}$

TABLE 4: Figures involved in the calculation of power consumption.

	Dual architecture				Single architecture	
	uC_{PIC}	RM_{Ember}	uC_{TI}	RM_{TI}	SoC_{Ember}	SoC_{TI}
I_0	$0.835\,\mu A$	$0.4\,\mu A$	$0.9\,\mu A$	$0.4\,\mu A$	$1\,\mu A$	$1\,\mu A$
I_1	$15\,\mu A$	—	$41\,\mu A$	—	—	—
I_2	$3.05\,mA$	$6\,mA$	$2.2\,mA$	$3.4\,mA$	$6\,mA$	$3.4\,mA$
I_3	—	$27\,mA$	—	$28.7\,mA$	$27\,mA$	$28.7\,mA$
I_{ACQ}	$1\,mA$	—	$850\,\mu A$	—	$1.1\,mA$	$1.2\,mA$
I_{SCI}	$0.5\,\mu A$	$200\,\mu A$	$0.5\,\mu A$	$200\,\mu A$	—	—
$Q_{0\to1}$	$15\,pC$	—	$16\,pC$	—	—	—
$Q_{0\to2}$	$0.39\,\mu C$	$12.4\,\mu C$	$10\,pC$	$51.57\,\mu C$	$12.4\,\mu C$	$51.57\,\mu C$
$Q_{2\to3}$	—	$9.94\,\mu C$	—	$40.95\,\mu C$	$9.94\,\mu C$	$40.95\,\mu C$
$Q_{3\to0}$	—	$3.3\,\mu C$	—	$13.6\,\mu C$	$3.3\,\mu C$	$13.6\,\mu C$
$t_{0\to1}$	$1\,\mu s$	—	$0.4\,\mu s$	—	—	—
$t_{0\to2}$	$128\,\mu s$	—	$0.4\,\mu s$	—	—	—
t_{ACQ}	$4.125\,\mu s$	—	$2.06\,\mu s$	—	$42.7\,\mu s$	$68\,\mu s$
t_{SCI_POLL}	$16\,\mu s$	$16\,\mu s$	$8\,\mu s$	$8\,\mu s$	—	—
$t_{SCI\_POLL\_ANSW}$	$4\,\mu s$	$4\,\mu s$	$2\,\mu s$	$4\,\mu s$	—	—
t_{SCI_REPORT}	$34\,\mu s$	$34\,\mu s$	$17\,\mu s$	$34\,\mu s$	—	—
t_{REPORT}	—	$8\,ms$	—	$8\,ms$	$8\,ms$	$8\,ms$
t_{POLL}	—	$6\,ms$	—	$6.8\,ms$	$6\,ms$	$6.8\,ms$

(iii) Current in power mode 0 of uC, RM, and SoC is several orders of magnitude lower compared to power modes 1, 2, or 3.

(iv) Time in sleep mode is several orders of magnitude larger than any other times.

Considering the former simplifications and application times between events (t_{SAMPLE}, t_{REPORT}, and t_{POLL}), the resulting energy balance between dual and single architecture for a given cycle is

$$Q_{CYCLE_{D-S}} = \frac{t_{REPORT}}{t_{SAMPLE}} \times Q_{SENSE_{D-S}} + \frac{t_{REPORT}}{t_{POLL}} \times Q_{POLL_{D-S}}$$
$$+ Q_{REPORT_{D-S}} + t_{REPORT} \times I_{SLEEP_{D-S}}, \quad (2)$$

where

$$Q_{SENSE_{D-S}} = Q_{uC_{0\to1}} + Q_{uC_{1\to0}} + I_{RM_0}$$
$$\times \left(t_{uC_{0\to1}} + t_{uC_{ACQ}} \right) + \left(I_{uC_1} + I_{uC_{ACQ}} \right)$$
$$\times t_{uC_{ACQ}} - Q_{SoC_{0\to2}} - Q_{SoC_{2\to0}}$$
$$- \left(I_{SoC_2} + I_{SoC_{ACQ}} \right) \times t_{SoC_{ACQ}}$$
$$+ \left(I_{RM_0} + I_{uC_1} - I_{SoC_2} \right) \times t_{SENSOR},$$

$$Q_{POLL_{D-S}} = Q_{uC_{0\to2}} + Q_{uC_{2\to0}} + Q_{uC_{1\to2}} + Q_{uC_{2\to1}}$$
$$+ \left(I_{uC_2} + I_{uC_{SCI}} + I_{RM_2} + I_{RM_{SCI}} \right)$$
$$\times \left(t_{SCI_{POLL}} + t_{SCI_{POLL_{ANSW}}} \right) + \left(I_{uC_1} \times t_{POLL} \right),$$

$$Q_{REPORT_{D-S}} = Q_{UC_{0\to2}} + Q_{UC_{2\to0}}$$
$$+ \left(I_{UC_2} + I_{UC_{SCI}} + I_{RM_2} + I_{RM_{SCI}} \right)$$
$$\times t_{SCI_{REPORT}} + \left(I_{UC_0} \times t_{REPORT} \right),$$

$$I_{SLEEP_{D-S}} = I_{UC_0} + I_{RM_0} - I_{SoC_0}. \quad (3)$$

Thus, when $Q_{CYCLE_{D-S}} < 0$, the dual architecture will be more power efficient than the single architecture and vice versa when $Q_{CYCLE_{D-S}} > 0$.

4. Experimental Method and Results

As mentioned above, there are different WSN simulation tools that focus on specific aspects of the network: latency times, bandwidth, collisions, message integrity, and so forth. According to the previous section analysis, we need to focus more deeply on the architecture of the node and associated states, than on the network characteristics. Thus, we used MATLAB suite to model energy consumption of real sensing nodes' hardware and simulate FSM operation.

Comparison between architectures has been done analyzing two real implementations with devices having similar

TABLE 5: Rate of consumption of each substate (considering that t_{report} = 8 hours, t_{SAMPLE} = 10 min, t_{POLL} = 4 min, t_{SENSOR} = 10 ms).

	Microchip-Ember	Texas Instruments
%$Q_{SENSE_{D-S}}$	33.707%	32.094%
%$Q_{POLL_{D-S}}$	0.773%	0.315%
%$Q_{REPORT_{D-S}}$	0.007%	0.002%
%($I_{SLEEP_{D-S}} \times t_{REPORT}$)	65.513%	67.589%

characteristics: both ZigBee standard chipsets and microcontrollers with 16 bit RISC architecture similar to MIPS, power supply ranges, integration of peripherals (ADC, serial communication interfaces, clocks, etc.), and memory capacity. Table 4 shows how theoretical analysis shown in Section 3 is specified for two different implementations of ZigBee standard (Texas Instruments and Ember, but now Silicon Labs) and for two different families of ultralow power microcontrollers (Microchip and Texas Instruments). (uC_{PIC} = PIC24F16KA102; RM_{Ember} = SoC_{Ember} = EM357; uC_{TI} = MSP430F2001; RM_{TI} = SoC_{TI} = CC2530. SoC manufacturers usually allow their devices to operate as RM running a specific firmware. Thus, in order to eliminate hardware dependencies in analysis, we decided to use the same chipset operating in different configurations in both architectures. The indicated energy consumption corresponds to the scenarios in which both architectures have optimized and similar performance: similar peripheral, clocks sources, and power configuration. It is important to remark that internal RTCC in PM_0 has been selected.)

For a given conditions and according to the analysis in Section 3, Table 5 shows the charge difference between dual and single architecture (%$Q_{X_{D-S}}$) of each substate, expressed in percentage contribution to the normalized total consumption per cycle. On one hand, it highlights the importance of sleeping and sensing processes related to total energy consumption evidencing their importance in autonomy maximization. It also proves the slight differences between chipsets, which together with the fact that information available about power consumption is more profuse for Microchip-Ember configuration leads us to choose it for further analyses.

4.1. Sensing and Reporting. When focusing on measurement process, there are two important tasks: data acquisition and reporting. Figure 3 represents how the power savings ratio (PSR) of the dual architecture versus single architecture (defined as PSR_{DSvsS} = $Q_{CYCLE_{D-S}}/Q_{CYCLE_S} \triangleq \Delta Q/Q$) varies depending on t_{SAMPLE}, t_{POLL}, and t_{SENSOR}. Values above zero indicate better performance of the dual architecture and vice versa when PSR_{DSvsS} is below zero.

It is appreciated that variation in t_{POLL} has reduced impact on PSR_{DSvsS}. The major effect comes from the variation of the time between measurements (t_{SAMPLE}) and the time needed to have valid sensor signal (t_{SENSOR}) [34]; the more time the node spends in sensing tasks, the more effective the dual architecture becomes. This fact is evidenced

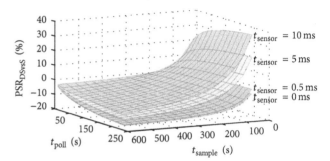

FIGURE 3: Variation of PSR_{DvsS} with t_{SAMPLE} and t_{POLL} (e.g., t_{REPORT} = 4 hours and several t_{sensor}).

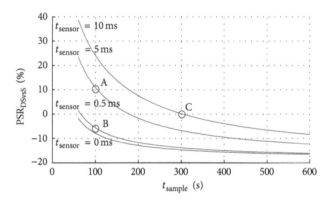

FIGURE 4: PSR_{DSvsS} versus t_{SAMPLE} (e.g., t_{REPORT} = 4 hours t_{POLL} = 4 min).

in Figure 4, where PSR_{DSvsS} is represented versus t_{SAMPLE} for various values of t_{SENSOR}.

We can clearly observe the impact of the measurement process on energy savings in the following example. Considering a sensor node getting one sample each 100 seconds from a sensor that needs 5 ms to provide a valid value (point A in Figure 3), the dual architecture would need 10% of energy less than single architecture. This effect is mainly derived from the higher flexibility in terms of clock sources of low power microcontrollers that is so far not available in SoCs (PIC24F16KA102 has five external and internal clock sources, providing 11 different clock modes with a minimum CPU clock speed of 31 kHz. Ember 357 has four clock sources with a minimum CPU clock speed of 6 MHz. The same happens to TI's hardware); that is, microcontrollers consider low power modes with slow clocks (PM_1) that are very convenient for sensing tasks. On the other hand if t_{SENSOR} is reduced to 500 us (point B in Figure 3), single architecture would be 6% more efficient. Finally, when sampling time t_{SAMPLE} exceeds 5 minutes (point C in Figure 3), for the conditions given (t_{REPORT} = 4 hours; t_{POLL} = 4 min; $t_{SENSOR} \leq$ 10 ms), single architecture will be always more efficient.

4.2. Rejoining and Polling Strategies. Regardless of the dual or single architectures, if it is assumable that the node is not connected to the network, a rejoin strategy can be more

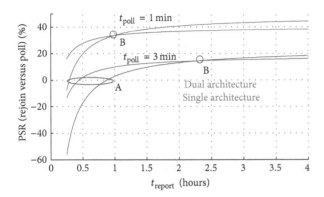

FIGURE 5: Comparison and single dual architecture with rejoining versus polling strategies (example for $t_{\text{SAMPLE}} = 1\,\text{min}$ $t_{\text{SENSOR}} = 5\,\text{ms}$).

optimal depending mainly on the reporting period (t_{REPORT}). This basically occurs when the overconsumption due to rejoin process compensates the accumulated energy consumptions of the polls. Figure 5 compares PSR between rejoining and polling strategies for single and dual architectures.

Intersection between lines with zero (points A in Figure 4) indicates the t_{REPORT} above which rejoining strategy would be more convenient for any architecture. Intersection between red and blue lines (points B in Figure 4) indicates the t_{REPORT} above which dual architecture is more efficient than single architecture.

As expected, the energy savings of rejoining strategy increases with time between reports, faster at the beginning, until reaching a final stable value. This is because increasing time between reports decreases relative impact of Q_{REJOIN} over the total. For this same reason, the final PSR is much more affected by the time between polls rather than by the value of Q_{REJOIN}.

4.3. Sleeping.
As we have seen in Table 5, with any given sampling/polling/reporting conditions, the current in sleep mode is a relevant variable that has major impact in node lifetime. Thus, it is evident that the primary goal of a low power system is being in sleep mode as long as possible [35]. Some authors propose adaptive runtime to maximize efficiency [36]. Indeed, it is common to perform nodal power consumption analysis according to sleeping duty cycle [37]. Given the presented FSM tasks, considering sleeping time that is several orders of magnitude higher than the time devoted to all other tasks, having a battery charged with Q_{BATT} and "n" being the number of reports performed by the node during its lifetime, charge will be drained as

$$Q_{\text{BATT}} = Q_{\text{INIT}}$$
$$+ n \times \left(\frac{t_{\text{REPORT}}}{t_{\text{SAMPLE}}} \times Q_{\text{SENSE}} + \frac{t_{\text{REPORT}}}{t_{\text{POLL}}} \right.$$
$$\left. \times Q_{\text{POLL}} + Q_{\text{REPORT}} + t_{\text{REPORT}} \times I_{\text{SLEEP}} \right). \tag{4}$$

Dual architecture with low power microcontrollers allows greater versatility to reduce sleep current, due to additional capabilities provided by a microcontroller: ultralow wakeup with external capacitor and radio module's totally powered off. (Frequently, microcontrollers have external interrupts based on discharged time of a capacitor. (See Microchip AN879 Using the Microchip Ultra Low-power Wake-up Module) or high impedance RC external circuits could be used in an low power interrupt. Note that the consumption for charging this capacitor is negligible.) Both architectures can also use an external RTCC to reduce to the maximum energy required for timing. (Low-Current High-ESR Crystals (such as Maxim DS1341) with I^2C communication and one output used to activate an alarm interrupt of the microcontroller.) Table 6 shows pros and cons of different sleep mode strategies, sleep current of hardware, and associated PSR of dual architecture versus single architecture.

For polling (node can receive messages) and rejoining (node cannot receive messages) configurations, we considered four sleeping strategies. Using internal or external RTCC (additional chip necessary) provides node's conscience about clock and calendar and high precision in wakeup timing. It can be useful to build time synchronized WSNs, to accurately monitor variables or to timestamp measurements. Internal WDT reduces current consumption and loses timing functionalities. Finally, ultralow power wakeup has the most inaccurate timing (that could be enough to form any applications) but greatly reduces current consumption.

Evidently, the more the silicon modules that can be powered off, the less the power consumption in sleep mode. Thus, due to its higher flexibility, the dual architecture can be very convenient in case the application requirements allow it; it is especially remarkable to note the PSR difference in the rejoining strategy with ultralow power wakeup.

4.4. Hardware Architecture Performance Comparison.
In order to range the importance of the issues described here, this section provides a hardware architecture performance comparison of well-known WSN platforms [38–40]. The methodology followed has been to model the hardware blocks of the platforms according to chip manufacturer specifications and calculate the expected battery lifetime in a realistic scenario. Table 7 show the life expectancy expressed in years and the ratio compared to the best performance architecture. (Test framework considered: $V_{\text{supply}} = 3\,\text{V}$; internal oscillator, main frequency = 8 mhz, secondary frequency = 1 MHz; External Oscillator, Crystal frequency = 32.768 kHz; $t_{\text{SAMPLE}} = 120\,\text{s}$, $t_{\text{POLL}} = 4\,\text{min}$, $t_{\text{SENSOR}} = 1\,\text{ms}$; $t_{\text{REPORT}} = 60\,\text{min}$; Battery type = LiMnO$_2$, model = 2032/5004LC, capacity = 210 mAh). Obviously, it is necessary to consider that older systems are at disadvantage as chipset performance improves every year.

According to the results in previous sections, dual architecture is more efficient than the single one for the given conditions. Also both Texas Instruments and Microchip-Ember provides the highest performance. As sensing duties are not exigent in terms of microcontroller requirements, we can observe the negative effect of oversizing them (SunSpot's microcontroller is very powerful) in terms of life expectancy.

TABLE 6: PSR$_{\text{DSvsD}}$ for several configurations (t_{SAMPLE} = 120 s, t_{POLL} = 4 min, and t_{SENSOR} = 1 ms).

	Sleeping strategy	I_{SLEEP} (Dual)	I_{SLEEP} (Single)		PSR$_{\text{cycle}}$ (DSvsS)	Pros and cons
		uC$_{\text{PIC}}$ + RTCC$_{\text{DS}}$	RM$_{\text{Ember}}$	SoC$_{\text{Ember}}$		
Polling	Internal RTCC wakeup	0.835 μA	0.4 μA	1 μA	5.68%	+ Node can receive messages + High precision in wakeup timing
	Internal WDT wakeup	0.585 μA	0.4 μA	0.8 μA	2.58%	+ Node can receive messages − Low precision in wakeup timing
	External RTCC wakeup	0.035 μA + 0.25 μA	0.4 μA	0.4 μA + 0.25 μA	0.78%	+ Node can receive messages + High precision in wakeup timing − Additional RTCC chip necessary
	Ultralow power wakeup	0.035 μA	0.4 μA	0.8 μA	−41.63%	+ Node can receive messages − The lowest precision in wakeup timing
Rejoining	Internal RTCC wakeup	0.835 μA	0	1 μA	−25.90%	− Node cannot receive messages + High precision in wakeup timing
	Internal WDT wakeup	0.585 μA	0	0.8 μA	−35.94%	− Node cannot receive messages − Low precision in wakeup timing
	External RTCC wakeup	0.035 μA + 0.25 μA	0	0.4 μA + 0.25 μA	−59.47%	− Node cannot receive messages + High precision in wakeup timing − Additional RTCC chip necessary
	Ultra low power wakeup	0.035 μA	0	0.8 μA	−90.66%	− Node cannot receive messages − The lowest precision in wakeup timing

TABLE 7: WSN hardware platform performance comparison.

	Platform	Hardware architecture		Life expectancy (Years)	Ratio (%)
		Microcontroller	Transceiver		
Dual	Texas Instruments	MSP43F2001	CC2530	2.75	100%
	Microchip-Ember	PIC24F16KA102	EM357	2.45	89.12%
	Iris-It (2008)	ATMega 1281	AT86RF230	1.03	37.42%
	Libelium (2012)	ATMega 1281	EM357	0.99	36.16%
	TelosB, Shimmer (2005)	MSP430F1611	CC2420	0.75	27.47%
	MicaZ (2004)	Atmega 1281	CC2420	0.42	15.11%
	Sun SPOT (2007)	AT91SAM9G20	CC2420	0.14	5.20%
Single	Texas Instruments	CC2530		2.13	74.34%
	Ember	EM357		1.42	48.90%

Also, comparing performance of platforms sharing the same transceiver (CC2420 and EM357), the influence of the microcontroller chosen is obvious.

5. Conclusions

WSNs are essential in the next generation of Internet where ubiquitous interconnected objects are available for interaction. Ubiquity means everywhere and anytime availability of sensing nodes implying wireless communication, energy harvesting, low power, and so forth; concepts that if not properly considered can lead to reduced systems' autonomy killing many real IoT applications. With these considerations in mind, low power consumption is one of the most important targets when designing IoT ready sensors.

This paper studies different sensor node hardware architectures, deepening in the power consumptions associated with each state of the runtime cycle and time-relationship

between them. It compares the energy consumption involved in the operation of a sensor node implemented using two different architectures: dual (based on a low power microcontroller and a radio module) and single (based on a system on chip). The specific finite state machine that describes the operation of sensing node is based on standard IEEE 1451 and the specific communications substates are modeled according to ZigBee Pro standard.

One important conclusion is that energy required in the sensing procedure has an important impact on this balance. There are some tasks, such as waiting for a valid sensor output (t_{SENSOR}) or acquiring the sensor data, which might require relevant amount of energy depending on the sampling rate (t_{SAMPLE}). This can turn dual architecture more efficient than the single one. One reason is that because low power microcontrollers in single architecture have higher flexibility than SoC architectures in terms of low power oscillator configurations, microcontrollers embedded in SoCs are usually not able to run with kHz oscillators. The second reason is because low power microcontroller peripherals are more optimized, something which can be especially relevant in case of using analog sensors that require the use of analog-digital converter (the same performance in terms of quality of the conversion requires less current and time in low power microcontroller than in SoC).

Considering temporal ubiquity requirements, if the IoT application does not require nodal availability at any time (for example to change sampling parameters), nodes can disconnect from the WSN. In case of ZigBee standard, this can be implemented using rejoining and polling strategies. In that case, when energy needed to rejoin exceeds consumption due to several polls, polling strategy turns to be more energy efficient. It also shows that, above a certain reporting period, dual architecture is more efficient because rejoining strategy allows to totally power off the radio module when not using it.

Power consumption in sleep mode has major impact on node lifetime, so there is a need to design a system with a current in sleep mode as low as possible. Again, dual architecture might be more convenient because low power microcontrollers are more flexible in terms of oscillator configuration and have additional low power modules such as ultralow-power wake-up module.

The main conclusion of the study evidences that, despite what could be considered initially and stated in datasheets, no architecture is always energetically more efficient than the other; deep contextualized system analysis is mandatory to squeeze batteries to the maximum. This paper provides generic guidelines that would help electronic designers in this analysis in order to decide the most energy efficient hardware architecture of sensor nodes. We also find it useful for firmware and even software developers in order to provide understanding about how IoT application requirements (e.g., reporting time) affect WSN performance and lifetime. Finally, a performance comparison of different WSN platforms attending to their hardware architecture evidences the impact of the issues just stated.

As a final example, making clear the importance of the analysis, if a sensor that polls for data every 4 min samples every minute a sensor that needs 5 ms to set up and reports data each 4 hours is implemented using a dual architecture, it would need 24% less energy than implemented using a SoC. But just changing sampling rate from 1 minute to 5 minutes would turn the situation making the dual architecture consume 6% more energy than single architecture.

References

[1] O. Mirabella and M. Brischetto, "A hybrid wired/wireless networking infrastructure for greenhouse management," *IEEE Transactions on Instrumentation and Measurement*, vol. 60, no. 2, pp. 398–407, 2011.

[2] O. A. Postolache, P. M. B. S. Girao, J. Mendes, E. C. Pinheiro, and G. Postolache, "Physiological parameters measurement based on wheelchair embedded sensors and advanced signal processing," *IEEE Transactions on Instrumentation and Measurement*, vol. 59, no. 10, pp. 2564–2574, 2010.

[3] V. C. Gungor and G. P. Hancke, "Industrial wireless sensor networks: challenges, design principles, and technical approaches," *IEEE Transactions on Industrial Electronics*, vol. 56, no. 10, pp. 4258–4265, 2009.

[4] C. C. Gómez, J. Paradells, and J. E. Caballero, *Sensors Everywhere. Wireless Network Technologies and Solutions*, Fundación Vodafone España, 2010.

[5] A. Sharma, K. Shinghal, R. Singh, and N. Srivastaya, "Energy management for wireless sensor network nodes," *International Journal of Advances in Engineering & Technology*, vol. 1, pp. 7–13, 2011.

[6] C. Knight, J. Davidson, and S. Behrens, "Energy options for wireless sensor nodes," *Sensors*, vol. 8, no. 12, pp. 8037–8066, 2008.

[7] R. Soua and P. Mine, "A survey on energy efficient techniques in wireless sensor networks," in *Proceedings of the Wireless and Mobile Networking Conference (WMNC '11)*, INRIA, Le Chesnay, France, 2011.

[8] J. E. Higuera and J. Polo, "IEEE 1451 standard in 6LoWPAN sensor networks using a compact physical-layer transducer electronic datasheet," *IEEE Transactions on Instrumentation and Measurement*, vol. 60, no. 8, pp. 2751–2758, 2011.

[9] IEEE Standard 1451.5, "IEEE standard for a smart transducer interface for densors and actuators—wireless communication protocols and transducer electronic data sheet (TEDS) formats," IEEE, 2007.

[10] C. Buratti, A. Conti, D. Dardari, and R. Verdone, "An overview on wireless sensor networks technology and evolution," *Sensors*, vol. 9, no. 9, pp. 6869–6896, 2009.

[11] ZigBee Alliance, "ZigBee Specification," Document 053474r17, 2008.

[12] R. X. Gao and Z. Fan, "Architectural design of a sensory node controller for optimized energy utilization in sensor networks," *IEEE Transactions on Instrumentation and Measurement*, vol. 55, no. 2, pp. 415–428, 2006.

[13] S. Bilouhan and R. Gupta, "Optimization of power consumption in wireless sensor networks," *International Journal of Scientific & Engineering Research*, vol. 2, no. 5, 2011.

[14] K. Akkaya and M. Younis, "A survey on routing protocols for wireless sensor networks," *Ad Hoc Networks*, vol. 3, no. 3, pp. 325–349, 2005.

[15] M. Al Ameen, S. M. R. Islam, and K. Kwak, "Energy saving mechanisms for MAC protocols in wireless sensor networks," *International Journal of Distributed Sensor Networks*, vol. 2010, Article ID 163413, 16 pages, 2010.

[16] S. M. Ahmad Madani, *Cross layer design for low power wireless sensor networks [Ph.D. thesis]*, 2008.

[17] P. Yu, L. Qinghua, and P. Xiyuan, "The design of low-power wireless sensor node," in *Proceedings of the IEEE International Instrumentation and Measurement Technology Conference (I2MTC '10)*, pp. 917–922, May 2010.

[18] T. R. Park and M. J. Lee, "Power saving algorithms for wireless sensor networks on IEEE 802.15.4," *IEEE Communications Magazine*, vol. 46, no. 6, pp. 148–155, 2008.

[19] F. Salvadori, M. de Campos, P. S. Sausen et al., "Monitoring in industrial systems using wireless sensor network with dynamic power management," *IEEE Transactions on Instrumentation and Measurement*, vol. 58, no. 9, pp. 3104–3111, 2009.

[20] S. Caban, G. José Antonio, and M. Rupp, "Measuring the physical layer performance of wireless communication systems," *IEEE Instrumentation & Measurement Magazine*, vol. 14, no. 5, pp. 8–17, 2011.

[21] C. Alippi, G. Anastasi, M. Di Francesco, and M. Roveri, "Energy management in wireless sensor networks with energy-hungry sensors," *IEEE Instrumentation and Measurement Magazine*, vol. 12, no. 2, pp. 16–23, 2009.

[22] Texas Instruments Incorporated, http://www.ti.com/product/cc2420.

[23] "XP Semiconductors N.V.," http://www.nxp.com/campaigns/i2c-bus/.

[24] "Silicon Laboratories Inc.," http://www.silabs.com/products/wireless/zigbee/Pages/zigbee-chips-em35x.aspx.

[25] "Texas Instruments Incorporated," http://www.ti.com/product/cc2530.

[26] P. H. Chou and C. Park, "Energy-efficient platform designs for real-world wireless sensing applications," in *Proceedings of the IEEE/ACM International Conference on Computer-Aided Design (ICCAD '05)*, pp. 913–920, November 2005.

[27] M. Gao, X. Pan, L. Deng, C. Huang, D. Zhang, and L. Ni, "A versatile nodal energy consumption monitoring method for wireless sensor networks testbed," in *Proceedings of the IEEE 17th International Conference on Parallel and Distributed Systems*, pp. 388–395, 2011.

[28] Castalia, http://castalia.research.nicta.com.au/index.php/en/.

[29] G. V. Merrett, N. M. White, N. R. Harris, and B. M. Al-Hashimi, "Energy-aware simulation for wireless sensor networks," in *Proceedings of the 6th Annual IEEE Communications Society Conference on Sensor, Mesh and Ad Hoc Communications and Networks (SECON '09)*, June 2009.

[30] P. Yu, L. Qinghua, and P. Xiyuan, "The design of low-power wireless sensor node," in *Proceedings of the IEEE International Instrumentation and Measurement Technology Conference (I2MTC '10)*, pp. 917–922, May 2010.

[31] H.-Y. Zhou, D.-Y. Luo, Y. Gao, and D.-C. Zuo, "Modeling of node energy consumption for wireless sensor networks," *Wireless Sensor Networks*, vol. 3, no. 1, pp. 18–23, 2011.

[32] E. Casilari, J. M. Cano-García, and G. Campos-Garrido, "Modeling of current consumption in 802.15.4/ZigBee sensor motes," *Sensors*, vol. 10, no. 6, pp. 5443–5468, 2010.

[33] B. Gholamzadeh and H. Nabovati, "Concepts for designing low power wireless sensor network," *World Academy of Science, Engineering and Technology*, vol. 45, pp. 559–565, 2008.

[34] W. S. Wang, R. O'Keeffe, N. Wang, M. Hayes, B. O. 'Flynn, and S. C. Ó Mathúna, "Reducing power consumption in metrics for building energy management apllications," in *Proceedings of the 23rd European Conference Forum Bauinformatik*, Cork, Ireland, 2011.

[35] A. Viswanathan and T. E. Boult, "Power conservation in ZigBee networks using temporal control," in *Proceedings of the 2nd International Symposium on Wireless Pervasive Computing*, pp. 175–180, University of Colorado Press, Boulder, Colo, USA, February 2007.

[36] J. Chern Lim and C. Bleakley, "AdaptiveWSN scheduling for lifetime extension in environmentalMonitoring applications," *International Journal of Distributed Sensor Networks*, vol. 2012, Article ID 286981, 17 pages, 2012.

[37] Y. W. Chung and H. Y. Hwang, "Modeling and analysis of energy conservation scheme based on duty cycling in wireless Ad Hoc sensor network," *Sensors*, vol. 10, no. 6, pp. 5569–5589, 2010.

[38] V. Madan and S. Reddy, "Review of wireless sensor mote platforms," *VSRD International Journal of Elecrical, Electronics & Communication Engineering*, vol. 2, no. 2, pp. 50–55, 2012.

[39] T. V. Chien, H. Nguyen Chan, and T. Nguyen Huu, "A comparative study on hardware platforms for wireless sensor networks," *International Journal on Advanced Science Engineering Information Technologgy*, vol. 2, no. 1, 2012.

[40] R. Lajara, J. Pelegrí-Sebastiá, and J. J. Perez Solano, "Power consumption analysis of operating systems for wireless sensor networks," *Sensors*, vol. 10, no. 6, pp. 5809–5826, 2010.

18

A Cross-Layer Security Scheme of Web-Services-Based Communications for IEEE 1451 Sensor and Actuator Networks

Jun Wu,[1,2] Ming Zhan,[3] Bin Duan,[4] and Jiang Liu[5]

[1] *Research Institute for Secure Systems (RISEC), National Institute of Advanced Industrial Science and Technology (AIST), Tsukuba 305-8568, Japan*
[2] *Global Information and Telecommunication Institute (GITI), Waseda University, Tokyo 169-0051, Japan*
[3] *School of Electronic and Information Engineering, Southwest University, Chongqing 400714, China*
[4] *College of Information Engineering, Xiangtan University, Xiangtan 411105, China*
[5] *School of Electrical and Electronics Engineering, North China Electric Power University, Beijing 102206, China*

Correspondence should be addressed to Ming Zhan; zmdjs@swu.edu.cn

Academic Editor: Mianxiong Dong

IEEE 1451 standard has been proposed to provide a common communication interface and transducer electric data sheet format for wired and wireless distributed applications in smart transducers (sensors and actuators). Currently, a unified Web service for IEEE 1451 smart transducers is a must. However, ensuring the security of web-services-based communications for IEEE 1451 smart transducers is an unsolved problem. In this paper, we proposed a cross-layer security mechanism that deals with the requirements of authentication, integrity, confidentiality, and availability across the communication process in IEEE 1451 smart transducers. The scheme contains three cross-layer components logically, including XML Encryption and Signature, SOAP Security Extension, and Web Services Description Language (WSDL) Security Checking. The former two components satisfy the requirements of confidentiality, availability, integrity, authentication, nonrepudiation, and freshness. The third component satisfies the requirement of availability, which can protect the system against denial-of-service (DoS) attack. The three cross-layer security components are integrated seamlessly in our scheme. To evaluate the overhead, we perform tests to evaluate the effect of message size on the performance of the access inquiry web service. The result supports the usefulness and feasibility of our scheme.

1. Introduction

In recent years, sensor and actuator have attracted a lot of attention recently due to their broad applications, ranging from industrial automation to environmental condition monitoring and control-to-intelligent transportation system to homeland defense [1–5]. A smart transducer is a compact unit containing a sensor or actuator element, a microcontroller, a communication controller, and the associated software for signal conditioning, calibration, diagnostics, and communication [6–8]. A smart transducer can enable novel application in and beyond measurement, monitoring, control, and actuating [9].

The behaviors to smart transducers generally call for distributed and remote architecture [10–12]. And these systems usually require a variety of networked interconnections and telecommunication technologies for measurement and control, and the devices are usually made by different manufactures. Therefore, common and reliable communication interface and data format are important for smart transducers. As a consequence, the Instrumentation and Measurement Society's Sensor Technology Technical Committee TC-9 at the Institute of Electrical and Electronics Engineers (IEEE) has been working to establish a group of smart sensor interface standards called IEEE 1451 [13–18]. IEEE 1451 standard is proposed to provide a common communication interface and transducer electric data sheet format for wired and wireless distributed applications. It will eliminate the issue of proprietary communication systems utilizing a wide variety of protocols, labels, semantics, and so forth, thus enabling a transducer application to exchange information with different smart transducers independently of a vendor.

From a utility perspective, unified definitions of common data minimize conversion and recalculation of data values for evaluation and comparison in many application systems.

Recently, the working group of Kang Lee, who is the Chairman of the IEEE Instrumentation and Measurement Society's Technical Committee on Sensor Technology and responsible for the establishment of the suite of IEEE 1451, proposed a unified Web service for IEEE 1451 smart transducers [19]. This work developed the IEEE 1451 standard to a new emerging unified Web service framework. An IEEE 1451 Network Capable Application Processor (NCAP) can be used as a Smart Transducer Web Services (STWS) provider, which provides asset of Web services for the STWS. STWS consumers, such as sensor alert system, OGC-SWE, or other applications, can find the STWS deployed and then invoke the STWS through Simple Object-access Protocol (SOAP)/Extensible Markup Language (XML) message. As a consequence, the use of Web service technologies provides the benefits of low implementation cost and ease of interoperability because Web services can implement service-oriented architectures (SOAs), which enable loosely coupled integration and interoperation of distributed heterogeneous system by using services as component elements in transducer networks. However, on the other hand, Web-services-based communication introduces the cyber security problem.

The importance of cyber security in sensor and actuator networks is widely recognized. Recently, schemes related to the cyber security for sensor and actuator networks have been widely investigated [20–24]. In particular, cyber security of Web-services-based communication for smart transducers must be implemented [25]. Security issues of communication for smart transducer are described in IEEE 1451.0. However, how the security issues are handled is up to the individual supplier and the responsibilities of communication protocol [13]. As a matter of fact, Web-services-based communication for smart transducers is a new emerging technology, in which few studies have been conducted for security. A common method of implement security is based on a secure transport layer or network layer, which typically includes secure socket layer (SSL), transport layer security (TLS), and network layer security (NLS). For example, TLS and NLS are recommended to secure TCP/IP-based communication for wireless sensor and actuator networks in IEEE 1415.5. However, these security schemes provide security only in a secure channel, and not in files or databases. Furthermore, these techniques do not correspond with the web services architecture in which the intermediaries can manipulate the messages on their way. Once using a secure transport layer, intermediaries are not able to control the message [26, 27].

The Web Services Security (WS-Security) [28, 29] standard was produced by Advancing Open Standards for the Information Society (OASIS) in 2004. The Web Services Security (WS-Security) is an essential component of the Web services protocol stack to provide end-to-end integrity, confidentiality, and authentication capabilities to web services. End-to-end message security assures the participation of nonsecure transport intermediaries in message exchanges, which is a key advantage for web systems and service-oriented architectures. Some security schemes corresponding

with WS-Security are proposed for e-mail system, enterprise services system, trust management, and so forth, but cannot be applied directly to smart transducers [28–31].

As a matter of fact, IEEE 1451 standards define a common communication interfaces for networked smart transducers, which include sensors and actuators. The research of sensor and actuator networks is an existing area. In this paper, IEEE 1451 sensor and actuator networks means the networked smart transducers which are based on the common interfaces of IEEE 1451. Because of the communication protocols and data format of IEEE 1451 sensor and actuator networks, the secure communication proposals should have their special features based on IEEE 1451 standards. On the other hand, this paper focuses on the Web services communication security. So the security topics of confidentiality, availability, integrity, authentication, nonrepudiation, and freshness are necessary for the IEEE 1451 sensor and actuator networks, which also must be based on the data format of IEEE 1451.

In this paper, we proposed a cross-layer security scheme for web-services-based communication for IEEE 1451 smart transducers. The rest of this paper is organized as follows. Section 2 analyzes the system architecture and security requirements of IEEE 1451 reference model. Section 3 presents the architecture and security measures of web services. Section 4 presents the proposed security scheme. Section 5 analyzes the security of the proposed scheme. Section 5 evaluates the implementation of the proposed scheme. Finally, Section 6 concludes this paper.

2. System Architecture and Security Requirements

2.1. IEEE 1451 Reference Model. IEEE 1451 standards define a common communication model to connect smart transducers to normalization of integrated, intelligent, and open distributed measurement and control systems (DMCSs). Figure 1 shows the IEEE 1451 reference model. The IEEE 1451 family of standards divides the parts of a smart transducer system into two general categories of devices. One is the Network Capable Application Processor (NCAP) that functions as a gateway between the users' network and the transducer interface modules (TIMs) [13–18]. In the IEEE 1451 reference model, smart transducers connect with DMCS users through the user communication network. The user communication network is outside of the scope of the IEEE 1451 family of standards. It may be anything that the user desires. The only requirement that is placed on the NCAP is that the NCAP has the appropriate network interface hardware and software [13].

The communications between NCAP and TIM are based on IEEE 1451.X communication modules in both sides, which provide the low levels of the communications protocol [13]. DMCS users interact with smart transducers through public application programming interfaces (APIs) [13]. The applications run in NCAP or remote DMCS system interact with transducers through public application programming interfaces (APIs).

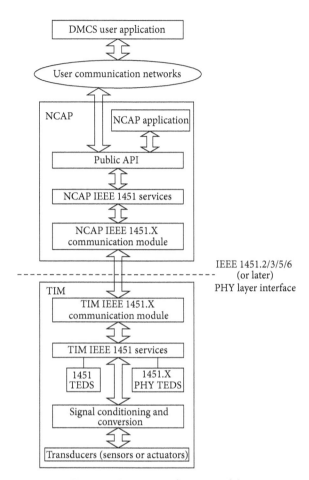

FIGURE 1: IEEE 1451 reference model.

2.2. Unified Web Service for IEEE 1451 Smart Transducers. Web services are typically APIs or web APIs that are accessed via Hypertext Transfer Protocol and executed on a remote system hosting the requested services. Qualities like simplicity, code reuse, and interoperability are also making Web services a *de facto* standard in the context of DMCSs [32]. The IEEE 1451 working group proposed a unified Web service for IEEE 1451 smart transducers recently [19]. In fact, in the reference model in Figure 1, the NCAP application module is logically an optional complement to provide the functions and service to pass information across the interface between the DMAC users and NCAP [33]. For mapping to Web services, the method introduced in [19] designed smart transducer Web services (STWSs) in the NCAP application services component. Hence, an IEEE 1451 NCAP provides a set of Web services for the STWS, which acts as an STWS provider. As shown in Figure 1, a common basis for the members of the IEEE 1451 family of standards is provided to be interoperable [13]. Hence, STWSs based on the IEEE 1451.0 standard have been defined using Web Services Description Language (WSDL). The DMCS user applications and STWS provider communicate with each other using SOAP/XML messages. The communications between NCAP and TIM are based on IEEE 1451.X [19].

2.3. Security Requirements. In this paper, we consider the security of the communication between the DMCS users and IEEE 1451 smart transducers purposely.

The security issues of the communication in the smart transducers are the responsibilities of IEEE 1451.X but not IEEE 1451.0 [13], and security in IEEE 1451.X is based on the specified communication protocol, such as bluetooth in IEEE 1451.5. However, the security of the communication between STWS consumers and STWS providers is an unsolved problem, which should be designed based on IEEE 1451.0 combined with Web services.

Recently, the security requirements of data exchange in sensor and actuator networks have been widely discussed, which include [34–37]:

(i) confidentiality: confidentiality or secrecy has to do with making information inaccessible to unauthorized users. A confidential message is resistant to revealing its meaning to an eavesdropper.

(ii) Availability: availability ensures the survivability of network services to authorized parties when needed despite denial-of-service (DoS) attacks. A denial-of-service attack could be launched at any OSI (open system interconnect) layer of a sensor network.

(iii) Integrity: integrity measures ensure that the received data is not altered in transit by an adversary.

(iv) Authentication: authentication enables a node to ensure the identity of the peer node with which it is communicating.

(v) Nonrepudiation: nonrepudiation denotes that a node cannot deny sending a message it has previously sent.

(vi) Access control: access control implement the process of identifying nodes as well as authorizing and granting nodes the access right to information or resources.

(vii) Freshness: this could mean data freshness and key freshness. Since all sensor networks provide some forms of time-varying measurements, we must ensure that each message is fresh. Data freshness implies that each data is recent, and it ensures that no adversary replayed old messages.

The above requirements are in conformance with the security requirements of data exchange described in ISO/IEC 29180 working draft [38], which is standard under development for security framework for ubiquitous sensor network.

In the above security requirements, access control can be performed based on access control scheme. The security access control scheme introduced in [23] is useful for IEEE 1451 smart sensors.

Other security requirements, which are confidentiality, availability, integrity, authentication, nonrepudiation, and freshness, should be implemented based on IEEE 1451.0 integrated with Web services.

IEEE 1451 standards defines six transducer services [13, 19, 33], which are *TimDiscovery, TransducerAccess, TransducerManager, TedsManager, CommManager*, and *AppCallback*.

Table 1 shows the security requirements of communication of the responding services.

TABLE 1: Security requirements of communication process.

Service	Security requirements for the communications
TimDiscovery	Availability, integrity, nonrepudiation, and freshness
TransducerAccess	Confidentiality, availability, integrity, authentication, nonrepudiation, and freshness
TransducerManager, TedsManager, and CommManager	Confidentiality, availability, integrity, authentication, nonrepudiation, and freshness
AppCallback	Integrity, nonrepudiation, and freshness

3. Web Services Architecture and Web Services Security

3.1. Web Services Architecture. Today, the ability to seamlessly exchange information between internal business units, customers, and partners is vital for success; yet most organizations employ a variety of disparate applications that store and exchange data in dissimilar ways and therefore cannot "talk" to one another productively. Web services have evolved as a practical, cost-effective solution for uniting information distributed between critical applications over operating system, platform, and language barriers that were previously impassable.

Web services [39] are in simple terms object methods exposed via HTTP using pure SOAP messages. The major components or layers of a Web Service Protocol Stack include

(1) Extensible Markup Language (XML) layer: providing a means for communicating over the Web using an XML document that both requests and responds to information between two disparate systems.

(2) Simple Object Access Protocol (SOAP) layer: a XML Messaging specification, which allows the sender and the receiver of XML documents to support a common data transfer protocol for effective networked communication.

(3) Web Services Description Language (WSDL) layer: playing an important role in the overall Web services architecture since it describes the complete contract for application communication.

(4) Universal Description, Discovery and Integration (UDDI) layer: a platform-independent, Extensible Markup Language- (XML-) based registry, which represents a way to publish and find web services over the Web.

Figure 2 shows the protocol stack architecture of Web Services.

3.2. Web Services Security. Web Services Security is based on open W3C-approved XML standards [40, 41], which provide the security foundation for applications of Web services. The standards are platform neutral, thus promoting

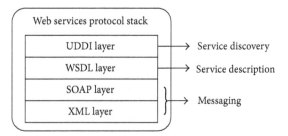

FIGURE 2: Web services protocol stack.

interoperability. Also, OASIS published the standards for defining the security expanding method for SOAP message exchange [42].

4. The Proposed Security Scheme

4.1. Basic Idea and Model. The basic idea and model of the proposed security scheme are shown in Figure 3. The goal of the security scheme is to satisfy the security requirements of the data exchange. The proposed approach can be viewed as "cross-layer design" at the messaging layer and description layer in Web Services protocol stack. The scheme contains three components logically, including XML Encryption and Signature, SOAP Security Extension, and WSDL Security Checking. The former two components satisfy the requirements of confidentiality, availability, integrity, authentication, nonrepudiation, and freshness. The third component satisfies the requirement of availability, which can protect the system against DoS attack. For mapping to Web Services, the security scheme is designed based on the layer architecture of Web services protocol stack. Also, the scheme is designed in conformance with the Web services security standard. Most important, the three components of the security scheme are based on IEEE 1415 transducer services, services API, and XML schema of API, respectively, which are defined in IEEE 1451 standards. As described in IEEE 1451.0, all text strings in the Transducer Electronic Data Sheet (TEDS) shall conform to W3C Recommendation Extensible Markup Language (XML) 1.0 (Second Edition).

4.2. Secure XML Messaging Layer. A security token represents a collection of claims, which is used to prove one's identity and provide the foundation for ensuring the confidentiality, integrity, nonrepudiation, and freshness of the data. Web Services Security standard defined several security tokens, including X. 509 certificate token, username/password token, Kerberos token, and SAML token. The security token most commonly used in DMCSs and sensor networks is username/password token [43–48].

Table 2 lists the notations used throughout the description of the security scheme for ease of reference.

4.2.1. Secure Messages of TimDiscovery. Figure 8 shows the protocol of secure message of *TimDiscovery*. For generating the signature, the client node first generates a fresh nonce R_U. Then, she computes the digital digest of her own password

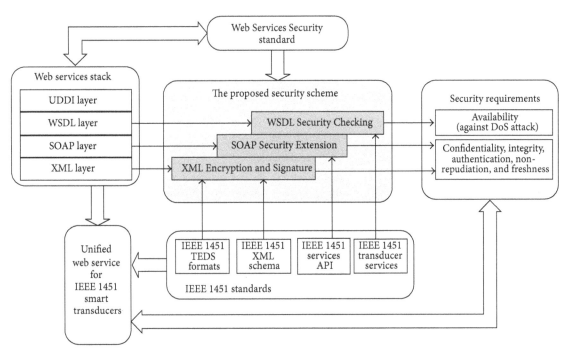

FIGURE 3: Basic idea and model.

together with the fresh nonce based on hash based message authentication code (HMAC). The password is stored in both the memory of client node and the server node. Clearly, the signature provides a nonrepudiation property. This is true because only the client node herself can generate it, and the fresh nonce guarantees its freshness. Next, nonce and created time are the additional elements to resist against the replay attack. Then, the client node generates a signature *RequestMAC*, which is for *RequestParameters*. *RequestParameters* is the original message of the access request. Next, the client node sends out *Username*, *ReqParameters*, *T*, R_U, and *RequestMAC*. After receiving the message from the client node, the server node retrieves the parameters from the message. Then, *S* computes the *RequestMAC'* based on the parameters from the message. After that, *S* verifies the signature through comparing *RequestMAC* and *RequestMAC'*. Then, a symmetric key is derived based on the password and a 16-bit random value G. Next, *S* computes the signature of response and the symmetric key. These values then are sent back to *U*. After *U* gets the message, *U* can derive the symmetric key.

4.2.2. Secure Messages of TransducerAccess, TransducerManager, TedsManager, and CommManager.
Figure 9 shows the protocol of secure message of *TransducerAccess*, *Transducer-Manager*, *TedsManager*, and *CommManager*. The client node *U* firstly generates a signature, which includes the generation of a fresh nonce R_U and the computation of the digital digest of her own password together with the fresh nonce based on HMAC. As a matter of fact, the generation process of the signature in this section is similar to the process of *TimDiscovery*.

TABLE 2: Notation used by the secure authentication protocol.

Notation	Meaning
U	A services consumer
S	A services provider
Key	Shared secret key between U and S for symmetric encryption and decryption
R_A	A nonce generated by entity A, usually it is a randomized value to defend replay attack
T	The created time of message
$Salt$	A random number to for derive the symmetric key
(M_1, M_2)	Concatenation of two messages
$HMAC\,(M)$	Calculate MAC for message M based hash function
$H\,(M)$	Apply one-way function to message M
$\{M\}_{Key}$	Encrypt message M by symmetric key algorithm with the secret key between user and service provider
$ReqParameters$	Parameters involved in the request
$ResParameters$	Parameters involved in the response

The password is stored in both the memory of client node and the sever node. Next, she generates a security token *ET* based on username/password method. Nonce and created time are the additional elements to resist against the replay attack. Then, she encrypts the *ReqParameters* based on the symmetric key. *ReqParameters* is the original message of the access request. Next, the client node sends out $\{ReqParameters\}_{Key}$, *ET*, and *ResponseMAC*. After receiving the message and the security token from client node, server

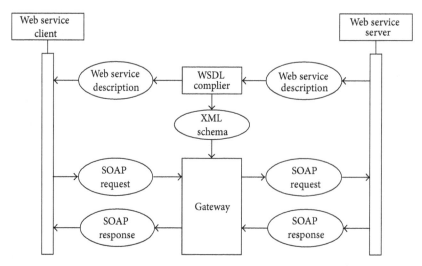

FIGURE 4: Integration of the CheckWay Web service firewall.

node retrieves the password by corresponding C from the local database, then calculates the PasswordDigest', compares it with PasswordDigest, and authenticates the identity of client node as being equal or not. After verification, the sever node S sends an access response message, including a signature of response parameters, *ResParameters*, to ensure the integrity and nonrepudiation. After getting the response message, U will verify the signature of *ResParameters* and then derive *ResParameters* from the message.

4.2.3. Secure Messages of AppCallback. The security requirements of *AppCallback* are as same as those of *TimDiscovery* except that *AppCallback* lacks availability. In the proposed scheme, ensuring availability is the responsibility of the security design of the WSDL layer. In addition, as defined in IEEE 1451.0 standard, *AppCallback* is implemented when applications that need advanced features exist [13]. *Appcallback* is implemented after *TimDiscovery*, which means that the key for symmetric encryption and decryption has already been generated when *AppCallback* is implemented. Hence, at XML messaging layer, the security mechanisms for securing message of *AppCallback* is as same as those of *TimDiscovery* but *key* generation is not needed.

4.3. Secure WSDL Layer. The security design of message layer cannot deal with the requirements of availability because the XML encryption and decryption can only ensure the confidentiality, availability, integrity, authentication, nonrepudiation, and freshness. Current Web services architecture does not consider validation of Web services messages against WSDLs during message processing. This could pose a potential security risk to enterprise servers hosting Web services. We secure the availability at the WSDL layer.

In fact, the most important aspect of a Web service is the service description using the Web Services Description Language (WSDL) that describes the messages, types, and operations of Web service and the contract to which the Web service guarantees it will conform [49]. WSDL plays an important role in the overall Web services architecture since it describes the complete contract for application communication. Smart transducer Web services (STWSs) in [19] are defined using Web services WSDL. WSDL is extensible to allow the description of endpoints and their messages regardless of what message formats or networks protocols are used to communicate. We secure the WSDL layer security based on the method in [50].

The considerations above regarding SOAP message validation lead to the Web service firewall, called CheckWay. Figure 4 shows the integration of a Web service firewall between Web service client and server. The security WSDL compiler gets the Web service server's Web service description, generates the corresponding XML message schema, "hardens" the description, and advertises the modified description to a Web service client. The CheckWay Gateway validates all SOAP messages against the schema, forwards the message if it is valid, and rejects the message if it is not. The next step is now to consider how to obtain an XML schema for the message validation and which problems regarding the firewalls performance emerge from the validation process. In order to answer the first question, a closer look at Web service client/server interaction and the Web service interface description is required. The compiling process is shown in Figure 5.

The SOAP message's structure belonging to a Web service description is defined by information spread all over the description document. The description must be traversed and the information necessary for a specific service or operation must be merged into a message definition.

5. Security Analysis

The basic secure authentication protocol for *TimDiscovery*, *TransducerAccess*, *TransducerManager*, *TedsManager*, *CommManager*, and *Callback* can provide a nonrepudiation property because only the client node herself can generate it, and the fresh nonce guarantees its freshness. Integrity property

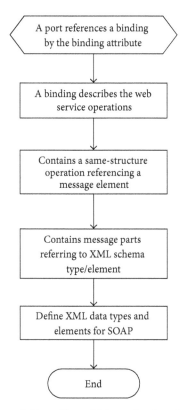

FIGURE 5: Compiling a Web service description.

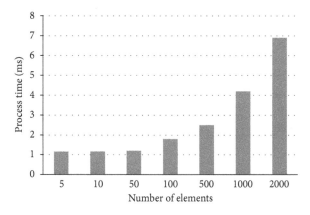

FIGURE 6: SOAP message length impact on process time.

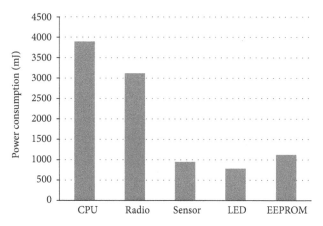

FIGURE 7: Power consumption on sensor.

can also be proved based on HMAC. Moreover, after the nonce and created time are added into the data packet, the receiver can check whether the nonce has been received before or whether the message is created in a very recent time. Thereby, nonce and created time combined into data packets can resist replay attack. Also, we consider the DoS attack model that consists in injecting bogus messages into the system. And before verifying PasswordDigest, only a hash computation needs to be implemented. At the same time, before verifying PasswordDigest, few values need be stored. Therefore, our protocol can resist DoS attack to some extent.

Beside the basic above security, the authentication protocols of *TransducerAccess*, *TransducerManager*, *TedsManager*, *CommManager* use both symmetric encryption and MAC for the message. Therefore, these protocols can provide confidentiality and authentication for the communications.

6. Implementation

6.1. Time Overhead of Process of CheckWay Gateway. In this section, we present the important aspect of the performance results. We evaluate the effect of message size on the performance of the access inquiry Web services of CheckWay gateway. A laptop is used to simulate the CheckWay gateway, which includes the Intel Core i5 M520 and 2 GB memory. In the implementation, we varied the message size by increasing the number of XML elements contained in the response message. As shown in Figure 6, the time consumption of CPU required to process an account inquiry request depends on the number of elements returned in the response message. The longest message is 400 times larger than the smallest message, but the increase in CPU consumption is less than 5-fold. Please note that in the implementation a SOAP message of 50 elements contains 1 KB of data, but the message itself has a length of 2.3 KB because of the XML tags.

6.2. Power Consumption of Sensor. It is very important to verify the feasibility of the implementation of the proposed scheme on resource-constrained sensors. In this subsection, we estimate the energy consumption of sensor using PowerTOSSIM [51], which is an energy modeling extension of TOSSIM for the simulation of MICAz mote. Here, we take *TimDiscovery* message authentication as the example for evaluation. The energy consumption is measured for five components: CPU, RADIO, LED, SENSOR, and EEPROM. We fix the time of execution equal to 1200 simulated seconds, which is because the motes in PowerTOSSIM take boot time of 10 seconds. In our scheme, storing security data performed by EEPROM component and computations performed by CPU component slightly increase the energy consumption, where radio transmission is not always necessary and accordingly the RADIO component energy consumption is greatly reduced. As shown in Figure 7, the energy consumption of our scheme is acceptable for resource-constrained WSNs.

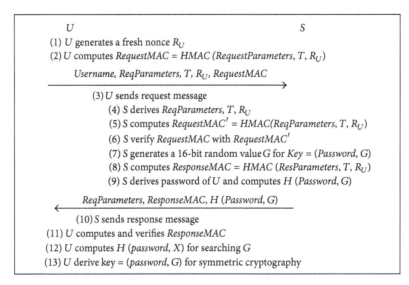

$$U \qquad\qquad\qquad\qquad\qquad\qquad\qquad\qquad S$$

(1) U generates a fresh nonce R_U

(2) U computes $RequestMAC = HMAC\ (RequestParameters, T, R_U)$

$\qquad\qquad Username,\ ReqParameters,\ T,\ R_U,\ RequestMAC$
$\xrightarrow{\hspace{8cm}}$

$\qquad$ (3) U sends request message

$\qquad\qquad$ (4) S derives $ReqParameters, T, R_U$

$\qquad\qquad\qquad$ (5) S computes $RequestMAC' = HMAC(ReqParameters, T, R_U)$

$\qquad\qquad\qquad$ (6) S verify $RequestMAC$ with $RequestMAC'$

$\qquad\qquad\qquad$ (7) S generates a 16-bit random value G for $Key = (Password, G)$

$\qquad\qquad\qquad$ (8) S computes $ResponseMAC = HMAC\ (ResParameters, T, R_U)$

$\qquad\qquad\qquad$ (9) S derives password of U and computes $H\ (Password, G)$

$\qquad\quad ReqParameters,\ ResponseMAC,\ H\ (Password,\ G)$
$\xleftarrow{\hspace{8cm}}$

$\qquad$ (10) S sends response message

(11) U computes and verifies $ResponseMAC$

(12) U computes $H\ (password, X)$ for searching G

(13) U derive key $= (password, G)$ for symmetric cryptography

FIGURE 8

$$U \qquad\qquad\qquad\qquad\qquad\qquad\qquad\qquad S$$

(1) U generates a fresh nonce R_U

(2) U computes $RequestMAC = HMAC\ (RequestParameters, T, R_U)$

(3) U computes $PasswordDigest = H\ (password, R_U, T)$

(4) U generates a security token $ET = (Username, PasswordDigest, T, R_U)$

(5) U computes $\{ReqParameters\}_{Key}$

$\qquad\qquad \{ReqParameters\}_{Key},\ ET,\ RequestMAC$
$\xrightarrow{\hspace{8cm}}$

$\qquad$ (6) U sends request message

$\qquad\qquad$ (7) S derives $PasswordDigest, T, R_U$ from ET

$\qquad\qquad\qquad$ (8) S computes $PasswordDigest' = H\ (password, R_U, T)$

$\qquad\qquad\qquad$ (9) S verify $PasswordDigest$ with $PasswordDigest'$

$\qquad\qquad\qquad$ (10) S decrypts $\{ReqParameters\}_{Key}$

$\qquad\qquad\qquad$ (11) S verify $RequestMAC$

$\qquad\qquad$ (12) S get $ResParameters$ from transducers according $ReqParameters$

$\qquad\qquad\qquad$ (13) S computes $ResponseMAC = HMAC\ (ResParameters, T, R_U)$

$\qquad\qquad$ (14) S encrypts computes $\{ReqParameters\}_{Key}$

$\qquad\qquad \{ReqParameters\}_{Key},\ ResponseMAC$
$\xleftarrow{\hspace{8cm}}$

$\qquad$ (15) S sends response message

(16) U computes and verifies $ResponseMAC$

(17) U decrypts $\{ResParameters\}_{Key}$ getting $ResParameters$

FIGURE 9

7. Conclusion

To secure the web-services-based communications for networked IEEE 1451 smart transducers, we proposed a cross-layer security mechanism, which is based on the layer architecture of Web services protocol stack. The security requirements are derived from IEEE 1451 and Web service communications, and the design is consistent with existing applications of IEEE 1451 web services communication utilities and an information security standard. Moreover, the scheme is designed in conformance with the Web Services Security standard. Most important, the three components of the security scheme are based on IEEE 1451 transducer services, services API, and XML schema of API, respectively, which are defined in IEEE 1451 standards. The effect of message size on the performance of the access inquiry web service is tested, which verifies the feasibility of our scheme. The proposed scheme provides an efficient reference security model of web-services-based communications for networked IEEE 1451 smart transducers.

Acknowledgment

The authors would like to thank the guest editor and anonymous reviewers for their helpful and constructive comments.

References

[1] E. Y. Song and K. Lee, "Understanding IEEE 1451—networked smart transducer interface standard—what is a smart transducer?" *IEEE Instrumentation and Measurement Magazine*, vol. 11, no. 2, pp. 11–17, 2008.

[2] K. Ota, M. Dong, and X. Li, "TinyBee: mobile-agent-based data gathering system in wireless sensor networks," in *Proceedings of the IEEE International Conference on Networking, Architecture, and Storage (NAS'09)*, pp. 24–31, Hunan, China, July 2009.

[3] J. Liang, X. Zeng, W. Wang, and H. Chen, "L-shaped array-based elevation and azimuth direction finding in the presence of mutual coupling," *Signal Processing*, vol. 91, no. 5, pp. 1319–1328, 2011.

[4] S. R. Rossi, A. A. de Carvalho, A. C. R. da Silva et al., "Open and standardized resources for smart transducer networking," *IEEE Transactions on Instrumentation and Measurement*, vol. 58, no. 10, pp. 3754–3761, 2009.

[5] B. Liu, H. Chen, Z. Zhong, and H. V. Poor, "Asymmetrical round trip based synchronization-free localization in large-scale underwater sensor networks," *IEEE Transactions on Wireless Communications*, vol. 9, no. 11, pp. 3532–3542, 2010.

[6] K. B. Lee and E. Y. Song, "Object-oriented application framework for IEEE 1451.1 standard," *IEEE Transactions on Instrumentation and Measurement*, vol. 54, no. 4, pp. 1527–1533, 2005.

[7] M. Dong, K. Ota, X. Li, X. Shen, S. Guo, and M. Guo, "HARVEST: a task-objective efficient data collection scheme in wireless sensor and actor networks," in *Proceedings of the 3rd International Conference on Communications and Mobile Computing (CMC'11)*, pp. 485–488, Qingdao, China, April 2011.

[8] L. Chen, W. Chen, B. Wang, X. Zhang, H. Chen, and D. Yang, "System-level simulation methodology and platform for mobile cellular systems," *IEEE Communications Magazine*, vol. 49, no. 7, pp. 148–155, 2011.

[9] H. Chen, G. Wang, Z. Wang, and H. So, "Non-line-of-sight node localization based on semi-definite programming in wireless sensor networks," *IEEE Transactions on Wireless Communications*, vol. 16, no. 1, pp. 108–116, 2012.

[10] M. Staroswiecki, "Intelligent sensors: a functional view," *IEEE Transactions on Industrial Informatics*, vol. 1, no. 4, pp. 238–249, 2005.

[11] K. Ota, M. Dong, J. Wang, S. Guo, Z. Cheng, and M. Guo, "Dynamic itinerary planning for mobile agents with a content-specific approach in wireless sensor networks," in *Proceedings of the 72nd IEEE Vehicular Technology Conference Fall (VTC2010-Fall)*, pp. 1–5, Ottawa, Canada, September 2010.

[12] G. Wang and H. Chen, "An importance sampling method for TDOA-based source localization," *IEEE Transactions on Wireless Communications*, vol. 10, no. 5, pp. 1560–1568, 2011.

[13] "IEEE standard for a smart transducer interface for sensors and actuators—common functions, communication protocols, and transducer electronic data sheet (TEDS) formats," IEEE Standards Board, IEEE Std 1451. 0-2007, 2007.

[14] "IEEE standard for a smart transducer interface for sensors and actuators—network capable application processor (NCAP) information model," IEEE Standards Board, IEEE Std 1451. 1-1999, 1999.

[15] "IEEE standard for a smart transducer interface for sensors and actuators—transducer to microprocessor communication protocols and transducer electronic data sheet (TEDS) formats," IEEE Standards Board, IEEE Std 1451. 2-1997, 1997.

[16] "IEEE standard for a smart transducer interface for sensors and actuators—digital communication and transducer electronic data sheet (TEDS) formats for distributed multidrop system," IEEE Standards Board, IEEE Std 1451. 3-2003, 2003.

[17] "IEEE standard for a smart transducer interface for sensors and actuators—wireless communication protocols and transducer electronic data sheet (TEDS) formats," IEEE Standards Board, IEEE Std 1451. 5-2007, 2007.

[18] "IEEE standard for a smart transducer interface for sensors and actuators - Transducers to radio frequency identification (RFID) systems communication protocols and transducer electronic data sheet formats," IEEE Standards Board, IEEE Std 1451. 7-2010, 2010.

[19] E. Y. Song and K. B. Lee, "STWS: a unified web service for IEEE 1451 smart transducers," *IEEE Transactions on Instrumentation and Measurement*, vol. 57, no. 8, pp. 1749–1756, 2008.

[20] B. Panja, S. K. Madria, and B. Bhargava, "A role-based access in a hierarchical sensor network architecture to provide multilevel security," *Computer Communications*, vol. 31, no. 4, pp. 793–806, 2008.

[21] L. Maccari, L. Mainardi, M. A. Marchitti, N. R. Prasad, and R. Fantacci, "Lightweight, distributed access control for wireless sensor networks supporting mobility," in *Proceedings of the IEEE International Conference on Communications (ICC'08)*, pp. 1441–1445, Beijing, China, May 2008.

[22] Y. Zhou, Y. Zhang, and Y. Fang, "Access control in wireless sensor networks," *Ad Hoc Networks*, vol. 5, no. 1, pp. 3–13, 2007.

[23] J. Wu and S. Shimamoto, "Usage control based security access scheme for wireless sensor networks," in *Proceedings of the IEEE International Conference on Communications (ICC'10)*, May 2010.

[24] K. Ota, M. Dong, Z. Cheng, J. Wang, X. Li, and X. Shen, "ORACLE: mobility control in wireless sensor and actor networks," *Computer Communications*, vol. 35, no. 9, pp. 1029–1037, 2012.

[25] K. B. Lee and M. E. Reichardt, "Open standards for homeland security sensor networks—sensor interconnection and integration trough Web access," *IEEE Instrumentation and Measurement Magazine*, vol. 8, no. 5, pp. 14–21, 2005.

[26] J. Viega and J. Epstein, "Why applying standards to web services is not enough," *IEEE Security and Privacy*, vol. 4, no. 4, pp. 25–31, 2006.

[27] E. Kleiner and A. W. Roscoe, "On the relationship between web services security and traditional protocols," *Electronic Notes in Theoretical Computer Science*, vol. 155, no. 1, pp. 583–603, 2006.

[28] Oasis Consortium, WS-Security specification, 2004, https://www.oasis-open.org/.

[29] Z. Wu and A. C. Weaver, "Using web services to exchange security tokens for federated trust management," in *Proceedings of the IEEE International Conference on Web Services (ICWS'07)*, pp. 1176–1178, Salt Lake City, Utah, USA, July 2007.

[30] M. Anlauff, D. Pavlovic, and A. Suenbuel, "Deriving secure network protocols for enterprise services architectures," in *Proceedings of the IEEE International Conference on Communications (ICC'06)*, pp. 2283–2287, Istanbul, Turkey, July 2006.

[31] L. Liao and J. Schwenk, "Secure emails in XML format using web services," in *Proceedings of the 5th IEEE European Conference on Web Services (ECOWS'07)*, pp. 129–136, Halle, Germany, November 2007.

[32] V. Viegas, J. M. D. Pereira, and P. M. B. S. Girão, ".NET framework and web services: a profit combination to implement and enhance the IEEE 1451.1 standard," *IEEE Transactions on*

Instrumentation and Measurement, vol. 56, no. 6, pp. 2739–2747, 2007.

[33] E. Song and K. Lee, "Smart transducer web services based on the IEEE 1451.0 standard," in *Proceedings of the IEEE International Instrumentation and Measurement Technology Conference (IMTC'07)*, May 2007.

[34] X. Chen, K. Makki, K. Yen, and N. Pissinou, "Sensor network security: a survey," *IEEE Communications Surveys and Tutorials*, vol. 11, no. 2, pp. 52–73, 2009.

[35] F. Hu and X. Cao, "Security in wireless actor & sensor networks (WASN): towards a hierarchical re-keying design," in *Proceedings of the International Conference on Information Technology: Coding and Computing (ITCC'05)*, pp. 528–533, April 2005.

[36] M. Shao, S. Zhu, W. Zhang, G. Cao, and Y. Yang, "PDCS: security and privacy support for data-centric sensor networks," *IEEE Transactions on Mobile Computing*, vol. 8, no. 8, pp. 1023–1038, 2009.

[37] A. S. Tanenbaum, *Computer Networks*, Prentice Hall, Upper Saddle River, NJ, USA, 4th edition, 2003.

[38] "Working Draft of ISO/IEC Draft Standard for Telecommunications and Information Exhange between Systems—Security framework for ubiquitous sensor network," ISO/IEC Unapproved Draft Std ISO/IEC, 29180, May 2008, http://isotc.iso.org/livelink/livelink?func=ll&objId=8158657&objAction=Open&vernum=1.

[39] M. MacDonald, *Microsoft .NET, Distributed Applications: Integrating XML Web Services and .NET Remoting*, Microsoft, Redmond, Wash, USA, 2003.

[40] W3 Consortium, XML Encryption specification, http://www.w3.org/.

[41] W3 Consortium, XML Signature specification, http://www.w3.org/TR/xmldsig-core/.

[42] A. Nadalin, C. Kaler, R. Monzillo, and P. Hallam-Baker, "Web services security: SOAP message security 1.1," OASIS Standard Specification, 2006.

[43] S. A. Kiprushkin, N. A. Korolev, and S. Y. Kurskov, "Distributed information measurement and control system for research and education in physics," in *Proceedings of the 2nd International Conference on Systems (ICONS'07)*, April 2007.

[44] J. Hieb, J. Graham, and S. Patel, "Security enhancements for distributed control systems," in *Critical Infrastructure Protection*, E. Goetz and S. Shenoi, Eds., pp. 133–146, Springer, Boston, Mass, USA, 2007.

[45] A. Aiello, D. L. Carnì, D. Grimaldi, and G. Guglielmelli, "Wireless distributed measurement system by using mobile devices," in *Proceedings of the 3rd IEEE Workshop on Intelligent Data Acquisition and Advanced Computing Systems: Technology and Applications (IDAACS'05)*, pp. 316–319, Sofia, Bulgaria, September 2005.

[46] A. Aiello, D. L. Carnì, D. Grimaldi, G. Guglielmelli, and F. Lamonaca, "Wireless distributed measurement system based on PDA and dynamical application repository server," in *Proceedings of the IEEE Instrumentation and Measurement Technology (IMTC'07)*, May 2007.

[47] L. Tao, H. Xu, and Z. Zhang, "Distributed inspecting and control system for motor vehicle safety performance," in *Proceedings of the International Conference on Intelligent Human-Machine Systems and Cybernetics (IHMSC'09)*, pp. 384–387, Zhejiang, China, August 2009.

[48] H. R. Tseng, R. H. Jan, and W. Yang, "An improved dynamic user authentication scheme for wireless sensor networks," in *Proceedings of the 50th Annual IEEE Global Telecommunications Conference (GLOBECOM'07)*, pp. 986–990, Washington, DC, USA, November 2007.

[49] D. Panda, "An Introduction to Service-Oriented Architecture from a Java Developer Perspective," http://www.onjava.com/pub/a/onjava/2005/01/26/soa-intro.html.

[50] N. Gruschka and N. Luttenberger, "Protecting web services from DoS attacks by SOAP message validation," in *Proceedings of the IFIP TC11 21 International Information Security Conference (SEC'06)*, May 2006.

[51] V. Shnayder, M. Hempstead, B. R. Chen, G. W. Allen, and M. Welsh, "Simulating the power consumption of large-scale sensor network applications," in *Proceedings of the 2nd International Conference on Embedded Networked Sensor Systems (SenSys'04)*, pp. 188–200, November 2004.

Permissions

The contributors of this book come from diverse backgrounds, making this book a truly international effort. This book will bring forth new frontiers with its revolutionizing research information and detailed analysis of the nascent developments around the world.

We would like to thank all the contributing authors for lending their expertise to make the book truly unique. They have played a crucial role in the development of this book. Without their invaluable contributions this book wouldn't have been possible. They have made vital efforts to compile up to date information on the varied aspects of this subject to make this book a valuable addition to the collection of many professionals and students.

This book was conceptualized with the vision of imparting up-to-date information and advanced data in this field. To ensure the same, a matchless editorial board was set up. Every individual on the board went through rigorous rounds of assessment to prove their worth. After which they invested a large part of their time researching and compiling the most relevant data for our readers. Conferences and sessions were held from time to time between the editorial board and the contributing authors to present the data in the most comprehensible form. The editorial team has worked tirelessly to provide valuable and valid information to help people across the globe.

Every chapter published in this book has been scrutinized by our experts. Their significance has been extensively debated. The topics covered herein carry significant findings which will fuel the growth of the discipline. They may even be implemented as practical applications or may be referred to as a beginning point for another development. Chapters in this book were first published by Hindawi Publishing Corporation; hereby published with permission under the Creative Commons Attribution License or equivalent.

The editorial board has been involved in producing this book since its inception. They have spent rigorous hours researching and exploring the diverse topics which have resulted in the successful publishing of this book. They have passed on their knowledge of decades through this book. To expedite this challenging task, the publisher supported the team at every step. A small team of assistant editors was also appointed to further simplify the editing procedure and attain best results for the readers.

Our editorial team has been hand-picked from every corner of the world. Their multi-ethnicity adds dynamic inputs to the discussions which result in innovative outcomes. These outcomes are then further discussed with the researchers and contributors who give their valuable feedback and opinion regarding the same. The feedback is then collaborated with the researches and they are edited in a comprehensive manner to aid the understanding of the subject.

Apart from the editorial board, the designing team has also invested a significant amount of their time in understanding the subject and creating the most relevant covers. They scrutinized every image to scout for the most suitable representation of the subject and create an appropriate cover for the book.

The publishing team has been involved in this book since its early stages. They were actively engaged in every process, be it collecting the data, connecting with the contributors or procuring relevant information. The team has been an ardent support to the editorial, designing and production team. Their endless efforts to recruit the best for this project, has resulted in the accomplishment of this book. They are a veteran in the field of academics and their pool of knowledge is as vast as their experience in printing. Their expertise and guidance has proved useful at every step. Their uncompromising quality standards have made this book an exceptional effort. Their encouragement from time to time has been an inspiration for everyone.

The publisher and the editorial board hope that this book will prove to be a valuable piece of knowledge for researchers, students, practitioners and scholars across the globe.

List of Contributors

Chunmei Ma and Nianbo Liu
School of Computer Science and Engineering, University of Electronic Science and Technology of China, Chengdu, Sichuan 611731, China

Gaurav Sharma, Suman Bala and Anil K. Verma
Computer Science and Engineering Department, Thapar University, Patiala 147004, India

Lei Wang, Zhuxiu Yuan and Zhenquan Qin
School of Software, Dalian University of Technology, Dalian 116621, China

Lei Shu
Department Multimedia Engineering, Osaka University, Osaka 565-0871, Japan

Liang Shi
School of Electronics Engineering and Computer Science, Peking University, Beijing 100871, China

Ning Yu, Lirui Zhang and Yongji Ren
School of Instrumentation Science and Optoelectronics Engineering, Beijing University of Aeronautics and Astronautics (Beihang University), Beijing 100191, China

Zusheng Zhang and Huaqiang Yuan
Dongguan University of Technology, No. 1 University Road, Songshan Lake Sci.&Tech. Industry Park, Dongguan, Guangdong 523808, China

Xiaoyun Li and Fengqi Yu
Shenzhen Institute of Advanced Technology, Chinese Academy of Sciences/The Chinese University of Hong Kong, 1068 Xueyuan Avenue, Shenzhen University Town, Nanshan District, Shenzhen 518055, China

Jun Wang and Deliang Yang
School of Electronic Information and Control Engineering, Beijing University of Technology, Beijing 100124, China

Jiliang Zhou
Shanghai University of International Business and Economics, Shanghai 201620, China

Guoxi Ma and Zhengsu Tao
Department of Electronic, Information and Electrical Engineering, Shanghai Jiaotong University, No. 800 Dongchuan Road, Shanghai 200240, China

Lina Xu and Chengchun Ni
School of Computer and Information, Hefei University of Technology, Hefei 230009, China

Na Xia
School of Computer and Information, Hefei University of Technology, Hefei 230009, China Engineering Research Center of Safety Critical Industrial Measurement and Control Technology, Ministry of Education of China, Hefei 230009, China

Fu Xiao, Jia Xu, Lingyun Jiang and Ruchuan Wang
College of Computer, Nanjing University of Posts and Telecommunications, Nanjing, Jiangsu 210003, China
Jiangsu High Technology Research Key Laboratory forWireless Sensor Networks, Nanjing, Jiangsu 210003, China
Key Lab of BroadbandWireless Communication and Sensor Network Technology (Nanjing University of Posts and Telecommunications), Ministry of Education Jiangsu Province, Nanjing, Jiangsu 210003, China

Guoxia Sun
College of Computer, Nanjing University of Posts and Telecommunications, Nanjing, Jiangsu 210003, China

Junghun Ryu and K. Wendy Tang
Department of Electrical & Computer Engineering, Stony Brook University, SUNY, Stony Brook, NY 11794-2350, USA

Eric Noel
AT&T Labs, USA

Jinbiao Chen, Yongcai Wang and Yuexuan Wang
Institute for Interdisciplinary Information Sciences (IIIS), Tsinghua University, Beijing 100084, China

Changjian Hu
NEC Laboratories, Beijing, China

N. N. Nik Abd Malik, M. Esa, S. K. Syed Yusof, S. A. Hamzah, and M. K. H. Ismail
UTM MIMOS CoE Telecommunication Technology, Faculty of Electrical Engineering, Universiti Teknologi Malaysia, 81310 Johor Bahru, Johor, Malaysia

Karen Miranda, Enrico Natalizio and Tahiry Raza indralambo
Inria Lille-Nord Europe, FUN Research Team, 40 avenue Halley, 59650 Villeneuve d'Ascq, France

Wenyang Guan, ChaoMa and Yue Li
College of Engineering, Swansea University, Swansea SA2 8PP, UK

Jianhua He and Zuoyin Tang
School of Engineering and Applied Science, Aston University, Birmingham B4 7ET, UK

Wei Wei
School of Computer Science and Engineering, Xi'an University of Technology, Xi'an 710048, China

Xiao-Lin Yang
College of Management Science, Chengdu University of Technology, Chengdu 610059, China

Pei-Yi Shen
National School of Software, Xidian University, Xi'an 710071, China

Bin Zhou
College of Science, Xi'an University of Science and Technology, Xi'an 710054, China

Ángel Asensio, Rubén Blasco, Álvaro Marco and Roberto Casas
Institute of Engineering Research (I3A) of the University of Zaragoza, 50018 Zaragoza, Spain

Jun Wu
Research Institute for Secure Systems (RISEC), National Institute of Advanced Industrial Science and Technology (AIST),
Tsukuba 305-8568, Japan
Global Information and Telecommunication Institute (GITI), Waseda University, Tokyo 169-0051, Japan

Ming Zhan
School of Electronic and Information Engineering, Southwest University, Chongqing 400714, China

Bin Duan
College of Information Engineering, Xiangtan University, Xiangtan 411105, China

Jiang Liu
School of Electrical and Electronics Engineering, North China Electric Power University, Beijing 102206, China

Printed in the USA
CPSIA information can be obtained
at www.ICGtesting.com
JSHW051440221024
72173JS00006B/1530